The Titans of the Twentieth Century

Also by Michael Mandelbaum

*The Four Ages of American Foreign Policy: Weak Power, Great Power,
Superpower, Hyperpower* (2022)

The Rise and Fall of Peace on Earth (2019)

Mission Failure: America and the World in the Post-Cold War Era (2016)

The Road to Global Prosperity (2014)

*That Used to Be Us: How America Fell Behind in the World It Invented and
How We Can Come Back* (with Thomas L. Friedman) (2011)

*The Frugal Superpower: America's Global Leadership in a
Cash-Strapped World* (2010)

*Democracy's Good Name: The Rise and Risks of the World's Most Popular
Form of Government* (2007)

*The Case for Goliath: How America Acts as the World's Government in the
Twenty-First Century* (2006)

*The Meaning of Sports: Why Americans Watch Baseball, Football, and
Basketball and What They See When They Do* (2004)

*The Ideas That Conquered the World: Peace, Democracy, and Free Markets
in the Twenty-First Century* (2002)

The Dawn of Peace in Europe (1996)

The Global Rivals (with Seweryn Bialer) (1996)

*The Fate of Nations: The Search for National Security in the Nineteenth
and Twentieth Centuries* (1988)

Reagan and Gorbachev (with Strobe Talbott) (1987)

The Nuclear Future (1983)

*The Nuclear Revolution: International Politics Before and
After Hiroshima* (1981)

*The Nuclear Question: The United States and Nuclear Weapons,
1946–1976* (1979)

The Titans of the Twentieth Century

How They Made History and the History They Made

Michael Mandelbaum

OXFORD
UNIVERSITY PRESS

OXFORD
UNIVERSITY PRESS

Oxford University Press is a department of the University of Oxford. It furthers
the University's objective of excellence in research, scholarship, and education
by publishing worldwide. Oxford is a registered trade mark of Oxford University
Press in the UK and certain other countries.

Published in the United States of America by Oxford University Press
198 Madison Avenue, New York, NY 10016, United States of America.

© Oxford University Press 2024

CIP data is on file at the Library of Congress
ISBN 978–0–19–778247–7

DOI: 10.1093/oso/9780197782477.001.0001

Printed by Sheridan Books, Inc., United States of America

To William P. Scott III, whom I first met at Garfield Junior High School, Berkeley, California, in the fall of 1958;

Mark F. Isenberg, whom I first met at the American International School, New Delhi, India, in the fall of 1963;

and Anne Mandelbaum, whom I first met at Yale University, New Haven, Connecticut, in the fall of 1967.

CONTENTS

———✦———

ACKNOWLEDGMENTS

———

I AM GRATEFUL TO THE friends and colleagues who took the time to give me the benefit of their expertise on one or more of the individuals discussed in the pages that follow: Nicholas X. Rizopoulos, Ralph Buultjens, James Kurth, and Leon Aron, Michael Burleigh, Derek Leebaert, Martin Kramer, Daniel Polisar, and George Walden. Any mistakes and, for better or worse, all the interpretations are my own.

Stephen Sears and Bart LaFaso of the Mason Library of the Johns Hopkins University School of Advanced Studies, and Michael Frimpong, stepped in to save the day when a computer malfunction compromised some of the chapters. I am greatly in their debt.

I am pleased to have been able to work, once again, with David McBride of Oxford University Press.

As with my previous books, my wife, Anne Mandelbaum, edited the manuscript for this one with characteristic scrupulousness and rigor, rendering it clearer and more coherent than it would have been without her meticulous and loving attention. I am immensely grateful to her for this, as well as her many other qualities of character and spirit, which are so numerous that it would require another book to record them all. Happily, I have been conducting the research for such a volume for the past fifty years.

Introduction

THIS BOOK ADDRESSES A QUESTION that, in the study of the past, is both difficult to ignore and impossible to answer definitively: what is the impact of individuals upon history? Thomas Carlyle's assertion that "the history of the world is but the biography of great men" surely goes too far in its emphasis on the individual. Karl Marx put it more accurately: "Men make their own history, but they do not make it as they please; they do not make it under self-selected circumstances, but under circumstances existing already, given and transmitted from the past." His appraisal, however, begs the question: what is the balance between men and circumstances?

Of that balance, two things—and perhaps only two—can be said with certainty: it will vary from historical moment to historical moment; and designating it can only be a matter of judgement, not fact. History is not, after all, a scientific experiment that can be run multiple times in order to measure different contributions to a particular outcome. It occurs only once. The chapters that follow, therefore, and especially the parts that directly concern the personal impact of the individuals discussed on the course of historical events, are exercises in historical judgement, not scientific conclusion.

Most people do not affect events beyond the scope of their personal lives. The chapters of *The Titans of the Twentieth Century* deal with eight people who did: Woodrow Wilson, the 28th president of the United States, who proposed a reordering of international politics after World War I; Vladimir Ilich Lenin, the leader of the Bolshevik Party that seized power in Russia in 1917 and created the Soviet Union; Adolf Hitler, the head of the Nazi Party that came to power in Germany in 1933 and proceeded, six years later, to plunge Europe into the deadliest and most destructive war in its long history; Winston Churchill, the prime minister of Great Britain during almost all of World War II, who insisted, against the odds, on resisting Nazi Germany; Franklin D. Roosevelt, the 32nd American president, who orchestrated the New Deal, the most sweeping program of reform in the history of the United States, and then led the country during the Second World War; Mohandas Gandhi, the leader of the twentieth-century Indian campaign for independence from the British Empire; David Ben-Gurion, a central figure in the Zionist movement that created a modern Jewish state in the Middle East and its first prime minister;[1] and Mao Zedong, the chairman of the Communist Party of China that won control of the country in 1949 and established the People's Republic of China.

Like the Titans of ancient Greek mythology, these men wielded great power. Like the mythical Titans, they ultimately relinquished it—in the democracies because of the verdicts of voters, the dictators through mortality. Not coincidentally, each of the eight modern Titans was a political leader. Other forms of influence have had deep and long-lasting effects on human society and are eminently worthy of the extensive study devoted to them through the years. Those who wield political power,[2] however, can have a wider, deeper, and more immediate impact on more people and events than those who exercise intellectual, or economic, or spiritual influence, as important as these three different modes of shaping history unquestionably are. All were men because no women had a comparable leadership role in the first half of the twentieth century, the period that this book covers for reasons explained below. Golda Meir, Indira Gandhi, and Margaret Thatcher—formidable leaders all—exercised power in the second half of the century.

Moreover, these eight are not the only twentieth-century leaders who could plausibly have been included in this book. Josef Stalin, while Lenin's disciple,[3] had the chief responsibility for the consolidation of the Soviet state and directed Soviet policy during World War II. Charles de Gaulle did more than anyone else to promote the political reconstruction and rejuvenation of France after its humiliation in that war. Harry S Truman, the 33rd American president, presided over the creation of an American foreign policy of global engagement in peacetime in the wake of the same war, a policy that broke with the precedent of American history and had an immense influence on the world in the second half of the twentieth century. Mustafa Kemal, known as Ataturk, built a secular Turkish state out of the ruins of the multinational Ottoman Empire. It is also worth noting that *The Titans of the Twentieth Century* includes no one from Japan, which was among the most important countries in the twentieth century by virtue of being the first non-Western state to harness the techniques of the Industrial Revolution and thereby become wealthy and powerful, and of having begun World War II in Asia and the Pacific. Japan began that war as part of its conquest of an Asian and Pacific empire on the largest scale in history during World War II. The Japanese conquests, although they did not survive the war, fatally weakened European imperial rule in that part of the world. A collective society, Japan did not produce leaders who stood out among their peers as the eight men portrayed here did.

The contemporaries of the men discussed in the pages that follow, as well as those who came after them, regarded each of the eight as supremely significant. One measure of a person's historical importance is the number of biographies written about him or her. Each of the eight has inspired many, and there will surely be more: of the making of books about them, no end is in sight. All eight achieved recognition as towering historical figures in other ways, and not only during their lifetimes but also, tellingly, after their deaths, when the incentives to exalt them in order to win their personal favor had disappeared. Their names were turned into adjectives, symbolizing particular qualities or beliefs: "Wilsonian" refers to a certain approach to international affairs, "Leninism" to a way of conducting politics. "Hitlerian" became a synonym for evil, "Churchillian" for courage and resolve. "Gandhian" denotes the embrace of nonviolence, "Maoist" a particularly disruptive approach to political life.

All eight fit the definitions of a term now overused but in this context appropriate: "iconic." The word, from the Greek *eikon*—"image"—refers either to a painting on wood displaying a holy figure in the Christian religion or, more broadly, to someone or something widely recognized and well established in the public mind, like the brand of a commercial product. Active in societies where literacy was not yet widespread, Lenin, Gandhi, and Mao relied on the propagation of images of themselves to generate support for their goals, and so fit the first definition.[4] Hitler, Roosevelt, and Gandhi became iconic in the second sense of the word. Germans referred to Hitler as simply the "Führer" ("the leader"), Roosevelt was widely known by his initials—"FDR"—the first American president to be so designated, and Indians referred to Gandhi with the honorific "mahatma"—*maha atma*, "great soul," in Hindi.

Lenin and Mao were embalmed after they died, and their tombs became pilgrimage sites. Democracy, unlike communism, does not lend itself to the veneration of dead leaders in this manner, but it does accord enduring recognition to its most influential political leaders in other ways. Institutions of higher education, for example, adopt their names: thus the (since renamed) Woodrow Wilson School of Public and International Affairs at Princeton University, Churchill College of Cambridge University, and Ben-Gurion University in Israel. Many Indian institutions are named after Gandhi. Franklin D. Roosevelt's profile adorns one of the most widely circulated coins in the United States.

* * *

The eight subjects of the chapters that follow belong, very roughly, to the same political generation. Each was born in the latter half of the nineteenth century: Woodrow Wilson, the oldest, in 1856; Lenin in 1870; Hitler in 1889; Franklin Roosevelt in 1882; Churchill in 1874; Gandhi in 1869; Ben-Gurion in 1886; Mao in 1893. Each of them put his personal stamp on the history of his country and the world in the first half of the twentieth century. Ben-Gurion and Mao, it is true, remained in power into the century's second half, with Ben-Gurion relinquishing office in 1963 and Mao dying in 1976. Both, however, had major historical achievements to their credit by midcentury.

The first half of the last century offered wider opportunity than was previously available for individuals to affect history. To be sure, political leaders before then—Alexander the Great, the Macedonian conqueror who lived in the fourth century BCE, for example, or Louis XIV, the French monarch of the seventeenth and eighteenth centuries—had wielded considerable power: in some cases, historians have called it "absolute." The earlier leaders lived, however, in traditional, mainly agrarian societies. They lacked the technologies—of transportation, communication, and coercion—to exercise the degree of control over those they ruled that their twentieth-century successors achieved.

Moreover, premodern monarchs generally aspired to rule for as long as possible over as much territory as possible but not, on the whole, to transform their systems of rule or the lives of those they ruled. While the world of tradition in which they lived was not static in every way, the scope of politically induced change fell well short of the dimensions it attained in the twentieth century. In the traditional world, nature—in the form of earthquakes, hurricanes, floods, droughts, and plagues—typically had broader, deeper, and more disruptive effects on everyday life than did the activities of those who exercised political power. In the twentieth century, political power expanded dramatically, and with it the capacity of individuals exercising it to make a personal imprint on events.

The French Revolution of 1789 and the wars that followed it marked the beginning of the end of the traditional political world; but at the conclusion of those wars, the victors attempted, with considerable success, to restore the political norms and institutions that had dominated Europe and the world before 1789. It was only in the first half of the twentieth century that the wide and deep personal impact on the course of history that the subjects of this book managed to make became possible. In that period, three world-shaking events—the two World Wars and the Great Depression—left the political and economic landscapes in ruins virtually everywhere.

By making use of the products of the ongoing Industrial Revolution, which began in the second half of the eighteenth century and gained momentum thereafter, the two wars had such destructive and disruptive effects that the traditional world simply could not be restored. In contrast to the aftermath of the French Revolution and the conflicts it spawned, the restoration of what had existed before was, in Europe at least, scarcely even attempted.[5] Similarly, although Europe and the world had experienced economic downturns before the 1930s, by that time the Industrial Revolution had created an international economy more tightly integrated and more financially vulnerable than ever before, making the Great Depression more damaging than its predecessors.

The three great upheavals acted as bulldozers, flattening previously standing political and economic structures. The two wars and the Depression weakened, ended entirely, or discredited, rulers, forms of government, sovereign borders, and methods of economic organization throughout the world. They thus created the opportunity for sweeping change. In particular, none of the eight history-making careers that are the subject of this book would have been possible without the two World Wars. Each man was not only affected by them; all except Gandhi took part, in one way or another, in one or both of the conflicts.

Some historical moments are more "plastic"—lending themselves to wider and deeper change—than others. The years between 1919 and 1950 can be seen, in retrospect, as exhibiting greater plasticity than any earlier period. The eight men featured in this book took advantage of this condition to introduce policies, institutions, and practices that departed in major ways from those they replaced. In so doing, they changed the world.

While history provided no shortage of ambitious political leaders before the first half of the twentieth century, in their ambitions and accomplishments the earlier leaders resembled architects working to renovate or modify existing structures. The eight men of this era were more like architects confronting a vacant lot: they were free to build *ab initio* according to their own often radical designs.

If the two World Wars and the Great Depression created opportunities for radical political innovations, they also enabled the rise to political power of men who entered political life precisely in order to make such innovations. The German sociologist Max Weber (1864–1920) divided political leadership into three types. Traditional leaders, typically hereditary monarchs, draw their authority from longstanding customs and traditions. For rational-legal leaders, authority rests on clear, firmly established procedures for allocating legitimate authority, as in democracies. The third type, which he called the "charismatic" leader, exercises power on the basis of his personal attributes. *Charisma* is a Greek word denoting a "gift of divine origin." Weber defined it, for the purpose of leadership, as

> a certain quality of an individual personality, by virtue of which he is set apart from ordinary men and treated as endowed with supernatural, superhuman, or at least specifically exceptional powers or qualities.[6]

Leadership based on personal qualities became more common in the first half of the twentieth century because the three great upheavals undercut the other two sources of authority. In so doing, they paved the way for the assumption of power by men with radical ambitions.[7] Both tradition and legal rules placed restraints on what leaders who depended on them for their power were able to do. In addition, traditional and rational-legal leaders had little incentive to overturn the orders from which they derived their authority, for that would, metaphorically, have cut off the branches on which they sat. By contrast, those relying on their personal qualities for the power they wielded were relatively free of such restraints and disincentives.

All of the political figures portrayed in this book relied, albeit in varying degrees, on personal qualities to accomplish sweeping changes. Lenin, Hitler, and Mao were avowed revolutionaries, with no allegiance to traditional or legal norms—although each claimed to be acting on behalf of the higher truths revealed by the ideology he professed. Gandhi and Ben-Gurion were democrats and the states they were instrumental in founding became democracies; but they initially aimed to overthrow imperial governance and with it the rules that the empire—in both instances the British Empire—had imposed.

Wilson, Roosevelt, and Churchill governed in established democracies and thus were bound by their countries' constitutional norms. None of the three had any desire to overturn those norms. All three did, however, exercise unusually broad authority compared with most of their predecessors and successors. This greater-than-usual power had something to do with their personal qualities but also, and more importantly, with the fact that they held office during national emergencies brought on by at least one of the three great twentieth-century upheavals. In emergencies, the scope for innovation tends to be broader than in ordinary times. Moreover, all of Churchill's and Wilson's and many of Roosevelt's major historical achievements took place in the realm of foreign policy, where democratic leaders have more leeway for the exercise of power than they do over domestic issues.

* * *

Each of the chapters that follow is divided into five sections. The first, entitled "The Life," provides a brief account of what is in each case a well-known and extensively documented life and career. It does not substitute for a full-scale biography, of which, for each individual, there are a number of good ones. Rather, it gives the reader who has little or no familiarity with the life in question enough information to appreciate the succeeding four sections.*

---

* Each chapter relies for basic information about the leader in question on a few of the many biographies that have been written about each one. A more comprehensive consultation is not necessary because *The Titans of the Twentieth Century* does not attempt to break new ground on the details of the individual lives. For the present purpose, the chapters need to convey only the basic facts of the life, which all biographies cover in more or less the same way, although of course they interpret these facts differently. In addition, as explained below, two of the five sections of each chapter—on "The Times" and "The Legacy"—do not deal directly with the biographical details of the subject's subjects at all but instead rely on other historical studies.

The second part, "The Times," presents the broad social and political forces—Marx's "circumstances already existing"—that did most to shape each individual's public life. It supplies, that is, the historical context in which he operated. In every case, the relevant forces include the impact of one or both of the two World Wars.

The third section of each chapter, "Leadership," comes in two separate although closely related parts. The first describes the ideas that the person brought to public life. For each of the eight, political ideas had unusual significance. For most of them, ideas had supreme importance, animating and defining their careers. The first half of the twentieth century was the great age of political ideas—for better and/or worse.

The second part of the third section of each chapter explores how he persuaded others of the worth of his ideas and of the urgent need to put them into practice. It also discusses the techniques each employed to enlist those with whom he had direct personal contact, as well as the many more with whom he did not, to follow and assist him in the pursuit of his goals. The first part of the third section, that is, tells what the subject of the chapter sought to do, while the second describes how he attempted, almost always successfully, to do it.

"Personal Imprint," the fourth of the five parts of each chapter, addresses directly the personal impact each man had on the history of his times. It specifies what he caused to happen that without him would likely not have happened, at least not in the way that it did. It offers, therefore, a necessarily subjective judgment about the aspects of twentieth-century history for which the individual career described in the chapter can be considered the *sine qua non*. The fifth and concluding section tells which of the man's accomplishments lived on after his death and which did not. The passage of time is a necessary condition for any such assessment, and for each of the eight men sufficient time has passed since he left the scene to make that assessment possible.[8]

Finally, although *The Titans of the Twentieth Century* concerns leaders, it is not intended to serve as a manual of leadership. It does not purport to tell those who aspire to lead organizations or political communities how to do so. There are many such books, and most have as their basic premise the conviction that leadership is a positive, constructive, valuable activity. Sometimes it is. Sometimes, however, leadership has disastrous consequences. Both kinds of leadership are in evidence in the pages that follow.

Five of the eight figures discussed here—Woodrow Wilson, Winston Churchill, Franklin Roosevelt, Mohandas Gandhi, and David Ben-Gurion—operated within democratic settings. They left democracy stronger than they had found it, both in their own countries and beyond. The other three—Vladimir Lenin, Adolf Hitler, and Mao Zedong—were tyrannical dictators. For them, a common—often the preferred—technique of leadership was coercion rather than persuasion. Indeed, the three were worse than tyrants: they were monsters—mass murderers who constructed political systems that caused, under their direction, the deaths of tens of millions of people. The twentieth century was in some ways a miserable period of history and to Lenin, Hitler, and Mao belongs the responsibility for much of that misery.

I

Thomas Woodrow Wilson

The Life

Thomas Woodrow Wilson was born on December 28, 1856, in Staunton, Virginia, to Thomas Ruggles Wilson and the former Jessie Woodrow. His father was a Presbyterian minister in Staunton who went on to hold several other pulpits in the South[1] and become a prominent figure in the American Presbyterian church. The religion in which Woodrow Wilson grew up played an important role in his life: in 1885, he married the daughter of another Presbyterian clergyman, Ellen Axson; he regularly attended church services and prayed privately; and the influence of his religious commitment affected some aspects of his public career.*

He attended Princeton College, graduating in 1879, studied law at the University of Virginia Law School where he began to call himself Woodrow rather than Tommy, and started practicing law in Atlanta. After a few years, he abandoned the law for an academic career, earning a PhD in history and politics in 1886—a degree then only beginning to be awarded—from the Johns Hopkins University in Baltimore, one of the first universities to offer it. He made the change because he wanted to be more active in public affairs than a life in the law seemed likely to permit, although at first he envisioned himself not as an officeholder but rather as a participant in the

---

* Of the eight leaders portrayed in this book, Wilson was the most conventionally religious, and his religion had the greatest influence on his public activities. Religion also played a major role in the life of Mohandas Gandhi, but Gandhi drew his religious beliefs from a variety of traditions, not just the Hinduism into which he was born and continued to practice in various ways throughout his life. See p. 160.

great political debates of his time: he aspired to be what subsequently came to be called a "public intellectual." His published writing attracted attention, particularly his book *Congressional Government*. In it, he criticized the fragmentation of authority in the American federal government mandated by the Constitution and advocated a greater concentration of power, along the lines of the British parliamentary system, in order to make the government function more effectively.

In 1890 he returned to Princeton as a member of the faculty and in 1902 became the president of the university. He devoted his presidency to promoting reforms through which he hoped to make Princeton a more intellectually serious institution, emphasizing two initiatives in particular: what was called the "Quad Plan," designed to make the residential halls more like Oxford and Cambridge colleges, and building a graduate college to be located at the center of the Princeton campus. Both encountered opposition, and Wilson was not able fully to realize either. Contributing to his failure was his stubborn insistence on having his way and his extreme reluctance to accommodate the preferences of others by compromise. These traits of character would recur during his presidency.[2]

Despite these setbacks, he acquired a reputation as a successful leader and made himself available for the Democratic nomination for governor of New Jersey in 1910. The nomination required the support of the politically conservative Democratic leaders of the state, which he secured. In the general election, however, when he had to win the favor of the far more numerous voters of New Jersey, Wilson presented himself as belonging to the other, less conservative wing of the party. He adopted the political identity of a Progressive.

The Progressive movement, which had Republican as well as Democratic adherents and of which he became a prominent champion, arose in the last decades of the nineteenth century in response to the rapid and sweeping changes the United States was then undergoing. Under the influence of what came to be called the Second Industrial Revolution, which brought the widespread use of oil for fuel, steel as a building material, and electricity for manufacturing and ultimately for use in the home, America's population became increasingly urban and its economy became more industrial. The country also had more foreign-born residents as the result of mass immigration, much of it from eastern and southern Europe rather than from the western part of that continent, from which most immigrants had come in the past.

These changes created new social and political problems. Several of them, including urban poverty, the power of unprecedentedly large industrial corporations, and the corruption of politics under the influence of big-city political organizations, particularly troubled the Progressives. To cope with these new developments, they favored a more extensive role for government in regulating private business than had been the norm in the United States. They also favored political reform to correct what they regarded as distortions of American democracy.

Wilson was elected governor and, in his single term, succeeded in enacting a progressive agenda: the passage of an employer liability and workman's compensation act as well as a corrupt practices act affecting candidates for office; the establishment of a commission to regulate public utilities; and the revision of election procedures.

His achievements as governor propelled Wilson into the contest for the Democratic presidential nomination in 1912. Obtaining it required winning the votes of two-thirds of the delegates to the party's convention, which was held in Baltimore that year. After forty-six ballots over six long days, Wilson received the requisite support. He entered the general election as the nominee of the weaker of the two major parties. Democrats had managed to elect only one president since the Civil War—Grover Cleveland in 1884 and again in 1892. In 1912, they still bore the stigma of the rebellion five decades earlier—the Confederate states had all opposed the Republican Abraham Lincoln in the election of 1860—which the continuing and overwhelming allegiance of white Southerners to the Democrats served to reinforce. The Northeast and Midwest—the sections of the country that had remained loyal, that had won the war, and that had become, in the wake of that conflict, the most economically dynamic parts of the United States—usually gave the majority of their votes to the Republicans.

In 1912, however, the Democrats—and their candidate—enjoyed a stroke of good fortune. The Republicans split into two camps. The 26th president, Theodore Roosevelt, decided not to support the reelection of his hand-picked successor, William Howard Taft, but instead to run for president himself on a third-party ticket.[3] Wilson was able to win the presidency with only 42 percent of the popular vote, the first president born in the South to be elected since James K. Polk in 1844.[4]

As he had done as governor of New Jersey, in the White House Wilson proposed, and largely passed, a progressive agenda. It included the first federal income tax since the Civil War; the establishment of a Federal Trade Commission to regulate business; the creation of the Federal Reserve Board to oversee the nation's monetary affairs; a child labor law; a law mandating an eight-hour workday for industrial workers; and the Clayton Antitrust Act to limit the size and power of big business.[5] He sought reelection in 1916 and achieved a narrow victory, the first Democratic president to win a second consecutive term since Andrew Jackson in 1832.[6] His campaign emphasized domestic issues, but by that time the greatest European war in a hundred years was in full swing.

World War I had begun in August 1914. It pitted a coalition consisting of Hohenzollern Germany, the Austro-Hungarian Habsburg Empire, and the Turkish Ottoman Empire, known collectively as the Central Powers, against Great Britain, France, and Imperial Russia— the Allied Powers. Americans reacted to the outbreak of war with a determination to stay out of it. Wilson declared that the United States would be "neutral in fact as well as in name . . . impartial in thought as well as action."[7]

From the start, however, a number of influential Americans of both parties, including members of Wilson's own administration, sympathized with Great Britain and the Allies. Another group opposed in principle direct American participation in the war.[8] The president himself belonged to neither faction. While he was an Anglophile, and Great Britain was the only foreign country he knew at all well, he initially sought not the victory of one side or the other but rather an end to the fighting. He launched, through his close associate Edward M. House, several attempts to mediate between the two coalitions, none of which succeeded.

Early on, Wilson conceived the major American war aim to be ensuring, whenever it ended, that no more such conflicts would occur.[9] That effort, which came into play when the war did end, turned into his principal contribution not only to World War I but also to world affairs more generally. It formed the basis for his personal imprint on the history of his time and beyond.

Neutrality as the United States practiced it turned out to favor the Allied Powers. America's neutral status did not prevent trade with the warring parties. Since the British Navy controlled the Atlantic Ocean, that meant trade almost exclusively with the Allies. Transatlantic trade boosted the American economy as the British, especially, bought more and more from the United States. Ultimately they required, and the Wilson administration authorized, American loans to finance their purchases. In this way America aided the Allied war effort and came to have a greater economic stake in the Allied countries than in the Central Powers. With its naval supremacy, Britain also imposed a stringent and punishing maritime blockade on the Central Powers, which the United States did not seriously oppose.

Germany found a means of counteracting British naval might with the newly invented submarine. Unable effectively to challenge the Royal Navy on the Atlantic Ocean's surface, the Germans could limit the benefits to the Allies of transatlantic commerce by attacking and sinking ships plying the Atlantic between North America and western Europe. To the Germans, submarine warfare represented a legitimate tactic that partially offset a major military disadvantage in their bitter struggle with their adversaries. Wilson and many Americans, however, objected to this form of warfare, regarding it as illegal and indeed barbaric.

On May 7, 1915, a German submarine sank the British luxury liner *Lusitania*. A total of 1,198 passengers died, including 128 Americans. The attack had a powerful political impact in the United States. It aroused deep and widespread resentment at Germany for having committed what was generally regarded as mass murder on the high seas.[10] Wilson sharply reprimanded the German government and insisted that it call a halt to surprise submarine attacks on surface ships.[11] For a time, it did. In January 1917, however, the German authorities decided to resume unrestricted submarine warfare,[12] and soon attacked American ships in defiance of Wilson's demand. In response to these attacks, the United States entered the war on the side of the Allies.

In his April 2, 1917, address to a joint session of Congress urging a declaration of war, Wilson emphasized the moral and legal reasons for fighting. "We will not choose the path of submission and suffer the most sacred rights of our nation and our people to be ignored or violated," he said, and added that "the right is more precious than peace, and we shall fight for the things which we have always carried nearest our hearts. . . ." By majorities of 82 to 6 in the Senate and 373 to 50 in the House of Representatives, the Congress voted to enter the war.

Wilson played only a minor role in the conduct of the war in Europe once the United States entered it, although he was prominently involved in the mobilization of American society for the conflict, which entailed a much-expanded economic role for the federal government. American troops arrived in force in France in the spring of 1918 and took part in the offensives that brought victory to the Allies in November of that year.

Even before the war ended, President Wilson set out his ideas for the postwar settlement, notably in three major speeches he delivered in person in the Capitol: his war message of April 2, 1917, before both houses of Congress; an earlier address to the Senate on January 22 of that year, in which he spoke of the need for a "peace without victory" to end the fighting; and an address on January 8, 1918, again to both houses of Congress, where he spelled out fourteen goals for the postwar world, which became known as the "Fourteen Points." The principles and proposals he presented came collectively to be called, in subsequent years, "Wilsonianism"[13]; and it is through the enduring salience of Wilsonianism in international affairs that Woodrow Wilson made his mark on the world.

The variety of proposals that he made were, in his view, all means to one great end: transforming the pattern of relations between and among sovereign states that had dominated Europe for centuries and had, in 1914, produced a catastrophic war, with the aim of preventing such conflicts in the future. The world could not afford more of them. He did not call World War I "the war to end all war"—words sometimes wrongly attributed to him[14]—but the phrase does express the unifying purpose of his various ideas and proposals.

To accomplish it, Wilson advocated changing the basis for constituting sovereign states. The belligerents in World War I were multinational empires, composed of whatever territories and peoples their rulers had managed to conquer and hold. Henceforth, Wilson said, sovereignty should be allocated according to the principle of national self-determination. The nation should form the basis for the state, replacing the planet's imperial dynasties.[†]

Wilson also wanted the new independent countries to be governed democratically. He did not give the same prominence to democracy in international affairs that it was to attain, especially in the foreign policy of his own country, in the decades following his active career. Nor did he offer any guidance on how to foster that particular form of government. He seems to have assumed that once states were composed of single nations, they would

---

[†] Wilson used the term "national self-determination" sparingly. John Milton Cooper Jr., *Woodrow Wilson: A Biography*, New York: Alfred A. Knopf, 2009, p. 6. The idea, however, had a prominent place in his thought. Points IX, X, and XIII of the Fourteen Points, for example, call, in effect, for national states for Italy, the peoples of the Habsburg Empire, and Poland.

become democracies more or less automatically. He certainly believed that undemocratic governments were incompatible with what was, after all, his supreme international goal: peace.[15]

Wilson also singled out as crucial for a peaceful postwar world the free flow of international commerce and the freedom of the seas that made it possible.[16] He advocated, as well, limitations on armaments, to reduce the chances for another terrible conflict.[17] Last but certainly not least, he called for some kind of international mechanism—what he described on January 22, 1917, as a "world league for peace"—through which the countries of the world could act together to prevent war.[18]

In January 1919, the victorious powers gathered outside Paris at Versailles to set the terms for organizing the postwar world. Wilson brought his blueprint for reconstructing the international order to the peace conference, having decided to represent the United States himself. He arrived in Europe—the first president to visit the continent while in office—to a rapturous reception. He was hailed as a savior, a secular messiah who could deliver the world from war.[19] He and the leaders of the other three victorious countries—Prime Ministers Georges Clemenceau of France, David Lloyd George of Great Britain, and Vittorio Orlando of Italy[20]—met together frequently and made the major decisions. In this way, they functioned as a kind of temporary, de facto world government. Their main business involved dealing with the three defeated Central Powers.

Of these, Germany was the most important because the most powerful. Wilson had promised a peace without victory,[21] but the terms the Germans had to accept resembled those that the winners of previous European wars had imposed on the losers. Germany lost territory, as had defeated powers in the past, including places where the people spoke German, identified as Germans, and wished to belong to a German state: national self-determination turned out not to apply to them. Clause 231 of the Peace Treaty that was signed at Versailles limited German military forces and stipulated, contrary to what almost all Germans believed, that Germany bore the responsibility for starting World War I[22] and therefore had to pay reparations to the Allies, just as France had had to pay after being defeated in the Napoleonic Wars in 1815 and the Franco-Prussian War of 1870–1871. Finally, German representatives had no say in devising the peace terms. They were simply presented with the Treaty and ordered to sign it.

As for the Habsburg Empire, it had begun to dissolve even before the guns fell silent, and several independent countries—which consisted very roughly but not precisely of single nations—emerged from it. Ottoman Turkey received treatment as harsh as did Germany in the Treaty of Sèvres of 1920, but a new Turkish government, led by a World War I general, Mustafa Kemal, managed to regain some of the territory Turkey had lost. A treaty recognizing independent Turkey's new borders was signed in Lausanne, Switzerland, in 1923, by which time Wilson had ceased to be president and the United States had withdrawn from active involvement in the political affairs of Europe.

Turkey did have to relinquish its provinces outside Anatolia, in the Middle East, but these did not become independent nation-states. Instead, they came under the control of Great Britain and France under a system of international "mandates," and these powers also retained their existing imperial territories. Far from giving up their non-European possessions, as a result of World War I the British and French in fact expanded them. The principle of national self-determination was not implemented outside Europe.

Wilson himself took the lead at the postwar conference in designing an international organization to keep the peace. The League of Nations was to have a General Assembly that every sovereign state would be able to join, a secretariat, and an executive council comprising the five victorious powers—Japan was included with the United States, Great Britain, France, and Italy—in addition to four other countries. Of all the different elements of the postwar settlement, Wilson imputed the greatest importance to the League. Once established, it would, he was confident, develop, grow, and embed itself in the fabric of international relations. He counted on it to cope with problems and difficulties that the peace treaties did not resolve, or that appeared independently of the postwar settlement. The creation of the League, he was convinced, would justify the enormous sacrifices that World War I had exacted. He regarded it as so important that he had it included in the peace treaties. That meant that when the United States Senate took up the Versailles Treaty—which the Constitution required a two-thirds majority of that body to ratify—it was deciding whether the United States would join the League of Nations. Here, Wilson experienced his greatest failure as president.

The debate over the League became heated and acrimonious, dividing the Senate into three factions. One supported the president and wanted the Treaty ratified as written and the League accepted as designed. A second adamantly opposed American membership in the League under any circumstances. A third was willing to contemplate membership, but only with reservations. Henry Cabot Lodge of Massachusetts, the Republican chairman of the Senate Foreign Relations Committee, offered fourteen of them.[23]

Much of the controversy that the proposal for American membership in the League aroused revolved around Article X of the League's charter. It read:

> The Members of the League undertake to respect and preserve as against external aggression the territorial integrity and existing political independence of all Members of the League. In case of any such aggression or in case of any threat or danger of such aggression the Council shall advise upon the means by which this obligation shall be fulfilled.

The wording raised the central question, among the senators and in the wider public, of whether the United States should accept the obligation to which this article committed League members. It also raised the prior question of just what that obligation was—that is, in what circumstances America would, if it joined the League, be obliged to go to war to counteract aggression.

Together, the partisans of the League and the group with reservations added up to two-thirds of the Senate; but Wilson would accept no reservations at all and those who supported reservations would not abandon them. So the Treaty did not win approval and the United States did not join the League of Nations.

In the midst of the battle over the League, Wilson decided to apply pressure to the reluctant senators by going over their heads with a direct appeal to the American public. For this purpose, he embarked, in September 1919, on a railroad journey across the country during which he delivered forty-two speeches in favor of League membership in twenty-one days. In Pueblo, Colorado, on September 25, he collapsed from exhaustion and had to discontinue his trip. A week later, on October 2, he suffered a crippling stroke. He was not only unable to save the League, he also could no longer carry out his presidential duties. He was bedridden for much of the rest of his presidential term and, in what can be seen in retrospect as an unrecognized constitutional crisis, his personal physician and his second wife, whom he had married in 1915 following the death of his first spouse the year before, served as his principal link to the world.[24] Even after leaving the White House, he never fully recovered, and he died on February 6, 1924.

The Times

World War I made Woodrow Wilson a world-historical figure. Had the war never taken place, or had the United States not entered it, he would be remembered as a president reasonably successful in enacting domestic legislation, one who broke decisively with the Democratic Party's Jeffersonian tradition of limited government. He thereby served as a bridge, in the construction of the American welfare state and the expansion of the power of government to regulate the economy, between the two Roosevelts, Theodore and Franklin, who occupied the White House before and after he did.

It was not just the fact of the war but its character that opened the historical space that Wilson filled. The conflict turned out to be vastly more destructive than was generally anticipated when it began. It involved larger armies than ever before. It made use of industrial weaponry—in particular, artillery and the machine gun—far more lethal than those that soldiers had employed to kill and maim one another in the past. Because the two warring coalitions were evenly matched, at least on the western front, with neither able to dislodge the other from the opposing lines of trenches that stretched from the North Sea across Belgium and France to the Swiss border, the conflict defied the initial expectations of a short war and dragged on for four terrible years. For much of that time, each side launched periodic frontal assaults on the other's entrenched positions, gaining little or no ground but suffering large numbers of killed and wounded. In all, about 20 million people died in World War I, half of them military personnel and half civilians.[25]

The war destroyed the old European political order. In 1815, in the wake of the previous great continental conflict, the wars against Revolutionary and then Napoleonic France at the end of the eighteenth century and the beginning of the nineteenth, the victors had gathered at Vienna and negotiated a restoration of the political arrangements in Europe that France had battered. This was possible because the partisans of the old order, the dynastic multinational empires of the continent in alliance with more liberal but still monarchical Great Britain, had won the war. A century later, they lost it.

The winners at the outset of the twentieth century were not inclined to restore to their thrones the emperors they had just sacrificed so much blood and treasure to defeat, and would have had great difficulty in doing so even if they had tried: the Romanovs had been unseated in Russia in 1917 and the nations that had constituted the Habsburg Empire had already begun to defect from it.

The old regimes had not only been defeated, they had also been discredited. Their policies had produced colossal failure. They had taken their countries into a spectacularly costly war and failed to win it. Of course, the leaders of the victorious powers had also led their countries into that disastrous conflict, which fostered the belief that not only the regimes of the losers but also the international rules and practices that had made World War I possible urgently needed to be replaced in order to prevent a recurrence of the horrors of 1914 to 1918.

Woodrow Wilson arrived in Europe offering a formula for replacing what could not and, it was widely accepted, should not be restored. That is why he received such an enthusiastic reception. He was in a position to make such an offer and have it both welcomed by the people of the continent and entertained seriously by their leaders not only because of his personal ideas for transforming international relations but also because of the office he held. The country he represented had come, during the war, to play a far larger role in European and international affairs than ever before.

Like World War I, the rise of the United States to a prominent place on the world stage made it possible for Woodrow Wilson to become an important historical figure outside the borders of his own country and beyond the confines of his own era. The American republic was, in its origins, a creation of Europe—of Great Britain, to be precise—and until 1815 played only a minor role in European great-power politics.[26] Following the conclusion of the American War of 1812 against Great Britain and the larger and more important Napoleonic Wars, of which that lesser conflict was an offshoot, a century passed in which the United States had little to do with the international politics of the European great powers. That changed with World War I, during the course of which America itself became a European power.

It was able to become a significant force in the affairs of the continent because over the preceding hundred years it had experienced rapid and substantial growth in the underlying bases of international power. It had pushed its western border from the Appalachian Mountains to the Pacific Ocean, and from north to south it came to encompass the vast territory from Canada to Mexico, the second of these countries diminished by the land the United States took from it in the war between the two countries of 1846 to 1848. The United States thereby became a country of continental scope, and its population increased as well. Through a high birth rate and mass immigration, from 1800 to 1900 the American population grew from 5 million to 75 million. In the wake of the Civil War, the Second Industrial Revolution, whose impact called the Progressive movement into being,[27] spurred high annual rates of economic growth that gave the United States, by the end of the nineteenth century, the largest economy in the world.

The major industrial innovations of that century also linked the United States more tightly to Europe. The two sides of the Atlantic had been connected since Europeans first began to make the long ocean voyage to North America, and from the time of the earliest settlements the settlers had depended on Europe for goods, immigrants, and capital. The revolutionary nineteenth-century advances in transportation and communication—the steamship, the railroad (which carried agricultural products from the American interior to its east coast for transoceanic shipment), and the telegraph produced ever-closer economic integration between the New World and the Old. For practical purposes, they substantially narrowed the ocean that separated the two.

The United States was therefore a looming offstage presence in World War I from the moment the conflict began. It was obvious that access to American resources—including the most valuable resource of all: manpower—would confer a major advantage on the side that gained it.[28] The Allies did manage to secure such access. First, they received imports relevant to their struggle in France. Ultimately, the United States came to finance much of the Allied, and especially the British, war effort. America had an economic interest in selling and lending to the Allies, but behind the historic decision to enter the war lay a different consideration: an idea about the American role in the world.

In the decades after the Civil War, the country's power and influence began to extend beyond its borders. The United States acquired a sphere of influence in Central America and the eastern Pacific and a modest empire as a result of its victorious war against Spain in 1898. It established an economic presence in China, along with those of the European great powers.[29]

The growth in American wealth and power made this possible, but under-lying it as well was the conviction, which was particularly strong among the minority of Americans who interested themselves in the world beyond North America, that being active abroad was important for their country.

Although all interested Americans did not necessarily agree on all the particulars of American foreign policy, they did agree that there should be one and that the country's values and traditions as well as its wealth made the exercise of influence abroad appropriate for it.[30] This proposi-tion commanded wide assent in the public attentive to foreign policy and established the broad context for Woodrow Wilson's wartime and, more importantly, postwar policies. He certainly concurred with it. He firmly believed that his country had a great deal to offer the world. Even while he hoped to avoid taking a direct part in the fighting in Europe, he favored, and began to think seriously about, a major American role in the settle-ment after the fighting had ended.[31] In general, therefore, the United States entered World War I because, among other reasons, Americans saw them-selves as a great power, with the obligations and opportunities that that status entailed.

Leadership

Like the other seven twentieth-century titans, Woodrow Wilson brought a set of ideas to the conduct of his public life, the ideas subsequently known collectively as Wilsonianism. His historical significance rests more heavily on these ideas than does that of the others. Lenin, Hitler, Churchill, FDR, Gandhi, Ben-Gurion, and Mao all put their ideas into practice—albeit to differing extents and not always to the benefit of those affected by them. Wilson, by contrast, only very partially succeeded in implementing his ideas about how the international order should be organized. Wilsonian ideas have had and continue to have a marked impact on the conduct of international affairs: that is his personal imprint on history. During his lifetime, however, the history of Woodrow Wilson's world leadership was largely the history of failure. He was an important prophet but an unsuc-cessful statesman.

This is not to say that Wilson failed in all his political projects. He enacted into law an ambitious agenda as governor of New Jersey. He was elected president of the United States, something only twenty-six men before him and seventeen in the century after he left office managed to accomplish, something that Wilson achieved twice. As president, he shepherded significant laws through the legislative process. Beyond America's borders, he aroused, for a time, passionate enthusiasm in much of Europe, enthusiasm both for himself and for what he was trying to do.

Wilson owed these successes in no small measure to his skill at public speaking. He was an orator in the style of the nineteenth century. He had to make himself heard, understood, and appreciated by large audiences, in person, without the benefit of electronic amplification. The people who came to hear him prized eloquence, and had more patience for extended discourses than subsequent, more distracted, generations. Unlike almost all of his successors in the presidency, Wilson wrote his own speeches, and he took great care in composing them. His understanding of the responsibilities of political leadership prominently included public education, and he regarded speeches as a major vehicle for this purpose. It was probably not irrelevant that the Presbyterian Church in which he grew up emphasized religious commitment of an intellectual rather than an emotional kind. The sermons he heard from his father and other ministers likely reflected this orientation.

In the positions of leadership that he held, Wilson saw himself as a reformer, and a bold one at that. His gifts as a speaker played an important part in the success he enjoyed in each of these positions—until he tried to implement his proposals for transforming international relations. Here he failed twice: once in the design of the postwar settlement at Paris, and again in his attempt to persuade the Senate to ratify the Versailles Treaty and bring the United States into the League of Nations. On both occasions, personal shortcomings hindered his efforts; but the two failures ultimately had deeper, indeed intractable, causes.

Like Clemenceau, Lloyd George, and Orlando, Woodrow Wilson arrived in Paris lacking power based on statutes or tradition that he could use to shape the deliberations of the peace conference, power of the kind that all four enjoyed in their domestic affairs. He could not enforce Wilsonian ideas. Nonetheless, he was confident that he could bend the conference's deliberations to his will and produce a settlement in conformity with the principles he had enumerated. He assumed that the United States had three sources of leverage. The late American entry into the war had tipped the military balance in favor of the Allies, which would, he believed (or at least hoped), give him outsized influence over the peacemaking. Moreover, the Allies, especially Great Britain, owed the United States $7 billion, and this, too, he thought, furnished the American president with the where-withal to enlist them in achieving his goals. Finally, the dramatic popular reception he received on the continent persuaded Wilson that, because the people of Europe had so enthusiastically hailed him, their leaders, who had ultimately to answer to their people, would fall in line with his plans.

Reasonable though these assumptions might have seemed at the beginning of 1919, none of them proved to be accurate. The Allies had sacrificed far more in blood and treasure than had the Americans and were not prepared to defer to Woodrow Wilson. He had failed to consult with the European leaders in formulating his vision of the peace settlement, and those leaders had, in fact, secretly agreed on a division among themselves of the territory they hoped to conquer in the war. Wilson might have been able to use the promise of debt relief to gain their assent when they disagreed with him, but American public opinion was not prepared to allow such relief. Finally, it turned out that the publics in the Allied countries who had received Wilson so warmly not only supported the idea of an enduring peace that he was promising, they also supported some of the peace terms on which their own leaders insisted, terms that conflicted with the Wilsonian vision. Not for the first time or the last, democratic public opinion proved to be neither of one mind nor internally consistent.

In addition to Wilson having less leverage than he initially imagined he had, some of his personal traits hurt his cause at Paris. He was prone to work, and to make decisions, alone, without seriously consulting even his own staff. This habit hindered his performance at the peace conference, where he had to deal with many complicated issues whose details he lacked the time to master.[32] He had always had difficulty cooperating with other strong personalities, a pattern that continued in his dealings with the leaders of the other victorious powers. He did not establish easy working relations with them, something that Franklin Roosevelt, the American president who presided over his country's policies in the Second World War, was always at pains to try to do.[33] The principal obstacles to a Wilsonian peace that Wilson confronted at Paris, however, had to do not with matters of personality but rather with national interests and the nature of international coalitions.

The parties to any coalition will have some overlapping interests—otherwise, they would not be allies; but they almost invariably have differing, often conflicting interests as well. In wartime, the shared interest in defeating the common enemy tends to submerge the differences. After the war is over, however, these differing interests often come to the fore. So it was with World War I. In its wake, Wilson discovered that America's allies had divergent and sometimes opposing preferences for the organization of Europe and the world. The differing positions proved difficult to bridge because they had their roots in two immutable factors: geography and history.

Crucially, France's geography and history divided Wilson from Clemenceau on the question of how to treat postwar Germany. With his country separated from Germany by the Atlantic Ocean, Wilson could favor, as he had said he did before the United States entered the war, a peace without victory. In the wake of the conflict, his goals for the former enemy included political reform, economic recovery, and international reconciliation. The French, by contrast, had just emerged from a bitter, costly war with Germany that they had come close to losing. France had in fact lost a war to the Germans within living memory, in 1871, and with it a slice of French territory, Alsace-Lorraine.

The French were destined, due to the unchangeable facts of geography, to live next to Germany; and it seemed to them all too likely that, after it recovered from the war, their dangerous neighbor would be able to build up its military forces to exceed those of France. Clemenceau made his overriding goal at the peace conference, therefore, the securing of a settlement that provided France—inevitably at German expense—with revenge, compensation, and above all safety.[34] That meant weakening Germany. He sought, that is, peace *with* victory.

Wilson had told the Senate in his "Peace Without Victory" speech that the aim of the postwar settlement had to be "not a balance of power but a community of power." Clemenceau put his faith in precisely what Wilson rejected. "There is an old system of alliances called the Balance of Power—this system of alliances, which I do not renounce, will be my guiding thought at the Peace Conference."[35]

Two other considerations obstructed Wilson's effort to obtain the kind of peace terms for Germany that he believed offered the best chance of avoiding a future European war. First, other commitments that he had made conflicted with such terms. For example, he had promised to provide the newly reconstituted Poland with an outlet to the sea. Creating one, however, requiring carving out some German territory for incorporation into Poland. This displeased the Germans, especially because it meant that ethnic Germans had to live, involuntarily, under Polish rule. Second, while both Wilson and Lloyd George sometimes spoke of a generous peace for Germany, and may at times actually have wanted one, American[36] and especially British public opinion wanted a harsh peace. Great Britain had fought the Germans for four long years, at great expense in lives and money, and its citizens were in no mood to be charitable to the nation responsible for the heavy price they had had to pay for victory. Democratically elected leaders being ultimately accountable to the people who elect them, on this issue the publics, not their leaders, had their way.[37]

Woodrow Wilson was willing to bend some of the principles he brought to Paris not only because he did not have sufficient power to prevail consistently in his disputes with the other leaders but also because he believed that the League of Nations, once established, would be able to resolve the problems that the peace conference either failed to settle or itself created. He could therefore justify, at least to himself, any compromises he had to make in order to bring the League into existence. For example, he acquiesced in the cession to Japan of Shandong, the German enclave in China, despite the clear violation of national self-determination that this represented, because that was the price of having Japan join the League.[38] The League's fate in the United States was decided not in Paris, however, but in Washington, in the halls of the United States Senate; and there, too, Wilson failed.

To the fight over the League he did bring well-established, widely accepted statutory power, as had not been the case at the peace conference. Presidential leadership in foreign policy, especially on issues of war and peace, had become standard practice in the United States over the decades since the birth of the republic. However, Wilson also had to operate under a constraint: the Constitutionally mandated requirement for a two-thirds Senate majority in order to ratify the Versailles Treaty and seal American membership in the League of Nations.

As with the overall settlement, Wilson's personal shortcomings contributed to his defeat in the League battle. He committed an act of political malpractice by doing nothing to try to obtain Republican support for the League before and during the peace conference. He chose a commission to accompany him to Paris, but none of its members had backgrounds or political connections that earned good will for Wilson and his settlement with his partisan opponents.[39] He had little communication with Republicans and the fact that their leader on foreign policy in the senate, Henry Cabot Lodge, harbored a deep personal animus toward the president did not help his cause. One of Wilson's personal traits, in evidence from his days at Princeton onward, also hampered him: his stubbornness. Once he made up his mind on an issue he seldom modified his position.[40] Had he accepted at least some of the Lodge reservations, he might well have secured the two-thirds majority in the Senate that he needed. Instead, he refused to accept any of them. Leadership in a democracy entails both persuasion and bargaining. For most of his career, Wilson did well at the first but poorly at the second.

One other personal factor made a difference in the League fight: Woodrow Wilson's health. His massive stroke in October 1919 rendered him incapable of carrying out his presidential duties. Even before that dramatic event, however, his health was deteriorating, and may have degraded his effectiveness as a leader. His difficulties at Paris and thereafter have inspired retrospective speculation that he may have suffered a series of undetected but debilitating mini-strokes before the massive one struck him, and that these medical events sapped his energy and impaired his concentration. It is conceivable as well that such episodes, if they occurred, also affected his temperament, making him even more resistant than he normally was to accommodating his political opponents.[41]

As with his inability to shape the peace settlement, and particularly the treatment of Germany, as he had initially wished, Wilson's failure to bring his country into the organization that he largely created had causes that went beyond his personal shortcomings. The League's fatal weakness, for the purposes of American accession to it, centered on Article X and the question of how binding an obligation it imposed on League members.

If the League's Charter meant that a member country had to go to war when the League so voted, the United States, as Wilson had recognized,[42] was highly unlikely to join—out of fear of becoming entangled in conflicts in which no American interests were at stake and because the American Constitution, the supreme law of the land, decreed that the Congress had the sole power to declare war. If, on the other hand, membership brought with it no such automatic obligation, the League could hardly be expected to keep the peace effectively. As a Republican senator who opposed membership under any circumstances put it, "What will your league amount to if it does not contain powers that no one dreams of giving it."[43]

Wilson tried to square the circle by telling the Senate Foreign Relations Committee that Article X imposed a moral rather than a legal obligation; but that did not clarify the matter. Depending on the interpretation of the article, the League was destined to be either unacceptable or impotent. Wilson never established a middle ground between these two possibilities, and it is difficult to see, in retrospect, how he could have done so.[†] He believed, and said, that once established and as it developed, the League would adapt its operations to fit the circumstances that it encountered; but that simply begged the question, on the most crucial issue, of exactly how it would adapt.

As he encountered opposition in the Senate, Wilson took comfort in the conviction that the people of the United States wanted what he wanted. He embarked on his speaking tour to mobilize public opinion, but his stroke ended not only his trip but any further public presidential efforts to rally the country behind him. Even if his health had permitted him to carry out such a campaign to a conclusion, however, it seems doubtful that he would have prevailed. The ultimate test of the popularity of his proposals, Wilson believed, would come in the 1920 presidential election. In that election, the successful Republican candidate, Senator Warren G. Harding of Ohio, opposed League membership and the Democratic candidate, Ohio Governor James M. Cox, did not vigorously support it. When the votes were counted, the Democrats, who were far more closely associated with the League, had suffered a crushing defeat.[44] The outcome of that contest had more than one cause, but it strongly suggested that the American public was not prepared to make the kind of international commitment that Wilson had thought necessary to prevent future wars and had worked to bring about. Woodrow Wilson's leadership ultimately failed not—or not mainly—because of the problems in the way he conducted it, but because the American people decided that they did not wish to go where he wanted to lead them.

[†] Underlying the problem that the League posed was the fact that the ultimate reason that states go to war is that they can. The structure of the society of sovereign states—the international system—permits war because that system is anarchic, without a supreme authority to enforce order. To abolish war requires creating such an authority—the equivalent of a world government—which is what the League, under one interpretation of Article X, would have become. Neither at the time that it was proposed, however, nor before or since have sovereign states, including the United States in 1919, shown any sign of being willing to surrender their sovereign independence to such an authority, which was what was ultimately at stake in the battle over the League. One observer characterized what Wilson was trying to do with the League as attempting to "preserve national sovereignty while suppressing its consequences." Quoted in William Widenor, *Henry Cabot Lodge and the Search for an American Foreign Policy*, Berkeley, California: University of California Press, 1980, p. 306.

The Personal Imprint

Its entry into World War I was the most significant foreign policy decision by the United States since Great Britain's thirteen North American colonies took up arms against the mother country and declared their independence 141 years previously. Woodrow Wilson was the public face of that decision: it was he who formally asked the Congress to declare war. Yet that epochal decision cannot be credited to him personally.

When the war began, he had wanted his country to stay out of it and he maintained that preference almost to the moment of its entry. One of his successors, Franklin D. Roosevelt, did all he could to support Great Britain in World War II before the United States officially became a combatant. Wilson did no such thing during World War I.

America was swept into the war not through presidential leadership but by the force of events. Submarine warfare aroused and angered the American public, turning it sharply against Germany. The undersea campaign against surface ships convinced Americans that their rights were being violated, which was the reason for war. At the beginning of April 1917, Wilson was responding to a public mood he himself had not created. Moreover, his cabinet unanimously favored asking Congress for a declaration of war. All in all, it is likely that whoever had been president at that moment would have acted as he did.

It is his ideas about the proper ordering of international relations that comprise the 28th American president's major, distinctive, and personal contribution to the international history of the twentieth and twenty-first centuries. To be sure, he did not conjure them out of thin air. Wilsonianism had pre-Wilsonian antecedents. The idea that nations should form the basis for states stems from the French Revolution. The Declaration of the Rights of Man of 1789 holds that: "The principle of sovereignty rests essentially in the Nation . . . no body of men, no individual, can exercise authority that does not emanate expressly from it."[45] During the nineteenth century, Italians and Germans consolidated national states, substantially changing the political map of Europe.[46]

Free trade and freedom of the seas had also been facts of international life before Woodrow Wilson included them in his Fourteen Points. Great Britain, with its robust economy, its willingness to reduce tariff barriers, and the maritime supremacy of its navy, underwrote both in the second half of the nineteenth century, which, not coincidentally, was the first great age of globalization. Nor was the idea of an international association to keep the peace Wilson's alone. During World War I, a number of prominent figures, including his two immediate predecessors in the White House, Theodore Roosevelt and William Howard Taft, floated the suggestion that there be a postwar international organization of some sort, although not necessarily the kind that Wilson ultimately proposed.

It was Woodrow Wilson, however, who brought together the component elements of Wilsonianism, who tried to make them the basis of post–World War I European and international politics, and who thereby put them firmly on the world's agenda, where they have remained ever since. In that sense, Wilsonianism comes personally from Woodrow Wilson. The ideas with which he made his mark were personal to him, and so would likely not have had the same historical role without his career. They are distinctively American and distinctively progressive, as was he, and very much in harmony with the intellectual bases of his public career and his own personality.

Wilson's ideas are distinctively American in that, like him, the founders of the United States were committed to remaking the world. They believed that they were embarking on an experiment in a form of politics different from, and better than, what the Old World practiced and that what they did would spread to other countries. "We have it in our power," one of the American Revolution's most ardent publicists, Thomas Paine, wrote, "to begin the world over again." For Thomas Jefferson, the nation's first secretary of state and its third president, that included abolishing the age-old custom of war. His Embargo Act of 1807 was designed to put pressure on Great Britain to accede to American demands by prohibiting all exports from the United States. In so doing, he was attempting to substitute economic leverage for military force—to achieve victory without war.[47]

Jefferson's tactic did not succeed, but the American impulse to transform international relations to make them more peaceful persisted, and in World War I and its aftermath found expression in Woodrow Wilson's ideas and his postwar diplomacy. Moreover, while Jefferson had presided over a weak country of marginal significance to the world's great powers, by the time of Wilson's presidency the United States had become, at least in economic terms, the greatest power of all. The world had to accord Wilson's ideas the kind of attention and respect that Jefferson's had not commanded.

Wilson was not only a representative American in this particular way, he also had a particular, and particularly American, political outlook that was in keeping with his international proposals. He was a progressive, and the progressive spirit informed Wilsonianism. The Progressive movement had as its fundamental premise the belief that the evolution of American society and the American economy required political adaptations through the creation of new institutions and policies. Wilson's ideas about international order rested on the same premise: historical trends, above all the Industrial Revolution, had made the venerable institution of war too costly for it to continue. He included the new international practices he deemed necessary to bring it to an end in his Fourteen Points; and the new institution he sponsored for this purpose was the League of Nations.

Wilsonianism owed its existence principally to Woodrow Wilson himself in a third way: it bore the stamp of his personality. He had the habit, while making decisions, of pondering the issue at hand alone and then announcing what he had decided. During the war, he did discuss matters at some length with his adviser Edward M. House, but then broke with him when the two men were in Paris. Thus Wilsonianism was largely the product of solitary deliberation and not, like so many other governmental initiatives, of extensive consultations and numerous committee meetings.[48]

Moreover, he believed that the purpose of public life—or at least his purpose in taking part in it—was to bring about improvement in the world.[49] He was by temperament a reformer, and acted as one as president of Princeton, as governor of New Jersey, and as president of the United States. Wilsonianism was an ambitious program for international reform. In addition, as a devout Christian he brought a religious sensibility to his public activities and with it the conviction that political issues have a moral dimension. Not surprisingly, he regarded his international program as furthering the cause of righteousness in the world.[50]

Woodrow Wilson combined a distinctively American faith in the mutability of international affairs, a progressive inclination to reform, and a temperament disposed to producing and promoting grand schemes on the basis of solitary reflection. The appearance and prominence of Wilsonian ideas during and after World War I were unlikely without this combination, and therefore without Woodrow Wilson himself as the American president during the years that he served. Others who might plausibly have occupied that position did not hold these ideas. Theodore Roosevelt, the leading Republican, who would probably have run for president again in

1920 had he not died suddenly on January 6, 1919, had little use for Wilson's approach to international politics. Roosevelt harshly criticized Wilson's European policies both during and after the war. Nor did he support the League as Wilson envisioned it. The former president did not believe that international relations could be transformed as Wilson proposed. As president, from 1901 to 1909, Roosevelt had based American foreign policy on balance-of-power considerations.[51] Most other Republicans shared his outlook.

By one common historical interpretation, Woodrow Wilson placed his personal stamp on the history of the twentieth century, albeit unintentionally, in yet another way. The postwar political dispensation that he took a leading role in designing had a major, unhappy result: it failed to keep the peace. Another great and destructive war broke out in Europe only two decades later. By this interpretation, the settlement had two principal flaws, the prevention of which would have avoided World War II: the harsh treatment of Germany, and the refusal of the United States to join the League of Nations.[52] Wilson sometimes seemed to favor more lenient terms for Germany and had passionately advocated American membership in the League, so those who insisted on those two features of the settlement must, according to this view, bear more responsibility than he does for the subsequent conflict. Nonetheless, by these lights his failures, despite his efforts, had a major, disastrous consequence. How plausible is this assertion?

The terms that the Germans had to accept at Paris certainly embittered them. They had expected postwar arrangements consistent with the Fourteen Points, which did not materialize. They considered the reparations imposed on them on the grounds that they had started the war to be unjust, and their postwar efforts to avoid paying what they were deemed to owe damaged their economy and those of the victorious powers as well. Adolf Hitler, the man most responsible for World War II, used the widespread German resentment of the Versailles Treaty to his political advantage in his rise to power in Berlin.[53]

World War II had, however, causes not directly descended from World War I, as well. Indeed, in the 1920s, especially with the Locarno Pact of 1925—a series of agreements in which Germany, France, Belgium, Great Britain, and Italy mutually guaranteed peace in Western Europe—the European powers seemed to have found a way to resolve their differences without war. The American-sponsored Dawes and Young Plans of 1924 and 1929, which restructured Germany's reparations obligations, offered a path out of the financial tangle that reparations had created. The slide to war began with the Great Depression, and the economic misery that it generated, which enabled Hitler to come to power in 1933. The Depression began a full decade after the Paris Peace Conference.

As for the League of Nations, its weakness as an organization to keep and enforce peace became evident with the Japanese invasion and occupation of Manchuria, in northwest China, in 1931. The League passed resolutions of disapproval but did nothing to stop Japan. The American government also strongly disapproved of what the Japanese had done and the League's members looked to the United States for more concrete actions. President Herbert Hoover and his senior officials did not, however, feel able to do more than assert that they would not recognize any territorial gains that Japan made by conquest.[54] There is no reason to believe that, had the United States belonged formally to the League, it would have responded more forcefully.

At Paris, Wilson had entertained the possibility of an Anglo-American security guarantee for France, which was far more important to Clemenceau than the League, and leading Republicans were sympathetic to such a measure;[55] but such a guarantee was never seriously considered.[56] In the wake of the Great War, as with the Manchurian episode, public support for American military intervention abroad was absent.

The Legacy

Woodrow Wilson's claim to major historical significance rests not on what he did but on what he said, not on what he caused to occur but on what he sought but failed to make happen. He failed to put his ideas about the international order into practice, but those ideas survived his departure from the center of global events, and they are his legacy.[§] Over the ensuing decades, they became more widely accepted and more extensively

---

[§] Wilson's historical reputation based on his domestic policies does not have a high standing in the twenty-first century. He believed in a racial hierarchy in the United States and presided over the resegregation of the federal workforce in Washington, D.C. These ideas and practices were decisively repudiated in the decades after his death. In addition, his domestic reforms expanded the federal government's role in the American economy, and those who believe that role to be far too extensive and intrusive have come to decry Wilson as the founder of what they call the "administrative state." For a criticism of his domestic policies, see Dan McLaughlin, "The Hater's Guide to Woodrow Wilson," *National Review*, March 16, 2022, https://www.nationalreview.com/2022/03/the-haters-guide-to-woodrow-wilson.

implemented. They owed their growing salience in no small part to their popularity in the United States, whose political culture, with its emphasis on progress and reform, they particularly suited. In the century after World War I, moreover, the United States became the most important country in the world, giving Wilsonianism a powerful champion. Wilson's ideas also gained in relevance because they met needs that the evolution of international society created, for which reason countries other than the United States came to embrace them.

Despite the rise in the popularity of his ideas, the world did not, in the century after Woodrow Wilson's death, abolish war or the power politics that Wilson had believed made war possible. Nor did the United States, which took his ideas the most seriously, conduct its foreign policy exclusively—or even, for the most part, mainly—along Wilsonian lines. One element of Wilsonianism, however, did attain hegemonic status. In the twentieth century, national self-determination became the only legitimate basis for statehood. The need for some principle for allocating sovereignty became urgent as the world's multinational empires, once the dominant political form on the planet, disappeared. The European empires of the German Hohenzollerns, the Austrian Habsburgs, the Turkish Ottomans, and the Russian Romanovs all collapsed as a result of World War I, although the Bolsheviks reconstituted the Russian Empire, ostensibly in the cause of anti-imperialism, under a new name—the Soviet Union.

After World War II, the British, French, Dutch, and ultimately the Portuguese overseas empires also ceased to exist. Finally, in the early 1990s, the communist multinational empire in Eurasia, which stretched from the middle of Germany to the Pacific coast of Russia, also came to an end. The world needed some way of redrawing its political boundaries and settled on the national principle to which Wilson, in his Fourteen Points and at the deliberations in Paris, had given pride of place.

Sorting the people of the world into distinct nation-states proved difficult because the world's population was not and is not divided into discrete, self-contained, homogeneous national units with clear boundaries between and among them. To the contrary, different peoples were and are intermixed, like a checkerboard or a tossed salad.[57] For that reason, drawing borders often became contentious and all too often led to bloodshed. An appreciable number of the armed conflicts during the century after the Paris Peace Conference had their roots in disputes arising from the intermixture of people bearing different ethnicities, religion, and nationalities, and the objections of some of them to the sovereign political units in which, with the end of empire, they found themselves placed.

At Paris, Wilson's secretary of state, Robert Lansing, had foreseen just such trouble. Of the principle of national self-determination, he said, "The phrase is simply loaded with dynamite. It will raise hopes which can never be realized."[58] No other, better formula for statehood being available, however, in the twenty-first century the national principle remained, at least in theory, the basis for drawing the world's international borders.

Democracy, too, became more common in the twentieth century, spreading in two distinct historical waves—the first after World War II and the second beginning in the 1970s and cresting in the late 1980s and early 1990s with the fall of communism in Europe. To be sure, it did not surge for the reason that Wilson had included it in his program for international reform. He had endorsed representative government because he believed that autocratic regimes could not be trusted to conduct peaceful foreign policies. The countries that adopted democracy, by contrast, did so not for the sake of peace but for a variety of reasons: because they came under the tutelage, or at least the influence, of the world's most powerful democracy, the United States; or because democracy seemed the political path to economic success; or because the alternative forms of government had, in one way or another, been found wanting.[59]

The free trade and freedom of navigation that Woodrow Wilson had included in the Fourteen Points also became more widespread in the second half of the twentieth century and beyond than had been the case in his day. The combination of the two came to be known as globalization. Advances in the technologies of transportation and communication toward the end of the century laid the basis for an expanding volume of cross-border flows of goods, money, and people. The United States supplied the open markets and naval support that Great Britain had provided for the globalization of the nineteenth century. As with democratic governance, countries did not adopt globalization-friendly policies in order to make the world safer, but rather to make themselves more prosperous; but adopting them did make the world more Wilsonian.

Wilson made the reduction of armaments one of his Fourteen Points on the presumption that weapons themselves cause wars. The presumption was and is a shaky one. No doubt the existence of weaponry makes war possible, and the more powerful the weapons to wage it are, the more destructive the war is likely to be; but armed conflict arises from political disputes.

Nations in conflict are not adversaries because they are armed; they are armed because they are adversaries.

The world did experience two periods of negotiated arms limitations after World War I, and in both cases the agreements came about in the context of a larger effort to reduce, or at least contain, the political differences among the signatories. The Washington Naval Treaty and attendant agreements of 1922 formed the basis for a general political settlement among the great powers in East Asia, as did the Locarno Accord in Europe. The Asian settlement came undone when Japan abandoned it for the sake of territorial expansion, beginning in Manchuria in 1931. Later in the century, in the 1970s and 1980s, the United States and the Soviet Union signed a series of nuclear arms control accords as part of an effort to moderate the tensions of the Cold War by limiting, although not ending, their global rivalry[60] and by stabilizing the kind of balance of military power that Wilson had sought to abolish. As with democracy and globalization, in both instances of arms control what Wilson had wanted came to pass, but not precisely for the reason that he had wanted it.

Similarly, the second half of the twentieth century became the great age of international organizations, but not exactly in the way that Wilson had envisioned. After World War II, a successor body to the League of Nations, the United Nations (UN), did come into existence, with the active support and participation of the United States. While in its basic structure the UN resembled the League, it was not granted the power to intervene in conflicts around the world that Wilson had wanted the League to have and that he considered the key to a peaceful world. Peace in Europe after 1945 rested on a balance of power between two opposing multinational coalitions. The United States led the Western coalition and provided a security guarantee to France—of the kind the French had sought but failed to receive after World War I—as well as to other Western European countries, through the North Atlantic Treaty and the integrated military force to which it gave rise, the North Atlantic Treaty Organization (NATO).

Reflecting the growth of the global economy and the increasing economic interactions among its member states, the most numerous and effective twentieth-century international organizations had as their purpose the fostering and regulating of economic cooperation among sovereign states, not peace and security. Wilson and the other leaders at Paris had devoted relatively little attention to economic matters, and the economic issue that they did consider at length, German reparations, did not promote international cooperation; quite the contrary. So international organizations proliferated after the second great war of the twentieth century but, as with democracy, globalization, and arms limits, not for an explicitly Wilsonian reason.

Wilsonianism's greatest impact has come through its deep and enduring influence on the foreign policy of Wilson's own country. "In the history of America's encounter with the world Woodrow Wilson is the central figure," according to one distinguished student of American foreign policy, and "Wilson towers above the landscape of modern American foreign policy like no other individual, the dominant personality, the seminal figure," in the judgment of another.[61] The commanding position that they impute to him stems from the fact that his ideas and his public career gave rise to a distinctive approach to foreign policy, one that the United States has intermittently followed.

Its emphasis on the promotion of American values rather than the country's national interests, and its aspiration to transform relations between and among sovereign states in order to make them more peaceful, earned this approach a title in addition to Wilsonianism: "idealism." It stands in contrast to what is sometimes called "realism," with its fixation on power, the approach to foreign policy that was normal in European history before World War I—and indeed at almost every other place and time— and that Wilson rejected and sought to transcend. For a great power to base its external relations on goals other than power represented something new in the world, and that is Woodrow Wilson's principal contribution to the world's history.

To be sure, manifestations of idealism had appeared before Wilson's moment on the world stage, notably Great Britain in the nineteenth century.[§] Moreover, considerations of power and security have governed the foreign policy of the United States since Wilson's time to a great extent—but not exclusively. Every president since Franklin Roosevelt has at least paid lip service to Wilson's ideas.[62] The Wilsonian approach has waxed and waned

---

[§] In 1876, for example, the British leader W. E. Gladstone aroused public sympathy for the Bulgarians seeking independence from the Ottoman Empire who were the victims of Ottoman atrocities. However, Gladstone was in opposition at the time and Britain did little to help the Bulgarians. The Wilsonian approach is also evident in the foreign policy of the twenty-first-century European Union insofar as the members of that organization are able to act collectively—which, in political and military affairs, is not very far.

over the decades but it has never disappeared, nor has it always been confined to the rhetoric of American officials.

In the two great conflicts in which the United States became involved after the Great War of 1914 to 1918, World War II and the Cold War, realism and Wilsonianism reinforced each other. The political and military contests with Nazi Germany and Imperial Japan in the first instance, and with international communism led by the Soviet Union in the second, were conflicts of both power and values. America's adversaries were seeking, wherever they could, both to expand the territory they directly or indirectly controlled and to impose political and economic systems different from and opposed to those of the United States. Waging those wars, hot and cold, was therefore both a Wilsonian and a realist enterprise.

Wilson himself has a personal connection to the second of these great global conflicts even though the United States entered it almost two decades after he died. He had several reasons for issuing his Fourteen Points when he did, among them the need he perceived to respond to the Bolshevik seizure of power in Russia in 1917. The communists were asserting that their form of governance would create a far more peaceful, just, and prosperous future than the one that the capitalist countries, the United States among them, would provide. Wilson presented his vision of the postwar international order in part as an alternative to the promises the Russian revolutionaries made, with the goal of keeping communist revolution from spreading across Europe as the Bolsheviks desired, expected, and actively sought to instigate. The Soviet-American rivalry after World War II was, as its core, a contest of competing political and economic systems.[63] The Fourteen Points may therefore be seen as a Western salvo in the opening round of the global competition between communism and liberal, capitalist democracy that dominated much of the second half of the twentieth century.

The heyday of Wilsonian foreign policy came in the quarter-century after the end of the Cold War, when the United States faced no major threats and so could devote its relations with other countries, to a greater extent than ever before, to the promotion of American values. In that period, its foreign policy featured two projects in particular that were informed by the Wilsonian spirit.

The United States used its armed forces to protect people in Bosnia, Somalia, and Haiti, where governments or local forces were threatening not only their political rights but also their lives. These operations had as their goal the securing of what had come to be called human rights, and so became known as humanitarian interventions. Official concern with safeguarding human rights began after, and as a result of, World War II, with the founding document being the United Nations Universal Declaration of Human Rights of 1948. Although not formally part of Wilson's program, it reflected the Wilsonian aspiration to make the world a better place for individual people and not simply, as with the realist approach, a safer place for sovereign states.[64]

In the post–Cold War period the American government also made serious efforts to foster in other countries one of the chief elements of the Wilsonian program: democracy. Both where the United States came to exercise direct control and in other places where representative government was absent, American authorities attempted, with at best limited success, to implant democratic institutions and practices.[65]

The post–Cold War era ended in the middle of the second decade of the twenty-first century. As China, Russia, and Iran came to pose threats to American interests and to the security of American friends and allies, power politics resumed.[66] Thwarting Chinese, Russian, and Iranian aspirations came to dominate the foreign policy of the United States, which once again, therefore, revolved around considerations of power. Wilsonian aims receded in importance. They did not, however, vanish entirely. Given the importance of democratic values and practices in American domestic affairs, they are unlikely ever to do so. For that reason, as long as the United States of America continues to be a major force in the world, Woodrow Wilson's legacy will remain alive in the affairs of the planet.

2

Vladimir Ilich Lenin (Ulianov)

The Life

The man the world came to know as V. I. Lenin was born Vladimir Ilich Ulianov on April 10, 1870, in Simbirsk, a city on the Volga River in the Russian Empire. He was baptized in the Orthodox faith. His father held the government position of inspector of schools. The senior Ulianov believed strongly in the importance of education and favored the reform of the Russian regime, but only within the framework of the existing imperial order.[1] His son came, therefore, from the segment of Russian society closest, in its cultural interests and political attitudes, to the European bourgeoisie.

Politics was not a subject of family discussion in the Ulianov household[2] and as a youngster Vladimir showed no interest in the subject.[3] He grew up as a willful, domineering[4] second son in a family of five children that was by all accounts a closely knit and affectionate one. He received both emotional and financial support from his parents and from his siblings, to whom he remained close to the end of his life.[5] He excelled in his studies, receiving a rigorous if narrow secondary education in which he mastered the Greek and Latin languages, among other subjects.[6]

In his teenage years, the Ulianov family suffered two major blows. In 1886, the father died of a cerebral hemorrhage at the age of 54.[7] Then, the next year, the eldest son, Alexander, who was studying science at St. Petersburg University, was arrested for taking part in a plot to assassinate the tsar. He made no effort to conceal or disavow his involvement and was tried, convicted, and executed in 1887. Alexander's activities and his fate placed a stigma on his family. They left Simbirsk and settled in another

Volga city, Kazan, where Vladimir entered the university. While he did study on his own and passed with distinction the examinations of the law faculty of St. Petersburg, and although he did do some minor legal work in the Volga region for a brief period[8] before moving to St. Petersburg, then the Russian capital, in 1893, from his university days onward he considered himself a professional revolutionary.[9] The 1863 novel *What Is To Be Done?* by Nikolai Chernyshevsky made a strong impression on him, with its themes of hostility to liberalism and the need for young Russians to devote themselves to freeing the Russian people from the oppression of their government. Chernyshevsky belonged to the agrarian-populist tradition of Russian radical politics, but Ulianov was not destined to become a populist: in the fall of 1888, he began to study seriously the writings of Karl Marx.[10]

A German from the Rhineland who lived from 1818 to 1883, Marx offered a comprehensive framework for understanding history, economics, and politics. It combined the English approach to political economy with the French revolutionary tradition and the ideas of German idealist philosophers, notably G. W. F. Hegel.[11] Conflict between social classes, Marx argued, acts as the motor of history, which unfolds in predictable stages.[12] In the stage that nineteenth-century Europe had reached, the principal conflict pitted the owners of capital, the bourgeoisie, against a new class that the Industrial Revolution had created, the manual workers in factories—the proletariat. The capitalist economy had an inevitable tendency to immiserate the workers, who would consequently overthrow the political dominance of the bourgeoisie and thereby usher in socialism, an ill-defined but morally superior type of society.

Ulianov not only read Marx's texts, he also translated some of them into the Russian language and began to write articles of his own interpreting and elaborating on the Marxian opus. For the rest of his life, he would be, among other things, a man of the written word, reading extensively[13] and generating for publication a stream of his own theoretical treatises, commentaries, and exhortations.

He modified Marx's teachings in two important ways, which would have profound consequences for his, Russia's, and indeed the world's future. First, while almost all of Russia's people lived in villages and engaged in agriculture, and the country had only the beginnings of the industrial economy that Marx had stipulated as necessary for the transition to socialism, Ulianov asserted, and attempted to document in his writings, that the country had become capitalist and so was ripe for an immediate revolution.[14] Second, while that revolution would be made in the name and in the interests of the workers, it was not they who would lead it. That task would fall to a disciplined, dedicated "vanguard" party of committed revolutionaries, some of whom, at least, would come from the ranks of the Russian intelligentsia.[15] The idea of such a party received its fullest statement in a pamphlet published in March 1902 with the same title as Chernyshevsky's novel. The author of this second *What Is To Be Done?* signed it "N. Lenin," and it was as Lenin that he was known thereafter.

He made his life's work during the early years of the twentieth century the creation and the shaping of the revolutionary party he had described. He became not only a theorist of revolution but also the organizer of the party that, he believed, was destined to carry it out in Russia. Lenin joined the Marxist movement in his country, which formed the Russian Social-Democrat Labor Party in 1902. At a conclave in 1903, however, it split, largely over Lenin's ideas and his insistence on his own primacy within its ranks.[16] His faction achieved a small, temporary advantage over its opponents on one particular vote[17] and so called itself the "Bolsheviks"— the majority—with their Marxist but non-Leninist rivals accepting the name "Mensheviks"—the minority.[18]

The life of the professional revolutionary came with costs for Lenin and others who chose it. Tsarist Russia was a police state in which their activities were illegal and for which they were punished if caught. That is why Lenin used pseudonyms: "Lenin" was not the only one. He was banished to Siberia for three years, living there from 1895 to 1898 in relative comfort compared to the conditions that awaited those sent to that region for most of the twentieth century, and then had to flee the country. He spent fifteen of the first seventeen years of the new century in enforced exile in Europe—prison awaited him if he returned to Russia—in Germany, France, England, Switzerland, and in the Polish part of the Habsburg Empire in the city of Krakow.*

---

* His European sojourns did not give him an affinity for Western political values or any real appreciation of the political conditions in Europe, which he more than once seriously misread. He and some of his Bolshevik colleagues "had spent long periods in the West.... But even as they lived in their midst, they had little contact with Westerners, for they led isolated existences in emigre communities and communicated only with the more radical elements of European socialism." Richard Pipes, *Russia Under the Bolshevik Regime*, New York: Alfred A. Knopf, 1993, pp. 236–237.

Revolution did come to Russia in 1905, on the heels of a military defeat. Japan's victory over Russian imperial forces provoked protests and unrest. The tsar was forced, grudgingly, to permit the establishment of a national parliament, the Duma. The Bolsheviks then living in Russia played almost no role in the events of 1905, although in their aftermath Lenin was able to return to the country for two years before going into exile again.[19]

Another series of military setbacks led to another, more sweeping revolution twelve years later. In World War I, Imperial Russian forces suffered major battlefield defeats at the hands of the German army,[20] damaging the prestige of the tsar and his government. The war caused economic hardship in Russia as well, and workers in the capital went on strike. Ordered to break the strikes, the soldiers of the local garrison refused. In conditions of near anarchy in St. Petersburg and elsewhere, the tsar abdicated, ending the 400-year reign of the Romanov dynasty,[21] and a provisional government took its place.[22]

Living in Zurich when World War I erupted, Lenin had favored a Russian defeat from the beginning[23] but had not anticipated the complete collapse of the tsarist regime. For the purpose of weakening the Russian military effort by inserting a rabble-rousing opponent of it into the country, the German government arranged for Lenin to travel back to his home country in early 1917, after a decade's absence. Once he arrived there, the Germans supplied the Bolsheviks with funding for the purpose of enhancing Russian opposition to the war.[24]

Upon returning, Lenin announced his "April theses," prominent among which was his indirect but unmistakable insistence, which surprised and dismayed many of his colleagues, that the Bolsheviks seize power immediately.[25] In the following months, they made several unsuccessful efforts to do so. Sought by the government for his seditious designs, Lenin went into hiding in Finland. Finally, on the night of October 24–25, Bolshevik forces succeeded in dislodging the government and seizing power in the capital. This did not occur through the kind of mass uprising that had taken place in February. What subsequently came to be known as the great October Revolution was, in fact, a coup d'état, executed by a handful of people and meeting almost no resistance.¶ Lenin later said that the Bolsheviks "found

---

¶ "… the two decisive October days were no more than an amateur police operation of ragtag Red Guards and Kronstadt sailors against a Provisional Government now so weak that there was nothing worth mentioning to overthrow." Martin Malia, *History's*

power lying in the streets and simply picked it up."[26] At first, what they did passed almost unnoticed outside the capital,[27] but it did serve to give the school inspector's son and dedicated Marxist from Simbirsk what he had devoted his life to seeking: political power.[28]

To take power and then to retain it, the Bolsheviks made a number of pledges for the purposes of securing the support, or at least neutralizing the opposition, of major segments of Russian society. They promised peace for the soldiers, land for the peasants, bread for the workers and other city dwellers, and self-determination for the non-Russians living in the Russian Empire. The tsar had failed or refused to provide any of these. In the end, the Bolsheviks kept none of their promises,[29] but making them probably did neutralize some of the potential opposition to their rule both before and after the coup.

For their new government, they established a single-party dictatorship that had Lenin as its undisputed leader. They shared power with no other group. They governed, they asserted, on behalf of the proletariat, but they had few workers in their ranks. Nor did they have any use for Western-style democracy. On October 27, Lenin signed a decree imposing censorship on the country.[30] A constituent assembly was elected shortly after the October coup for the purpose of drafting a constitution for Russia. Lenin summarily dismissed it in January 1918 after a single meeting, and it never convened again.[31]

In economic matters, the government moved to implement what later became known as "War Communism." The term suggested a set of emergency measures necessary in the extraordinary circumstances of wartime, but in fact they were not occasioned by war and represented Lenin's ideas for ordering the Russian economy.[32] War Communism involved taking control of banks and major industries, an attack on private property of all kinds,[33] and the seizing of grain from Russia's vast population of peasants. It also began the practice of appointing loyal Party members to monitor economic activity.[34]

Not least important for life under the new regime, with Lenin's enthusiastic support and following the tsarist precedent the Party set up a

---

Locomotives: Revolutions and the Making of the Modern World, New Haven and London: Yale University Press, 2006, p. 270. "The 'storming' of the Winter Palace, which took place all day, consisted actually in small groups of the bolder among the Bolshevik soldiers and sailors squeezing into the building, there being disarmed by the Junkers, but in the process of haranguing them about the uselessness of defense." Adam B. Ulam, *Lenin and the Bolsheviks: The Intellectual and Political History of the Triumph of Communism in Russia*, London: Secker and Warburg, 1966, p. 370. (Published in the United States in 1965 under the title *The Bolsheviks*).

secret police force with the mission of enforcing Bolshevik political orthodoxy and stamping out dissent, using coercion and repression for these two related goals. The Bolsheviks called the new body the "Extraordinary Commission for the Struggle Against Counterrevolution and Sabotage," and it came to be known by the acronym formed by the initial letters of the first two words of its title: the Cheka. Under a series of different names, a secret political police force was to remain a major feature of the regime Lenin founded for the nearly seventy-five years of its existence.[†]

For the purpose of defending, consolidating, and expanding their power in Russia, and with the hope of extending what they anticipated would become a European-wide proletarian revolution, the Bolsheviks, under Lenin's leadership, launched several major initiatives between 1918 and 1921. In early 1918, the new government ended the war with Germany. Lenin deemed withdrawal from the conflict necessary for the survival of the regime: the Bolsheviks had already moved the capital to Moscow, the tsarist seat of power before Peter the Great had built St. Petersburg at the beginning of the eighteenth century as his window on the West. They did so in order to place the government farther from the war front.[35] Imperial Germany forced the Bolshevik government to pay a high price in territory to obtain peace. By the terms of the Treaty of Brest-Litovsk, signed on March 3, 1918, Russia relinquished the Ukraine, the Baltic provinces, and Finland. It became, temporarily as it turned out, a dramatically smaller country.[36]

Brest-Litovsk extricated Russia from World War I but did not bring peace to the country. A Civil War began, with three separate armies, known collectively as the "Whites,"[37] seeking to oust the Bolsheviks—the "Reds"—from power. The war raged for three years, from December 1917 to November 1920, causing immense suffering and inflicting vast damage. An estimated 15 million people died,[38] perhaps 90 percent of them civilians who perished from hunger and disease as well as from the fighting.[39]

The Civil War ended with the victory of Lenin's forces. They were able to win because their opponents were dispersed and divided and had forfeited the potential support of the non-Russians by refusing to countenance independence for them. The Bolshevik side had shorter lines of communication

---

[†] A secret police force to impose political orthodoxy had operated in tsarist Russia, before the Bolshevik revolution, and such an organization was reestablished and strengthened under the second leader of post–Soviet Russia, Vladimir Putin. Through considerable political upheaval, therefore , and despite some seismic political changes from the nineteenth century to the twenty-first, Russia remained a police state.

and supply and managed to win over a sufficient number of former tsarist officers and soldiers[40] to prevail in the conflict. Neither side generated enthusiasm for its cause among the Russian population as a whole.[41] In addition, while the other European governments had no liking for Lenin and his colleagues and for the most part would have welcomed their defeat, those governments did not provide the kind of military assistance that could have tipped the balance in the fighting in favor of the Whites.[42] As a bonus for the new regime, Germany's ultimate defeat in World War I made it possible for the Red Army to reoccupy and reclaim much of the territory that the Bolsheviks had had to relinquish at Brest-Litovsk.[43]

The Germans had occupied the Ukraine but abandoned it after the armistice of November 1918. In early 1920, forces from the newly reconstituted sovereign state of Poland arrived there in an effort to recapture lands that had belonged to the Polish commonwealth before its eighteenth-century partition and disappearance as an independent country. The Bolshevik government sent troops to prevent this, and Lenin decided to advance further westward and conquer all of Poland. He believed that this would trigger a workers' revolution across Europe that, as a good Marxist internationalist, he anticipated and indeed expected his party's seizure of power in Russia to inspire.[44] The assault failed, in part because Lenin had underestimated the power of Polish nationalism to motivate resistance to the Red Army. The Polish forces stopped that Army outside Warsaw, and Poland survived as an independent country. For that and other reasons, Lenin's revolution did not spread westward.[45]

A year later, under the combined impact of the Civil War and Bolshevik economic policies, the country was caught up in an economic crisis so deep that it placed the regime in peril. The countryside was resolutely opposed to, and actively resisted, the government's economic policies, and peasants were withholding their produce, threatening mass hunger in the cities.[†]

[†] ". . . the Soviet regime was near collapse, not in the sense that there was an organized adversary ready to overthrow it—the Red Army had eliminated any such direct threat—but in the sense that the Bolsheviks could not continue their current course without the human and material fabric of the country disintegrating beneath them." Martin Malia, *The Soviet Tragedy: A History of Socialism in Russia, 1917–1991*, New York: The Free Press, 1994, p. 143. "In 1921, economic output did not even reach one sixth of the pre-1914 level; the 1921 grain harvest came in at one half of the 1913 level. Russia would go from world grain exporter (1913) to cannibalism (1923)." Stephen Kotkin, *Stalin: Paradoxes of Power, 1878–1928*, New York: Penguin Books, 2015, p. 405. See also Richard Pipes, *The Russian Revolution*, New York: Alfred A. Knopf, 1990, p. 735.

To preserve his government, Lenin ordered the domestic equivalent of Brest-Litovsk, retreating from the economic policies it had sought to impose after seizing power.[46]

In what became known as the New Economic Policy (NEP),[47] the regime shifted from requisitioning grain to taxing it while allowing individual peasants to keep, and to sell, much of what they grew. The government also permitted private trade in nonagricultural products.[48] The Bolsheviks had defined the socialism that they had taken power to implement as the negation of capitalist practices and institutions,[49] but Lenin decided that necessity—that is, his retention of power—required the resumption of some of these practices in the reconstituted Russian Empire that they had reorganized, in 1922, as the Union of Soviet Socialist Republics.

When he authorized the NEP, Lenin had less than three years to live and even less time than that in which to continue his active leadership of what he caused, in March 1918, to be renamed the Communist Party.[50] He had had recurrent problems with his health, he had been seriously wounded by an assassination attempt on August 30, 1918, and he suffered strokes in May and again in December 1922. There followed a particularly severe stroke on March 10, 1923, which left him unable to speak: he communicated only through handwritten notes. He died on January 21, 1924.

The Times

Lenin's political ideas belonged to the broad nineteenth-century tradition known as socialism. Socialism, in turn, emerged from the impact on Europe of the greatest source of disruption in human affairs in 10,000 years: the Industrial Revolution. The vast expansion of usable power that made it possible led to, among other things, steady and substantial economic growth for the first time in human history, migration on a large scale from the countryside to the city, and the creation of large factories that employed salaried workers. It also led to marked and visible economic inequality that, because the conviction that it was divinely ordained had lost its grip on European societies, caused steadier and more readily mobilized resentment than ever before. All this fostered the conviction, which underlay socialism, that new political practices and institutions were needed to cope with the radically new social and economic circumstances.

Many parties and programs have borne the label "socialist,"[51] but they divide roughly into three categories. Utopian socialism involved the creation of small, often relatively isolated, voluntary communities that operated according to a particular set of principles. Their principles distinguished these communities from the society as a whole, and usually included material equality and considerable social cooperation.[52] Democratic socialism, the second category, became a property of a number of sovereign states, initially in Western Europe and North America. (Many members of the twenty-first-century European Union fit into this category.) In countries following the political practices that define democracy—regular free and fair elections and the protection of liberty—democratic socialism retained a major economic role for free markets while adding a variety of social welfare programs, old-age pensions prominent among them. The programs came to be known, collectively, as the welfare state, and became integral parts of Western democratic governance in the twentieth century. The American Progressive movement of which Woodrow Wilson was a leading figure, although not calling itself socialist, belonged broadly to this tradition.[53]

Marxian socialism, the third variant, to which Lenin pledged his allegiance early in his life, followed Karl Marx's teachings, with their emphasis on class struggle, revolution, and, after 1917, Lenin's idea of the political dictatorship of a communist party.

Marx's teachings appealed to Lenin because they promised the overthrow of the existing political and social order. They promised, that is, revolution; and Lenin was a revolutionary before he became a Marxist. His deep animus, even as a teenager, toward the tsarist regime—no doubt enhanced, perhaps even created, by his brother's fate at its hands—predisposed him to an ideology that ordained that regime's end.

Marx's opus appealed to him as well because its forecast had—or so Marx claimed—a scientific basis. In the last decades of the nineteenth century, the scientific enterprise enjoyed high prestige in Europe, including among Western-oriented Russians such as the Ulianovs.[54] One of the most important and influential scientific treatises ever published, Charles Darwin's *On the Origin of Species*, which set forth his theory of evolution, had appeared in 1859. Marx's sometime coauthor Friedrich Engels expressed the scientific claims of Marx's works by calling his collaborator "the Darwin of the social sciences."[55]

Marxism held yet a third attraction for Lenin: it offered him the prospect of seizing and wielding political power. "The philosophers have only interpreted the world, in various ways," Marx wrote in 1854, "the point, however, is to change it."[56] From an early age, Lenin aspired to change the world. In Marx's writings on politics, economics, and history, he found the tools he needed for this project; and change the world he certainly did.

Inconveniently, Marxism offered a formula for revolution in the most economically advanced—that is, the most industrialized—parts of Europe, in particular in Marx's home country of Germany. Lenin's Russia, however, was the least advanced country on the European continent. Lenin solved this problem in his own mind with the belief, which he held even after events had shown it to be erroneous, that by taking power in Russia the Bolsheviks would trigger the kinds of revolutions across Europe that Marx had prophesied. The history of the twentieth century, in fact, demonstrated that only in less advanced countries could groups acting in Marx's (and later also Lenin's) name achieve political control. No such group, however, would have come to power anywhere without the events of October 1917 and thereafter in the Russian Empire; and those events would never have transpired without the impact of the First World War.

The war had a pulverizing impact on Russia. Its army suffered major battlefield defeats at German hands. The defeats discredited the tsarist regime—the tsar had assumed personal command of the army in August 1915[57]—which led to his abdication. The conflict produced widespread social and economic dislocation, with severe inflation and hundreds of thousands of peasants taken off the land they farmed and sent to the front. By arming them, moreover, the regime gave them potential power that, in the autocratic Russian political system, they had never before had.

A military mutiny in the midst of the government's military and economic failures triggered the fall of the monarch. With the massive disruption that the war brought, and absent a tsar at its head, the entire imperial political structure disintegrated.[58] Only in the conditions of near anarchy that the war created in Russia could a group as few in number as the Bolsheviks, and one with a political program as extreme as theirs, hope to gain power. The number of politically active Russians was, after all, small; those of them committed to Marxism constituted only a modest fraction of that total; and the Bolsheviks were a minority of Russian Marxists. Without World War I, Lenin would be remembered now, if remembered at all, as a politically marginal early-twentieth-century Russian radical who was something of a crank.

Still, Russia was not the only country devastated by the war, nor the only one to lose it: Germany, to take the most prominent example, had a similar experience. Yet neither in Germany nor in any other warring country did anything like the successful October coup take place. In combination with the impact of the war, it was the special characteristics of Russia that made this possible.

To use a once common term that has fallen out of favor, Russia was, as both Marx and Lenin acknowledged, backward in comparison to the countries to its west.[§] There was in Europe at the time of the Bolshevik revolution, as there had been for centuries, a kind of "cultural gradient" sloping downward from west to east, with Great Britain and France, the most advanced countries, at one end and Russia, the least, at the other.[59]

Russia was politically backward in the sense that it was more autocratic, with fewer restraints on the power of the hereditary monarch who ruled the country, possessed fewer and weaker political institutions other than the monarchy, and had a smaller segment of the society taking an active part in its public life, than was the case to the west. Russia's economy had proportionately more agriculture and less industry, with more peasants and fewer workers and a smaller middle class, than were to be found beyond its western borders. Socially, the country lacked the intermediate organizations between the citizens and the government that developed in Europe and North America and that came to be known, collectively, as civil society.[60]

Because of its political, economic, and social backwardness, Russia fielded the largest but, on the whole, the least militarily effective army of any of the major combatants in World War I. The German army, the product of a more advanced society, was therefore able to defeat it. In addition, Russia's political backwardness produced an unusually radical intelligentsia, of which Lenin and his colleagues were exemplars, because its members were unable to participate in political life and so never had to modify their ideas in response to the assumption of responsibility for governing, as occurred among radicals in the West.[61]

As a consequence of the absence, or weakness, of modern Western institutions, the collapse of Russia's autocratic regime created a vacuum, which the Bolsheviks proceeded to fill. In October 1917, their numbers were modest[62] and they possessed only negligible military forces. Few Russians were aware of their political program and fewer still actually supported it; but the other organized political groups in the country were no more formidable. The fall of the governments in the other defeated powers in World War I left a variety of claimants to power and a series of institutions through which they could hope to exercise it.[63] The end of tsarism left

---

[§] Lenin did not have a high opinion of Russian culture or the Russian people. "He had never like[d] Moscow because it was so much less Westernised than Petrograd. Physically and culturally Moscow embodied traditional Russian values. For Lenin, this was no recommendation at all." Robert Service, *Lenin: A Biography*, Cambridge, Massachusetts: The Belknap Press of Harvard University Press, 2000, p. 345.

nothing.^ε This gave Lenin an opportunity that his would-be imitators in other countries did not have. His skills as a leader enabled him to take full advantage of this opportunity.

Leadership

Lenin's political career rested on a bedrock of ideas. He devoted himself to absorbing them, modifying them, publicizing them, and, in his final seven years, putting them into practice. Most notably for his political leadership, he spent a good deal of time and effort trying to persuade others that his ideas were both useful and accurate reflections of reality and that the others should therefore join and follow him. In this undertaking, he enjoyed enough success to create the Bolshevik Party, which then succeeded in taking power in Russia.

The ideas he adopted were those of Karl Marx, but the two major changes to Marx's account of Europe's and the world's past, present, and future that Lenin made convinced him of the feasibility of seizing power in his home country: the creation of a disciplined, secretive vanguard party to act on behalf of the class that Marx had identified as the driving force behind what would be history's culminating revolution—the proletariat; and the assertion that decidedly nonadvanced, largely peasant Russia was ripe, in Marxist terms properly understood (that is, as he interpreted them), for an immediate revolutionary transformation.[64]

In developing and promoting his ideas, Lenin combined dogmatism with flexibility, both of them arising from his overweening intellectual and political self-confidence. On the one hand, he was certain that Marxism had the status of scientific truth. He was certain as well that his own version of Marxist ideology was the only legitimate one, and before 1917 he engaged in fierce polemics against Russian Marxists who did not accept

---

^ε ". . . in the course of 1917 all of old Russia's structures—the state, the army, the Empire, the local administration, the economy, and both the urban and rural societies—came apart simultaneously." Malia, *The Soviet Tragedy*, pp. 96–97. See also *ibid.*, p. 134. "The February Revolution had many striking features that distinguish it from other revolutionary upheavals. But the most striking of all was the remarkable rapidity with which the Russian state fell apart. It was as if the greatest empire in the world, covering one-sixth of the earth's surface, were an artificial construction, without organic unity, held together by wires all of which converged in the person of the monarch. The instant the monarch withdrew, the wires snapped and the whole structure collapsed in a heap." Pipes, *The Russian Revolution*, p. 336.

his views in their entirety. On the other hand, he did not hesitate to make major revisions in the Marxist outlook as Marx himself had presented it, all the while assuming that his own contributions were entirely faithful to Marx's theories, despite the fact that they were not.[65] On matters of doctrine, Lenin was a stranger to doubt.

In addition to his unshakable conviction that he was right, several other features of his personality were central to Lenin's leadership because they became features of the regime that he founded. One was his belief that in political affairs the ends always justify the means. He regarded any measure that furthered the cause of the revolution to be acceptable, indeed all but mandatory.[66] The Bolsheviks engaged in bank robberies, took money from the capitalist and imperialist German government that was at war with Russia, and, in an effort to win public support, made promises they had no intention of keeping. Lenin showed no qualms about engaging in any of this. He did not, of course, invent this approach to public policy and to life more generally; but his embrace of it ensured that it would be embedded in the conduct of public affairs in the Soviet Union for decades to come.

Another conspicuous feature of Lenin's personality with implications for Soviet policy was his predilection for hatred.[67] Anyone who questioned or opposed his ideas, and all those associated with the old regime, were, he firmly believed, his mortal enemies, with no redeeming features, worthy, in most cases, of destruction.[68]

For this reason, in order to achieve his goals, he particularly favored the use of coercion and violence. Nor did he regard these tactics as regrettable necessities to be used as sparingly as possible.[69] Once the Bolsheviks had gained power, he displayed conspicuous enthusiasm for the use of force against his political enemies—who, because his Party's program was so radical, were numerous.[70] Violence and coercion by the government against the people it governed became normal, indeed pervasive, in the state that he founded.[71] Here, the Soviet state differed from the tsarist regime Lenin had despised: he, his colleagues, and their successors shed far more blood than the Romanovs ever did.

Leadership involves persuasion, and Lenin had success in persuading people in small but crucial numbers first to join the Bolsheviks and adopt the Party's political program—which he had created—and then, after the October coup, to follow the course that he favored. He made converts, no doubt mainly of those already disposed to radical politics, through his vigorous, colorful, sometimes learned, occasionally arcane, and often angry writings.[72] He was also able to impose his will on the Party by dint of what, by all accounts, was a very forceful personality. He could have what sometimes seemed an almost hypnotic effect on those within his personal orbit. According to the leading historian of the Russian Revolution,

> ... this unattractive man glowed with an inner force that made people quickly forget their first impressions. His strength of will, indomitable discipline, energy, asceticism, and unshakable faith in the cause had an effect that can only be conveyed by the overused term "charisma."[73]

Lenin's mastery of the Party stemmed as well from his virtuosity at managing organizational issues. He devoted most of his waking hours to Party matters, indeed was preoccupied with them to the exclusion of virtually everything else. He paid close personal attention to every detail of Bolshevik affairs. Again and again, he outmaneuvered actual and potential critics and rivals, through both his bureaucratic adroitness and his willingness to spend as much time as was needed to prevail. An old saying has it that the trouble with socialism is that it takes too many evenings. Lenin was willing to spend all of his evenings working for the cause: he had no higher use for them.[74]

Once the Party had seized power, Lenin gained another source of authority within its ranks: his impressive record, at crucial junctures in the history of the revolution, of being right.[75] In particular, events had proven him right about seizing power in October 1917, and right about surrendering extensive territories to the Germans at Brest-Litovsk in exchange for peace: the regime was able to recover most of the lost territory after the Western powers defeated Germany in 1918. This record made the Bolsheviks, whose membership expanded rapidly once they had taken power, even more disposed to accept Lenin's judgment and submit to his demands than had been the case before the October coup.

The prerevolutionary Bolshevik Party was not a mass movement, but once in power it, and Lenin, had to lead a country of more than 125 million people. The skills and the traits of personality that he had deployed to good effect within the Party did not have a comparable impact on the Russian and non-Russian masses. He was not a compelling public speaker: the outstanding orators of the revolutionary period were Alexander Kerensky, the leader of the Provisional Government, and Leon Trotsky, a Marxist who joined the Bolsheviks only in 1917 and later served as minister of both foreign affairs and war.[76]

While he claimed to speak *for* the workers, Lenin had no great ability to speak persuasively *to* them, or to Russia's vast reservoir of peasants, either. Nor was he even particularly well known outside the capital for the first several years after his party executed its coup.[77] Because Lenin lacked the capacity to sway the Russian population and, more importantly, because the Communist program ran counter to the beliefs, wishes, and interests of almost all Russians, once in power the Party depended for governing not on persuasion but on coercion on a large scale.

The Communist Party relied on Lenin even after his death. It organized and promoted a cult with him at the center.[78] It made his likeness ubiquitous, producing, distributing, and posting in public places and in printed material stylized portraits and busts of him. The regime frequently referred to things he had said or written, using his words to justify its policies. It placed his embalmed body in a mausoleum in the heart of Moscow, and thousands of people filed past it each week.

Lenin's tomb became a kind of pilgrimage site,[79] and Lenin himself more broadly the object of the kind of veneration that religions have commonly accorded their holy figures.[80] His omnipresent image recalled the iconography common in the Russian Orthodox Church—images being especially important in Russia because so many of the believers could not read. His sayings and writings attained the status of the sacred texts that are central to many faiths.[81] The authorities changed the name of the former capital from Petrograd to Leningrad—from Peter's city to Lenin's—and communism's official doctrine added his name to its title: it became Marxism-Leninism.

The veneration of the supreme Bolshevik leader began even before his death. He did not encourage it, but, when he was in a position to do so before his strokes all but ended his active leadership, he did not put an end to it either.[82] Its full elaboration came only after he had died. From the 1930s to the 1950s, his successor, Josef Stalin, created his own cult that partially eclipsed Lenin's; but after Stalin's death, his successor Nikita Khrushchev attempted to discredit him, and part of the campaign to do so involved glorifying Lenin once again.[83]

The cult of Lenin had two principal purposes: it provided a source of common belief and common allegiance, and thus of political cohesion, for the surviving Communists. It also sought to cultivate in the Russian population the belief that the Communist Party had the right to rule by giving the people an object on which they could focus the kind of devotion to which their religious tradition had accustomed them.[84] The creation of the cult also acknowledged, indirectly and perhaps unintentionally, the momentous changes that Lenin had personally caused to occur during his lifetime.

The Personal Imprint

Of the eight men portrayed in these pages, Vladimir Ilich Lenin has a good claim to have had the greatest influence. He was the prime mover behind the October 1917 coup in Russia that set twentieth-century history on a path, which continued long after his death, that was radically different from the one it almost surely would have followed in the absence of the events in Petrograd of that month. Without that coup, the Soviet Union would not have come into existence. Without Soviet sponsorship, the international communist movement either would not have arisen or would have been a far less formidable political force than it turned out to be. The Russian Revolution counts as one of the causes of World War II in Europe in that the specter of communism in Germany helped Adolf Hitler, who started that war, come to power.[85] The Second World War, in turn, spread Marxist-Leninist governance beyond the Soviet borders. The Red Army imposed it in Eastern Europe as a consequence of that war. Mao Zedong's Communists would not have been able to take control of China in the wake of the war in Asia without Soviet assistance.[86] Eventually, sixteen countries,[87] with more than a third of the world's population, came to have communist political and economic systems.

Communism in power had two signal achievements. Implanted as it invariably was in backward countries like Russia rather than in the advanced industrial states where Marx had anticipated that revolutions would take place, Marxist-Leninist regimes presided over the broad process known as modernization: the transition from agricultural to industrial economies and from a population living predominantly in the countryside to much of it inhabiting cities.

Urban-industrial societies are generally wealthier than rural-agrarian ones, and under communism people became, on the whole, less poor. In non-communist countries, however, this transition made people richer than their counterparts governed by Marxism-Leninism, and raised their standards of living higher while doing so with far less bloodshed than occurred where communist parties held power.

Bloodshed on a large scale is communism's second major achievement. Other communist governments adopted the widespread use of violence and repression that Lenin and his Bolshevik colleagues had embraced, and for the same declared purposes: to defend their regimes, to root out enemies, and to enforce their preferred policies in order to build socialism. As a result, communism in power became an exercise in mass murder.

The grand total of deaths that Marxist-Leninist regimes perpetrated across the twentieth century cannot be precisely calculated: the relevant statistics in these cases are often unreliable or unavailable. By the most serious effort to arrive at the overall figure, however, communism killed almost 100 million people.[88] No natural disaster or outbreak of deadly disease in human history, with the possible exception of the Bubonic Plague of the fourteenth century, inflicted death on that scale, and it all goes back, ultimately, to Lenin. Epidemiologists refer to the person in whom an infectious disease first appears, and from whom it spreads, as "patient zero." If communism is seen as a man-made version of a deadly pandemic, its own patient zero was Vladimir Ilich Ulyanov, known as Lenin.

Lenin had a direct personal impact only on events in his lifetime, but that impact was a profound one. The Bolshevik Party was his personal creation. His revision of Marx's ideas called it into being. He became its unchallenged leader, a particularly impressive accomplishment because for most of the period between its establishment and early 1917, he had to exercise his leadership from abroad. It was his personal creation that seized power in Petrograd in October. No other group had the daring and the zeal to attempt the coup that the Bolsheviks carried off.

Or rather, to put it more precisely, only Lenin himself had the daring to do so. When, upon returning to Russia, he insisted on overthrowing the Provisional Government as soon as possible, virtually every other member of the Bolshevik inner circle opposed the idea, deeming it reckless and doomed to fail. Lenin cajoled, threatened, pleaded, and argued until he won them over.[89] Without his personal insistence, the October coup would not have taken place.[90]

Lenin had little directly to do with the operation that ousted the Provisional Government on the night of October 24–25: he was, in fact, in hiding across the border from Petrograd in Finland in the days leading up to it.[91] It was Trotsky who orchestrated the seizure of power. He, along with Lenin, was indispensable for what took place. As one historian put it, "The Bolshevik putsch could have been prevented with two bullets."[92]

In the new state that the Bolsheviks established, Lenin became the leading figure. During the early years, the Party organized the government and selected its priorities according to his vision. He had far more influence on the first five years of what became the Soviet Union than any other individual.[93] As with the decision to seize power, however, on three crucial initiatives of the new regime, Lenin's preferences encountered serious resistance from his colleagues. In each case he was at first more or less isolated in his position. As with the October coup, for each of the three initiatives, employing both his political skills and his high prestige in the ranks of his fellow Communists, he eventually prevailed over the opposition within the Party. Each of the initiatives, therefore—the Treaty of Brest-Litovsk, the attack on Poland, and the New Economic Policy—bears his personal stamp. None would have taken place without him.

Lenin's insistence that the new regime had to make peace with Germany at almost any price was not at all popular among his colleagues. The terms the Communists ultimately accepted at Brest-Litovsk validated their reservations. Not only did the treaty deprive Russia of much of its territory, by signing it the self-proclaimed champions of the workers also experienced the humiliation of submitting to an arch-enemy of the workers' cause—the autocratic, reactionary, imperial German government.

Other Party leaders advocated continuing to fight, or at least not agreeing to accept such drastic conditions for withdrawing from the World War.[94] The critics, like Lenin, believed in the imminence of a Europe-wide proletarian revolution and thought that if they held out against German militarism, perhaps by waging guerrilla warfare, the workers would rise up against the German government and German soldiers would abandon it.[95] Dispatched to negotiate with the German officials responsible for the peace talks, Trotsky attempted to appeal over their heads to the German troops to abandon the Kaiser and join the Bolsheviks.[96]

When the failure of such tactics became apparent, Lenin got his way:[97] the Communist regime signed what amounted to a document of surrender. In so doing, it probably saved the revolution, which was what Lenin had argued was at stake. Without Brest-Litovsk the German army might well have swept even farther east and, if it had, could easily have crushed the Bolsheviks and done away with their still-precarious government.

Lenin also had little support from the other high-ranking Communists in calling for an attack on Poland to hasten revolution both there and further to the west. The others doubted that a Russian assault would have the consequences that Lenin predicted. Once again, the Party acceded to Lenin's wishes.[98] In this case, however, events proved him wrong and the skeptics right. Polish nationalist sentiment prevailed over the class consciousness on which the Bolshevik leader was counting to motivate the Poles.[99] Rather than switching sides to foster the victory of the proletariat across Europe, the Poles fought—successfully—to defend their newly obtained national independence.

On yet a third occasion, Lenin advocated a course that almost all the other prominent Bolsheviks opposed. It was he who proposed the New Economic Policy, with its retreat from communist economic principles and practices and return to major features of the capitalist system he and his associates believed they had overthrown. In this way, it paralleled the Treaty of Brest-Litovsk, the dictated peace with Germany. As with that agreement, the NEP seemed to Lenin's colleagues to violate their Party and their government's very reasons for being: the abolition of capitalism was, after all, the purpose to which they had devoted their lives.[100] For Lenin, however, the reinstitution of private property, private trade, and private profit, no matter how distasteful, was necessary to keep the Communists in power. Without what he acknowledged was a step backward in what, as a Marxist, he believed to be history's destined progression, Russia faced economic disintegration.

As with the October coup, Brest-Litovsk, and the Polish campaign, Lenin got his way.[101] As with the treaty with Germany, moreover, in retrospect his position seems justified in the sense that, had the government pressed ahead in 1921 with the radical economic policies it had introduced, it might well have lost its grip on political power. Lenin therefore not only made the Russian Revolution, he also saved it. As with Brest-Litovsk as well, the retreat proved not to be permanent, although the negation of the NEP and the return, with a vengeance, to the original Bolshevik economic policies took place after Lenin had died, under the leadership of his successor, the Georgian-born Josef Djugashvili who took the name Stalin—"man of steel." For that and other reasons, an assessment of Lenin's historical legacy has to reckon with what the Soviet Union became in Stalin's time.

The Legacy

Lenin did more than any other individual to create what he intended to be, and believed to be, the first workers' state. That state became the Union of Soviet Socialist Republics, which endured for seven decades. It follows, therefore, that the Soviet Union represents Lenin's principal historical legacy. That proposition has not, however, gone unchallenged.

Lenin dominated post-tsarist Russia for five years, from the October coup in 1917 to his first serious strokes in 1922. His successor Josef Stalin exercised supreme power for far longer, from the second half of the 1920s to his death in 1953. Under his leadership, many Soviet institutions and practices took the forms they would maintain until the end. So influential was he that the type of communist governance in his time came to be known as Stalinism.

Stalin certainly built much of the edifice called the Soviet Union: he was, to use a metaphor, its contractor. Did he build it according to Lenin's blueprint? Was Lenin the architect of what the Communists termed "real existing socialism" on the territory of what had been the Romanov Empire? Was Stalinism, that is, a faithful continuation of Leninism? Assessing Lenin's legacy depends on the answers to those questions.

One school of thought holds that the policies that Stalin imposed on the state deviated from what Lenin had wanted and planned. According to this point of view, Stalinism, with its industrial-scale repression and bloodshed, broke with the more humane form of socialism that Lenin would have built had he lived and that a number of his Bolshevik disciples would have created had they, rather than Stalin, succeeded him at the head of the Communist Party. The case for radical discontinuity between Lenin and Stalin rests to a great extent on two pieces of evidence.[102]

The first is what is known as "Lenin's Testament," a handwritten note of December 1922 that evaluated several of the leading Bolsheviks and said that "Comrade Stalin, having become General Secretary, has concentrated unlimited power in his hands, and I am not convinced that he will always manage to use this power with sufficient care." A few days later, there appeared an addendum: "Stalin is too crude, and this defect, which is entirely acceptable in our milieu and in relations among us as communists, became unacceptable in the position of General Secretary. I therefore propose to comrades that they should devise a means of removing him from this job. . . ."[103]

The other piece of evidence is the New Economic Policy of 1921, which retreated from the harsh and radical economic measures of the period of War Communism. Lenin prevailed on his reluctant colleagues to authorize it and is even said to have foreseen at one point that it would endure for a long time.[104] In fact, it lasted for seven years. With Lenin gone, Stalin reversed the country's economic direction and returned to the initial policies, at great cost in human suffering.

It is, of course, impossible to know what Lenin would have done, and chosen not to do, had he remained the Soviet leader for as many years as his successor actually held power. (Had Lenin lived as long as Stalin did, he would have died in 1945.) The historical record, however, strongly suggests that even in that case the Soviet Union would have evolved in roughly the way that it, in fact, did.

The assertion that Stalin was an illegitimate usurper of Lenin's position does not stand up to the facts. Lenin's testament included unflattering appraisals of a number of his senior colleagues. It seems, in retrospect, to express the conviction of a dying man that none of his potential successors, and not only Stalin, was worthy of his mantle.[105] Moreover, it was Lenin himself who gave Stalin the high positions that the Georgian Bolshevik held through 1924.[106] Lenin respected, trusted, and promoted Stalin, who would never have been in a position to gain control of the Communist Party apparatus, and thus make himself the country's undisputed leader, without Lenin's patronage.[107]

As for the NEP, Lenin said at the outset that it was intended to be a temporary set of arrangements, and that was the understanding of most of his colleagues. It was put in place to provide a "breathing space" for Russia's new rulers to avoid economic disaster and consolidate their power.[108] Had it continued much beyond the point at which Stalin terminated it, it would have entrenched the very capitalist practices that the Bolsheviks had seized power to extirpate. It would thereby have obstructed the socialism that Lenin was committed to building. In addition, extending the NEP indefinitely would have greatly strengthened its principal beneficiary— Russia's peasantry. The agrarian sector of Russian society would have had the economic basis for political leverage on, and even a measure of political independence from, the ruling Communist Party. A long-term NEP would, that is, have threatened the Party's monopoly of power, which Lenin considered an inviolable principle.[109]

Had the Bolsheviks lost power, twentieth-century Russia would surely have developed differently than it did. As long as the Communists remained in charge, however, and even with a politically active Lenin presiding, a radically different history seems implausible. Stalin asserted, after reaching the pinnacle of power, that he was the best of all Leninists. A comparison between what he did and Lenin's initiatives demonstrates that he had a good case for this claim.[110] Stalinism conformed in large part to the spirit, and in very important ways to the letter, of Leninism.[111]

Stalin's pattern of leadership did differ from Lenin's in some respects. For much of his political career and especially before seizing power and in the months immediately afterward, for example, Lenin had to win support from the other prominent Bolsheviks for his preferred initiatives; he generally did so through his formidable powers of persuasion. (In power he relied on coercion for dealing with non-Bolsheviks.) Stalin, once he had consolidated his power, had no need to persuade anybody of anything. Still, the single-party dictatorship and the centralization of power through which Stalin exercised his absolute power originated at the inception of Bolshevik rule, with Lenin in charge.[112] Lenin fashioned the tools that Stalin subsequently used. Stalin put them to terrible use, but here, too, the difference with Lenin is merely one of degree.

By the second half of the 1930s, Stalin's orders commanded unquestioning obedience because by then all inhabitants of the Soviet Union knew that the penalty for opposing or even questioning what the leader decreed was likely to be death. In Lenin's day, the regime had observed a taboo against killing Party members.[113] Stalin did away with it. At Stalin's order, millions of people were executed—not for any real crimes but for the purpose of protecting and expanding his and the Communist Party's power.[114] His campaign of terror[115] ravaged the Party, the military, and the ranks of Russians with technical expertise or knowledge of the outside world as well as killing many people belonging to none of these groups, while achieving at least one of its goals: it suppressed any hint of dissent, let alone active opposition, within the country.[116]

Lenin's direct victims numbered in the hundreds of thousands, not the millions,[117] but the toll exceeded the death count of any previous such campaign and the earlier victims of Bolshevik terror died for the same reasons as the later ones. Lenin caused to be killed[118] people who opposed, or were suspected of opposing or of planning to oppose, the Party and its policies, or who had neither planned nor carried out any such activities but whose deaths would discourage anyone else from even considering doing so.[119]

The first supreme leader of the Soviet Union enthusiastically endorsed the use of terror to secure the Communists' grip on power and enforce its policies.[††] He regarded it as a normal and useful method of governance.

[††] "The evidence shows that Lenin, its most determined instigator, regarded terror as an indispensable instrument of revolutionary government. He was quite prepared to resort to it preventively—that is, in the absence of active opposition to this rule." Pipes, *The Russian Revolution*, p. 790. "Terror served the Bolsheviks not as a weapon of last resort, but as a

In Stalin's time, the responsibility for carrying out the terror fell to the se-cret police, an organization that Lenin founded.[120] In Stalin's day, those branded enemies of the revolution (that is, of the regime) but spared ex-ecution were dispatched to camps where they were forced to labor under terrible conditions. These camps were established while Lenin lived and ruled.[121]

Stalin's economic policies also followed the guidelines that Lenin had set down. Most notoriously, Stalin presided over the forced collectiviza-tion of agriculture. Beginning in 1928, millions of peasants were forced off their land and sent to collective farms. Russia's 25 million peasants were herded into 280,000 of these farms.[122] Because they resisted, collectiviza-tion amounted to an internal war by the regime against rural Russians. The cost in lives lost and ruined was immense and included a famine, caused by the Communist assault on the countryside, that killed, by different estimates, between 5 and 11 million people.[123]

During his lifetime, Lenin had regarded the Russian peasantry—by his ideological lights a reactionary and superfluous class—as an obstacle to the creation of socialism as he envisioned it, and had acted accordingly. He had opposed the institution of private property, including the private owner-ship of land. Once in power, he had ordered the requisitioning—that is, the confiscation—of the grain that peasants grew and on which they depended for their livelihoods, at below-market prices or with no compensation at all.[124] He believed, based on very little evidence, that rural Russia had a class structure[125] and that the rich peasants, called kulaks, were the enemies of socialism and had to be eliminated. (In the end, the regime dispossessed all peasants.) While he had pushed through the NEP, which restored some of the prerevolutionary practices in the countryside, he had left no doubt about his hostility to the people who lived there;[126] and after his death, the regime mustered enough force to put his ideas and his attitudes about agri-culture and those who engaged in it into practice.[127]

Soviet nonagricultural economic policy followed the same pattern. While Stalin formally inaugurated the central plan controlling all sig-nificant economic activity, Lenin's hostility to private property and pri-vate trade as well as his aspiration for the Party to exercise unchallenged

---

surrogate for the popular support which eluded them. The more their popularity eroded, the more they resorted to terror, until in the fall and winter of 1918–19 they raised it to a level of indiscriminate slaughter never before seen." *Ibid.*, p. 792.

authority everywhere[128] made planning entirely compatible with his economic and political outlook. Even during the NEP, according to one of his biographers, he wanted to move toward a "uniform economic plan for the entire state."[129]

In foreign as well as domestic policy, Stalin followed Lenin. Stalin's foreign policy unfolded in two stages, both of which had Leninist precedents. In the 1920s and 1930s and during World War II, he sought to conciliate the capitalist powers. He authorized the Molotov-Ribbentrop agreement with Nazi Germany of August 1939, by the terms of which the two dictators pledged to maintain peaceful relations with each other. They also carved up and ultimately annexed the territory between their two countries, acting as the European powers had traditionally done before World War I. When Hitler violated the accord and launched a massive attack on the Soviet Union on June 22, 1941, Stalin made common cause with the capitalist United States and with capitalist and imperialist Great Britain.

Lenin had carried out comparable policies, making peace with Imperial Germany at Brest-Litovsk and then, after World War I had ended in a German defeat, signing a treaty with the Germans at Rapallo in 1922 as well as concluding a secret agreement to engage in military cooperation with the Weimar regime.[130] Stalin could therefore legitimately claim to be carrying out a Leninist foreign policy during the two decades between Lenin's death and the end of World War II; and both, not coincidentally, were conducting the kind of foreign policy typical of countries weaker than their neighbors[131]—protecting themselves by attempting to conciliate stronger and politically hostile powers while seeking to augment their own strength by allying with other countries.[132]

The Soviet Union emerged from World War II as one of the two mightiest powers on the planet. Stalin and his successors used their relative strength to prosecute a broad-ranging conflict with the United States, a conflict akin to the rivalries that powerful states had pursued with one another for centuries. Soviet participation in the Cold War also conformed to Lenin's view of world politics. As a devout Marxist, he believed conflict between the global revolutionary socialist movement and the capitalist world to be unavoidable. Stalin also pursued an ideological foreign policy, installing or encouraging the installation of Marxist-Leninist regimes wherever possible. Here, too, he was acting as an authentic Leninist, following the precedent, albeit with far greater success, of Lenin's ill-fated Polish campaign of 1920.

Not only its inception, therefore, but also the 70-year-long life span of the Union of Soviet Socialist Republics counts as a monument to Lenin.[133] The demise of the state that Lenin founded also had connections with its founder. Three great historical forces toppled it, all of which included elements of Leninism.

Lenin believed, with Marx, that the evolution of the capitalist economy would immiserate the workers, and that that would ultimately doom the political system that presided over it. In the 1980s, it was the development of the communist economic order, however, and the resulting Marxist-style contradiction between economics and politics, that started the process that brought down communism in Europe. Communism failed to provide the economic growth that its leaders had promised and on which they counted to win a measure of public tolerance for their rule and to generate the resources to compete with the capitalist West. What became known as "the era of stagnation" in the Soviet Union inspired a series of reforms that, rather than revitalizing the economic and political systems that Lenin and Stalin had built, had the ultimate effect of destroying them.[134]

Lenin also believed that the imperialist policies of the capitalist powers would upend them by leading to wars, such as World War I, between and among them. In the end, however, it was communist imperialism, and specifically the forces of anti-imperialism—in communist parlance, the forces of national liberation—that caused first the Soviet empire in Europe and then the Soviet Union itself to come apart. Given the opportunity in 1989, the countries of Eastern Europe—Poland, Hungary, Czechoslovakia, the German Democratic Republic, Bulgaria, and Romania—overthrew the communist regimes that Moscow had imposed on them and defected from the Soviet sphere of influence.

As for the Soviet Union itself, what Lenin had pronounced the first workers' state was in fact a communist-style multinational empire, a descendant, with some modifications, of the empire of the Romanovs. The Russian-dominated Communist Party controlled the non-Russians within the Union. The Bolsheviks did not deliver the national self-determination that they had promised in 1917, but they did organize the state along national lines. The major non-Russian nationalities had their own designated Soviet republics, indigenous cadres held key positions in the republican governments, and the republics enjoyed extensive linguistic autonomy.[135] All this sowed the seeds of the nationalist sentiment, which was present to varying degrees in the Ukraine and Belarus, in the Baltic region, in the

Caucasus and in Central Asia, that underlay the secession of the fourteen non-Russian provinces in 1991. What had been the Soviet Union splintered into fifteen separate sovereign states, with half the former Soviet population living in an ethnically far more homogenous Russia.

Finally, it was largely the initiatives of the supreme Bolshevik leader, Lenin himself, that created the Soviet Union and largely the initiatives of his last Communist successor, Mikhail Sergeyevitch Gorbachev, that subverted it. Under the spell of the Lenin cult that portrayed him as a kind of philosopher-king, Gorbachev drew inspiration from what he took to be Lenin's example and considered Lenin a model for his own efforts at reform. Lenin had bequeathed a hyper-centralized structure of power to the state that he founded, and Gorbachev used the power that that structure placed in his hands to implement political and economic changes that, entirely unintentionally, brought to an end the Soviet era in Russian and world history. With the end of that era came the disappearance of the institutional legacy of Vladimir Ilich Lenin.

3

Adolf Hitler

The Life

Adolf Hitler was born on April 20, 1889, to Klara and Alois Hitler. The husband was a minor customs official of the Austro-Hungarian Empire who was stationed on the border with Germany. By all accounts, the son had warm relations with his mother but got along badly with his father.[1] An indifferent student, Adolf ended his formal education at age 16 , although he continued to read widely on his own for most of the rest of his life.[2]

His father wanted the son to follow in his own footsteps as an Austrian civil servant but the younger Hitler aspired to be an artist.[3] He moved to Vienna in 1908 and twice tried to enter the Academy of Fine Arts there, but his application was rejected both times. During his stay in the Habsburg capital he had no regular job and was often short of money, at one point living in a hostel for the indigent, the kind of residence that would be called in American parlance a "flophouse."[4] He ultimately managed to scratch out a living by making and selling postcards and sketches of scenes of the city. In 1913, to avoid conscription into the Habsburg army, he moved to Munich,[5] in Germany; but when war broke out the next year, despite the fact that he remained a citizen of Austria-Hungary not the German Reich, he enlisted in a Bavarian, that is, a German, regiment.[6]

Military service transformed him: he became an enthusiastic soldier.[7] He served as a dispatch runner—a messenger between commanders in the rear and the troops on the front lines in the trenches in France—a task that exposed him to danger. He was wounded and hospitalized, suffering temporary blindness, and received medals for bravery. The German high command's decision to give up fighting in November 1918 shocked and distressed him,[8] as it did many Germans. He remained in the army after the armistice and was assigned to duties involving propaganda, an activity considered necessary because of the presence of revolutionary sentiment in Munich, where an abortive communist coup took place in 1919—an event that appalled him as well as the military leaders. As part of his duties, Adolf Hitler, who had previously demonstrated no particular abilities in any field, discovered a remarkable talent for public speaking,[9] which was to become the key to the political career on which he embarked soon thereafter.

He joined the National Socialist German Workers' Party (NSDAP, commonly known as the Nazi Party), a small, obscure, radical nationalist political grouping, receiving membership card number 555.[10] He quickly established himself as its star attraction, drawing crowds to his speeches. He became the party's leader, its symbol, and its leading political asset. He concentrated power over its operations in his own hands. Under his direction, it presented itself as a "volkspartei," which purported to represent not simply one class or interest group or religion but rather the entire German people.[11] The Party organized its own paramilitary force, the Sturmabeleitung (SA), which used violence to promote its fortunes and its program.[12]

That program, which Hitler propagated through his speeches, featured vehement opposition to the postwar political settlement that the victorious Allies had imposed on Germany through the Treaty of Versailles of 1919; rejection of the Weimar Republic, the democratic political system established after the defeat; and intense hostility to communism and to Jews, whom he deemed responsible for Bolshevism as well as for many other ills.[13] His strident version of nationalism and antisemitism, while not necessarily commanding majority support, had wide currency in Bavaria and throughout Germany.[14]

In 1923, Hitler felt strong enough to attempt to seize power forcibly in Bavaria. His effort to do so became known as the "Beer Hall Putsch" because it involved marching on an auditorium in a tavern. The coup failed and Hitler was arrested, tried for treason, convicted, and incarcerated. He used the trial as a platform from which to broadcast his views, making himself more widely known to Germans. Initially sentenced to five years in prison, he served only one, in less than arduous conditions.[15] During that time, he dictated his political testament, published under the title *Mein Kampf* (My Struggle). Emerging from prison, he revived the Nazi Party, which had languished in his absence. Chastened by his failure to seize power by extra-parliamentary means, he altered his strategy for gaining power and began to compete in elections.

For most of the 1920s, the Nazis remained a marginal if loud and violent presence in German public affairs, but the onset of the Great Depression at the end of the decade broadened the constituency for their particular brand of extreme nationalism. During 1932, five elections took place. In March, Hitler ran in a runoff election for the presidency of the republic but lost to Paul von Hindenburg, a World War I general, by 53 percent to 37. In a parliamentary election in July, the NSDAP reached its high point in the Reichstag, the German legislature, winning 230 seats with 37 percent of the total vote. Another election followed in November, and the Party's performance declined to 196 seats with 33.1 percent of the vote.[16]

After that election, the leaders of the conservative parties struggled to form a government and decided to include the Nazis in a governing coalition. Hitler insisted that, as a condition of his party's participation in the government, he had to become its head, the chancellor. President Hindenburg at first resisted appointing him but finally agreed. On January 30, 1933, Adolf Hitler took office. While the Nazis engaged in considerable street violence as well as conducting electoral campaigns, unlike Lenin and the Bolsheviks, Hitler came to power entirely legally.

He moved quickly and with remarkable success to consolidate all power in his own hands. He used the outbreak of a fire in the Reichstag building on February 27, whose origins remain unclear although a Dutch vagrant was tried and executed for it,[17] to persuade President Hindenburg to grant him extraordinary powers. He held another election on March 4 in which, amid violence against the Nazis' opponents, his party gained a majority of the seats in the legislature. He and his followers then cajoled and intimidated the other parties into passing the Enabling Act on March 23, which did away with the Weimar Republic's constitutional restraints on the power of the government. Germany became a dictatorship.[18]

All other political parties were abolished, and the once formidable trade unions were dissolved. Rival political leaders as well as Jews, communists, and others whom Hitler considered the enemies of his regime were arrested and put in detention centers that became known as "concentration camps."[19] Two more events completed the new order in Germany that the Nazis put in place. On June 30, 1934, the "Night of the Long Knives,"

Hitler ordered the killing of a number of political figures including the leader of the SA, which had become too powerful for the Nazi leader's comfort. For this purpose, he used the Schutzstaffel (SS: "Protective Echelon"), which functioned initially as a personal guard for him and acted in this instance with the complicity of the army.[20] Then, in August of that year, President Hindenburg died and the office was combined with the chancellorship. The only remaining potential source of opposition to Hitler had disappeared.

Through these events, the Weimar Republic gave way to the Third Reich, a government in which Hitler exercised supreme and unchallenged power. He did not exercise it in an orderly fashion. Keeping late hours and frequently ignoring the details of administration, he followed the habits and the lifestyle that he had developed as a would-be artist, without a regular job, during his years in Vienna.[21]

The government consisted of multiple agencies with overlapping jurisdictions and no clear lines of authority between and among them. Hitler used this chaotic design to play off different groups and factions against one another, thereby retaining his own authority.[22] He had come to be known, first in the Nazi Party and then in Germany as a whole, as the "Führer" ("the leader"), and the one unshakable rule in the Third Reich was that the Füehrer's word was law. Subordinates sometimes undertook initiatives without him but never against him.[23]

Hitler made the first priority of his government expanding German military might. He raised defense spending, which had the side-benefit of increasing economic activity and thus reducing the unemployment that the Great Depression had created. Between 1933 and 1935, overall output rose by 25 percent.[24] Whereas 6 million people were jobless in 1933, by 1936 that number had fallen to 1 million.[25]

He then turned his attention to dismantling the widely resented post–World War I political settlement that the Allies had imposed through the Versailles Treaty, opposition to which he had made central to his political program from the first day he entered politics. That settlement had placed limits on how many troops and what kinds of weapons Germany could have and where they could be deployed. Hitler renounced the Treaty's "demilitarization" clauses in March 1935. France and Britain, the authors of the limits he abandoned, did nothing.[26] The following year, again contrary to the postwar settlement, Hitler sent forces into the Rhineland, the German territory on the west bank of the Rhine River bordering on France, tilting the military balance between the two countries in a direction favorable to

Germany. Again, France and Britain took no effective steps to stop or roll back Hitler's illegal initiative.[27]

In 1936 as well, Nazi Germany intervened militarily in the Spanish Civil War on the side of the forces of General Francisco Franco, which were attempting to unseat the republican government of that country. German military assistance helped the rebels prevail. Also in that year, Germany signed agreements with Italy and Japan, two other countries seeking to overturn the post–World War I political arrangements. In 1940, the German alignment with the two other revisionist powers became the tripartite Axis Pact.[28]

The dismantling of the postwar settlement accelerated in 1938. In March, Germany annexed the German-speaking Austria that had emerged from the ruins of the far larger, polyglot Habsburg Empire after World War I, a measure known as the *Anschluss* ("Union"), which most Austrians enthusiastically welcomed.[29] In the summer, Hitler demanded that Czechoslovakia, another new multinational country carved out of Austria-Hungary after the war, cede its ethnically German territories to the Third Reich. The Czech government wanted to resist this demand but needed French and British support to have a chance of keeping its country intact. Rather than providing such support, British Prime Minister Neville Chamberlain made three trips to Germany to negotiate with Hitler.[30]

At the last of them, at Munich in September, with the Italian Fascist leader Benito Mussolini also present, Chamberlain and French Prime Minister Edouard Daladier gave the Füehrer what he wanted.[31] In five years, Hitler had overturned the political arrangements in Europe that had existed when he assumed power and in so doing had gathered almost all Germans into a single state—his state. He had done all this without firing a shot.*

If one major part of Hitler's political program involved disassembling the Versailles Treaty, another—equally important to him—called for assaulting Germany's Jews. The Nazis persecuted them from the moment Hitler had come to power, forcing them out of the civil service and universities. On the night of November 9–10, 1938, there took place

---

* The avoidance of war at Munich pleased much of the world, but not Hitler himself. "He felt cheated of the greater triumph which he was certain would have come from the limited war with the Czechs which had been his aim all summer." Ian Kershaw, *Hitler, 1936–1945: Nemesis*, New York: W.W. Norton, 2000, pp. 122–123.

a nationwide attack on Jewish-owned stores and buildings as well as synagogues. An estimated 30,000 Jews were arrested and sent to concentration camps. The episode became known as *Kristallnacht*—the "Night of Broken Glass."[32]

Hitler's international activities were far from finished. In March 1939, he seized the remaining territory of Czechoslovakia.[33] With this step, he crossed a line. The takeover had nothing to do with rectifying the perceived injustices of the postwar settlement and it violated the assurance that he had given to Chamberlain and Daladier at Munich that the concessions they made to him there fully satisfied his ambitions. The two leaders, and their countrymen, discovered that the German leader had lied to them. Public opinion in Britain, especially, turned sharply against Germany.[34] The British and French issued a guarantee to defend the country that was clearly the Third Reich's next target: Poland.

In late August 1939, to the world's astonishment, Germany signed a non-aggression agreement with the country Hitler had consistently reviled, the Soviet Union. The Nazi-Soviet Pact included a secret protocol dividing between them the territories that lay between the two countries.[35] Freeing the Third Reich as it did from any concern about Soviet intervention, the Pact cleared the way for a German attack on Poland on September 1. Thus began a six-year period in which Hitler was continuously engaged in waging war. At first, he achieved spectacular success. Germany conquered Poland in three weeks.[36] Josef Stalin's Soviet Union seized the territory that the Nazi-Soviet Pact had allotted to it, and Germany imposed a brutal occupation on the Poles, wantonly murdering, with Hitler's approval, its nobility, its clergy, and its Jews.[37]

While pledged to defend Poland, Great Britain and France undertook no military initiatives for this purpose. After Poland's defeat, there followed seven months of military inactivity, known in England as the "phoney war" and in France as the *"drôle de guerre."* In May 1940, however, Germany occupied Belgium and Holland. Most importantly, its army, the Wehrmacht, attacked France not where the French expected it to strike, from the north, but rather to the south, through the Ardennes Forest. Tank formations with close air support broke through France's defenses in that region and moved with lightning speed[38] all the way to the English Channel.[39] Rather than attacking the retreating forces, Hitler ordered a pause in the German offensive, with which his generals concurred. This enabled the British to evacuate most of the troops they had sent to help defend France, and some French soldiers as well, at the

Channel port of Dunkirk.[†] That was the only consolation for the Allies. Thoroughly beaten, the French surrendered.

Hitler's Wehrmacht had achieved in four weeks what the Kaiser's army had failed to accomplish in four long years in World War I.[40] Twelve years after that war had ended in a German defeat, Nazi Germany faced no armed opposition on the European continent.

Great Britain, however, now led by Winston Churchill, who had become prime minister in May 1940, held out. Britain was one of the few countries for which Hitler had some regard. He had not expected the British to go to war for Poland and consistently hoped to come to terms with them. He was prepared to leave them with their overseas empire while Germany dominated mainland Europe.[41] Churchill's refusal to accept such an arrangement infuriated him. Hitler decided to subdue the British militarily and launched a bombing campaign to this end. He also ordered preparations for a cross-Channel invasion, which required German air superiority to succeed. The ensuing Battle of Britain took place in the air over the Channel and southern England. By failing to win it, the Germans lost that battle. The Royal Air Force proved a match for the German Luftwaffe. Hitler abandoned the plan for invading Britain and turned his attention to the east.[42]

He decided to attack the Soviet Union. For that purpose, the Third Reich deployed a force of 3.2 million Germans, supplemented by troops from allied countries,[43] and thousands of tanks and other motorized vehicles. On June 22, 1941, that force launched Operation Barbarossa, named for a twelfth-century Holy Roman Emperor. Three army groups struck eastward. The northern one aimed at Leningrad, the Soviet name for the old imperial capital St. Petersburg. The center group headed for Moscow, while the southern group moved through Kiev, with its ultimate intended destination being the oil fields of the Caucasus.

Barbarossa achieved sweeping early success, rapidly pushing back and frequently encircling the unprepared Soviet forces, which Stalin's purges of the Red Army and his abandonment of some of the country's western

---

[†] Hermann Goering, the head of the Luftwaffe—the German air force—asserted that his planes could finish off the British and French troops at Dunkirk. They did not. The British escape was a fateful moment. "If the British Expeditionary Force had been lost, it is almost inconceivable that Churchill would have survived the growing pressure from those powerful forces within Britain that were ready to seek terms with Hitler." Kershaw, *Nemesis*, p. 297.

defenses after 1939 had severely weakened. In July, 89 of 164 Soviet divisions had been knocked out of the war or crippled and only nine of twenty-two tank divisions were operational.[44] By the autumn, 3 million soldiers of the Red Army were German prisoners of war, a high proportion of whom did not survive their captivity.[45] Hitler and his associates had expected the Red Army, and the Soviet regime, to collapse under the German onslaught; but while both were severely battered, neither disintegrated.

By December, with the cold weather setting in, the Wehrmacht had reached Leningrad but had not occupied the city. German forces had progressed to the outskirts of Moscow (German troops were within 12 miles of the city on December 2)[46] but had not captured it, and had taken Kiev but had not invaded the Caucasus.[47] On December 5, the Red Army managed to launch a limited counterattack outside Moscow. The German army was not well equipped for a Russian winter, its leaders having assumed that the war would have ended by the time that season arrived; and its troops were spread out over such a broad front that they were vulnerable to the attacks that Soviet partisans and regulars were still able to launch. The German commanders wanted to withdraw to what they regarded as more defensible positions, but Hitler forbade this.

On December 7, 1941, while the German assault was bogging down in Russia, Japan attacked American naval forces at Pearl Harbor, Hawaii. The United States immediately declared war on Japan but not on Germany. Four days later, however, on December 11, Hitler himself declared war on the United States. He would thenceforth have to contend not only with the vast spaces and large population of the Soviet Union but also with the increasingly mobilized technological prowess, and the land, naval, and air forces, of the democratic colossus of North America. In the end, the two major decisions he made in 1941—to wage war against both the Soviet Union and the United States—assured his defeat.

Meanwhile, thanks to Barbarossa, Germany occupied most of the European part of the Soviet Union in addition to the countries it had previously conquered. The treatment of the people whom the Third Reich now had at its mercy proved to be, if anything, more brutal than the fate the Poles had suffered.[†] Orders were given to liquidate all the functionaries

---

[†] For details, see Michael Burleigh, *The Third Reich: A New History*, New York: Hill and Wang, 2000, pp. 512–567. Hitler made it clear that the war in the east was to be "a *Vernichtungskrieg*, an ideological war of destruction, in which all the conventional rules of war concerning prisoners, occupation, and so on were to be disregarded, political commissars shot out

of the Soviet system and the Soviet intelligentsia as well.[48] Detachments of the SS roamed the captured territory rounding up Jews and others considered undesirable and murdering them, often after forcing the victims to dig their own graves.[49] Berlin decided that more systematic and effective methods were needed to deal with the vast majority of Europe's Jews who now had the terrible misfortune to fall under Nazi control. This led to the construction of six camps in Poland to which Jews were transported by rail from all parts of the continent and killed, most of them by herding them into small, crowded buildings, unleashing poison gas on them, and then burning their corpses. By the time the Nazis had finished, an estimated 6 million Jews had died.[50]

The fighting in the east continued in 1942, with large German losses,[51] and at the end of that year the tide of war began to turn against Germany. Beyond Europe, in North Africa, British troops led by General Bernard Montgomery defeated an army led by one of the Wehrmacht's ablest commanders, Erwin Rommel, at El Alamein in Egypt. In the same month, an American army entered the field for the first time, also in North Africa, in Morocco and Algeria. British bomber aircraft struck German cities, taking a heavy toll in lives.[52]

The most important battle of that year, perhaps the most important battle of the war, took place in European Russia, at Stalingrad, a city on the Volga River. Hitler made it the main object of the 1942 campaign and hurled a large army against it. The troops on both sides fought doggedly and courageously. The combat became the most intense and murderous of the entire war, as the rival forces battled over individual buildings in the ruins of the city. In November, the Red Army succeeded in encircling and cutting off the Germans forces that were attacking Stalingrad. Despite Hitler's order forbidding it, on February 2, 1943, with his troops starving,[53] the German commander, Field Marshal Friedrich Paulus, surrendered. Germany's momentum was broken. It had lost the military initiative and was never to regain it. Thereafter, World War II became, for the Third Reich, a defensive struggle in which the numerically superior

---

of hand, and the civilian population made subject to summary execution and collective reprisals." Alan Bullock, *Hitler and Stalin: Parallel Lives*, New York: Alfred A. Knopf, 1992, p. 760. German policy in the territories captured in Barbarossa included "extermination of leading strata, deprivation of rights and enslavement of the remaining mass of the population." Sebastian Haffner, *The Meaning of Hitler*, Translated by Ewald Osers, Cambridge, Massachusetts: Harvard University Press, 1979, p. 133.

and increasingly better-armed allies, slowly and at great cost in human life, ground down the Wehrmacht.

In July 1943, at Kursk in Russia, in the largest tank battle ever fought, the Red Army again prevailed. In September, American and British forces conducted an amphibious landing in Italy and began to fight their way up the Italian peninsula.

The next year, 1944, brought one military disaster after another for the Third Reich. Soviet armies continued to push German forces westward, back toward Germany. American, British, and Canadian forces landed in northwest France, on beaches in Normandy, on June 6th (later known as D-Day), opening a second front against the Germans on the European continent. On July 20, German army officers succeeding in detonating a bomb in a conference room where Hitler was present. The blast injured him but he escaped with his life. In December, the Third Reich launched its final offensive of the war, in the Ardennes region where German tanks had attacked France so successfully four years earlier.[54] The offensive failed.[55]

As Germany went from one defeat to another, Hitler ceased to appear in public. At the beginning of 1945, he retreated, with a small staff, to a bunker underneath the garden of the chancellery building in Berlin. His orders became increasingly detached from the military realities on the ground. In the first four months of that year the opposing coalition executed a pincer movement against Germany, with the Americans and the British advancing from the west and the Red Army coming from the east. At the same time, Allied bombing was reducing German cities to rubble. By the end of April, the Russians had entered Berlin and were within a few blocks of Hitler's bunker. On April 30, realizing that all hope for a reversal of fortune had vanished and determined to avoid both falling into the hands of his enemies and repeating the surrender of November 1918 that he had spent his entire political career reviling, Hitler committed suicide with his own pistol. A few days later, the remnants of the regime did surrender. The Reich that he had promised would last for a thousand years had not reached its thirteenth birthday.

The Times

The career of Adolf Hitler, like the victory of the Bolsheviks in Russia, would not have been possible without the First World War. In the absence of that war, it seems likely that he would have continued on the aimless, unsuccessful, anonymous course that his life followed during his years in Vienna.[56] Being a soldier transformed him personally, and the outcome and aftermath of World War I gave him a purpose and a vocation while creating the conditions in which he was able to come to power. He also adopted as his goal saving Germany from the disgrace and political bondage that, as he (and not he alone) saw it, the postwar settlement had inflicted on it. Overthrowing the Versailles Treaty and restoring Germany to what he deemed to be its rightful place in Europe became fundamental parts of the platform of the Nazi Party. Germans joined and supported it because they shared those goals and believed that Hitler could achieve them. The war and its consequences, in short, gave him an agenda and a following.

More broadly, the massive death and destruction that the war caused had the effect of shattering and discrediting the imperial political system that had led Germany into the conflict. The old regime collapsed and the Kaiser fled to Holland. Of course, the conflict had severely damaged all the countries that waged it, but unlike Great Britain and France, Germany also lost the war, which made its trauma all the greater. Moreover, the defeat came, for the German public, suddenly and unexpectedly, but the victorious Allies did not occupy Germany. These circumstances gave credibility to the postwar charge, on which Hitler insisted, that Germany had been betrayed—"stabbed in the back"—a phrase that Hindenburg used in 1919.[57]

The Germans expected—or at least chose to believe—that the terms of the postwar peace settlement would display generosity toward them and that they would have a voice in devising it. In their understanding, it would embody the spirit of the American president Woodrow Wilson's Fourteen Points.[58] Instead, at the Paris Peace Conference in 1919 the leaders of the victorious coalition, including Wilson himself, designed a peace treaty that the Germans regarded—both at the time and subsequently—as unduly harsh and grossly unfair.[59]

Germany was required to give up territory, including territory inhabited by ethnic Germans who did not want to belong to the new countries to which the settlement assigned them. Germans also had to pay reparations to the victorious powers, which the treaty justified on the grounds that their country was guilty of starting the war. The origins of World War I have remained a contentious issue among historians for more than a century, but in its immediate aftermath few Germans accepted the responsibility for the conflict that the Versailles Treaty imputed to them. The Treaty aroused widespread and enduring resentment among Germans, and Hitler and the Nazi Party made exploiting it central to their political strategy. The Party distinguished itself in the 1920s by the vehemence of its opposition to the postwar settlement.[60]

The Nazis opposed not only the Versailles Treaty but also the successor political system to the imperial Reich, the shaky democracy known as the Weimar Republic (1918–1933), which had accepted and then attempted, albeit often grudgingly, to implement the Treaty's terms. Many Germans, and certainly Hitler and the Nazis, regarded the Weimar Republic as having been born in sin. Thus, a democratic government in a country that had never before been a full-fledged democracy began life burdened with the responsibility for what a very large number of its citizens regarded as a national humiliation. The wish to avoid paying reparations contributed to economic policies that resulted in German hyper-inflation in 1923,[61] which saddled the new regime with another damaging reputation—for ruinous economic incompetence.[62]

Weimar never commanded the robust, wholehearted allegiance of a clear majority of the people it governed. Its widely perceived illegitimacy made the Nazis' emphatic opposition to it politically advantageous to them. In German democracy's permanently weakened condition—another consequence of World War I—Hitler was able to dispatch it quickly and with relative ease when he came to power in early 1933.

World War I also affected the Western democracies in ways that made it possible for Hitler to leave the mark he did on European and world history. Over the course of the 1920s, more and more people in Great Britain, and to a lesser extent in France, came to believe that fighting the war of 1914 to 1918 had been a mistake.[63] The cost of the conflict, they concluded, had far exceeded any benefits that had accrued, even to the victors. They also came to believe, in growing numbers, that the postwar settlement had in fact treated Germany unfairly.[64]

These two sentiments combined to underpin the policy that Britain and France conducted toward Nazi Germany from 1935 until the middle of 1939, the policy of appeasement.[§] Appeasement had as its purpose avoiding another major European war by refraining from responding

---

[§] Two other considerations contributed to British appeasement. "Britain's interests overseas in the Empire and in the troubled Far East, alongside a prevalent concern about the threat of Bolshevism, encouraged a more pro-German stance completely at odds with French

forcefully to Hitler's sequential dismantling of the Paris settlement, and thus acquiescing in what he did. By allowing measures that rectified what they had come to see as the wrongs of the Versailles Treaty, appeasement's proponents expected, or at least hoped, to satisfy the Germans and preserve the European peace.

Thus, the British and the French—who felt obliged to follow the British lead since they were unwilling to risk war with Germany without Great Britain as an ally[65]—effectively did nothing when, in 1935, Hitler renounced the disarmament requirements that the Allies had imposed in 1919, when he sent troops into the Rhineland in 1936, and when he annexed Austria later that same year. In 1938, at Munich, they more or less compelled the government of Czechoslovakia to surrender to Hitler the parts of their country that he was demanding. The leadership of the Soviet Union, although unconcerned with the ethical ramifications of the postwar settlement and impervious to public sentiment in their now communist country, also pursued a policy of appeasement toward Germany, which found explicit expression in the Nazi-Soviet Pact of August 1938.[66]

Appeasement proved costly to the democracies. They ultimately had to stop Nazi Germany's expansion by military means, which required six terrible years of war. Had they adopted a forceful rather than a conciliatory approach to Hitler's demands before 1939, they might have prevented the bloodshed and destruction of 1939 to 1945. Hitler might have backed down in 1935 or 1936, or encountered serious internal opposition, particularly from the upper ranks of the army, which harbored some discontent about his threat to go to war over Czechoslovakia in 1938.[67] Or, if war had come on those occasions, Hitler might have been defeated at a far lower cost than the war that began in September 1939 ultimately involved. Even during that month, when the war in Europe began, because most of its forces were participating in the invasion of Poland, Germany had weak military defenses to its west, which Britain and France might have exploited.[68] They did not try to do so.

At every point at which Hitler took another step toward primacy in Europe until the final German absorption of Czechoslovakia in the spring of 1939, the British and French leaders decided that their publics would not support measures to check him because such measures had the potential to

---

diplomacy and to Hitler's direct advantage." Ian Kershaw, *Hitler, 1889–1936: Hubris*, New York: W. W. Norton, 1999, p. 553.

lead to another war. In this way, the legacy of World War I, with its terrible loss of life, discouraged policies that might have avoided World War II, or at least made such a conflict easier for the anti-Nazi coalition to win.

Powerful though its impact was, however, World War I alone did not create the conditions under which Hitler and the Nazis were able to take control of Germany. In the second half of the 1920s, conditions in Germany and Europe stabilized.[69] The peace settlement, with some modifications,[70] seemed to take hold. Then came the Great Depression, the worst economic downturn in modern history.[71] It hit Germany particularly hard because that country depended heavily on loans from the United States and trade with its neighbors, both of which contracted sharply.[72] Without incoming loans and export markets, economic activity plummeted and unemployment soared.[73]

The German people became ever more distressed, angry, and politically polarized. Germany also became a more violent place, as two political parties—the Nazis and the Communists—fielded paramilitary forces that the parties' leaders did not hesitate to send into action.[74] In these new circumstances, the Nazis' political fortunes improved dramatically. In the last pre-Depression parliamentary elections, in 1928, they received 809,000 votes and won 12 parliamentary seats. In the elections of 1930, with the severe economic downturn in full swing, their numbers were 6,400,000 votes and 107 seats.[75] The Depression enhanced Hitler's public appeal, raised his political standing, and brought him to the threshold of power.

He did not cross that threshold and into the chancellor's office unaided, however. Nor could he have done so: on the eve of assuming power he had the support of only one-third of the German public.[76] Hitler owed his ultimate political ascent to the other parties and their leaders on the right of the German political spectrum.[77]

They, and in particular the devious former chancellor, Franz von Papen, brought the Nazis into a governing coalition and acceded to its leader's demand that he become the chancellor.[78] They did so on the basis of two misconceptions. The first of these was that Hitler was one of them.[79] He did share their contempt for Weimar democracy and their horror of communism;[80] but unlike many of them, he felt no nostalgia for the prewar Reich and was in fact not a conservative but a revolutionary, as his gruesome efforts to remake Germany demonstrated.[81]

German conservatives also mistakenly—and in some cases fatally[82]—believed that, once in office, they could control Hitler.[83] They could not and did not. They believed that by installing him in the chancellery in Berlin, they were advancing their own careers. In fact, they were ending them. He turned on them and banished them from power. They suffered, on the whole, less than the politicians of the left (not to mention the Jews), but political life in the Third Reich turned out to be radically different from what they had anticipated on January 30, 1933.

One German institution in particular played a supporting role in Hitler's assumption of power and a far larger one in what he did with that power: the army. Descended from the Prussian army, the instrument by which Prussia raised itself to the status of a European great power in the eighteenth century and unified Germany in the nineteenth, it had consistently wielded more extensive political power and domestic influence than the armed forces of any other European country.[84] It involved itself deeply in the public life of the Weimar Republic, and almost never in a way that strengthened German democracy.[85]

The failure of his attempted putsch in 1923 convinced Hitler that he could not come to power over the objections of the army; and while the army did not put him in office in 1933, neither did it attempt to block him.[86] He earned its support after becoming chancellor by making his highest priorities expanding the armed forces through increasing military spending and breaching the treaty-imposed limits on the German military.[87] He further enhanced his standing with the military by his assault on the leadership of the Nazis' paramilitary arm, the SA, during the Night of the Long Knives and his subsequent reduction of its numbers. At its peak, the SA had fielded over 3 million men and its leader, Ernst Roehm, wanted it to supplant the Wehrmacht as the nation's principal military force. By having Roehm killed, Hitler removed a threat both to his personal leadership and to the primacy of the army.[88]

Subsequently, the Füehrer gained complete control of the army,[89] to the extent that during the war he directed its operations personally, often bypassing or overruling the generals. This meant that during the Third Reich, civilian control of the military was probably stricter and more effective than at any previous point in German history—which did not, of course, make for a peaceful foreign policy.

With Hitler's patronage, the German army became once again what it had been from the middle of the nineteenth century through 1918: the most powerful in Europe, if not in the world.[90] As such, it served as the instrument of the Nazis' greatest and most terrible achievement: the conquest of most of Europe. While it was the SS that took the lead in carrying out the murderous rampages in the territories to the east that Germany conquered, the army sometimes also took part in them and in any case was well aware of what was taking place and did not try to put a stop to it.[91] Along with the First World War and its aftermath, therefore, and the Great Depression and the machinations of conservative German politicians, the German army bears responsibility for the political power that Hitler acquired and the uses to which he put it.

Leadership

Adolf Hitler was a man of ideas, which he sought, with an alarming degree of success, to impose on the world. His ideas informed his political party's program and guided his policies in office. Like most political figures, he did not have a fully elaborated philosophy of history, politics, and statecraft, but he did have a worldview; and that worldview had, in the end, a profound impact on German, European, and world history.

He presented himself, when he entered politics, as a German nationalist. As a "volkisch" nationalist he represented, in his own mind, the interests of the entire German people. While not born a citizen of the German Reich, he became, as well, a fervent German nationalist, regarding the Germans as superior to other people and thus entitled to a privileged position, a position of superiority—indeed of dominance—in the world.

His nationalist program therefore involved, in the first instance, restoring Germany to its rightful place in Europe, from which World War I and the subsequent peace settlement had, in his view and that of most of his countrymen, dislodged it. A full restoration of this kind required doing away with the Weimar Republic, which, by accepting that settlement, had become complicit in the humiliation of 1919. He railed against those who had surrendered to the Allies, whom he called, after the month in 1918 in which Germany surrendered, "the November criminals." Most Germans disliked the settlement, and many disliked the Republic. Hitler appealed to them by making himself the most outspoken and extreme political opponent of both.[92]

He was also an extreme and outspoken antisemite. Antisemitism was central to his worldview: it had a more important place in his thinking than was imaginable—or at least than was imagined—before he came to power. To be sure, hostility to Jews was common in Europe for centuries before the

Third Reich came into existence. It generally increased in intensity from the western to the eastern part of the continent: the British version being for the most part and for most of history the mildest, the Russian incarnation the most severe as the site of recurrent murderous attacks on Jewish communities known as "pogroms." Germany before Hitler, while never philo-Semitic, was by no means the worst country in Europe for Jews.[93]

For most of European history, antisemitism had a religious basis: the Jews were anathematized for scandalously resisting becoming Christians and denying Christian dogma. In the modern era, prejudice against Jews also came to have a social basis. It involved excluding them from a range of social positions and activities as well as resentment at the successes they achieved in the professions when and where they were allowed to enter them.[94] After the Russian Revolution, some antisemites, Hitler among them, linked the Jews to the Bolsheviks.[95]

Hitler's antisemitism, however, belonged to a different and far more toxic category. He regarded Jews, incorrectly from a scientific point of view, as a distinctive race that passed on its invidious characteristics from generation to generation. Although the Jewish people formed a tiny part of the overall population of Europe, these characteristics, which Hitler never fully specified, made them, in his view, a mortal threat to everyone else. He used the metaphor of germs and disease in describing them, calling the world's Jews a "bacillus"—with, by implication, the potential to infect the whole world.[96] This made his assault on them, in his own historical cosmology, an act of self-defense: given the threat they posed, they had to be eliminated.[97] This he proceeded to try to do.

In the long and bloody history of antisemitism, nothing like what Hitler perpetrated had ever occurred. His own personal antisemitism qualifies as perhaps the most lethal idea that anyone has ever had. Just how and where it originated is not known, and can never be known.[98] It belongs not to the history of ideas but to the realm of psychopathology;[99] and the individual psyche in question shut down on April 30, 1945, never to reopen.

From the 1920s, Hitler emphasized another idea that had profound real-world consequences: the Germans' need for living space (*lebensraum*). They had to seek it to the east, and Operation Barbarossa had the effect of putting the idea into practice, at horrible cost to the people already living in the territories he designated for German expansion and occupation.[100] He regarded those territories as the German equivalent of the British imperial domain in India,[101] although the British did not engage in the large-scale murder of the Indians whom they governed.

Underlying his various ideas was a master concept: war. It was for Hitler not simply a metaphor for life: it *was* life.[102] The world, he believed—in an extreme version of Social Darwinism, itself the corruption of the modern theory of evolution—was divided into separate races that engaged in an ongoing struggle for survival with one another. What economically determined social classes were for Lenin, races were for Hitler. Hitler's warlike policies thus followed the laws of nature as he claimed to understand them.[103]

In the face of this inevitable, permanent struggle, he devoted his career, again from his own perspective, to ensuring that Germany would prevail. Only the strong would survive and, for Hitler, only the strong *deserved* to survive. At the end, with the regime he had built crashing down on his head, he suggested that the Germans' failure in the war that he had started demonstrated their weakness. (His own massive responsibility for the disaster apparently failed to occur to him.) The fate of the weak, he believed, was to perish, and he more than once suggested that, in the event of defeat, this is what would happen to the Germans. The history of Europe, while hardly one of uninterrupted peace, is not, needless to say, a history of constant, titanic wars to the death among its constituent nations. The power that Hitler held in Germany, however, and what he did with it, made European history conform to this particular idea for a dozen dreadful years.

Some of Hitler's ideas appealed to most Germans and others—including antisemitism, although not necessarily his own annihilationist version— appealed to at least some of his countrymen. His task as an aspiring and then actual leader was to persuade people that he was the man to put the ideas they favored into practice. How did he accomplish this?

He had, by most accounts, a varying impact on people who had direct personal encounters with him. He could come across as a self-centered bore, droning on about subjects of interest to him but not to his listeners, turning his opinions and prejudices into monologues.[104] On the other hand, in his political career before becoming chancellor, he was able to persuade Germans of substance, and from higher social strata than he, to support him and his party, sometimes financially.[105] Moreover, on some who came into direct contact with him he had a mesmerizing effect.[106] Such people, including high Nazi officials, became his devoted followers.

The key to Hitler's political success, however, lay in his impact on the vast majority of Germans who had no direct, personal connection with him. He reached them through his oratory—in rallies and eventually through the new medium of radio; and as a public speaker, he had a magnetic, galvanizing effect on his listeners.[107] In his many large rallies, that effect stemmed not only from his words but also from the stagecraft involved. Such gatherings were carefully orchestrated pageants, designed both to evoke awe in the participants and to make them feel a part of a mighty, irresistible movement.[108] A speech by Hitler was always the centerpiece of these events. His speeches did not appeal to the listeners' reason through carefully structured arguments, but rather aimed to arouse their emotions—above all their anger.

He and the Nazi Party attended carefully to the manner in which he presented himself, both in the rallies and elsewhere. He and they also paid careful attention to his public image, especially in the press.[109] In this way, he resembled less a traditional, conventional politician than the figure that technology had created at the same time that Hitler was building his political career: the movie star. Such people often appear unremarkable in everyday life, but projected on a large screen they become magnetic personalities. So it was with Hitler and his rallies; and as with movie stars, people came to feel an intense personal connection with him even though they had never met him.[110] He embodied charismatic leadership.[111]

All the emphasis in Nazi public events and propaganda fell on the person of Hitler himself. He was widely known not by his name but by his self-appointed title: the Füehrer. In his presence, and then in ordinary encounters between and among Germans, the Nazi salute—the outstretched right arm and the phrase "Heil Hitler"—became common, and ultimately more or less mandatory. It began within the Nazi movement and spread to the wider population after the Nazis assumed power.[112]

Hitler's style of leadership had three particular features that helped him gain power and then use it for such catastrophic purposes. He was a shrewd political operator. "Among all the prominent figures of the Weimar period," according to one distinguished historian (who was hardly an admirer of the Third Reich), "he is the only one of whom it can be said unequivocally that he possessed political genius."[113] He read situations perceptively and judged accurately the opportunities they provided him.[114] He also excelled at assessing other leaders, understanding their strengths and, what was more relevant for his rise, their weaknesses.[115]

In addition, Hitler had a penchant for acting boldly, shunning compromises and half-measures. He said of himself, "I always go to the outermost limits of risk, but never beyond."[116] This served him well, for example, when he insisted that he be made chancellor in exchange for including the Nazi Party in a governing coalition in 1933. Finally, the emotion that animated him, on which he relied, and that he sought to inspire in others, was hatred. His devoted acolyte and propaganda chief Josef Goebbels, upon meeting him in 1926, recorded him as saying, "God's most beautiful gift bestowed on us is the hate of our enemies, whom we in turn hate from the bottom of our hearts."[117] Other leaders might attempt to generate respect or affection for themselves: Hitler felt acutely, and aimed to instill or enhance in his followers, hatred of others.

Frequently during Hitler's twelve-year reign and recurrently thereafter, a particular set of questions has arisen: how could Germany have embraced him as their leader and followed him loyally for so long in pursuit of such destructive, horrific ends?[118] How could the nation that gave the world Beethoven and Goethe, a political community traditionally governed by the rule of law if not full-fledged democracy, a highly educated people at the forefront of world science, have attached itself to a rabble-rousing outsider who made, for the most part, no secret of what he intended to do? And how could the Germans have maintained that attachment all the way to the bitter, violent, bloody end in 1945?

The appearance of a more or less equally bloodthirsty communist regime in the Russian Empire has occasioned less astonishment, for Russia was always on the backward fringe of the European continent, politically and economically as well as culturally if not in artistic terms. It was far from the center of European civilization.[119] Germany, by contrast, was located at the center; yet it, too, produced a barbarous regime.[120]

In one sense, the reasons for this awful historical episode are clear enough: war, defeat, hyper-inflation, and depression had battered German society and radicalized German politics, creating a political opening for Hitler. He became the country's leader through a series of contingent events driven by the calculations (or miscalculations) of Germany's venal, short-sighted, anti-democratic conservative politicians. The support he commanded before becoming chancellor and thereafter stemmed in no small part from the fact that many Germans agreed with many of the views and policies that he espoused.

Even those who did not support the Nazi program in its entirety were favorably impressed by Hitler's early successes.[121] By the end of 1938, he had revived the country's economy, restored its political and military standing in Europe, and recovered territory lost in 1919, and had done so without war.[122] And, of course, both when things were going well for Hitler and then when they went badly, the Nazis suppressed opposition through ruthless coercion.[123]

All those things are true, and yet together they seem less than wholly adequate to explain how so many Germans could have remained faithful to the Third Reich for so long, faithful even as it brought death, destruction, and ruin into their lives.¶ In this way, the historical phenomenon of Adolf Hitler, which depended for its existence on Germans' fidelity to him, is likely to remain not only horrifying but also, somehow, mysterious.[124]

Personal Imprint

The history of Germany from 1933 to 1945, and the history of Europe and much of the world for the last half of that twelve-year span of time, is history that Adolf Hitler personally caused to happen.[††] He set in motion great and terrible events that would not have unfolded—at least not when and as they did—without him. Lenin's legacy lasted longer, but Hitler had

---

¶ An example: Hitler ordered his staff to burn his body after his death. When he committed suicide in his bunker beneath the Reichschancellery, on April 30, 1945, the Red Army had occupied most of Berlin and was shelling the Chancellery building. Nonetheless, staff members carried the body to the garden above ground and burned it, endangering their own lives while doing so. Ron Rosenbaum, *Explaining Hitler: The Search for the Origins of His Evil*, New York: Random House, 1998, p. 65. This did not, however, mean that they had decided, like their leader, to die there and were thus indifferent to the danger. Having discharged their last duty to the Füehrer, a number of them then fled the bunker to try to escape the Russians.

†† "The eruption he unleashed was stamped throughout almost every one of its stages, down to the weeks of final collapse, by his guiding will." Joachim C. Fest, *Hitler*, Translated by Richard and Clara Winston, New York: Vintage Books, 1975, p. 3. "In him an individual once again demonstrated the stupendous power of a solitary person over the historical process." *Ibid.*, p. 7. ". . . the things which happened in his time are inconceivable without him, in every respect and in every detail." Joachim Fest, quoted in Kershaw, *Hubris*, p. 601. ". . . he had an enormous impact and left a more indelible mark upon the century than any other dictator, a Lenin or a Stalin or a Mao." John Lukacs, *The Hitler of History*, New York: Alfred A. Knopf, 1997, p. 51.

a wider and deeper immediate personal impact on the twentieth century than any other individual.

He created and dominated the Nazi Party.[125] As German chancellor he had supreme and unchallenged authority. While he did not supervise the day-to-day operations of the Third Reich carefully, he set its direction and decreed its major policies. He also made the major decisions in German foreign policy and made them by himself.[126] He felt no need to consult his cabinet—which never convened after February 5, 1938—or the circle of Nazi officials close to him. He had absolute confidence in his superior expertise on all matters of statecraft. Leaders of the Wehrmacht had reservations about some of his military initiatives, but he overrode them. While the Nazi program of the 1920s clearly foreshadowed the measures of the 1930s to dismantle the post–World War I settlement, Hitler decided on the timing and the general approach that Germany adopted.[127]

He authorized the pact with the Soviet Union of August 1939, the war against Poland the following month, and the attacks on Western Europe of May 1940. It was he and he alone who made the fateful, world-changing decisions of 1941: the launch of Operation Barbarossa on June 22 and the declaration of war against the United States on December 11. What Hitler did was not entirely foreign to Germany's politics and history. Germans in general were dissatisfied with the terms of the Versailles Treaty, and expansion to the east had been a war aim in World War I, an aim that the Wilhelmine Reich briefly attained with the Treaty of Brest-Litovsk with Lenin's new Soviet government on March 3, 1918, before the German defeat in November eliminated the territorial gains that that Treaty had brought. Still, the combination of Hitler's personal, deeply held convictions and his singularly powerful position in Germany make it plausible to surmise that in his absence World War II in Europe would not have taken place.[128]

Hitler's leadership in foreign and military affairs differed from his role in domestic affairs in that, in matters of war and peace, he involved himself far more deeply in the details of policy. Indeed, he made decisions not only on questions of grand strategy, the normal province of commanders-in-chief, but also on military operations—the deployment of troops and the direction of battles.[129] To the conduct of Germany's war, especially after 1941, he brought detailed, intense oversight. In this way Hitler's work habits, for the first time in his life, came to resemble those of people with full-time jobs, although he still kept hours different from those of most office or factory workers.[130]

He was well informed about some of the technical aspects of the military arts[131] and deserves a share of the credit for the initial German military successes. He supported the unorthodox "Plan Yellow" devised by General Erich von Manstein, which involved attacking France through the Ardennes, that brought an unexpectedly swift and decisive victory in May and June of 1940.[132] In the winter of 1941, Hitler forbade any evacuation of the advanced positions to which Barbarossa had brought the German army, and in retrospect some historians have judged that this "halt order" prevented the kind of disorderly, punishing retreat in which Napoleon's armies had engaged in similar circumstances in 1812.[133]

On the other hand, his refusal ever to countenance tactical withdrawals, even when trading space for time made military sense, hampered the German military effort.[134] He believed that willpower counted for everything in war and that retreat of any kind signaled a weakening of the will, leading to defeat.[135] Willpower does indeed matter in war, but so do other factors that Hitler resisted taking into account. He also rejected the military advice that Barbarossa concentrate on capturing Moscow, a center of arms production as well as the Soviet capital, which, if accomplished, would have strengthened the German position at the end of 1941, perhaps decisively.[136] To cite a final example, he refused to order the total mobilization of German society for war.[137]

His greatest impact on World War II came through his wider strategic decisions, and here his mistakes were responsible for Germany's defeat. Bismarck, the country's greatest nineteenth-century statesman, had made it a cardinal rule to avoid two-front wars, and World War I had vindicated that rule[138]: imperial Germany had waged war both to the east and to the west and had suffered defeat. With Barbarossa and then the declaration of war with the United States after Pearl Harbor, Hitler repeated that mistake, which raises the question of why he did so.

For all his verbosity, he had a secretive aspect to his personality. He was not in the habit of confiding his private calculations and innermost thoughts to anyone else. He left very few documents from which to reconstruct his process of decision making.[139] For that reason, the available records do not give a clear picture of his thinking in launching the attack on the Soviet Union. Several motives seem to have been at work.

He certainly never intended to honor the nonaggression pact with Stalin that he had authorized in August 1939. Before that agreement he had made intense hostility to Bolshevism central to his political program.[140]

In that sense the attack of June 1941 did not come, or at least should not have come, as a complete surprise. Crucially, he believed that the Wehrmacht would quickly overwhelm the Red Army, which Stalin's purges had weakened.[141] He was not alone in this belief.[142] The German high command concurred. The American Secretary of War Henry Stimson reported to President Franklin Roosevelt the consensus within the American military that the Soviet Union would be able to fight for only three months before succumbing.[143] In addition, Hitler felt a personal urgency about achieving the goal of gaining "living space" for the German people. He was convinced that this could only be done under his leadership—it could not be left to a successor—and that he had only a limited time to live. He therefore had to act promptly.[144]

Not least important, he saw smashing the Soviet Union as a way of finally bringing Great Britain to terms. The British were holding out, he reckoned, in the hope that they would get help in their struggle against the Third Reich. The defeat of the Bolsheviks, he expected, would extinguish that hope and he would finally be able to make the kind of arrangements with His Majesty's Government for which he had hoped since the 1930s.[145]

The Wehrmacht did not destroy the Red Army, and the chances for the short war in the east that Hitler had envisioned evaporated. That makes his decision to declare war on the United States after Pearl Harbor, when the initial failure of Barbarossa was already becoming apparent, particularly puzzling. True, he had told the Japanese that he would join them if they made war on America, but he was hardly noted for keeping his word;[146] and in any event, Japan had not obliged him by fighting the Soviet Union after he had attacked it, instead observing the nonaggression pact with Moscow that Tokyo had signed in April 1941. In the immediate aftermath of the Japanese attack, it was far from clear that President Roosevelt would be able to persuade his country to enter the war against Germany, which had not, after all, taken part in that attack. Churchill feared that the United States would confine itself to waging war in the Pacific.[147] Hitler's declaration of war on December 11 did Churchill and Great Britain an enormous favor.[148]

Hitler seems to have assumed that the Third Reich would ultimately have to fight the United States and to have decided that it would be advantageous to do so while the Americans also had to contend with Japan.[149] In addition, the United States was already effectively involved in the European war, with its navy helping to protect ships carrying supplies to

Great Britain.[150] In 1917, the German General Staff decided to resume unrestricted submarine warfare despite understanding that this would very likely bring the United States into World War I on the side of Britain and France—as indeed it did—based on the calculation that the Americans would not for months be able to do more damage to Germany than they were already doing.[151] Hitler may have made the same calculation about the United States in December 1941. Earlier, he had been careful not to provoke the Americans.[152] Having declared war, he could and did feel free to authorize frequent submarine attacks on shipping in the Atlantic, which put Britain's lifeline to North America in jeopardy for a time.[153]

In major wars, especially if they are long wars, victory almost always goes to the side with superiority in war material, manpower, and financial resources.[154] Hitler's two decisions in 1941 ensured that the coalition opposing Germany would be broad enough to enjoy those advantages.[††] Yet Germany still had a way, or so Hitler hoped and believed, to gain at least some of its goals: by dividing that coalition. He took as a favorable precedent the way Frederick the Great of Prussia escaped defeat in the Seven Years' War in 1762, when the Russian Empress Elizabeth died and her successor and nephew, Peter III, withdrew from the anti-Prussian coalition.[155] He regarded the alliance of the democracies with the Soviet Union as an unnatural one and counted on its breaking apart—as it ultimately did, but only after Hitler was dead and Germany defeated.

What blocked any possibility of a compromise with one of his major adversaries in World War II was Hitler himself. This is another way in which he personally contributed to the German defeat. He had shown himself to be so deceitful and aggressive, and had carried out policies so

---

[††] Hitler came closer to winning the war he started than is often recognized. In early December 1941, the Wehrmacht had advanced to the gates of Moscow. Then, on December 5, the Red Army launched, for the first time, a successful if limited counterattack. Had the Germans captured Moscow, while Stalin and the Communist leadership would have fled eastward, they would have had difficulty presiding over effective resistance to the Germans. In that circumstance, the British might well have replaced Churchill with a leader willing to accept the terms that Hitler was offering—the preservation of the British Empire in exchange for the acceptance of German hegemony in Europe. Had that happened, the United States might have decided to confine itself to securing the Western Hemisphere, thereby giving Hitler the outcome he sought. In part because he had not sufficiently concentrated German forces on Moscow, Hitler did not succeed in capturing it; and on December 7 came the Japanese attack on the American fleet at Pearl Harbor, Hawaii and, a few days later, Hitler's declaration of war on the United States, which ultimately ensured his defeat.

barbaric, that none of his enemies would trust him. The twentieth century differed from the eighteenth in a number of ways that made the kind of diplomacy in which the great powers of the earlier era routinely engaged difficult if not impossible to conduct in World War II. Still, if Hitler had been a more conventional, less murderous leader, perhaps there would have been a chance for a compromise of some kind.[156] Of course, if he had been a more conventional political leader, he would not have started the war in the first place.

Hitler's most distinctive mark on the history of the twentieth century, and the one for which he will longest be remembered, is his campaign to murder all of Europe's Jews. Although his raging animus against them was clear and constant, the tactics he employed against the people he considered his—and Germany's, and the world's—mortal enemies changed over time.[157] Upon coming to power, the Nazis persecuted and imprisoned German Jews but also permitted them to leave the country, albeit after confiscating their property. With the conquest of Poland and then of most of the European part of the Soviet Union, a far larger number of Jewish people came under his control. As late as the summer of 1940, plans were being discussed for sending them all far away: the island of Madagascar in the Indian Ocean was the favored destination.[158] Mass killings started as soon as Barbarossa took place, however, and in the second half of 1941, or perhaps early 1942, the Nazis settled on the "final solution:"[159] extermination of every Jew they could seize by shipping them by rail (in inhuman conditions) to the death camps in Poland and killing them there.

No doubt deliberately, Hitler left an exceedingly thin record of this deed. No written order from him for the annihilation of the Jews has come to light, and it is likely that none ever existed. He never visited a death camp, or even spoke explicitly in public about what Germans were doing in the east.§§

---

§§ Hitler was indifferent to German deaths as well. "Casualties, which any responsible commander worries about all the time, never seem to have concerned Hitler for a moment. When he was told of extremely high losses among junior officers in an operation just concluded, his only comment was: 'But that's what the young people are there for.'" Gordon A. Craig, *Germany 1866–1945*, New York: Oxford University Press, 1978, p. 756. "He never visited a field-hospital, nor the homeless after bomb-raids." Kershaw, *Nemesis*, p. 500. See also Lukacs, *The Hitler of History*, p. 194.

Yet there is no doubt about his personal responsibility for the genocidal war against the Jews.[160] He had made his obsessive hatred of them central to his program from the moment he embarked on a political career. At the outset of the war he hinted at what was to come: "If Jewry succeeded in again provoking a world war, it would end in the destruction of the Jews."[161] He repeated the warning on other occasions.[162] Subordinates issued orders for organizing the system of mass killings in his name.[163] It is inconceivable, given the realities of the Third Reich, that such an enterprise could have been undertaken against his wishes or indeed without his authorization. No one else in Germany was in a position to cause what befell Europe's Jews during his time in power, and it is difficult to imagine any other figure wanting to do what he caused to be done. He did not do the killing himself: thousands of people, mostly Germans but other nationalities as well, carried it out. Still, in the end, the verdict of the writer Milton Himmelfarb rings true: "No Hitler, no Holocaust."[164]

The Legacy

Adolf Hitler left a legacy both powerful and unique: it was, and remains, entirely negative. He achieved the opposite of what he intended.[165] His conquests, his party, and his political program did not survive him. His goals were entirely discredited, ultimately even—and most importantly—in Germany itself.[166] Unlike after World War I, the German people did not embrace, nor did their leaders pursue, the aim of overturning, by force if necessary, the political and territorial settlement imposed after World War II. Hitler's posthumous reputation could hardly be worse. It is a mark of the extreme distaste in which he came to be held that the name "Adolf" almost completely disappeared in Germany and elsewhere: no parent wished to encumber a son with it.

The contrast between posterity's treatment of Hitler and its view of the nineteenth-century figure whose career most closely approximates his is instructive. Napoleon Bonaparte also ruled as an autocrat at home and installed puppet governments abroad. Napoleon conquered most of Europe through bloody wars that brought death and destruction on a large scale and were waged at his whim. Yet many of the legal and administrative changes he brought to France have endured. His historical reputation is a mixed one,[167] but he has serious, credible defenders. Hitler does not.[168] Subway and railway stations in Paris bear the names of Napoleon's victorious battles. It is inconceivable that any public place anywhere would be named after the location of Hitler's most notable achievement: Auschwitz.

The geopolitical results of Hitler's war epitomize his wholly negative legacy. Instead of conquering Europe, Germany was itself conquered. After 1945, it lost approximately one-quarter of its prewar territory[169] and was occupied by Germany's conquerors—Great Britain, France, the United States, and the Soviet Union—countries that, with the partial exception of Great Britain, Hitler had considered bitter enemies populated (or controlled) by racial inferiors.

Germany was subsequently divided into two separate states: the democratic German Federal Republic in the west and the communist German Democratic Republic (GDR) in the east. "As long as I live," he had declared, "Germany will not suffer the fate of the European states inundated by Bolshevism."[170] After his death, and as a direct result of his policies, that is precisely what happened, for three-and-one-half decades, to 17 million Germans living in East Germany. Once militarily the most powerful state in Europe, and probably the world, the two Germanys found themselves largely disarmed and deprived of the capacity to act independently in matters of war and peace.

Hitler had envisioned sending millions of Germans to colonize the territories that the Wehrmacht had overrun to the east. Instead, virtually all Germans living to the east of what became postwar Germany—most of them in Central Europe, the Baltic region, and the western part of the Soviet Union—many of whose families had lived there for centuries, were evicted. They were forced to flee, at great loss of life, to postwar Germany.[171]

The perverse consequences of Hitler's years on the world stage— perverse, that is, from his point of view—were on vivid display in Europe. His war diminished not only Germany's role in Europe but also Europe's role in the world. The two non-European or partly European members of the victorious coalition—the United States and the Soviet Union— came to control the continent's political fortunes. The Nazi era had another perverse consequence in Europe: at the zenith of his military success, Hitler had imposed a kind of unity on Europe. In the years after 1945, the western part of the continent once again became more closely integrated than was historically normal, but did so in a decidedly anti-Hitlerian way. Integration came about peacefully and voluntarily, through economic cooperation rather than military domination. While Germany played a leading role in what is now the European Union,[172] moreover, it did so in a manner entirely alien to the Third Reich: hesitantly, reluctantly, often acting in concert with France, and by virtue of economic prowess rather than military power.

The two postwar German states themselves also embodied Hitler's negative legacy. Each was designed to be radically different from the Third Reich. The GDR embraced the communism that he had despised, but as a communist country became a police state and so had a family resemblance to Hitler's regime. The Federal Republic bore no such resemblance. Its constitution provided for the decentralization of power, in order to avert the concentrated authority that Hitler had wielded to such devastating effect. That constitution, known as the Basic Law, also sought, successfully as it turned out, to make it difficult to bring down governments, the constant turnover of ministries having been a source of weakness in the Weimar Republic.[173]

The two political parties that emerged as the strongest ones in the Federal Republic, the Christian Democrats (CDU) and the Social Democrats (SPD), had been outlawed in the Nazi era. Their postwar leaders, Konrad Adenauer of the CDU, the initial chancellor, and Kurt Schumacher, the first leader of the SPD, and Willy Brandt, the first member of that party to serve as chancellor, had suffered imprisonment or exile during that era.[174]

The Federal Republic did have one particular, and unwished for, continuity with the Third Reich. Before 1933, Germany had played host to a lively, creative community of writers and artists of all kinds. It had also had an impressive cadre of scientists. The country was a world leader—if not the world leader—in both spheres. Hitler's regime crippled Germany's artistic and scientific life because it did not permit free inquiry and free expression and because many of those at the forefront of the arts and sciences were Jewish, the fortunate among whom went into exile. Almost none returned after 1945, and Germany did not replace them. While the Federal Republic was not only open but also positively hospitable to the arts and sciences, the country did not recover its position of global eminence in either.[175]

Hitler's war also had an impact on the political organization of the world that went counter to what he had wanted. Far from wishing to bring an end to multinational empires, he was willing to allow the British to keep theirs and envisioned turning Eastern Europe into a German imperial domain.[176] Defeat compelled Germany to give up the territories it had conquered and had the same consequence for the vast empire Japan had assembled in Asia.[177]

In the quarter-century after 1945, the overseas empires of Great Britain and France also disappeared. The two powers relinquished them because the war had weakened them, which made keeping their imperial possessions too costly, and the dissolution of Europe's major land-based empires after World War I had already set a precedent for the end of empire. There was, however, another reason for the conclusion of the two countries' imperial careers, stemming directly from the war against the Third Reich: having opposed Hitler in part because of the Nazis' brutal domination of non-Germans, it became difficult to justify their own dominance, although it was far less brutal, of foreigners who had never volunteered for and were increasingly dissatisfied with British and French rule.

Hitler came closest to achieving what he set out to do in his war against the Jews. The assault he launched not only killed upwards of 6 million of them, it also destroyed the centuries-old Jewish communities of Eastern Europe. In the wake of the greatest disaster the Jewish people had ever suffered, however, came their greatest modern accomplishment: the revival of Jewish sovereignty in the Holy Land, where it had originated, in the form of the state of Israel. Hitler and his deeds are sometimes said to have made possible, entirely contrary to his intentions, the creation, in 1948, of the Jewish state.[178] This is incorrect.[179]

Zionism, the national movement of the Jewish people, predated the Third Reich by decades, and the hope of returning to the original home-land, enshrined in prayers, had formed a part of Judaism for two millennia. True, the news of what had befallen the Jews of Europe in the first half of the 1940s, once it became known, did engender sympathy for those who had survived; but that sympathy was not responsible for the emergence of the state of Israel. Crucial diplomatic support for its establishment, for example, came from the Soviet Union, whose supreme leader, Josef Stalin, had no sympathy for Jews (and very little for anyone else).

Nor did the decision of the United Nations General Assembly on November 29, 1947, to authorize the partition of Mandatory Palestine and thus of a Jewish state ensure that state's existence. The next year, when the Jewish community in Palestine proclaimed statehood upon the expiration of the British Mandate, it was invaded by several Arab armies, which it managed to defeat at considerable cost. It was the determination, the bravery, and the sacrifices of the Jews of Mandatory Palestine that created the state of Israel. In fact, the destruction of all but a fragment of European Jewry inflicted a huge setback on Zionism: the leaders of the Zionist movement had counted on those who were lost to populate the new Jewish state, as many of the all-too-few who survived, in fact, did.[180]

Hitler's negative legacy extended to the creation of international norms. The rule of law was absent in the Third Reich. Hitler believed in, and practiced, his version of the law of the jungle, in which the strong obliterate the weak. In response, after the war the victorious powers put Nazi leaders on trial for war crimes in the German city of Nuremburg and other venues.[181]

Similarly, Hitler had taken the basic unit of social and political life to be the collective. He made his goal the triumph of the German race, as he defined it. The fate of individual Germans, not to mention non-Germans, did not matter to him. In reaction, the United Nations enacted the International Declaration of Human Rights, designed— although often honored in the breach—to protect individual persons.[182] The Nazi efforts to exterminate the Jews gave rise to a new term for such an endeavor—"genocide"—and led to a convention making it a violation of international law.

Measured by body count, the Third Reich does not qualify as the worst political movement of the twentieth century. Communism killed more people. Certainly Mao and arguably Stalin presided over more murders than did Hitler if combat deaths in World War II are omitted from his total.[183] Yet it is Hitler who has the worst historical reputation of all of them.[184] This is so in part because he lost his war, his regime came to an end, and his crimes were fully exposed: communism escaped that fate. In addition, Hitler explicitly endorsed murderous inequality. The rhetoric of Marxism-Leninism, by contrast, is suffused with the aspiration to universal equality and brotherhood. The reality proved to be radically different, but communism, unlike Nazism, seems to have received global credit for its professed good intentions.[185]

Hitler's overtly malign intentions, and the project of genocide that followed from it, count, finally, as the principal reasons for his singular personal status after 1945.[186] He became the symbol of evil, assuming a role in the public imagination held, in the Christian world and in more religious times, by the devil, or the anti-Christ.[187] He and his works came to stand for ideas and policies to be avoided, or if necessary resisted, at all costs. A phrase that came into usage, particularly among Jews, in response to the Holocaust summarizes, in two words, the world's posthumous assessment of Hitler and the essence of his historical legacy: "Never Again."

4

Winston Leonard Spencer Churchill

The Life

Winston Churchill was born on November 30, 1874, at Blenheim Palace in Oxfordshire, England. His parents were Randolph Churchill, the second son of the Duke of Marlborough, whose ancestral home Blenheim was, and Jennie Jerome Churchill, the daughter of a wealthy New York businessman, Leonard Jerome. Randolph Churchill was a prominent political figure in the Conservative Party who rose to become the chancellor of the exchequer and leader of the House of Commons.[1] In 1886, however, he offered his resignation as a political tactic designed to enhance his political standing, unexpectedly had it accepted, and never held ministerial office again. He died in 1895, at the age of 45.[2]

His parents neglected young Winston, but he nonetheless idealized them. He remained close to his mother as an adult and wrote an admiring biography of his father. As a child, Winston Churchill decided that he wanted to be either a soldier or a politician.[3] He became both.

After passing through the Harrow School, one of the institutions of secondary education for the sons of the British elite, he entered Sandhurst, the Royal Military Academy. Upon finishing the prescribed course of studies, he secured a commission as a lieutenant in the Fourth Hussars, a cavalry regiment, and was posted to Bangalore, in south India—then a hundred years away from becoming the high-tech hub of the Asian subcontinent. There, he spent his days in drill, playing polo, and pursuing a course of self-education. He read books of history, philosophy, and economics that he had not encountered during his formal schooling.[4]

He did not remain tethered to his regiment. Using family connections,[5] he managed to involve himself in three late-nineteenth-century imperial wars against local forces challenging British rule:* on the northwest frontier of imperial India, near the border with Afghanistan, in 1897; in the Sudan, where he took part in Britain's last cavalry charge at the Battle of Omdurman in 1898; and in South Africa, where the British fought the Dutch settlers, the Boers, in 1899 and 1900. In the Boer War, he was taken prisoner but escaped and fought in several major battles. From these three conflicts emerged what would become major features of the rest of his life.

The first was war. He was caught up in five of them: in addition to the first three, he held high positions in the British government during the World Wars of the twentieth century. It was in the last of these wars that he made his personal mark on the history of his country and the world.

The second lifelong theme to emerge from these early years was danger. At the least, he did not shy away from it, he often thrived on it, and sometimes he even seemed to court it. Churchill was exposed to gunfire several times in India and Africa, and again in World War I in France. He had brushes with death during peacetime as well. As a child he contracted pneumonia and initially seemed unlikely to survive it.[6] At age 19, he took a 29-foot fall from a tree and was unconscious for three days.[7] As an adult, he took up flying and was involved in several accidents.[8] He was hit by a car and seriously injured in New York City, on Fifth Avenue, in 1931.

Third, the imperial wars in which he fought made Churchill a writer. He adopted a dual role in all three, as both a soldier and a war correspondent— something unthinkable in our own day but not unheard of in late-nineteenth-century Britain. He filed reports of the fighting with London newspapers and afterward wrote books about all three wars.[9] Thus began a career as a journalist and author to which he devoted a large part of his life.

He wrote thirty-seven books in all. In addition to the biography of his father in 1906, his works include a four-volume biography of his distinguished ancestor John Churchill, the first Duke of Marlborough, who defeated the French at the Battle of Blenheim in 1704 (published from 1933 to 1938); a five-volume history of World War I (*The World Crisis*, 1923 to 1931); a six-volume history of World War II (*The Second World War*, 1948

---

* Odd as it may seem to a twenty-first-century reader, Churchill belonged to a social class, and lived in an era, in which young men pulled strings to enter rather than avoid combat. Young Israelis are the exception to this pattern.

to 1954); and four volumes of *The History of the English-Speaking Peoples*, which he began before World War II but published afterward, from 1956 to 1958. In 1953, he received the Nobel Prize for Literature.

To be sure, especially as time went on, the production of these works more closely resembled a factory than a lone author sitting at his desk. Churchill usually dictated the texts rather than writing them by hand[10] and had multiple secretaries, research assistants, and sometimes even ghost writers.[11] Still, the books always reflected his ideas and for the most part were in his words. He also wrote prolifically for magazines and newspapers.[12] For much of his life, his writing served as his chief source of income, and a necessary source because he adopted an aristocratic lifestyle but lacked the inherited wealth to support it that most of the upper ranks of the British aristocracy generally enjoyed.[13]

Fourth, and finally, Churchill's military exploits, his accounts of them in writing, and the lectures he gave about them (in one such lecture, in New York, he was introduced by Mark Twain) made him famous in Britain before he had reached the age of 25. He continued to be famous, a person of whom most of his countrymen had heard and of whom many had opinions, sometimes strong and not always favorable ones, for the next sixty-five years.[14]

He left the army and began his political career by winning election to the House of Commons in 1900 as a member of his father's Conservative Party. He sat in that body, with a two-year interruption from 1922 to 1924, for sixty-three years. He did not, however, belong to the same party for all that time. In 1904, unhappy with the weakening of the Conservatives' commitment to the policy of free trade, he defected to the opposition Liberal Party.[15] The Liberals won a landslide victory in the 1906 election, and Churchill held a series of increasingly important ministerial positions in the governments they formed from that year through the First World War: under secretary at the Colonial Office (1906–1908), president of the Board of Trade—which carried with it cabinet rank (1908–1910)—and home secretary (1910–1911). In 1911, he was appointed First Lord of the Admiralty, putting him in charge of Britain's most important military arm, the Royal Navy. He held that office when his country entered World War I in 1914.

His position at the Admiralty made him one of the two members of the cabinet who wielded the greatest influence over the military operations in the war, along with Lord Herbert Kitchener, a commander in both the

Sudan and South Africa conflicts, who oversaw the army.[16] The war on the western front quickly turned into a bloody stalemate, with the French and British troops arrayed against the opposing Germans in long parallel lines of trenches in northern France and Belgium that stretched from the North Sea to the Swiss border. Each side undertook costly offensives without gaining much ground.

In an effort to win the war by circumventing the trenches, the British government launched a major initiative in a different theater. Churchill became one of the architects and champions of the Dardanelles campaign in the spring of 1915. It aimed to seize control of the strait of that name that connects the Black Sea to the Mediterranean, to land soldiers on a beach called Gallipoli on the peninsula between the Dardanelles and the Aegean, and then to push north to Constantinople, the capital of the Ottoman Turkish Empire, which was allied with Germany. The attack failed, with serious losses, and the troops that had landed were withdrawn.[17] Historians have since debated whether better tactics and more effective leadership could have made the operation successful, and whether, if so, it could have achieved its larger goals of knocking the Turks out of the war and relieving pressure on Britain's imperial Russian ally. Whatever might have happened, what did happen was a major setback, and much of the blame fell on Churchill—not entirely justly because, although he was one of the officials responsible for the expedition to Turkey, he was not the only one.[18] The Dardanelles campaign and other shortcomings in the Liberal cabinet's conduct of the war led to the formation of a coalition government with the Conservatives. In light of the failure at Gallipoli, as well as because a number of Conservatives resented and distrusted him for having deserted them a decade previously, Churchill was not included in the new cabinet.

Bitter at what he regarded as unfair treatment, and frustrated because he no longer had any influence over Britain's war policy, he went to France at the age of 41 to serve as an officer in the trenches. He spent twenty-three weeks there, between December 1915 and May 1916.[19] In October 1916, David Lloyd George, a Liberal parliamentarian from Wales to whom Churchill was close and who influenced him on domestic issues, became prime minister, and in July 1917 he appointed Churchill minister of munitions, a post he held when the war ended, in November 1918, and into 1919.

In the wake of World War I, Britain and the other members of the victorious coalition had to decide how to deal with two once-powerful European countries—Germany, which had lost the war, and Russia, where a revolution had brought to power a small group of adherents to an extreme version of Marxism who were known as Bolsheviks.[20] Churchill had views, which he made emphatically clear, on the proper approach to both. He favored a generous peace with Germany. Lloyd George and the American president Woodrow Wilson seemed at times to agree, but public opinion in Britain and the United States, as well as in France, demanded harsh treatment for the defeated Germans. The peace treaty with Germany, signed in the Paris suburb of Versailles, required the Germans to pay reparations to compensate for the damages the victors had suffered at their hands.[21] Churchill called the treaty's economic clauses "malignant and silly to an extent that made them obviously futile."[22]

As for Russia, he considered the Bolsheviks a menace, a potentially serious ideological and political threat to the rest of the world, and advocated substantial assistance to the forces opposing them in the Civil War that broke out after their seizure of power. His efforts notwithstanding, the Bolsheviks won that war and consolidated their hold over the former Russian Empire.[23]

From 1919 to 1921, Churchill held the position of minister for defense and air and then became colonial secretary in 1921 and 1922. In that capacity, he presided over the disposition of the Middle Eastern territories that Britain had acquired from the defeated and disbanded Ottoman Empire.

After the war, his political fortunes followed a roller-coaster pattern. He retained his seat in the House of Commons in the general election of 1918 as a Coalition Liberal. In the next election, however, in 1922, he lost it and failed on two subsequent occasions to return to the House. Finally, he switched parties again, stood for election as a Conservative in 1924, and won. The second switch came about because he was disturbed by the increasingly close association of the Liberals with the Labour Party, which he strongly opposed because it professed allegiance to socialism. He was also aware that the Liberal Party was a declining force in the national political life, and it did, in fact, give way to Labour as the chief alternative to the Conservatives.[24] The suspicions of him in Conservative ranks—because, among other things, of his party switching—had not entirely dissipated and indeed would persist for more than a decade; but Prime Minister Stanley Baldwin named Churchill chancellor of the exchequer, the second most important cabinet position, which he held from 1925 to 1929, when an election turned the Conservative government out of office.

Churchill spent the next ten years in parliament but without a ministerial portfolio, even though the Conservatives formed the government for most of that time. He referred to this period as his "wilderness years." During the 1930s, British policy in Europe, and specifically toward Germany, became increasingly important. Here again, Churchill had clear views that he did not hesitate to express forcefully. Early on, he saw Adolf Hitler,[25] who came to power in Germany in January 1933, as a major, ominous threat to the peace of the continent and to Britain's interests and values. Churchill's was a voice in the wilderness, however. The British government did not act on his warnings. It did not, for example, embark on as ambitious a program of rearmament as he recommended.

As Hitler systematically dismantled the political and military restrictions that the post–World War I settlement had imposed on Germany, the Conservative government responded by doing, essentially, nothing. This was the policy of appeasement,[26] which had several sources: the fear of another war like the one fought between 1914 and 1918; a sense that the postwar settlement had treated Germany unfairly and that modifying it was proper; the conviction that the Soviet Union and communism posed a greater threat than Germany and Nazism; and the need to devote the resources available for external policy, which the Great Depression had diminished, to safeguarding the British Empire.

Appeasement reached its apogee in September 1938, when Great Britain and France actively cooperated with Hitler by putting pressure on Czechoslovakia to cede part of its territory to him. At the time, Churchill called that episode "a total and unmitigated defeat."[27]

The British public, averse to another war, generally supported the government's European policy. When, however, six months after Munich, Hitler violated the pledge he had made there not to seek any additional territory and proceeded to annex the rest of Czechoslovakia, public opinion shifted sharply. The British people turned away from alignment with the government's policy and toward the approach Churchill had advocated. The government changed course: Britain along with France extended a guarantee to the country that was clearly next on Hitler's agenda, Poland. When he attacked Poland at the beginning of September 1939, the second great European war of the twentieth century began.

In recognition of the sea change in British opinion, and of the need for a government capable of waging the war that seemed imminent, the Prime Minister, Neville Chamberlain, whose name would forever be associated with Munich and British appeasement, appointed Churchill to the position he had held at the outset of the previous war, First Lord of the Admiralty. The appointment took effect on September 3, the first day of World War II in Europe. The new First Lord took up his duties with his customary alacrity and had a hand in a military operation in Norway in the spring of 1940. That operation failed,[28] but Prime Minister Chamberlain received the bulk of the blame for it.[29] Rising public dissatisfaction with the conduct of the war made new leadership in the cabinet seem necessary. There was an effort to form a government of national unity, as in World War I, that included representatives of the main parliamentary opposition, the Labour Party; but the Labour representatives would not serve under Chamberlain[30] and he resigned. Two principal candidates to succeed him emerged: Churchill and Foreign Secretary Edward Wood, Lord Halifax. Chamberlain himself, still very influential among Conservative Members of Parliament (MPs), favored Halifax, who, however, demurred. On May 10, 1940, therefore, four decades after he had first entered the House of Commons, Winston Churchill became the king's first minister.

Churchill assumed the office in perilous circumstances for Britain, which quickly became much worse. On May 10, the German army invaded and swiftly conquered the Benelux countries. At the same time, it launched an assault on France. The German offensive pierced the French defenses and headed rapidly for the English Channel, trapping the bulk of the French army and the sizable British Expeditionary Force that was fighting alongside it. British war plans had assumed that the French would stand firm against Germany as they had for four years in World War I. Churchill made five flying visits to France in the weeks after May 10 to assess France's military prospects and to urge its government and people to keep fighting. His efforts were in vain. French resistance collapsed.

As the end of that resistance began to seem imminent, Churchill ordered the evacuation of as many British and French troops as could be saved, and more than 338,000 did manage to escape to England through the Channel port at Dunkirk. It was a formidable logistical feat, although, as Churchill told the House of Commons, "wars are not won by evacuations."[31]

After the fall of France, Nazi Germany faced no armed resistance on the European continent. Only Britain, along with its dominions[32] and its empire, opposed Germany. The British government had to reckon with the possibility of a German invasion of the British Isles. Hitler in fact set in motion a plan for such an invasion, but to carry it out successfully Germany had to control the airspace over southern England. The fight to establish control became known as the Battle of Britain, which took place from July to September of 1940. The courage and skill of the Royal Air Force won that battle by avoiding losing it. The Germans did not obtain mastery of the skies and so could not invade. "Never in the field of human conflict," Churchill observed, in acknowledging the Air Force's achievement, "have so many owed so much to so few."[33] An intense German bombing campaign against English cities known as the Blitz followed, from September 1940 to May 1941,[34] and German air attacks continued into 1944, first with aircraft and then with V-2 rockets; but after the Battle of Britain, the Germans never threatened to conquer the country.

In the second half of 1941, two events, triggered by decisions Hitler made, relieved Britain's isolation in opposing Germany and, ultimately, caused his defeat. On June 22, 1941, he launched Operation Barbarossa, a full-scale assault on the Soviet Union.[35] Despite his anti-Bolshevik history, Churchill had begun thinking about making common cause with the communist regime as early as June 1940 and had sent a message to that effect to the Soviet dictator, Josef Stalin.[36] When Barbarossa began, Churchill swiftly declared British solidarity with the Soviet Union and provided as much support as Britain could supply.[37] "I will unsay no word I have spoken about it," he said of the communist regime, "but all this fades away before the spectacle which is now unfolding." One of the time-honored principles of power politics—my enemy's enemy is my friend—guided his actions. "If Hitler invaded hell," he said, "I would make at least a favorable reference to the devil in the House of Commons."[38]

From the outset, Churchill had recognized that Britain's success against Germany, perhaps even its survival, depended on receiving considerable assistance from the United States. He made it one of his highest priorities to secure such assistance. He made contact with the American president, Franklin D. Roosevelt, exchanged numerous messages with him, and journeyed across the Atlantic Ocean to Nova Scotia, Canada, to meet with him in July 1941. The decisive moment for the Anglo-American partnership came, however, five months later, on December 7, when Japanese forces attacked the American fleet at Pearl Harbor, Hawaii. The American Congress voted for a declaration of war the next day—but against Japan, not Germany. It was Hitler who, on December 11, declared war on the United States,[39] which thereupon formally and wholeheartedly joined the British in their struggle against the Third Reich.

The early part of 1942 brought more setbacks to Great Britain. Long believed to be impregnable, British Singapore fell to Japan in February. In March, the Japanese army took control of Rangoon, the capital of Burma, a country Churchill's father had annexed in 1886 when serving as the secretary of state for India.[40]

In that year, however, the tide of the war began to turn, as the armed forces of Great Britain and its two allies, the United States and the Soviet Union, achieved several important military victories. In two major naval engagements against Japan in the Pacific—the Battle of the Coral Sea in May and the Battle of Midway in June—the American navy first held off the previously victorious Japanese and then achieved a clear victory. The Red Army turned back the major German offensive of 1942 at Stalingrad, on the Volga River in the heart of European Russia, and managed to trap the German Sixth Army there. That Army surrendered in February 1943, the first large German military force to do so in World War II. The surrender dealt a psychological as well as a military blow to Germany.[41] In November, British forces commanded by General Bernard Montgomery defeated troops led by the previously successful German general Erwin Rommel at El Alamein, in Egypt.[42] That same month, American forces landed in French North Africa and saw their first combat of the war in what was called Operation Torch.

In January 1943, Churchill met Roosevelt in the Moroccan city of Casablanca, and the two issued a demand for Nazi Germany's unconditional surrender. For Great Britain, the most important military engagement of that year took place at sea: the contest for control of the Atlantic shipping lanes, which were Britain's lifeline to North America. At the beginning of the year, German submarine attacks had reduced the volume of supplies reaching the British Isles from North America to dangerously low levels. In six weeks between March and May, however, American and British naval and air forces defeated the anti-submarine campaign.[43] In 1943, as well, American and British forces entered Europe by a side door, moving from North Africa to Sicily and then north to the Italian peninsula.

Churchill and Roosevelt met again in November 1943, in Cairo, where they were joined by the Chinese leader Chiang Kai-shek, to discuss the course of the war in Asia and its political future. The British and American leaders then traveled on to Tehran to meet with Stalin. Churchill and Roosevelt agreed to mount an invasion of France the following year, and thus to initiate the second front in Europe for which the Soviet leader had been pressing since the United States had entered the war and about which Churchill had consistently expressed reservations.

Accordingly, on June 6, 1944, Operation Overlord took place at Normandy, on the French coast. A combined operation of the United States, Great Britain, and Canada, it was the largest amphibious assault in the history of warfare. The Allies successfully established a beachhead, moved ground forces ashore in large numbers, and began their march, against bitter German resistance, to Germany.

Even before then, Churchill, while maintaining his deep involvement in Britain's conduct of that war, turned his attention to the politics of Europe in the war's aftermath.[44] He traveled to Moscow in October 1944 to try to work out postwar arrangements with Stalin, and continued his efforts to shape those arrangements thereafter.[45] The most contentious postwar political issue turned out to be the status of Poland, which was the main subject of the discussions at the second meeting of the three principal Allied leaders at Yalta, on the Black Sea in the Soviet Union, in February, 1945.

The country mattered to all three of them: Britain had gone to war on its behalf; the population of the United States included a sizable contingent of people of Polish descent whose views counted with the American government; and Poland had served as a corridor for a German invasion of Russia twice in a quarter-century. (Stalin and the communists resisted the second invasion but had welcomed the first.)[46] The Red Army occupied Poland on its way to Germany and thus controlled its political fate. Churchill and Roosevelt wanted the Poles to be able to determine their own political future, and at Yalta Stalin promised that free elections would be held there, but he reneged on that promise. After the war, Soviet forces imposed a communist government and Poland became, unwillingly, a Soviet satellite.

On April 30, with Russian troops only a few blocks from his underground bunker in Berlin, and with British and American armies having penetrated deep into Germany from the west, Hitler committed suicide. A few days later, on May 8, Germany surrendered, although the war in the Pacific would continue for another three months. On July 17, the leaders of the three principal allies—Harry Truman had become the American president upon Franklin Roosevelt's death in April—reconvened in Potsdam, a suburb of Berlin. Eight days later, Churchill traveled back to London to await the results of the British general election, the first to be held since 1935. He did not return to the conference. Instead, he was replaced by Clement Attlee, whose Labour Party won a resounding electoral victory. Having entered the cabinet as the conflict began, having led Great Britain through five arduous years of it, having devoted thousands of hours to overseeing the country's military efforts and traveled tens of thousands of miles in pursuit of the diplomacy involved, Churchill's direct role in World War II had come to an end.

After his party's defeat he became the leader of the parliamentary opposition. He was among the first to warn of the worsening conflict with the Soviet Union, using the term "iron curtain" to describe the division of Europe between communist and non-communist countries.[47] Just as he had after World War I, he advocated generous treatment of Germany in the wake of the second great war.[48] He also spoke favorably of the prospect of European unity of some kind, but did not believe that Britain should be an integral part of whatever form it might take.[49]

He became prime minister again in 1951 and sought a summit meeting with the American and Soviet leaders to try to modify the hostility of the Cold War.[50] He did not succeed in arranging one. He resigned in April 1955 and died ten years later, on January 24, 1965. He received a state funeral, only the third nonroyal English person to be so honored.[51]

The Times

Winston Churchill lived a very long[52] and eventful life, a life that was embedded in the history of Great Britain in the first half of the twentieth century. That history shaped his career, and his career, in turn, did more than that of any other Briton to shape British history. Early on, he conceived a sense of responsibility for the destiny of the United Kingdom. He therefore chose a public life, spent virtually all of his adult years in the House of Commons at the center of policymaking, and for many of those years held positions of authority—ultimately of supreme authority.

Even if he had never become prime minister, any history of Great Britain from the beginning to the middle of the twentieth century would have had to devote attention to him. His was as long and wide-ranging a career as any public figure in a democracy has ever had.[†] That career involved him in all three principal aspects of the public business of Great Britain in his era: its domestic affairs, its Empire, and its part in the international politics of Europe.

British internal affairs during Churchill's era, like those of the other countries in Western Europe and North America, were largely taken up with coping with the economic and political consequences of the two world-changing developments of the second half of the eighteenth century: the French Revolution and the Industrial Revolution. The first of these placed on Europe's agenda the idea that the people, not hereditary monarchs, should rule. Britain had long since curtailed the monarch's authority but had to answer the question of who should be allowed to vote. In the early decades of Churchill's career, that general question had as its specific focus the vote for women. The champions of female suffrage did not, on the whole, regard him as a friend of their cause. He nonetheless supported votes for women when the matter came before the House of Commons in 1918.[53]

The Industrial Revolution, in conjunction with the political currents set in motion by the French Revolution, created more complicated and productive but less stable national economies, which displayed more pronounced, more visible, and politically more explosive inequalities of wealth than had been present in the agricultural era. This imposed an economic agenda that had two parts: one had to do with how much social protection the government should provide. The House of Commons had to decide the dimensions of what came to be known as the welfare state. Here, Churchill's inclination throughout his career was to be generous, although he firmly opposed the most generous version of social protection, socialism. The other part of the twentieth-century economic agenda involved economic management to promote stability, a task that thrust itself on Western governments with the Great Depression. As chancellor of the exchequer from 1925 to 1929, Churchill held the cabinet office with the

---

[†] His career overlapped, and intersected, with those of the other seven men whom this book discusses. As an MP, he met Woodrow Wilson in Paris in 1919; he pressed for military intervention against Lenin and his Bolsheviks after World War I; he confronted Hitler in partnership with Franklin D. Roosevelt; he denounced Gandhi, with whom he had a single personal encounter; he gave active support to the Zionist cause to which Ben-Gurion devoted his life; and he served as prime minister at a time when Mao led China.

chief responsibility for devising and carrying out the relevant policies; but he relinquished that office in time to escape the Depression's worst effects.

"I shall devote my life to the preservation of this great Empire," Churchill wrote to his mother from Bangalore in December 1897.[54] He certainly exerted himself on its behalf, and did so long after he had finished with the imperial wars with which he began his career. Yet that career coincided with the decline and fall of the British Empire. At its zenith during his early years, he lived to see it all but disappear. During his lifetime, Britain's right to govern millions of foreigners without their democratic consent came sharply into question—although he himself did not question it— and the power needed to sustain that governance ebbed away. He did what he could to stem the downward course of the Empire, but in this aspect of his public life he failed entirely.

The most contentious imperial controversies in Churchill's era con- cerned Britain's oldest imperial possession, Ireland, and its largest one, India. He had a family connection to Ireland. His grandfather, the sev- enth Duke of Marlborough, served as the Lord Lieutenant—the equiv- alent of a viceroy—there from 1876 to 1880. The Duke's son, Winston's father Randolph Churchill, assisted him, and in his 1930 memoir Winston Churchill reports it as the scene of his earliest childhood memories.[55]

In the nineteenth century, the Liberal Party proposed home rule for Ireland, and the Conservatives, including Randolph Churchill, opposed it. The dispute over home rule became a major cleavage in British politics. During his parliamentary career, Winston Churchill had some ministerial responsibility for policing Ireland and employed harsh tactics against the independence movement;[56] but as a Liberal, he broke with his father's po- sition on home rule and departed from his own staunch advocacy of the continuation of imperial rule elsewhere by helping to negotiate the 1921 agreement that partitioned the island, with the six northern counties re- maining part of the United Kingdom and the rest becoming independent.[57]

India, the jewel in the imperial crown, was different. It held a spe- cial place in Churchill's political outlook even though he never returned there after leaving his regiment in 1899,[58] and his direct experience of the country even while living in it was a limited one.[†] After World War

---

[†] Geoffrey Best, *Churchill: A Study in Greatness*, London: Hambledon and London, 2001, pp. 110, 157–158. The Indians Churchill encountered when he lived in that country consisted chiefly of maharajahs and servants. Then and in subsequent years, he did not come to know educated Indians such as Gandhi and Nehru, who were his intellectual and

I, Indian agitation for independence became increasingly serious and the independence movement, led by Mohandas Gandhi, grew larger and more powerful. In the second half of the interwar period, the British negotiated with Gandhi and his colleagues and offered concessions, including eventual dominion status, which fell short of full independence. The Indians rejected the British proposals on the grounds that they did not go far enough. Churchill, for his part, opposed these same proposals, and did so vigorously and vocally, as going too far. In the 1930s, he was as sharply at odds with the government of his own party over India as he was over its policies toward Europe, Germany, and Hitler. He did not believe that India was ready for full self-government, or, it may be inferred from what he said and wrote, that it ever would be.[59] "India," he said in 1931, "is a geographical term. It is no more a united nation than the Equator."[60]

For the major steps in the separation of India from Great Britain, Churchill had no direct responsibility.[§] He did not hold office until the end of the 1930s and the Conservatives, although he led them, were out of power in 1947 when a partitioned British India became independent India and Pakistan. Churchill did not like what happened but could not prevent it.

Indeed, with the exception of Ireland, Britain voluntarily relinquished virtually no territory while he held office. To the contrary, in fact, his one period of direct responsibility for the country's overseas possessions came at an anomalous moment in its twentieth-century imperial history when, rather than contracting, the Empire actually expanded.

As colonial secretary in 1921 and 1922, where his responsibilities did not include India because it came under the jurisdiction of the India

---

political peers. That may help to account for his insistence that India was incapable of successfully managing its own affairs.

[§] He was prime minister during a serious famine in Bengal in 1943, but the war and other factors may well have prevented measures that could have alleviated the hunger. "The problem [of the famine] lay in the destruction of rail and road links by the same typhoon that caused the famine; Japanese control of countries such as Burma, Thailand and Malaya; the high prices for rice charged by Bengali merchants who preferred to hoard it as prices rose; and other such factors largely beyond Churchill's control in London." Andrew Roberts, "'The Cambridge Companion to Winston Churchill': A Review," July 6, 2023, The Churchill Project, Hillsdale College, https://winstonchurchill.hillsdale.edu/packw ood-cambridge-companion. Still, Churchill did not make coping with the impact of the famine a high priority. Geoffrey Wheatcroft, *Churchill's Shadow: The Life and Afterlife of Winston Churchill*, New York: W. W. Norton, pp. 280–281.

Office, he had to decide what to do with the Middle Eastern possessions of the Ottoman Empire that Britain and France had divided between themselves after World War I. From a conference in Cairo in March 1921 emerged a new disposition of the British-controlled territories. Three Ottoman provinces were combined to form Iraq, and lands east of the Jordan River became Transjordan. The British chose two sons of the sharif of Mecca as the monarchs of the new states. Churchill acted, literally, as a kingmaker.[61]

One hundred years later, the two countries still existed within the borders that the British had drawn, although only Jordan had a king. The territory between the Jordan and the Mediterranean became the British Mandate of Palestine. In that territory, Churchill, a strong supporter of Zionism, the Jewish national movement, endeavored to deliver on the promise made during World War I by the Foreign Secretary, Arthur Balfour, in what became known as the Balfour Declaration, "to facilitate the achievement" of a Jewish national home there.[62] A century later, after many vicissitudes, which included efforts by successive British governments to renege on that promise,[63] the Jewish state of Israel stood as a thriving, stable democracy in an unstable, undemocratic region. The contemporary Middle East may therefore be said to be, at least in small part, the handiwork of Winston Churchill.

During his political lifetime, the defining events for Churchill, for his country, and indeed for the world took place, or at least began, in Europe: the two World Wars. At the beginning of his career, he had reason to expect not to be involved in armed conflict on the continent. It was British policy to avoid fighting in Europe if at all possible. Specifically, Great Britain pursued a centuries-old policy of offshore balancing, deploying its diplomatic and financial resources to prevent any single power from achieving continental domination.¶

¶ In 1936, Churchill wrote a letter describing the policy: "British policy for four hundred years has been to oppose the strongest power in Europe by weaving together a combination of other countries strong enough to face the bully. Sometimes it is Spain, sometimes the French monarchy, sometimes the French Empire, sometimes Germany. I have no doubt who it is now. But if France set up to claim the over-lordship of Europe, I should equally endeavour to oppose them [sic]. It is thus through the centuries we have kept our liberties and maintained our life and power." Quoted in Martin Gilbert, *Churchill: A Life*, New York: Henry Holt and Company, 1991, p. 555.

Occasionally, the rise of a potentially hegemonic power required the British to do more than underwrite an opposing coalition, and specifically to send their own troops to fight on the continent. Churchill's ancestor, the first Duke of Marlborough, fought in Europe at the outset of the eighteenth century. The Duke of Wellington led a multinational force that administered Napoleon's final defeat at Waterloo in 1815. As the twentieth century dawned, however, the British had waged no major war in Europe since then and had taken part in only one lesser conflict, against Russia in the Crimea from 1853 to 1856.

Preserving the continental equilibrium on which Britain depended required a large British military presence in Europe twice during Churchill's political career, on both occasions to resist a German bid for mastery of the continent. He became deeply involved in both conflicts, as anyone prominent in British public life in those years was bound to do: both were, for Great Britain, all-consuming supreme national efforts. Moreover, Churchill, unlike many Englishmen (including members of the aristocracy), felt comfortable with Europeans and at home in Europe, at least in France,[64] which was a major British ally in both wars. He also had connections, initially through his mother and subsequently through visits there, with Britain's other great democratic ally in both conflicts, the United States. In addition, unlike any other twentieth-century leader, he held high office in both World Wars.[††]

In the midst of war, Churchill was in his element. It would be wrong to characterize him as a war-lover[65] but in wartime he seemed to feel most fully alive and war provided him the opportunity to use to the maximum his considerable talents.[66] He had a keen interest, and developed considerable expertise, in strategy, tactics, and weaponry.[67] He had an instinct for useful military innovations: before and during World War I, he pressed for the incorporation of the tank and the airplane into British military operations. It was in war, furthermore, that he made his mark on the history of the twentieth century. Some personalities stand out in time of war. While he was a formidable public presence in peacetime as well, that was true of Winston Churchill.

[††] Franklin D. Roosevelt, his American counterpart in World War II, had served as assistant secretary of the navy in World War I, which was a responsible position but not as influential as the one Churchill held for the first ten months of the war—First Lord of the Admiralty.

Leadership

Although a prolific writer, Churchill cannot properly be said to have been a man of ideas. He subscribed to no overarching doctrine akin to Woodrow Wilson's design for reconstructing international politics, Lenin's and Mao's versions of Marxism, Hitler's racism, or Ben- Gurion's Zionism. Such comprehensive worldviews historically have not appealed to the English, at least not to English conservatives, and especially not to English Conservative politicians.

Instead, Churchill had a set of attitudes, which he held throughout his career, that informed his approach to public affairs.[68] At home, he counted, in his Liberal period but thereafter as well, as a radical.[69] The more appropriate term in the contemporary context would be "reformer." He accepted the hierarchical features of British society but believed that the upper echelon of that society, into which he had been born, had an obligation to improve the lives of those less favored: the French term *noblesse oblige* is not inappropriate here.[70] He also had strong personal sympathy for the underdogs, the downtrodden, and the victims of unfairness.[71] Most importantly, he was deeply committed to, and always defended, the core values of the British political system, above all liberty.[72]

Where his country's policies beyond its borders were concerned, Churchill was a British patriot.[73] He considered it right, indeed necessary, that Britain be a great power. This was so because, he believed, British greatness and British goodness went together: British power had made the world a better place than it would otherwise have been and that power therefore served the interests and promoted the welfare of people far beyond Great Britain. He took the British Empire to be an outstanding example of this beneficence: he did not doubt that the peoples of the world, like those in his own country, were ranged in a natural hierarchy and that in the world, as in the British Isles, it was the duty of the people at the top to bestow benefits on those situated lower down.[74] The Empire provided a framework for doing just that. It furnished better government to its subject peoples, Churchill believed, than they could have contrived by themselves.[‡‡]

[‡‡] Best, *op. cit.*, pp. 106, 137–138. In his 1930 memoir, Churchill wrote of England's "high mission to rule these primitive but agreeable races for their welfare and our own." Winston Churchill, *My Early Life: A Roving Commission*, New York: Charles Scribner's Sons, p. 104. His commitment to the Empire does not win favor in the present, anti-imperial

Since Britain did not aspire to govern any part of Europe, the considerations that determined his attitude toward the Empire did not apply there. Churchill opposed his government's policy of appeasing Germany in the 1930s because it conflicted with what he saw as the requirements of the time for successful offshore balancing. He was revolted, as well, by the Nazi treatment of Jews and other minorities. Not least important, he saw Hitler as a mortal threat to the liberty that he held dear and had always defended.

Individuals secure the opportunity to apply their ideas or attitudes to public affairs by reaching the pinnacle of the political systems in which they find themselves. A person ascending to supreme leadership in Great Britain, as in the United States, holds membership, successively, in three distinct groups, which become smaller in number as he or she rises. The first of them is the political nation, which includes all those with interest and experience, and who participate actively (beyond simply voting) in public life. The second group, far fewer in number, consists of those who, by their talents, determination, and good fortune hold positions of influence and visibility that make them eligible for the most powerful position. Moving from this second group to the very top requires political skill and effective self-promotion but also good fortune, since there are at any time a number of people who can reasonably aspire to the highest political office, the third and ultimate group, which has room, however, for only one of them at a time.

Winston Churchill inherited his position in the British political nation. His family had been prominent in the affairs of the kingdom for the better part of two centuries before he was born. He lifted himself into the second tier through his ability. His distinguishing quality, according to his wartime cabinet colleague and postwar political opponent Clement Attlee, was his extraordinary energy.[75] He put in long hours in his various ministerial positions and traveled frequently as part of his official duties. His physical stamina and powers of concentration gave him an enormous capacity for work.[76] He could absorb information quickly and in large volume.[77]

He also had a wide-ranging curiosity and constantly generated ideas for proceeding more effectively with whatever activities he was supervising.[78] His energy and creativity combined with his considerable ambition, the writing and speaking that kept him constantly in the public eye, and his

---

age; but while he staunchly supported the British role in India, he also criticized what he regarded as its excesses. He denounced, for example, the Amritsar massacre of 1919.

eloquence—he was a gifted and powerful speaker[79] in an era when oratory mattered a great deal—to make him a formidable public figure. Even those who disliked him and did not wish to see him advance acknowledged this.

He could be brusque and insensitive in personal interactions and hard on those who worked for him;[80] but there are also many recorded instances of his kindness, consideration, and generosity. He inspired loyalty. Those closest to him tended to be devoted to him.[81]

Yet but for the extraordinary circumstances of May 1940, he would not have become prime minister.[82] He made political enemies, and even many who were not hostile to him had serious reservations about his suitability for the highest office in the land. For Churchill's manifest talents had drawbacks as well. He was described as having *"les défauts de ses qualities"*—the faults of his virtues.[83] His ambition, and the way he pursued it during the course of his career before 1940, fostered the perception among some critics that he was unscrupulous: to switch parties was unusual in British politics and he did it not just once but twice.[84] His creativity and enthusiasm for fresh ideas and new measures, it was thought, led him to endorse unsound schemes such as the Dardanelles operation. His rhetorical arsenal included a cutting wit that could wound and alienate those on the receiving end of it.[85] For Churchill himself, political differences did not mean personal animosity:[86] others were not as charitable.

The two Conservative prime ministers who preceded him in office, both of whom appointed him to major cabinet positions, stated, privately and at different times, the case against him. Stanley Baldwin acknowledged his "imagination, eloquence, industry, ability" but added that he lacked "judgement and wisdom."[87] Neville Chamberlain called him "a brilliant wayward child." §§

---

§§ Gilbert, *op. cit.*, p. 486. An example of Churchill's capacity both to inspire and to exasperate was his plan to take part directly in Operation Overlord. He arranged to be aboard a warship that would be bombarding Normandy from just off the coast but was ultimately talked out of it. The episode illustrates his courage and his desire to be in the middle of whatever action was under way, but it was also irresponsible to run such a risk given his governmental duties. Also of note was the letter that King George VI wrote in order to dissuade him. In it, the king said: "I am a younger man than you, I am a sailor and as King I am the head of all these Services. There is nothing I would like better than to go to sea, but I have agreed to stay at home; it is fair then that you should do exactly what I should have liked to do myself?" Quoted in Andrew Roberts, *Churchill: Walking With Destiny*, New York: Viking, 2018, p. 890.

Churchill assumed the leadership of His Majesty's government in the desperate straits of the spring of 1940, when the nation badly needed the assets he brought to the position and could not afford to deny it to him because of his liabilities. Only in such dire circumstances could he have risen to the top of the British political system.[88]

As a wartime prime minister, Churchill excelled. Perhaps no democratic leader in history has ever brought more pertinent experience to the task of directing his country's military and diplomatic efforts. To that task, and despite Britain's limited military options in the second half of 1940 and for months thereafter, he took an emphatically active rather than a passive approach.[89] He became a fount of ideas for military initiatives. He ordered that bright red labels be printed with the phrase "ACTION THIS DAY" stamped on them and affixed them liberally to the steady stream of memoranda he dispatched.[90]

His most important role as leader of the British government, especially in the early, perilous days of his leadership, was to keep up the morale of the British people—to sustain, that is, the public will to continue to resist Nazi Germany in deeply unfavorable military circumstances. The military initiatives he ordered were intended to have this effect (among others)—to show the British (and the Americans as well) that Britain could and would fight back against the Third Reich. To help bolster the spirit of the public (and in sharp contrast to his adversary, Hitler),[91] he made himself publicly visible, visiting parts of London and other cities after they had been bombed to demonstrate solidarity, compassion, and defiance.[92]

Churchill did the most to promote public support for continuing the war against Germany through his speeches, both in the House of Commons, which were reported in the newspapers although not broadcast, and over the radio. Eight decades later, with the occasions on which they were delivered far in the past and the people who originally heard them long gone, his words still resonated.[93]

The rolling cadences of Edward Gibbon's *Decline and Fall of the Roman Empire* and the romantic patriotism of Thomas Babington Macaulay's *History of England*, which he had read as a young army officer in Bangalore, had long since shaped Churchill's writings, and they seeped into his speeches as well. The tone might have seemed old-fashioned and out of place in a different context; but in the circumstances in which they were given, they struck exactly the right note, telling the prime minister's listeners what they needed to hear to rally them to the monumental task at hand.

He did not attempt to hide the dangers the country faced or deny the military reverses its armed forces had suffered. He told the House of Commons on October 8, 1940 that

> No one can predict, no one can even imagine, how this terrible war against German and Nazi aggression will run its course or how far it will spread or how long it will last . . . death and sorrow will be the companions of our journey; hardship our garment; constancy and valour our only shield.[94]

He made unmistakably clear, though, that he was determined to persevere and that they should be as well. On June 4, 1940, he told the House of Commons: "We shall fight on the beaches, we shall fight on the landing grounds, we shall fight in the fields and in the streets, we shall fight in the hills; we shall never surrender."[95] He explained how great the stakes of the conflict were and why, it followed, Britain could not afford to lose it. If Hitler were to win, he said on June 18, 1940,

> then the whole world, including the United States, including all that we have known and care for, will sink into the abyss of a New Dark Age, made more sinister, and perhaps more protracted, by the lights of perverted science.[96]

He also imparted, in the midst of very trying times, hope for success and indeed optimism about the long-range prospects for the war.[97] Finally, he cast the British people, in 1940, in a historically crucial and heroic role. In the June 18th speech, he urged: "Let us therefore brace ourselves to our duties, and so bear ourselves that, if the British Empire and its Commonwealth last for a thousand years, men will still say, 'This was their finest hour.' "[98] There can be no doubt that he himself believed what he said.

The impact of his words did not lend itself to precise measurement, but those who heard them and observed the British response to them generally concluded that Churchill's rhetoric had the cumulative effect that he intended.[99] Of all his contributions to victory in World War II, they count as perhaps the most important one. As President John F. Kennedy said in making him an honorary citizen of the United States, borrowing the words of the American wartime broadcaster Edward R. Murrow, "he mobilized the English language and sent it into battle."[100]

Personal Imprint

Leaders in democracies, where power is limited and dispersed, generally have less personal influence over events and people than do dictators, whose power is concentrated and far less inhibited. The British version of democracy, however, affords to officials other than the prime minister opportunities for making a personal mark. The system of cabinet government gives ministers, who are themselves elected members of parliament, some latitude for personal authority in their departmental responsibilities; and Churchill, with his energy and activist temperament, used that authority in the cabinet positions he held before 1940.

At the Board of Trade (1908–1910), he established labor exchanges. At the Home Office (1910–1911), he promoted penal reform.[101] At the Admiralty (1911–1915), he instituted measures that prepared the Royal Navy for the First World War.[102] As chancellor of the exchequer (1924–1929), he put Britain back on the gold standard, a measure that came to be considered a mistake—although, to be fair to Churchill, one that had strong support from Treasury officials and within the Conservative Party.[103]

Democratic leaders tend to assume greater individual authority in time of war, and Churchill was no exception. Even from 1940 to 1945, however, he operated within definite limits. He was responsible to his war cabinet (which was smaller than the full cabinet) and to the House of Commons as a whole.[104] He sometimes disagreed with his chief military advisors but, unlike Hitler, he never overruled them when they strongly opposed what he wanted to do.[105] From 1942 onward, he had to coordinate his war policies with those of the Soviet Union and especially the United States, and as the war went on, the American forces in the field grew larger and larger, giving President Franklin Roosevelt greater political weight in his dealings with Churchill. Especially in wartime, political influence rests on military power, which depends ultimately on the size of a country's population and of its economy; and on both these counts Britain's wartime partners, when fully mobilized, far exceeded Great Britain's.[106]

For reasons of strategy, domestic morale, and personal temperament, Churchill was eager, upon becoming prime minister, to take the offensive wherever possible. Given Britain's military position in 1940, the possibilities were severely circumscribed. He sought to foment guerrilla resistance to the Germans on the continent through the formation of the Special Operations Executive, which he ordered to "set Europe ablaze."[107]

He also favored commando-style raids, the attack on the German-held French port of Dieppe in August 1942 being perhaps the best known although not one for which Churchill was directly responsible.[108] These operations may have heartened the British and other people resisting or occupied by Nazi Germany, but they did not have appreciable military effects and did not materially affect the course of the war.[109]

Churchill also authorized the bombing of German cities as a way of striking the German homeland, and this campaign continued, in concert with the American air force, to the end of the war. In retrospect, while the impact on the German war effort was not negligible, neither was it as great as Churchill had initially hoped and that the leaders of the Royal Air Force maintained.[110] Also a concern, a minor one during the war but of greater importance afterward, was the morality of killing civilians in this way.[111]

On the larger issues of grand strategy, Churchill was consistently skeptical about, to the point of actually resisting, a cross-Channel amphibious landing on the French coast followed by a frontal attack on Germany through France. He favored, instead, a "peripheral strategy" featuring an assault through the Balkans, the "soft underbelly" of the continent. He was wary of the casualties that the British army might incur in a more direct attack, with the slaughter of World War I always in his mind,[112] as it would have been for any British leader in World War II. Franklin Roosevelt, who had his own set of calculations and incentives, concurred on this point and authorized, contrary to the wishes of his military chiefs, the American campaigns in North Africa, Sicily, and Italy in 1942 and 1943; but Roosevelt then insisted on launching Operation Overlord in June 1944. In 1945, Churchill wanted the American and British armies to head for Berlin as fast as possible, in order to arrive there before the Red Army. Dwight D. Eisenhower, the Supreme Allied Commander in Europe, declined to do so on the grounds that by the terms of the Yalta agreement the Western allies would not be able to retain the territory it captured in such an operation even if it were successful.

As prime minister, Churchill devoted considerable time to personal diplomacy. In particular, he sought to establish good working and personal relationships with the leaders of both of Britain's two principal allies. Of the two, Franklin D. Roosevelt received much more of Churchill's time, and for good reason. Upon becoming prime minister in May 1940, Churchill had two urgent and related goals: one was to keep Britain engaged in resisting Hitler; not less important was to persuade the United States to become an

active belligerent on the British side. Without large-scale American participation in the war, Churchill knew, Great Britain could not hope to prevail
and might not even be able to survive as an independent country.

He corresponded with Roosevelt frequently: nearly 2,000 written
messages passed between them.[113] He encountered the president in person
eleven times and spent a total of 113 days in his company.[114] In August 1941,
he traveled to Nova Scotia (he made four subsequent Atlantic crossings
during the war),[115] where the two men signed what came to be known
as the Atlantic Charter, a joint statement of war aims issued before the
United States formally entered the war. It was a mark of Churchill's need
for good relations with Roosevelt, and of Britain's need for broad support
in the United States, that the Charter included a pledge to "respect the
right of all peoples to choose the form of government under which they
will live," a principle that the prime minister, a devoted supporter of the
British Empire, did not in fact favor.[116]

Roosevelt did do what Churchill wanted him to do, although perhaps
not as quickly as the prime minister hoped. The United States dispatched
aid to the British war effort, first in a trade in which Britain received some
aging American warships in exchange for American access to British military bases in the Western Hemisphere, then under the Lend-Lease program, by the terms of which the British did not have to pay immediately for
the supplies and armaments the Americans shipped to them. The president
authorized joint military talks and intelligence-sharing with the British.[117]
Even before Pearl Harbor, the United States took an active part in the war
in the Atlantic, its navy protecting convoys carrying cargoes for Britain and
its government assuming responsibility for the defense of Iceland. And, of
course, America ultimately did become a full-fledged belligerent against
Germany.

None of that was due mainly to Churchill himself.[118] It was, in the end,
the Japanese attack on Pearl Harbor and Hitler's subsequent declaration of
war that precipitated the United States fully and formally into World War
II. Roosevelt, who acted according to his own beliefs and calculations—in
both of which he had supreme confidence—was not a person to be cajoled
or charmed into doing something he did not wish to do. Churchill did affect Roosevelt's calculations by making it clear, by his words and deeds in
1940 and 1941, that Britain was committed to seeing the war through to
the end and that whatever assistance the United States sent would therefore not be wasted.[119] Moreover, while the public perception, during the

war and afterward, of the degree of mutual admiration, trust, and genuine friendship between the president and the prime minster was sometimes exaggerated, Churchill did establish a good enough relationship with Roosevelt to manage the issues that divided them—the future of the Empire, for example, and the strategic course the Allies should follow—without seriously impairing the war effort.[120]

With Stalin, he spent far less time. He traveled to Moscow twice, in August 1942 and October 1944, and met the Soviet leader at three summit conferences. Churchill had less success in establishing a personal relationship with Stalin and ultimately failed to obtain what he sought from him. The major issue on which Churchill tried to steer or persuade the communist dictator was the shape of postwar Europe, and especially the political organization and geopolitical alignment of Poland. Here, Churchill had to labor under three handicaps: Stalin did not trust him, and indeed did not trust any "capitalist" leader or perhaps anyone at all; the two had opposed goals—Stalin wanted to control as much of Europe as possible, Churchill sought to minimize Soviet control;[121] and Stalin's Red Army, by virtue of its counteroffensive against the Germans, occupied more and more of Eastern and Central Europe as the war proceeded, including, by the war's end, all of Poland.

That meant that Stalin could impose whatever territorial and political settlement he chose on the Poles, and he ultimately imposed what neither Churchill nor Roosevelt nor the Polish people wanted: a communist government. Churchill's diplomacy failed with Stalin not because of any personal shortcomings on the prime minister's part or errors in his approach, but because of the resolutely anti-Western character of the communist ideology that shaped Stalin's worldview and above all because of the realities of power at the end of World War II and immediately afterward.

Churchill's greatest contribution to the war effort, and his deepest imprint on the history of his times, came not through the military initiatives he set in motion, or in his dealings with Roosevelt and Stalin, but rather in his leadership at home during the period of maximum peril for Great Britain. That period began when France fell even as he became prime minister in May 1940, and lasted until the early days of December 1941.

True, Britain had ceased to be the only country at war with the Third Reich six months before the second date, on June 22, 1941, when Germany attacked the Soviet Union. Until December of that year, however, it appeared that Hitler might well achieve his goals in Operation Barbarossa: shattering the Red Army, destroying the communist political apparatus that Lenin and Stalin had built, occupying all of European Russia, and then turning back to Britain with the expectation that Churchill would be replaced by someone disposed to make the deal the German leader had sought even before the war in Europe began—an arrangement in which the British would accept German domination of the continent in return for a promise to be allowed to retain their empire. At that point, Hitler could reasonably have believed that the United States would decide not to challenge him and instead confine itself to the Western Hemisphere.

In the first week of December, however, the German drive on Moscow stalled and the Red Army managed to counterattack. It became clear that the swift, decisive victory on which Hitler had counted was out of reach: the war would be a long one, and in a long war the side with the larger population and greater economic resources, in World War II the anti-Hitler coalition, would have a major advantage. Before that turning point, and especially for Churchill's first year-and-a-half as prime minister, Great Britain faced the gravest possible danger. In his first few months in that post, the prospect of a German invasion of southern England was all too real. While Britain could not have won the war in 1940, the British could have lost it,[122] with all the terrible consequences—and not only for Britain—that would have flowed from a Nazi triumph.

In late May, the idea of approaching Hitler through his ally, the Italian dictator Benito Mussolini, surfaced and the War Cabinet,[123] a subset of the cabinet as a whole, discussed it. Halifax, who had supported the policy of appeasement before the war, favored exploring the possibility of negotiating with the Nazi leader.[124] Neville Chamberlain, no longer prime minister but still an important cabinet member[125] with considerable influence among Conservative Members of Parliament—many of whom still did not entirely trust Churchill[126]—was at first noncommittal.

Churchill adamantly opposed the idea.[127] He was certain that Hitler would never offer terms consistent with Britain's self-respect and long-term safety. Even if the British were to enter into the agreement that Hitler had floated, in which they kept their empire while acceding to his domination of Europe, there was no reason to believe the German dictator would keep his word. Moreover, the mere appearance of negotiations with

Hitler, even indirectly, would, he believed, weaken morale in Britain and give the Americans the impression, at best, that the British will to fight was faltering.[128] Moreover, he warned, negotiations, once begun, would place Britain on a slippery slope, with the British position becoming progressively weaker.[129] In retrospect, each of these scenarios seems all too plausible,[130] and it was far from clear at the time that Churchill's position would prevail.

The deliberations took place in the War Cabinet, but at one point Churchill convened the cabinet members who did not belong to the smaller group and delivered a rousing presentation stating his own views. He received enthusiastic approval for it. He reported this response to the War Cabinet and eventually prevailed: no negotiations with Hitler, direct or indirect, took place. At the same time, the evacuation at Dunkirk lifted the country's spirits and reinforced its determination to continue the fight against Germany.[€]

Had someone else been prime minister—Halifax, for example—British policy in the late spring of 1940 might have taken a decidedly different course,[131] with profoundly negative consequences for the resistance to Hitler. Even in the absence of such a departure, it is far from clear that another prime minister could have sustained British morale in those dark days as Churchill did. Certainly, no one else had anything like his combination of bulldog determination and inspirational eloquence. In his history of Great Britain from 1914 to 1945, A. J. P. Taylor, a historian hardly given to adoring treatments of politicians, especially Conservative ones, called Churchill "the saviour of his country."[132] By his refusal to bow to the German onslaught, he saved more than Britain; and it was with his leadership in the months that came thereafter to be called, using his words, the British people's finest hour, that he earned that accolade.

[€] Best, *op. cit.*, pp. 130–131. In his book *Five Days in London: May 1940* (New Haven, Connecticut: Yale University Press, 1999), the distinguished historian John Lukacs traced the deliberations about negotiations and portrayed the episode as a crucial one in the history of World War II, the moment when Britain came closest to losing it. In a review of the book, the equally distinguished historian Michael Howard doubted that the episode was as important as Lukacs had maintained, on the grounds that negotiations would probably not have taken the course that Churchill feared and that it was Dunkirk that counts as the turning point for continuing the war. Michael Howard, "Turning Point," *The National Interest*, Spring 2000.

The Legacy

In one way—a way that mattered greatly to him—Winston Churchill's public career counts as a failure. The world in which he grew to manhood, in which he made his name, whose principal features he valued and that he did all he could to preserve, disappeared. When he was born, the government scarcely touched the everyday lives of the British people and was generally uninvolved in the economy. London was the seat of the largest empire on Earth. For that reason, among others, Churchill's country could claim to be the greatest of the great powers.

By the time he died, by contrast, the country had acquired expensive programs of social protection, its major imperial possession—India—had gained independence, and the other parts of the empire had followed or were about to do so, and Britain had fallen from the ranks of the great powers, a decline made painfully evident in the abortive military operations at Suez in 1956.[133]

To be sure, that account overstates the case where domestic issues were concerned. In the course of his career, Churchill had consistently favored measures to assist the less fortunate,[134] had approved some of the social measures the country adopted, and had even sponsored several of them. The Labor government that replaced his in 1945 established the most important of these programs, the National Health Service; but during that election campaign Churchill had himself advocated a nationwide health program.[135]

Where the Empire was concerned, however, Churchill did fail—definitively. He waged a rearguard battle against giving it up, or even, in the case of India in the interwar period, modifying its system of governance. He declared in 1942 that he had "not become the King's first minister to preside over the liquidation of the British Empire."[136] It was liquidated all the same, although he was spared what would have been the additional pain of presiding over it himself.

The Empire ended because Britain, exhausted by the two World Wars, lacked the resources or the political will to keep it. In Churchill's political lifetime, the cost of retaining it rose as populations once content with British rule, or at least not actively opposed to it, began to mobilize for the purpose of overthrowing it. That is what took place in India.[137] The British government decided not to try to hold on forcibly, a decision that looks wise in retrospect, especially in light of France's different experience. In the wake of World War II, the French made the opposite decision in Indochina and Algeria, fought bloody, expensive, dispiriting wars in both places, and in the end had to give up their imperial possessions there nonetheless.

The Labour government that came to power in 1945 relinquished control of what had been British India in 1947, dividing it into independent India and Pakistan, for another reason: it had ceased to believe in the morality as well as the practicality of empire. That general shift in sentiment proved to be one of the most important global trends of the twentieth century. When the century began, the proposition that the various peoples of the world were unequal in fundamental ways and that some of them had the right, indeed the responsibility, to rule others had wide currency. Churchill shared this view. By century's end, it was more or less discredited almost everywhere.[138] Britain could not ignore this trend and did not seriously attempt to do so.

Churchill did believe that Britain could govern peoples indigenous to Africa and Asia more efficiently and fairly than they could govern themselves.[139] He predicted that a British withdrawal from India would precipitate massive bloodshed,[140] and so it did in the riots between Hindus and Muslims surrounding partition.[141] By the end of World War II, however, the time when such considerations could have bolstered a determination to remain an imperial power had passed. Whether the British Empire was a force for good, as Churchill always believed, or an agent of repression and selfish enrichment, as its opponents contended, had become a strictly historical question. Whether Europeans could govern Africans and Asians better than they could govern themselves ceased to matter: Europeans could no longer govern them at all. Empire became, for the democracies at least, an anachronism. In that sense, Churchill outlived his own historical era.[142]

Great Britain's fall from the ranks of the great powers, where it had been firmly lodged for most of Churchill's life and where he had no doubt it ought to remain, came about because his country no longer had the power to sustain that position. Nor, it turned out, did any country occupy the top rung of the international system other than the two other members of the victorious coalition in World War II that became, after the war, the nuclear superpowers.[143]

The loss of empire also contributed to the end of Britain's career as one of the great powers, for the empire supplied, beyond its economic benefits, one of the fundamental ingredients of power: soldiers.[144] The British were able to mobilize for battle in both World Wars Asian and African troops in large numbers.[145] With the end of empire, its military potential plummeted.

Churchill, and others among his countrymen, believed that Britain should, despite its demotion in the international hierarchy, continue to play a leading role in global affairs after 1945,[146] and he sought substitutes for great military power and empire that would enable it to do so. British officials hoped that the Commonwealth, the successor organization to the Empire consisting of former imperial possessions turned independent countries, would enhance Britain's global influence. Churchill himself emphasized the importance of what he called the "special relationship" with the United States, which he and others hoped would become a permanent partnership through which Britain could exercise some version of its previous influence.[147] He also promoted, through his last great multivolume history, the idea of an association of the English-speaking peoples.[148] None of these initiatives, however, restored the international power and status that Churchill had taken to be normal, natural, and desirable.[149]

If he did not manage to preserve the British international role that was part of his political inheritance, Churchill did leave a powerful and enduring legacy in other ways. The postwar world counts as part of that legacy inasmuch as without him, Hitler might have won the war in Europe and that victory, however long it lasted, would have had awful consequences. Given the brutality of the Nazi occupation of the territory that the Third Reich conquered, especially to Germany's east, Churchill's warning of a "New Dark Age" does not seem hyperbolic.

A Nazi victory would have had the severest impact on Europe: Hitler's defeat, by contrast, left the western part of the continent (although not the Soviet-dominated east) free to build a community of prosperity, liberty, and cooperation in the decades after the war, one of the most remarkable and beneficial developments in Europe's long history. While it was the Soviet Union and the United States that lifted the Nazi yoke from Europe, it was Great Britain, led by Churchill, that held out against Germany long enough for those two giants to enter the war and win it.

As World War II has receded into history, as the world has changed and those with personal memories of that conflict have passed from the scene, Churchill's political achievements have loomed less large in the public consciousness. His personal reputation, however, has endured, and he shows no sign of being forgotten. That reputation, to be sure, has undergone the usual posthumous vicissitudes, with sometimes acerbic critical appraisals[150] joining the sometimes adulatory treatment he received during his lifetime and thereafter. Still, in Great Britain, the United States, and elsewhere he has remained, in the eyes of a great many people—most of whom were not alive during World War II—an epic, almost mythic figure.[151] This is so because he came to embody several timeless values.

One of them is political in character: the defense of freedom, both national and individual, against those bent on destroying it. The forces of repression did not vanish from the Earth with the end of the Third Reich and for that reason this feature of Churchill's historical reputation has remained all too relevant.[152]

Churchill also came to represent two eternally invaluable personal characteristics. One is resilience. Throughout his life, he incurred setbacks but recovered, gathered his forces, and returned to the projects in which he had been engaged.[153] He suffered recurrent bouts of depression—which he called his "black dog"[154]—but still had a remarkably active, productive life. He experienced political reverses as well, including taking the blame for the Dardanelles fiasco, failing to win a parliamentary seat in three successive elections between 1922 and 1924, and spending a decade out of office; but he never gave up, and he reached the top of the British political system at the moment of the country's greatest trial. Not least important, Britain had suffered a crushing military defeat when he came to power in May 1940. He did not downplay the gravity of the nation's peril, but by his determination to persist in the war he rallied the British people for this purpose.

Finally, Churchill came to symbolize courage. He displayed physical courage throughout his life, from his early service in the three colonial wars[155] to his term as prime minister, when he made it clear that in the event of a German invasion he would personally resist and was prepared to die fighting if need be.[156] He also displayed moral courage, taking positions on public policy that he thought right even when they made him unpopular and subjected him to scorn and hostility. Churchill himself considered courage the supreme virtue,[157] and it is always crucial and almost always in short supply. During World War II, in the decades that followed, and no doubt far into the future, whenever courage is needed, people have looked and will look for inspiration to the life and works of Winston Churchill.

5

Franklin Delano Roosevelt

The Life

Franklin Delano Roosevelt was born on January 30, 1882. His father, James Roosevelt, a gentleman farmer and businessman living in the Hudson Valley of New York State, could trace his ancestry to seventeenth-century Dutch settlers of New York. His mother, the former Sara Delano, the father's second wife, was 26 years younger than her husband.[1] Her father had prospered in the China trade. As a child, Franklin led a comfortable, privileged life, and a cosmopolitan one: he was tutored in both French and German[2] and in his childhood traveled to Europe no fewer than nine times.[3] He attended the Groton School in Massachusetts, a college preparatory school for the sons of the American elite, and then went on to Harvard, where he was a student leader and president of the undergraduate newspaper *The Crimson*.[4] He attended the Columbia Law School and briefly practiced law, although with an eye to entering politics.[5]

In 1905, he married Eleanor Roosevelt, a distant cousin who was given away at the ceremony by her uncle Theodore Roosevelt, then the president of the United States. The couple had six children, five of whom survived. The marriage suffered a blow when she discovered Franklin's infidelity, but the two stayed together and Eleanor played a major role in her husband's political career.[6] That career, inspired by the example of cousin Theodore and the importance of public service instilled by the headmaster of Groton, the Reverend Endicott Peabody,[7] began in 1910 with his election to the New York State Senate and his reelection two years later. Despite his admiration for the Republican president to whom he was related, Franklin

Roosevelt adopted the partisan allegiance of his father and became a Democrat.

When Woodrow Wilson won the presidency in 1912, he appointed the younger Roosevelt to be assistant secretary of the navy, a post he held through both of Wilson's terms in office, including the years when the United States took part in World War I.[8] In a federal government far smaller than it would later become (in part because of Franklin Roosevelt's own policies as president), his position was important and influential. He was one of the four senior civilian officials overseeing the American military.[9] He did well enough in the post,[10] and became sufficiently widely known and well respected, to become the Democratic nominee for vice president in 1920—at 38 the youngest person ever to secure a major-party nomination for that office. The Democratic ticket lost badly that year, but Roosevelt seemed launched on a promising career in national politics.

Then he suffered a severe setback. In August 1921, he contracted polio. Despite strenuous physical therapy, he lost, permanently, the use of his legs, although he was ultimately able to manage a semblance of walking over short distances with heavy metal braces on his legs and the use of a cane, sometimes also leaning on another person (often one of his sons) for support.

Still, he did not give up his political ambitions. He reappeared in the political arena at the 1924 Democratic National Convention to nominate New York Governor Al Smith for president.[11] In 1928, with Smith the presidential candidate (Roosevelt again gave the nominating speech), he himself was drafted for the New York governorship and narrowly won. He was handily reelected two years later.[12] In the spirit of both Theodore Roosevelt and Woodrow Wilson, he compiled a generally progressive record as governor,[13] becoming a champion of old-age pensions and establishing a scheme to provide work for the unemployed.[14] To compensate for his limited mobility, his wife traveled on his behalf and spoke for him around the state.[15]

Smith lost in 1928, and Roosevelt managed to secure the Democratic presidential nomination for the next election, in 1932. With the Republican incumbent Herbert Hoover deeply unpopular because of the devastating impact of the Great Depression on the American economy, Roosevelt won the presidency by a wide margin.[16] The result was less an affirmation of him than a repudiation of Hoover.[17]

In his speech accepting the nomination, Roosevelt promised a "new deal" for the American people,[18] and that phrase became attached to the sweeping program of legislation that his administration passed for the purpose of combating the effects of the Depression. Much of it was enacted in the first hundred days[19] after his inauguration on March 4, 1933.[20] The New Deal addressed, among other problems, the country's stricken financial system: Roosevelt declared a bank holiday immediately after taking office, Congress established the Federal Deposit Insurance Corporation to assure people that their bank deposits were safe, and the administration took the United States off the gold standard.

The flurry of legislation included as well new programs and agencies to reduce the unemployment that was ravaging the country: the Civilian Conservation Corps, the Federal Emergency Relief Act, the Public Works Administration, and the Works Progress Administration among them. The Roosevelt administration also instituted more extensive government regulation of the economy than ever before. The Securities and Exchange Commission came into existence to govern stock issues, the Glass-Steagall Act separated commercial from investment banking, the National Recovery Administration created a series of regulations for industry, most of which turned out to be short-lived, and the Agricultural Adjustment Administration promulgated regulations on American agriculture, which proved to be longer-lasting.[21] Organized labor increased its power and influence as a result of the New Deal, becoming a major force in both the economic and the political life of the nation.[22] Perhaps the most important item of legislation during the first Roosevelt term was the Social Security Act of 1935, which established the right of every American to an old-age pension and quickly became indispensable for millions of people.

The New Deal represented by far the greatest peacetime expansion of the role of government in American history. Through its various initiatives, the federal government involved itself more deeply in the country's economic life than ever before, with the aims of stabilizing and regulating economic activity, goals that had come to seem urgent because of the Depression. Perhaps most importantly, the Roosevelt program established the responsibility of the federal government for the welfare of individual citizens as a precept of American life. That is its most significant long-term consequence. In the short term, it succeeded in relieving some of the effects of the Depression. The fact that the government was exerting itself in novel ways to counteract them lifted the country's spirits. More concretely, economic conditions did improve in noticeable ways.[23]

For this reason, the New Deal received a vote of confidence in the 1936 presidential election: Roosevelt was resoundingly reelected.[24] His second term, however, proved less productive than his first. The economy slumped again, because, according to the retrospective consensus, the Roosevelt administration prematurely reduced government spending.[25]

In addition, the president initiated two political battles that he failed to win. The nation's Supreme Court had struck down a number of New Deal measures, including the National Recovery Administration, on the grounds that they violated provisions of the United States Constitution. To overcome this opposition, in February 1937, Roosevelt proposed legislation stipulating that for every one of the nine members of the Court age 70 or older, he would be able to appoint an additional justice. The measure generated serious resistance, and the Congress refused to back the president.* Having encountered increasing opposition to his proposal from congressional Democrats, most of them from the South, he tried to defeat several of them in Democratic primary elections in advance of the 1938 congressional elections but achieved little success.[26] In that same year, a Roosevelt bill for reorganizing the federal government died in Congress.[27] By 1938, however, his attention was turning increasingly to foreign affairs.

Upon assuming office, Roosevelt had inherited an American policy of opposition to Japanese encroachment on China. In 1931 Japan had set up the puppet state of Manchukuo in the Chinese province of Manchuria. The Hoover administration refused to recognize it, a policy that its

---

* Ted Morgan, *FDR: A Biography*, New York: Simon & Schuster, 1985, pp. 472–474. Roosevelt "had expended a large part of his political capital on a failed enterprise. He had given a winning cause to conservatives long opposed to him, and had seen former allies, even some of the strongest progressives, join them." Frank Freidel, *Franklin D. Roosevelt: A Rendezvous With Destiny*, Boston: Little, Brown and Company, 1990, p. 239. Despite the failure of what came to be known as his "court-packing" initiative, the Court's opposition to the New Deal came to an end. On a crucial decision in March 1937, one justice changed his vote so that the Court upheld the statute in question, which relieved some of the pressure for changing the number of justices and so became known as "the switch in time that saved nine." Freidel, *op. cit.*, p. 234; David M. Kennedy, *Freedom from Fear: The American People in Depression and War, 1929–1945*, New York: Oxford University Press, 1999, p. 334. Then a number of the older justices voluntarily retired, enabling Roosevelt to choose successors better disposed to his program. Ultimately, he appointed eight men to the Supreme Court.

successor continued.[28] In 1937 Japan went farther, invading North China. The Roosevelt administration wanted to avoid a military conflict with Japan but felt pressure from the American public to assist the Chinese,[29] so it began to send aid to China and to impose restrictions on American exports to Japan. The president himself paid more attention to events in Europe.

There, Hitler steadily dismantled the political and military arrangements that had emerged from the Paris Peace Conference after World War I: in 1935, renouncing the demilitarization clauses Germany had accepted, in 1936, sending military forces into the Rhineland and annexing Austria, and in 1938, with the cooperation of Great Britain and France at a meeting in the German city of Munich, taking over the German-speaking parts of Czechoslovakia. Then came the fateful year 1939. In March, contrary to the German dictator's assurances at Munich, Germany took control of the rest of Czechoslovakia. Britain and France thereupon promised to defend the country that loomed as his next target—Poland. In August, Nazi Germany and the Soviet Union, previously bitter ideological enemies, signed a non-aggression pact that divided the countries that had the misfortune to be located between them. On September 1, Germany attacked Poland, and Britain and France declared war on Germany. Two decades after World War I had ended, Europe was again at war.[30]

Franklin Roosevelt regarded these events with growing dismay and increasing concern for the security of the European democracies and the interests of the United States; but his capacity to affect events on the other side of the Atlantic was severely limited both by the modest size of the American armed forces[31] and by the prevailing attitude of the American public. While a majority in the United States favored the cause of the British and the French over that of the Germans, most Americans did not want the United States to become directly involved in the war.[32]

By 1939, a substantial majority had concluded that their country's participation in World War I had been a mistake, one that it strongly desired not to repeat.[33] As tensions in Europe rose and then war broke out, opposition to American intervention appeared across the political spectrum. The opposition ranged from some on the left, who rejected war as an instrument of American statecraft, to others on the right, who wanted no part of Europe's political quarrels.[34] An organization called "America First" was formed to oppose direct involvement in the European conflict and the celebrated aviator Charles Lindbergh became the most prominent advocate of staying out of the war.[35] To guard against the experience of World War I,

Congress passed a series of Neutrality Acts forbidding arms sales and loans to the belligerent countries, the provision of which was regarded in retrospect as having drawn the United States into the fighting in 1917.

A turning point in Roosevelt's—as well as America's and the world's—assessment of the unfolding events in Europe came with the swift and unexpected fall of France in May and June 1940. Nazi Germany's triumph made the world suddenly appear to many Americans, including the president, to be a far more dangerous place. Roosevelt decided to seek what none of his thirty predecessors as president[36] had had, a third term, and he won it. During the course of the campaign, in a bow to the prevailing sentiment in the electorate, he made a categorical pledge: "I have said this before, but I shall say it again and again and again: 'Your boys are not going to be sent into foreign wars.'"[37] He proceeded thereafter, however, to do everything he believed he could within the constraints of public opinion to assist a beleaguered Great Britain.

When the war in Europe began, Roosevelt had proclaimed American neutrality but had made it clear that, although his country would not join the fighting, he and many of his fellow countrymen wanted one side and not the other to win it. "Even a neutral," he said, "cannot be asked to close his mind or his conscience."[38] As the war continued, and especially after the defeat of France and his own electoral victory in November 1940, he spoke in increasingly explicit and urgent terms about the stakes the conflict held for the United States, and specifically about the danger that a German victory would present to America.[39]

While moving cautiously, he managed to take a series of steps to aid the British. He secured the repeal of some of the provisions of the Neutrality Acts.[40] He arranged to send old destroyers from the United States Navy to Great Britain in exchange for the rights to British military bases in the Western Hemisphere.[41] When the British ran out of money to pay for imports from the United States, he persuaded Congress to authorize the Lend-Lease program, by whose terms payment for British purchases was deferred—in many cases permanently.[42] The United States also sent military assistance to China and, after the German attack of June 22, 1941, to the Soviet Union as well, through the Lend-Lease program.

In July 1941, Roosevelt traveled by ship to Placentia Bay, Newfoundland, in Canada, to meet with the British Prime Minister Winston Churchill, the first of nine times they were together on four different continents.[†]

[†] Between 1941 and 1945, they met in North America (Canada and the United States), Africa (Casablanca and Cairo), Asia (Tehran), and Europe (Yalta). By July 1941, the two

The two leaders signed a declaration of principles that came to be called the Atlantic Charter. It was the equivalent of a joint declaration of war aims, a counterpart to Woodrow Wilson's Fourteen Points for World War I even though the United States had not yet entered the war.[43]

In addition to aligning his country ever more closely with Great Britain, Roosevelt initiated military measures to prepare the United States for war and then to move it, subtly and unofficially, into the ongoing military conflict with Germany. He persuaded the Congress to appropriate funds for rearmament, with an emphasis on the production of aircraft.[44] He succeeded in passing the Selective Service Act, establishing the first peacetime draft in American history, and then renewing it—by a single vote in the House of Representatives.[45] He also authorized, without publicizing them, military talks between the American and British high commands.[46] In the interest of keeping the Atlantic Ocean safe for the transport of civilian goods and military materiel to Britain, he ordered American forces to Iceland and Greenland.[47]

Also to safeguard Britain's Atlantic lifeline against attacks on shipping by German submarines, the American navy began patrolling further into the ocean from the east coast of North America and escorting transatlantic convoys to and from points increasingly far to the east.[48] In this way the United States began taking part in the maritime war between Great Britain and Germany.[49] Churchill told his associates that Roosevelt had told him at Placentia Bay that "he would wage war but not declare it."[50]

The formal American entry into World War II, however, came as the result of events in Asia, which Roosevelt had not only not fully anticipated but had also, in fact, sought to prevent. In July 1941, Japanese forces moved into the southern part of Indochina. In response, the United States tightened its economic sanctions on Japan and cut off all Japanese access to American oil, a potentially crippling blow to that country's economy and armed forces.[51] Preoccupied with the conference in Newfoundland, the president did not realize how restrictive the new round of sanctions was; but once having imposed them, he concluded that relaxing them would not sit well with the strongly anti-Japanese and pro-Chinese American public.[52]

---

had been corresponding for the better part of two years. Placentia Bay was technically their second personal encounter: they had attended the same dinner party in London in 1918, an occasion that Roosevelt remembered but Churchill did not. Morgan, *op. cit.*, p. 195.

Negotiations between the United States and Japan in an attempt to resolve their differences continued through the fall, but the Japanese government decided on a military campaign to seize the oil fields of Southeast Asia and included in the plan of the campaign an attack on the United States itself. The attack came on December 7, 1941, against the American fleet at Pearl Harbor, Hawaii.[†] The next day, at the president's request, Congress declared war on Japan. On December 11, Hitler declared war on the United States. Franklin D. Roosevelt had become, officially, a war president.

Immediately after Pearl Harbor, the United States began to mobilize for war. As in World War I, special agencies were created to coordinate war-related activities. To a far greater extent than in World War I, the national economy converted to the production of weaponry and other war materiel. On December 29, 1940, Roosevelt had committed the country to becoming "the great arsenal of democracy,"[53] and it supplied much of the equipment used by the British armed forces and the Red Army of the Soviet Union[54] as well as by the American military itself. Because it was essential to manufacture tanks, ships, airplanes, and wheeled vehicles on the largest possible scale, major corporations played a prominent role in war production.[55]

The war economy had one particular unanticipated but welcome effect: it put an end, finally, to the Depression. With millions of people joining the armed forces and millions more working in factories making what the people in uniform needed in order to fight, unemployment dropped to very low levels; and despite the emphasis on war production, civilian consumption in the United States rose.[56]

The war had an impact on American society as well, with long-term consequences for the kind of country the United States was and was to become. Before the war, the vast majority of Americans of African descent lived in the South, where their ancestors had been slaves. During the war, many moved to the North, to work in the defense industries that were mainly located outside what had once been the Confederacy. They thereby escaped the legal segregation of the South and earned more money than

---

[†] "The [American] military knew Japan was on the march, but believed it would attack Burma or Thailand. They had a mind-set that a small country like Japan would never make a first strike against a big power like the United States. If the Japanese were crazy enough to fight the United States, they would attack the Philippines. They would never attack Pearl Harbor, it was too far away and too well defended." Morgan, *op. cit.*, p. 610.

had been possible there. The war also drew women into the workforce in larger numbers than ever before.

The president neither decreed nor foresaw the economic and social impact of the war. He did have ultimate responsibility, however, for two wartime policies that came in for some criticism during the war and for much more in the years thereafter. A total of 125,284 Japanese Americans living on the West Coast were removed from their homes and sent to bleak camps inland on the grounds that, because they might be loyal to the Japanese enemy, they posed a threat to national security. Roosevelt signed the executive order authorizing this measure and the Supreme Court upheld it. No evidence of subversion or serious disloyalty ever emerged, and decades later the Congress voted to issue a formal apology and pay compensation to the victims of the forced relocation.

World War II included a Nazi war of extermination against Europe's Jews. The Jews who had a hope of leaving Europe were desperate to do so, and a favored destination was the United States. Restrictions on immigration limited the number who managed to escape to America, however. Roosevelt was well aware of the perils European Jews faced and could have taken steps to rescue many of them by making immigration easier and more widely available, but he did not.[57] Almost nine decades later, his inaction on this issue remains a major blot on his presidential record.

As for the war itself, with the president as commander-in-chief making the major decisions, America's European campaign began in North Africa with Operation Torch in the late fall of 1942. From there, American and British forces proceeded to Sicily and then to the Italian peninsula. The most important Anglo-American military operation of 1943 took place not on land but over, on, and under the Atlantic Ocean. German submarine warfare was severely interfering with the flow of weapons and other supplies to the British Isles. In six weeks between March and May of that year, American and British forces succeeded in dramatically reducing the number of ships the Germans were able to sink, thereby making safe the crucial highway of Anglo-American military cooperation.[58]

In Italy, the Allies reached Rome on June 4, 1944, but by then the focus of their military efforts had shifted to the north. On June 6, Operation Overlord began. From a starting point in southern England, American, British, and Canadian forces under the command of the American General Dwight D. Eisenhower crossed the English Channel and landed in Normandy on France's northwest coast. An amphibious assault against defended territory of the kind they conducted is the most difficult of all military undertakings, and Overlord was the largest and most complicated one ever launched. It succeeded in landing more than 150,000 soldiers in France on what became known as D-Day. Joined eventually by many more—ultimately 2 million Americans served in the European theater— the Allied troops pushed eastward, against stiff German resistance, to Germany itself. The Red Army assaulted Nazi Germany from the east and on May 8, 1945, after Adolf Hitler had committed suicide, the Germans surrendered.

In the Pacific, in the six months after Pearl Harbor, Japanese forces scored one victory after another, capturing Wake Island, Guam, several is- land chains, Burma, Malaya, Singapore, the Philippines, Borneo, and Java.[59] Two major naval engagements stopped their rampage. In the Battle of the Coral Sea on May 3, 1942, a clash of aircraft carriers in which, for the first time in the history of maritime combat, the two opposing fleets did not come within sight of each other, the United States held its own.[60] Then, a month later at the Battle of Midway on June 3, 1942, American naval airpower scored a decisive victory, knocking out four Japanese carriers. Japan never regained the military initiative in the Pacific war.[61]

Roosevelt decided to fight the Japanese in three theaters. The United States supported Chiang Kai-shek's Chinese forces against the Japanese invaders in China. In the southwest Pacific, Army General Douglas MacArthur advanced to the Philippines, from which the Japanese had evicted him shortly after Pearl Harbor. In the central Pacific, the Navy fought its way toward the Japanese archipelago by capturing a series of is- land chains: the Solomons, the Gilberts, the Marshalls, and the Marianas. From the last of these, the United States Air Force bombarded the Japanese islands. On August 6, 1945, it dropped, on the city of Hiroshima, a newly fabricated atomic bomb, the product of a secret, elaborate, and expen- sive American program of research and development that Roosevelt had authorized called the Manhattan Project. On August 9, another such bomb struck Nagasaki. On September 2, in a ceremony on the American battleship *Missouri*, which was anchored in Tokyo Bay, Japan officially surrendered.

The United States fought World War II as part of a coalition, which required of Franklin D. Roosevelt active diplomatic engagement with the leaders of America's two coalition partners. Besides Placentia Bay, his most significant bilateral meeting with Churchill took place in Casablanca in

January 1943, at which he called for Germany's unconditional surrender. Roosevelt and Churchill met with the Soviet leader Josef Stalin twice. In Tehran in late 1943, they agreed that the Americans and British would initiate a "second front" of the European war in France in 1944, in what turned out to be Operation Overlord. In February 1945, at Yalta on the Black Sea in the Soviet Union, the three discussed a wide range of issues including the postwar futures of Germany and Poland.

In 1944, Roosevelt decided to run for a fourth presidential term and won it. He took office in January, 1945, with his third vice president. John Nance Garner, a former speaker of the House of Representatives from Texas, had filled the position in the first two terms. Henry Wallace of Iowa, a farmer, publisher, and scientist who had served as secretary of agriculture during those two terms, succeeded Garner in the third. For the fourth term, Harry S Truman, a senator from Missouri, replaced Wallace.

Franklin D. Roosevelt did not live to see the end of the war. By the time of the 1944 presidential campaign, his health had begun seriously to deteriorate. He looked haggard and he tired easily.[62] A physical examination in March 1944 revealed that he had advanced heart disease.[63] On April 12, 1945, he died of a massive cerebral hemorrhage at his home in Warm Springs, Georgia.

The Times

Two great global shocks made Franklin D. Roosevelt president of the United States and enabled him, in that office, to make a major mark on the history of the twentieth century. The first shock came partially, and the second entirely, from outside North America. Both demanded, or seemed to demand, a vigorous American response, which Roosevelt led in both cases.

Although the stock market crash of 1929 in the United States weakened the American economy, much of the impetus for the Great Depression of the 1930s came from Europe. World War II had European origins as well, although it began in East Asia and the attack that precipitated American entry into the war came from across the Pacific, not the Atlantic.

Roosevelt gained the presidency because of these two shocks. He would not have been elected without them. He owed his first two presidential terms to the Depression and his policies to cope with it, and his third and fourth terms to the war. Moreover, the Depression and the war loosened the normal constraints on the American presidency, creating a sense of national emergency that afforded Roosevelt greater scope for the personal exercise of authority, and for innovations in public policy, than were available to almost all of his predecessors and to every one of his successors in that office, who governed in less troubled times.

The Great Depression began as a banking crisis in Europe and the United States.[64] As banks failed, so too did businesses that relied on them for credit, which put their employees out of work. Without salaries, these former workers had no money to spend, which crippled more businesses by depriving them of customers. Prices collapsed, further damaging businesses and making debt unmanageable.

The country had experienced economic downturns before, but this one turned out to be the worst of them in no small part because mistaken policies carried out in response to it by the American government (and other governments as well) only served to worsen economic conditions. Following the economic orthodoxy of the day, governments reduced spending when, in order to revive economic activity, they should have expanded it, and raised interest rates rather than lowering them.[65]

The Depression inflicted massive damage on the American economy. By 1933 unemployment stood at least at 30 percent of the workforce and was perhaps even higher. In the previous three years, 5,000 banks had failed, destroying 9 million individual accounts. Total nonagricultural production had fallen to less than half its level in 1929.[66] A sense of desperation, even hopelessness, gripped the country, creating the political conditions in which Roosevelt could become president and implement the New Deal.

He became the Democratic nominee for the office in 1932 for some of the same reasons that Woodrow Wilson had done so twenty years earlier. As the governor of the nation's then-most-populous state, Franklin D. Roosevelt was an obvious candidate for the nomination. Moreover, he was neither a Catholic nor a Southerner, two groups heavily represented in Democratic ranks but no member of which, it was then widely believed, could be elected to the country's highest office. While belonging to neither group, he was acceptable to both: he had decent relations with the Catholic-dominated Democratic organization of New York and had nominated the Catholic Al Smith for the Democratic nomination twice; and, having built a home and a polio rehabilitation center in Warm Springs, Georgia, where he spent a good deal of time, he had ties to the South as well.[67]

Under normal circumstances, Roosevelt, or indeed any Democrat, would have had great difficulty being elected president. The Republican Party had dominated national politics since the Civil War. Only two members of Roosevelt's party had won the presidency in the seventy-two years since that war had begun: Grover Cleveland, a very conservative Democrat, and Woodrow Wilson, who had benefited in 1912 from the split in Republican voters between the incumbent William Howard Taft and his predecessor, Theodore Roosevelt.[68] Franklin Roosevelt had himself expressed the opinion that only an economic cataclysm could put a Democrat in the White House.[69] The Great Depression was such a cataclysm, and that is what it did.

Once Roosevelt was elected, the severity of the Depression made the country willing to try more sweeping measures than any previously enacted. The New Deal flouted the economic and political orthodoxy that prevailed in 1933, and this was possible because Herbert Hoover had hewed faithfully to that orthodoxy and had signally failed to rescue the country. In his 1932 campaign, Roosevelt had called for "bold, persistent experimentation."[70] Most people in most places most of the time do not wish to take part in experiments that affect their livelihoods; but in the desperate circumstances of 1933, Americans and their representatives in Congress, a majority of whom were Democrats as the result of the 1932 election, were willing to try the ones that Roosevelt proposed.

The Roosevelt presidency would have come to an end with the completion of his second term but for the war in Europe. Although the president was not in the habit of confiding his innermost thoughts or deepest political calculations to anyone else, it does seem that until well into the election year 1940 he was leaning against running again. The fall of France in May and June apparently made him change his mind.[71] That shocking event caused the stakes for America in the conflict on the other side of the Atlantic to seem much higher, and the chances that the United States would be able to stay out of it much lower, than had been the case when both France and Great Britain were opposing Germany. Without the war, it is difficult to see how Roosevelt would have persuaded American voters to abandon the informal rule, in effect since George Washington voluntarily stepped down in 1796, that presidents do not serve more than two terms.[72]

The fall of France took place just before the Republican National Convention and had a great deal to do with its selection of its own presidential nominee. Wendell Willkie, a New York utilities executive originally from Indiana, had never held elective office. Beyond his attractive personal characteristics, he appealed to the delegates to the convention because he did not share the determination to steer clear of Europe's quarrels that had wide currency within his political party. That sentiment appeared to many Republicans to have been overtaken by events.[73] The Willkie candidacy meant that, in the 1940 election, the country had a choice between two men both of whom regarded the events in Europe as crucial for the United States, and neither of whom subscribed to the principled noninterventionist view of Charles Lindbergh, the members of America First, and many others.

While the same man occupied the White House between 1940 and April 1945 as the one who had served as president between 1933 and 1940, the job changed fundamentally. The war gave Franklin Roosevelt—or, perhaps more accurately, forced him into—a second distinct presidency. True, he continued to operate at the center of events, some of the same people had positions of responsibility,[74] and the role of the federal government again expanded[75] to cope with what qualified, like the Great Depression, as a national emergency.

Still, the differences between the two presidencies stand out: "Dr. New Deal" had different responsibilities and purposes than "Dr. Win the War."[76] Whereas during the first presidency the Roosevelt administration had as its principal goal ending the Depression, which meant above all increasing employment, in the second the overriding aim was winning the war, and the principal economic means to that end was the large-scale production of armaments.

The two FDR presidencies rested on different political foundations as well: groups that had opposed the New Deal supported his efforts to bolster the British and stop Nazi Germany. In 1940, the president added two prominent Republicans to his administration. He appointed Henry Stimson, who had served as Herbert Hoover's secretary of state, to be the secretary of war and chose Frank Knox, the 1936 Republican vice-presidential candidate, to be secretary of the navy.[77] Eastern Republicans, for whom the first two Roosevelt terms seemed a dangerous and highly undesirable exercise in social engineering and even socialism, and Southerners, who, although mainly Democrats, had turned against Roosevelt's legislative agenda in his second term, became enthusiastic advocates of aiding the British and confronting Hitler.[78] On the other hand, the progressives, who had staunchly supported Roosevelt's domestic program beginning in 1933, had reservations about the foreign policy he began to pursue toward Europe. Some progressives actively opposed it.[79]

To cite another political difference between the two Roosevelt presidencies, in both of them, the president brought into responsible positions people not ordinarily part of the government, but they were very different kinds of people. In the first era, he often consulted a "brain trust,"[80] individuals whose stock in trade was ideas, many associated with universities. In the second, leaders of major businesses helped direct the economic side of the war effort. These men sometimes accepted only nominal salaries and thus became known as "dollar-a-year men." In addition to having little in common, each group disliked and distrusted the other. The sharp changes in the political underpinnings of his presidency, and Roosevelt's ability to navigate them, testify to his flexibility, adaptability, and political dexterity—all useful qualities for a leader to possess.

In the United States, as in other countries, war tends to concentrate power. World War II gave Franklin D. Roosevelt extraordinary power by American standards, both at home and especially in conducting the nation's policies abroad. The war vested great authority in his office and therefore in him personally. Because the World War took place, as the name by which it came to be known suggests, on a global scale, the decisions he acquired the authority to make had wide, deep, and long-term repercussions. The Great Depression made Roosevelt a major figure in the history of the United States. World War II made him, like Hitler and Churchill (and Josef Stalin as well), a major figure in the history of the world.

Leadership

Franklin D. Roosevelt was not a man of ideas in the way that most of his fellow twentieth-century titans were. He never made his living by developing and criticizing ideas, as the one-time academic Woodrow Wilson did. No powerful idea inspired and informed his political career, as Marxism did for Lenin's, antisemitism did for Hitler's, nonviolence did for Gandhi's, and Zionism did for Ben-Gurion's. Yet ideas did matter to him. He read widely. He was acquainted with, if not necessarily deeply versed in, the intellectual currents of his time. He had an interest in, and welcomed, political and economic ideas of all kinds.[81] He pioneered the use of experts from outside the government—his "brain trust"—to supply him with suggestions and plans for governing.[82]

To the task of sorting through the ideas he encountered, Roosevelt brought a twofold approach. First, no single idea dominated his thinking. It was eclectic—he routinely entertained different points of view; and he was pragmatic rather than dogmatic, favoring whatever would help him achieve his goals.[83] His willingness to set aside the economic orthodoxy that had shaped Herbert Hoover's policies toward the Great Depression made the New Deal possible.

Second, while, like Winston Churchill, he came from the upper reaches of his society, never displayed anything other than pride in his background and ancestry, and certainly did not seek to transform his country radically to make it more egalitarian, he did have a persistent sympathy for the underdogs, the downtrodden, and the victims of misfortune in the United States. In 1933, a very substantial fraction of the American population belonged to one or more of these categories. In his 1932 campaign, he vowed to help "the forgotten man at the bottom of the economic pyramid." Like Churchill, he approved of and indeed successfully promoted reforms to help the disadvantaged.

Roosevelt became one of the giants of the twentieth century because he managed to translate into public policy the ideas that he deemed useful and his impulse to assist the less fortunate, as well as his conviction that the survival of an independent Great Britain and the defeat of Nazi Germany had the greatest importance for the United States. That required political skill, and Roosevelt was nothing if not a skillful politician, effective both in interpersonal settings and in appealing to the American public as a whole.

In small groups and one-on-one meetings, he excelled at winning people over through his affable, friendly, informal manner.[84] He had a generous supply of that hard-to-define but powerful trait of personality known as charm. (He also had a streak of vindictiveness, although he seldom showed it publicly.)[85] He convinced people whom he met that they had established a personal connection with him.[86] Whether he reciprocated that sentiment is open to doubt: some who observed him closely and at length concluded that for him relationships tended to be purely transactional.[§] In general,

---

[§] Harold Ickes judged Roosevelt to be "cold as ice inside." Derek Leebaert, *Unlikely Heroes: FDR, His Four Lieutenants, and a World Made Anew*, New York: St. Martin's Press, 2023, p. 146. Ickes also said of him, "Beneath all his outward charm and cordiality he was cold and calculating. . . ." John Lamberton Harper, *American Visions of Europe: Franklin*

those observers and historians who wrote about him found his character difficult to penetrate and his inner life entirely inaccessible.[87]

He was adept at sizing people up, assessing their strengths and weaknesses and deciding what roles they might be able to play in his life.[88] He attracted talented aides, sometimes individuals whom others had overlooked,[89] and inspired loyalty, often intense loyalty, on the part of those who worked for and with him.

For all his attractive qualities, he had some unattractive ones as well. More than most politicians, he could be less than straightforward in his dealings with others. He himself said so:

> I am a juggler, and I never let my right hand know what my left hand does. I may have one policy for Europe and one diametrically opposite for North and South America. I may be entirely inconsistent, and furthermore I am perfectly willing to mislead and tell untruths if it will help win the war.[90]

War is, to be sure, an exceptional circumstance in which departures from accepted norms are sometimes preferable to respecting them, but Roosevelt resorted to dissembling in other circumstances and for other purposes as well.[91]

For example, he sometimes gave the impression to someone that he favored that person's preferred course of action on a particular issue and then turned around and conveyed a similar assurance to someone else with the opposite preference on the same issue. He was capable of acting deviously even toward close associates and major national figures. In the months leading up to the 1944 Democratic National Convention, the president assured Henry Wallace that he wanted to run with him again in the fall election, all the while working behind the scenes to remove Wallace from the ticket.[92] These tactics could and did create mistrust, resentment, anger, and hurt feelings.

Moreover, Roosevelt's duplicity carried over into his method of administration. He sometimes contrived to produce overlapping bureaucratic authority, with different agencies and departments believing that he had put

---

D. Roosevelt, George F. Kennan, and Dean G. Acheson, New York: Cambridge University Press, 1994, p. 20. Roosevelt's personal secretary Marguerite "Missy" LeHand said that he "was really incapable of personal friendship with anyone." Leebaert, *op. cit.*, p. 39.

them in charge of the same areas of policy.[93] This tactic enhanced the control he could exercise, by playing one party off against another, but it could sow confusion and was hardly a formula for administrative efficiency.

Yet all things considered, he was good at his job.[94] He kept himself well informed about the issues, foreign and domestic, with which he had to deal.[95] He made the decisions the he needed to make, and on the whole these decisions served him and the country well: the New Deal was enacted into law and it eased the worst effects of the Depression; and the United States, with its allies, won the Second World War. Measured by the results he achieved, Roosevelt counts as a superb leader.

His success as president rested on his success as an electoral politician; and, with his four victories in presidential contests, he earned the distinction of being the most successful politician in American history. Winning those elections required winning the affection, the respect, or at least the votes, of millions of people. As with individuals whom he encountered directly, Roosevelt was able to establish a sense of personal connection with the public at large.

He made good use of a new technology, radio, on which he relied to circumvent the nation's largely Republican-owned newspapers by speaking directly to the American people.[96] As president, he delivered occasional radio addresses on the major issues of the day that became known as "Fireside Chats." As the name implies, they gave listeners the sense that the president was speaking personally to them in the comfort and intimacy of their living rooms. He had a knack for choosing homely but vivid figures of speech to communicate his points. Among the most celebrated of them was his reference to a garden hose in his remarks promoting the Lend-Lease program:

> Suppose my neighbor's home catches fire . . . if he can take my garden hose and connect it up with his hydrant, I may help him to put out his fire. Now, what do I do? I don't say to him before that operation, "neighbor, my garden hose cost me $15; you have got to pay me $15 for it." . . . I don't want $15—I want my garden hose back after the fire is over. . . . In other words, if you lend certain munitions and get the munitions back at the end of the war, . . . you are all right.[97]

His public addresses had a powerful impact. They enhanced his popularity, which formed the basis for his political effectiveness. Because of what he said to them directly, large numbers of American felt a personal tie to him. The Hoover White House employed one person to respond to letters addressed to the president. After Roosevelt took office, the number assigned to this task increased to seventy.[98] Beyond popularity, Roosevelt's speeches, and his public image more generally, generated widespread trust in both his motives and his judgment. **

Hitler and Churchill also made electronic means of communication central to their methods of leadership, but for different purposes. Hitler delivered a message of anger and hatred, Churchill one of resolution and defiance. The message that Roosevelt's audience received, the sentiment that he successfully cultivated, was confidence:[99] confidence in him, in themselves, in their country, and in the future. In his first Inaugural Address, he told the country: "Let me assert my firm belief that the only thing we have to fear is fear itself." During and as a result of the New Deal, and during and as a result of what the United States did in World War II, Americans did recover their confidence.[100] That was the most important consequence of Franklin D. Roosevelt's leadership.

A particular question hovers over any assessment of Roosevelt's leadership, and indeed of his political career and his life: what difference did his polio make? It surely had a substantial impact. It is hard to imagine a more severe blow to someone entering the prime of his life and accustomed to vigorous physical activity than being deprived of the use of his legs, thus rendering him, for many basic human activities, helpless. In the confessional political climate of the third decade of the twenty-first century, anyone in his position would have to respond to inquiries about it. With norms of privacy for public figures far more restrictive in the first half of the last century, Franklin D. Roosevelt did not have to do so.

Nor is there any record of his personal reflections on what had befallen him. Some who knew him, and others who studied his life, have concluded that his condition made him more serious, more determined, more patient, and more compassionate than he had been before the summer of 1921.[101] Such speculation makes sense, but there is no record of Roosevelt himself having said anything to this effect.

** ". . . the secret of [Roosevelt's] political genius was that he knew exactly what the public needed to hear. It amounted to . . . a personal declaration by the President that took into account the feelings of the people, and especially their fears." Saul Bellow, "In the Days of Mr. Roosevelt," in Bellow, *It All Adds Up: From the Dim Past to the Uncertain Future*, New York: Viking, 1994, p. 23.

It is also logical to suppose that, in the depths of the Great Depression, the public saw him as a living metaphor for the nation as a whole: stricken by a cruel and arbitrary affliction, just as America had been stricken by the Depression, he pulled himself together and overcame it, encouraging millions of Americans to believe that this was possible for them as well.[102] His polio, and the way he managed to adapt to it, could well have served as a source of inspiration and hope for an economically ravaged people.

The difficulty with such an interpretation is that in the 1920s, 1930s, and 1940s it was possible to conceal a handicap such as his, and he made every effort to do so. He could walk, after a fashion and with help, and stand at a lectern, and on major public occasions that is what he did. He did not allow himself to be photographed in a wheelchair, or permit pictures to be taken of the heavy metal leg braces he wore in public.[103] Just how many Americans knew of his handicap is unknown, but it is likely that most did not.[104] How it would have affected his public career if, as would certainly be the case in the present century, the wider public had been aware of his condition, is a question that cannot be answered.

The Personal Imprint

The New Deal stands as the great domestic achievement of the Roosevelt era. It counts as Franklin Roosevelt's personal achievement, but not his alone. National legislation in the United States requires collaboration between the executive and legislative branches of the American government, which is seldom entirely smooth, and with the public as a whole at least indirectly involved as well. The president played a crucial role in each of these arenas.

The proposals for New Deal legislation emanated from the executive branch, which Roosevelt, as the chief executive, controlled. Like all presidents he nominated, and could fire, everyone who worked in it: they were his appointees. He relied on them to propose ideas and draft laws embodying them. He himself, however, decided which ideas should go forward and when and how to present them to the Congress, where the Constitution requires majority votes in both the House of Representatives and the Senate to turn a bill into a law.

Once they were submitted to Congress, the White House had to steer the proposals through committees to reach the floors of the two bodies for votes on them. Here, the president acted as navigator and salesman.

He assumed responsibility, along with Vice President Garner—who, as a former speaker, knew the House of Representatives well[105]—for persuading members of Congress to support what he proposed. Although the legislation could pass with only the votes of members of his own Democratic Party, which held the majority in both chambers, such support did not always come easily. Congressmen and senators operate more independently of party discipline in the United States than do legislators in other political systems—the British one for example. Roosevelt could not count on automatic majorities for whatever he submitted: he had to work, and to make compromises and adopt congressional suggestions, to obtain the necessary votes.[106]

Public attitudes also affected the fate of his legislation. A member of Congress's vote on a particular bill depended, then as now, on that person's perception of how favorably his or her constituency regarded it. Professional politicians ordinarily place a high premium on securing reelection to the offices they hold. This disposes them to conform to the wishes of the voters, who have the power to prolong or end their careers as public officials. Here, Roosevelt's robust popularity made a difference. His sponsorship of legislative proposals, especially in his first term, generally assured public approval of them; and public approval inclined legislators to vote for them.

To obtain the passage of the various elements of the New Deal, therefore, Roosevelt relied on his judgment about what the country needed and what the political traffic would bear. He also relied on his formidable powers of persuasion, which he applied to members of Congress but also, through his Fireside Chats, to the American public. These are essentially political skills.[107] While the Great Depression created the context in which the New Deal became politically feasible, it did not pass by itself. The country's dire economic conditions made possible the sweeping changes that it embodied, but President Roosevelt's political skills—as formidable and effective as those deployed by any American president—made the New Deal a reality.

It had an enormous impact on American life. The maximal assessment of its impact credits it with having saved capitalism and democracy in the United States. In 1933, the influential English economist John Maynard Keynes wrote to Roosevelt that the president had become

the trustee for those in every country who seek to mend the evils of our condition by reasoned experiment within the framework of the

existing social system. If you fail, rational change will be gravely preju-
diced throughout the world, leaving orthodoxy and revolution to fight
it out.[108]

Certainly, the New Deal stabilized the economy and upheld the political
order. In the 1930s, a number of American political figures in the United
States gained significant followings by promising far more radical economic changes than Roosevelt implemented. They included Huey Long,
governor of, and later senator from Louisiana, whose "Share Our Wealth"
program promised every family a household grant of $5,000 and various
other benefits; Francis Townsend, a California physician whose Townsend
Plan proposed to furnish a monthly stipend of $200 to every American
over the age of 60; the novelist Upton Sinclair, who ran for governor of
California on a platform he called End Poverty in California (EPIC), the
terms of which included forming workers' and farmers' cooperatives to
control idle factories and land; and Father Charles Coughlin of Detroit,
an antisemitic priest with a large radio audience whose National Union for
Social Justice called for the nationalization of major industries.[109]

The success of the New Deal limited the political traction each of them
was able to gain.[110] In some European countries, by contrast, the Great
Depression did destroy democracy. Whether or not Franklin D. Roosevelt
actually saved democratic government and the free-market economic
system in the United States, he certainly provided both with useful protection in dangerous times. [††]

In conducting the nation's foreign policy, Roosevelt had more leeway,
because his office had more power, than he did in domestic affairs. Yet
whereas in instituting the New Deal he acted boldly, from the late 1930s
until Pearl Harbor, in matters of foreign policy he proceeded with cau-
tion: he enjoyed a tailwind in public opinion in the first case but confronted
a headwind in the second. The American people wanted to combat the
effects of the Depression and were willing to support major—indeed, by
the standards of American history, radical—measures for that purpose. By

---

[††] Leebaert, *op. cit.*, pp. 54–55. Roosevelt singled out big businessmen—individual
capitalists—as his political adversaries but never the capitalist system itself. Nor was it true,
as his political opponents sometimes charged, that in criticizing business, he was acting as
a traitor to his class. He saw himself as a gentleman farmer not a businessman, and indeed
had some of the disdain for commerce (his personal commercial initiatives did not succeed) that British aristocrats, who lived off the land they owned, had for upstart merchants.

contrast, although the public sympathized with Great Britain and France rather than Germany as their quarrel escalated and ultimately erupted in open warfare, most Americans remained, until the moment that Japan attacked Hawaii, opposed to the United States becoming directly involved in the fighting in either Europe or Asia.

The direction of Roosevelt's policy was clear. With the destroyers-for-bases deal, the Lend-Lease law, and the naval operations in the northwest Atlantic, he wanted to give as much assistance as possible to those opposing Nazi Germany and to oppose, as well, Japan's depredations in China. He proceeded in that direction, however, at an uneven pace, one that was slower than the British and some of his countrymen wished. He was always mindful of the example of Woodrow Wilson, whose foreign policy after World War I failed for lack of public support.[111] Roosevelt was guided by the need not to get too far ahead of public sentiment; and until December 7, 1941, the public seemed more reluctant to become involved in European affairs than was the president. [++]

It was telling that Roosevelt frequently justified what the United States was doing for Great Britain as part of a policy of strengthening the British so that they could win the war by themselves, thereby avoiding the pattern of World War I in which America sent troops to fight on the continent.[112] His country did not, of course, avoid fighting in the war; but the military and economic assistance Roosevelt caused to be sent to Britain and, after June 22, 1941, to the Soviet Union, helped them avoid defeat at the hands of Nazi Germany until the moment when the United States joined them in active combat. The president's leadership was indispensable in getting them that assistance.

When the United States officially entered the war, Roosevelt acquired even more personal authority, as the American president does in wartime as the constitutionally designated commander-in-chief of the armed forces.[113] Having served in a high position involving military affairs in World War I, and with his extensive familiarity with Europe, he had had more previous experience relevant to that job than any other American president.

[++] Historians have debated whether Roosevelt could have moved farther faster to aid Britain without forfeiting public support for himself and his policies. For the case that he could have so moved, see Lynne Olson, *Those Angry Days: Roosevelt, Lindbergh, and America's Fight Over World War II, 1939–1941*, New York: Random House Trade Paperback Edition, 2014, pp. 193, 344. For the contrary position, see John A. Thompson, *A Sense of Power: The Roots of America's Global Role*, Ithaca, New York: Cornell University Press, 2015, p. 155.

He exercised his authority judiciously, intervening in military matters less often, and meeting with his senior commanders less frequently,[114] than did his wartime counterparts Hitler, Stalin, and Churchill. Roosevelt did, however, make the important decisions about American war policy, and what he decided regularly encountered opposition, often from the country's military leaders. The dissent that these decisions elicited make it all the more impressive that in retrospect they largely appear to have redounded to the benefit of the United States and its wartime goals.

Before December 7, 1941, Roosevelt sent military supplies to Britain in the face of doubts that, in the wake of the fall of France, the British could avoid being conquered by Germany and despite objections, then and later, from American military leaders that the weaponry the United States was shipping across the Atlantic was urgently needed by America's own armed forces.[115] His decision, after the Germans launched Operation Barbarossa, to dispatch military assistance to the Soviet Union[116] similarly encountered opposition, not only on the grounds that the Red Army would not be able to hold out against the *Wehrmacht* and that the United States itself needed the weaponry but also on the basis of widespread dislike of the Soviet regime among Americans, in particular for its assaults on religion.[117]

Roosevelt's greatest strategic failure came before the attack on Pearl Harbor, and indeed helped to trigger the attack. He wanted to avoid direct military conflict with Japan in order to be able to concentrate on Europe. His policies toward the Japanese, however, and particularly the total embargo on the sale of American oil to them in the summer of 1941, unintentionally contributed to the Japanese government's decision to launch an assault on the United States in Hawaii.[118]

Despite the fact that that attack came from an Asian power with which, as of December 8, 1941, the United States was at war, Roosevelt chose to give priority to the European theater. He approved sending the American army first to North Africa and then to Italy even though those campaigns qualified as diversions from the main business in Europe: attacking and defeating Germany.[119] This particular decision stemmed from the need to attend to the principal responsibility of any American commander-in-chief in wartime: keeping his country committed to the fighting. Roosevelt calculated that maintaining such a commitment required that the American public see its army in action in 1942, when an invasion of northern Europe was not militarily feasible.[120]

At the Casablanca Conference with Winston Churchill in 1943, Roosevelt demanded that Germany surrender unconditionally, a demand that came as a surprise in some quarters. It was intended to assure Stalin that the democracies would prosecute the war to the end rather than making a separate peace with Hitler at Soviet expense,[121] and signaled a determination to avoid what then seemed to have been a mistake at the end of World War I. At that time, the failure to occupy Germany had made it possible for Germans to claim that the German army had not really been defeated on the battlefield, but rather had been "stabbed in the back" by perfidious politicians, a claim that Hitler emphasized and exploited.[122]

The main military thrust at Germany via France had to be preceded by a large-scale amphibious landing on the French coast, and Roosevelt resisted pressure from Stalin to launch it in 1942 and 1943—the correct decision in retrospect—because the American armed forces were not prepared for such an ambitious operation; but he then overruled Churchill's wish to postpone it further, which would have prolonged the war, and settled on 1944 for what became Operation Overlord.

Roosevelt also did well in choosing his senior military leaders. He personally selected George C. Marshall to be the army's chief of staff in 1939,[123] and Marshall performed superbly in that position, coming to be known as "the organizer of victory." He designated Dwight D. Eisenhower as the supreme commander of Overlord. Marshall had wanted the assignment, but Roosevelt decided that it required considerable political skill, since it involved coordinating a number of military leaders with strong personalities, and he considered "Ike" to be the best politician among the generals. Eisenhower, like Marshall, justified Roosevelt's faith in him.[124] The president created a separate command for General Douglas MacArthur in the southwest Pacific out of a sense of obligation to recapture the Philippines, which Japan had overrun in early 1942, but also because of his wariness of MacArthur, a military man with political ambitions of his own. Keeping him out of the country and fully occupied suited Roosevelt's political purposes.[125]

Two other wartime decisions affected the course of the war in its final months and had an even greater impact on the postwar period. The president authorized the Manhattan Project, a large, secret, and expensive program to produce weapons based on unlocking the energy at the heart of matter.[126] A different chief executive might not have grasped the importance of what scientists told Roosevelt about the military potential of atomic energy, or might have been reluctant to commit resources on so large a scale, in the midst of a great war, to an enterprise that was not guaranteed to succeed. The atomic bomb brought the war in the Pacific to a conclusion without an invasion of the Japanese archipelago, and nuclear weapons profoundly shaped military strategy and great-power relations in the postwar world.[127]

Roosevelt's replacement of Henry Wallace by Harry Truman as vice president in his fourth term also had major and unforeseen consequences. Truman presided over the postwar policies that, in concert with (and in response to) those of the Soviet Union, led to the Cold War. Wallace had a more benign view than did Truman of America's wartime ally and thought it more important to perpetuate the wartime cooperation with Stalin. Indeed, Wallace became so disenchanted with Truman's policies that he ran against him as an independent candidate for president in 1948, losing badly, with members of the Moscow-dominated American Communist Party playing major roles in his campaign. Had Wallace and not Truman become president when Roosevelt died, American policy toward the Soviet Union might well have taken a different course, at least for a time.

During the war, Roosevelt also acted as America's chief diplomat. He dealt directly with other leaders and here, too, what he did and what he did not manage to do had a pronounced effect on events. His most intensive personal diplomacy involved the prime minister of Great Britain. The two men had some things in common: upper-class backgrounds, reformist impulses in domestic politics, and experience supervising their countries' navies. Above all, they shared a deep personal commitment to defeating Nazi Germany.

They also had differences. Roosevelt opposed the perpetuation of the British Empire, to whose continued existence Churchill was passionately devoted.[128] Churchill wished to avoid committing forces to a cross-Channel landing in France and a subsequent confrontation with the Germany army in northwest Europe for as long as possible—perhaps indefinitely. Roosevelt considered such a strategy essential for winning the war.

Above all, however, the two men knew that they needed each other, because the closest possible Anglo-American cooperation was indispensable to securing the goal of supreme importance to both of them: victory. While their affection for each other was sometimes exaggerated,[129] what mattered for their relationship was the mutual understanding they needed to make it work. They did so,[130] for which both deserve credit.

The president and the prime minister disagreed about two other national leaders, and in retrospect Churchill's judgment appears superior to Roosevelt's. Churchill found General Charles de Gaulle, the leader of the French during the war, a difficult person with whom to deal but also recognized the importance of having an independent French leader in exile and supported de Gaulle in that role. Roosevelt, by contrast, took a disliking to the Frenchman, suspecting him of dictatorial ambitions, and at first gave him little attention or respect.[131] De Gaulle turned out, despite (or perhaps because of) his abrasive personality, to be the man that France and the Western democracies needed.

Roosevelt had a higher regard than did Churchill, by contrast, for the Chinese leader, Chiang Kai-shek.[132] The United States provided military support to Chiang's forces that were opposing Japan in China despite accurate reports of the incompetence of his commanders and the corruption of his regime. To be sure, the president had good reasons for trying to bolster Chiang. Chinese troops engaged a large Japanese force that might otherwise have been deployed elsewhere against the Allies.[133] Moreover, Roosevelt's vision of a postwar world kept in order by the "Four Policemen"—the United States, Great Britain, the Soviet Union, and China—presumed a major role for the Chinese government in Asia.[134] As with de Gaulle, Roosevelt did modify his view of Chiang as the war went on, but overall his direct dealings with the Chinese leader did little to achieve American goals in Asia either during the war or afterward.

Like Churchill, Roosevelt tried, through correspondence and two personal encounters at Tehran and Yalta, to establish a cordial personal relationship with Josef Stalin. The president sought at first to ensure that the Soviet Union would remain in the war against Hitler. As victory drew closer, he tried to cultivate the Soviet dictator, even going so far as to seem to side with Stalin against Churchill,[135] to ensure that the Red Army would participate in the anticipated invasion of Japan[136] and that the politics of postwar Europe would be as acceptable as possible to the United States. He knew that the Soviet Union would have a powerful presence there and assumed—wrongly, as it turned out—that the American troops on the continent would all return home and stay home, making Soviet good will exceptionally important. He devoted particular attention at Yalta to attempting to preserve maximal independence for Poland, a country that the Red Army occupied on its way to Berlin.[137]

Roosevelt did not bring Stalin around to his way of thinking on Poland or Eastern Europe more generally. Nor, such evidence as there is of Stalin's thoughts suggests, did the president establish a personal rapport with the Soviet dictator. Roosevelt seems to have overestimated the impact of his powers of persuasion and his personal charm, which had served him well in American politics, on someone very different from the bureaucrats, legislators, and voters of the United States.[138] As the subsequent unfolding of the Cold War was to show, Roosevelt's efforts with Stalin, like Churchill's, failed; but other approaches, by them or other leaders of their countries, probably would not have succeeded either.[139]

In the end, the Allies did win the war, and their victory counts as perhaps the most important development of the twentieth century. The United States made a major, indeed indispensable, contribution to that outcome, sending military supplies to Great Britain and the Soviet Union to help prevent Nazi Germany from conquering them, launching a second front in Europe, driving into Germany, and defeating Japan in the Asia-Pacific theater. As the American president, Franklin D. Roosevelt decisively shaped the American war effort and thereby left a deep personal imprint on the history of his times. With the New Deal, he changed America. Through the war, he changed the world.

The Legacy

The Roosevelt era changed the balance of partisan power in American politics. From the Civil War until 1932, the Republican Party had almost always controlled the presidency[140] and had held majorities in the Congress. From 1932 through 1964, Roosevelt's Democrats won seven of the nine presidential elections and controlled both houses of Congress for most of that time. Roosevelt added the major industrial states to what was known as the "solid South" in his electoral coalition, and that coalition had a long life. From 1968 through 1988, while the Republicans won four of the five presidential contests, with that coalition the Democrats held the House of Representatives continuously until 1994 and the Senate for most of that time.

The Republicans dominated the seven decades after 1860 because they had pursued what the country deemed to be the correct policy during one of the formative events in American history—the Civil War. The Great Depression had a similar impact on American voting habits and this time the Democrats, the sponsors of the New Deal, earned the gratitude and trust of the electorate. The response to the Great Depression, for which Franklin D. Roosevelt had the primary responsibility, had as great an effect on politics as on policy. The Republicans eventually established something like political parity with the Democrats,[141] but they did so by accepting, in its broad outlines, what the Democrats had accomplished between 1933 and 1936. Dwight D. Eisenhower broke the Democratic grip on the White House in 1952 because of his credentials in military and foreign policy but also because he made it clear that he would not attempt to abolish the programs that the Roosevelt administration had put in place.[142]

So sweeping were the goals and institutions of governance wrought by the New Deal and World War II that they brought into being a third version of the American republic.[§§] The first, which bound thirteen separate British colonies scattered along the Atlantic coast of North America into a single democratic state, emerged from the Revolutionary War. The victory of the Union over the Confederacy in the Civil War gave birth to the second republic, which eliminated the chattel slavery that was radically inconsistent with principles upon which the first one had been founded and set the United States on the path to becoming a dynamic urban and industrial country.

Roosevelt presided over the creation of a third American republic, whose defining characteristic is a far more extensive, intrusive, and ambitious federal government than the country had had in its first century and a half of existence. That government regulates a wide variety of activities and furnishes a social safety net for American citizens[143] that notably includes Social Security as well as government-assured health care for those aged 65 and older, a benefit that was added in 1965. In the third republic, the federal government also has responsibility for moderating the vicissitudes of the economy as a whole, an undertaking tentatively begun, although not officially embraced, in the Roosevelt years.[144]

The expansion of the federal government turned its home, Washington, D.C., from a sleepy Southern town into a bustling, wealthy metropolis dotted with the kind of grand public buildings found in the great capitals of Europe such as London and Paris. What Washington became and, of greater importance, the significance of what happens there, are legacies of Franklin D. Roosevelt.

[§§] I owe the following analysis to James Kurth.

He did not leave to the wider world the legacy that he had intended. Postwar international politics turned out not to conform to his vision for it. While not a wholehearted, uncritical Wilsonian, he had enough regard for Wilson's ideas to act as the moving force behind the establishment of the United Nation; but such peace as the planet enjoyed after World War II had little to do with the efforts of that organization. His idea of the four policemen—the United States, Great Britain, China, and the Soviet Union—cooperating to keep the peace[145] came to nothing. Britain fell out of the first rank of global powers, Chiang's China had not belonged there in the first place, and the two countries that remained, whose military might and global political reach made them "superpowers,"[146] did not cooperate with each other.

The Cold War disappointed Roosevelt's hope for at least a *modus vivendi* between the democracies and Stalin's communist state. Whether, had the president lived to serve out his fourth term, the two countries would have had a more cordial relationship and, relatedly, whether Roosevelt himself would have taken the tack that Harry Truman adopted or instead pursued the course that Henry Wallace preferred, are frequently posed questions that do not, of course, admit of definitive answers.

It is perhaps worth noting, however, that Franklin Roosevelt, for all his efforts at conciliation and accommodation, was not naïve about Stalin or the communist system. He would, had he lived, have experienced and had to respond to the Soviet initiatives in Central and Eastern Europe that turned the Soviet Union, in American eyes, from an ally into an adversary. He would, in addition, have surrounded himself with at least some of the advisors who counseled Truman to pursue the policies he did. It is worth remembering as well that, personalities aside, the hostility between the United States and the Soviet Union had deep political roots.[147]

Yet Roosevelt did leave his mark on American foreign policy. The institutions through which the United States conducted it after 1945, and in particular with which it waged the Cold War, carried over from World War II or were reassembled in its aftermath. Foremost among them was the War Department, renamed the Department of Defense, housed across the Potomac River from the Capitol in the Pentagon, the largest office building in the world that was constructed in sixteen months from September 1941 to January 1943.

Roosevelt's foreign-policy legacy includes, as well, the fusion of two distinct American approaches to the world. One of them, favored by

Theodore Roosevelt, emphasizes the centrality of power in international relations, the inevitability of war, and the consequent need for formidable armed forces. Although he sometimes seemed to glorify armed conflict, the first President Roosevelt appreciated the importance of peace but believed that the best way to assure it was through a stable balance of power between and among countries. He endeavored, during his presidency, to contrive such a balance in East Asia.[148] Woodrow Wilson, the apostle of the other approach, sought to abolish war by transforming both sovereign states so that the people who inhabited them had the power to choose their governments, and the international system as a whole, for which his favored vehicle was the League of Nations.[149]

Franklin Roosevelt knew and admired both men and combined their different outlooks in his own foreign policy.[150] He understood the significance of military and political power but he also embraced Wilsonian principles such as national self-determination, which was expressed in his opposition to European empires. The Atlantic Charter that he and Churchill signed included a number of these principles, incorporating some of Wilson's Fourteen Points.[151] His version of a Wilsonian international organization, the United Nations, partook of both approaches. It had universal membership but also an important subdivision, the Security Council, where the most powerful countries held sway. From his time onward, American foreign policy, under all his successors, included elements of both traditions. The United States built a formidable military force and deployed it first to defeat Nazi Germany and then to counterbalance the Communist bloc led by the Soviet Union; but the country also never abandoned the aspiration to remake the world along Wilsonian lines and indeed made periodic efforts to do so.[152]

When the United States confronted undemocratic regimes seeking to increase the territories under their control and their political influence, as in the Second World War and the Cold War, it was possible to pursue the two approaches simultaneously. At other times, the two coexisted uneasily or even were in conflict, as when America aligned itself with undemocratic regimes for the sake of offsetting a more powerful common adversary.[153] The fidelity to both, and the unwillingness to sacrifice either, however, which began with Franklin Roosevelt, endured.

Finally, the second President Roosevelt wanted the United States to play a prominent role in world affairs after the war and so it did, although it was not precisely the role he had envisioned. The extensive political and military engagement after 1945 owed a great deal to Josef Stalin, of course, but America's global presence had an economic dimension as well, the basis for which was laid in the Roosevelt era. His administration passed and then reauthorized the Reciprocal Trade Administration Act, which served as the legal charter for the substantial increase in American international trade in the 1950s and thereafter.[154] It took the lead in writing, at a conference in Bretton Woods, New Hampshire, in the summer of 1944, the rules that governed postwar cross-border flows of money in the first postwar decades, an activity in which, like trade, the United States became deeply engaged.[155]

The expansive American participation in global affairs in peacetime after 1945 broke with the precedents of American foreign policy[156] as sharply as the New Deal had departed from the earlier norms of American domestic governance. That global role affected, sometimes decisively, every international issue and the foreign policy of every other country in the world; and it had its origins in the ideas and the policies of Franklin Delano Roosevelt.

6

Mohandas Karamchand Gandhi

The Life

Mohandas Karamchand Gandhi was born on October 2, 1869, in the city of Porbandar in Gujarat, a western part of British India located on the Indian Ocean. In the stratified social order of the subcontinent known as the caste system,[1] his family belonged to the Modh Bania *jati*, or subcaste. Its members customarily earned their livings as merchants, but Gandhi's father, like his father before him, was employed in the service of the local native ruler.[2] The Modh Banias occupied a middle position in the caste system: they were not situated at the top, but Gandhi's family had a relatively comfortable existence, more so than the vast majority of Indians.

Mohandas received his schooling locally and was married, following the Indian custom, at the age of 13 to a girl a few months older: the marriage would produce four sons and last for 61 years until her death in 1944. In 1888, at age 19, he traveled to London to take up the study of law, which was thought likely to assure him a good position in the local government when he returned.[3]

In London, he found himself in a far more cosmopolitan environment than the one in which he had been raised. He met people and was exposed to ideas he would never have encountered had he stayed at home. He lived frugally and walked everywhere, a habit he maintained as much as possible for the rest of his life.[4] There he adopted his first cause: vegetarianism. While growing up, he had avoided meat and eggs out of religious custom, but in London he concluded that such a diet had wider benefits, of which the public should be made aware.[5]

Most importantly for his subsequent career, his sojourn in the capital of the British Empire began his lifelong devotion to the never-ending task of personal spiritual improvement. He came to regard himself, even—indeed especially—when he was deeply involved in the movement for Indian independence, as less a political leader than a pilgrim, seeking the way of truth.

He qualified as a lawyer and returned to India, but his legal career did not prosper there. For that reason, in 1893 he accepted an assignment in South Africa, to which, since it was part of the Empire, Indians could move in search of economic opportunity. He agreed to work for businessmen originally from Gujarat (Muslims, not Hindus, as it happened) who needed someone with legal training who could function in both the English and the Gujarati languages. He intended his time in that country to be brief, a year at most. He remained, ultimately to be joined by his wife and family, for twenty-one.[6]

In South Africa, he became involved in efforts to defend the position of Indians living there against the policies of the local, all-white government. He lobbied and petitioned the government on behalf of the Indian community. He did not demand all the rights of citizenship—the right to vote, for instance. He acted, moreover, as a loyal subject of the British Empire. During the Boer War (1899–1902), he organized a corps of stretcher-bearers to help provide medical support for the British Army in its successful fight to control all of South Africa.[7]

In 1906, for the purpose of restricting Indian immigration—South African whites resented economic competition from hard-working Indians[8]—the government of the state of Transvaal passed an ordinance requiring everyone of South Asian origin to register with the government and to carry the registration certification at all times. Gandhi objected, and after failing to persuade the authorities to revoke the ordinance he announced that Indians would refuse to obey it. He declared that he himself was willing to go to jail rather than comply with the new law. At the end of the following year he was tried and convicted and, in July, 1908, sent to prison.[9]

Thus began the technique that would make Mohandas Gandhi world-renowned and would have a pronounced impact on the history of South Asia and significant effects on the course of public policy in other parts of the world during the twentieth century.[10] Initially called passive resistance, it came to be known as "civil disobedience." Gandhi had his own term for it, derived from the Sanskrit language: *satyagraha*, which means, roughly, "truth force."

It involved openly and peacefully violating a law considered unjust and voluntarily accepting the legal consequences of doing so, often incarceration. It had as its purpose protesting a particular law while respecting the principle of the rule of law, with the hope of persuading those responsible for the law to change it. While the decision to commit an act of satyagraha was (and is) always an individual one, in South Africa, and later, on a far larger scale, in India, Gandhi inspired and led many who engaged in it. In addition, while the Indian community in South Africa came from different regions, religions, and castes, he managed to unite most of them in opposition to the registration law. He created, that is, an ecumenical movement.

In 1913, he mounted another satyagraha campaign, this one involving indentured laborers from India. The legislature had passed laws designed to limit their numbers by, among other measures, encouraging, through a special tax, their return to India after the end of the contracts that had brought them to South Africa. Gandhi led more than 2,000 previously politically inactive miners on a strike, and the strike spread to include other Indians as well. The episode broadened the constituency for his method of protest to encompass the poorest members of the Indian community, with whom he had previously had little contact. He was arrested three times in three days and spent six weeks in jail.[11]

In his years in South Africa, Gandhi's interests and activities went beyond satyagraha. Having adopted English customs and ideas while in London, he began to reconsider them and moved toward a simpler style of life. He founded two communities to put into practice the values and the manner of living to which he was drawn. He began the practice of periodically fasting, both for the purpose of spiritual renewal and later, in India, in the service of political goals.[12] He also founded a newspaper, *Indian Opinion*,[13] and wrote extensively for it while keeping up a large volume of correspondence. His name became increasingly well known in India and he established connections with influential people there, in particular with Gopal Krishna Gokhale, a prominent figure in the new national movement in the country.[14]

In 1909, Gandhi published a short book entitled *Hind Swaraj* (Indian Self-Government). In it, he not only advocated the goal expressed in the title but also laid out in detail the economic and social views at which he had arrived, which rejected much of what the British, the Industrial Revolution, and modernity in general had brought to the Indian subcontinent.[15]

Having found his life's vocation in service to Indians, he decided to pursue it in the mother country and left South Africa for India, arriving at the beginning of 1915. His sojourn on the African continent had transformed him. He had come as an Anglicized lawyer. He left as a trail-blazing social and political activist with far different ideas about the proper values and customs of social and economic life than those with which he had arrived. His change of dress expressed this transformation. Upon arrival he had worn the kind of suit appropriate to an aspiring British lawyer. By the time he left he had adopted the standard dress of rural India, a loin-cloth and a shawl. He had become the person who, over the next three decades, would leave his mark on the history of the twentieth century.

Gandhi spent his first year back in India reacquainting himself with his native land.[16] Or rather, he acquainted himself with much of it for the first time since his previous experience had been confined to the western part of the country and to a narrow stratum of Indian society. He visited places he had never seen and made contact with poor Indians, whom he had not previously encountered. He founded an ashram, like the two communities he had established in South Africa, a place for people to conduct their lives in the simple manner that he considered spiritually healthy.[17] He became involved in three local issues. In 1917, he sought to help peasants in Bihar, in the northern part of the country, who were being forced to grow indigo, a plant from which dye is extracted, on disadvantageous terms.[18] There, his civil disobedience consisted of refusing an order to leave the district. The following year he supported farmers in his home territory of Gujarat in a dispute with the government and organized a workers' strike against textile mill owners in the Gujarati city of Ahmedabad.[19]

In the wake of World War I, the British government instituted, with the Montagu-Chelmsford Reforms, political changes that gave Indians wider participation in governing their country,[20] thereby initiating a process that would culminate, three decades later, in the end of British rule on the subcontinent. At the same time, however, the British passed the Rowlatt Act, which extended and enhanced the emergency powers the government had wielded during the war.[21] The protests against the Rowlatt Act made Gandhi a prominent figure throughout the subcontinent.[22]

One protest took place in the city of Amritsar in the Punjab in northwest India, on April 13, 1919. There, a crowd of at least 10,000 people gathered in a semi-enclosed area known as the Jallianwallah Bagh. The assembly was entirely peaceful, but violence had erupted in the city a few days earlier. A British general, fearing that the gathering would turn into an insurrection, ordered his troops to fire on the crowd. Approximately 380 Indians died and 1,200 more were wounded.[23] The episode shocked and angered Indians throughout the country, all the more so because many British officials in India and much of the British public itself supported the general.[24]

The events of 1919 strengthened the position of those Indians who wanted to end British rule. This, in turn, endowed the principal organization in the subcontinent committed to Indian self-government, the Indian National Congress, with increased importance. The Congress had begun in 1895 as an association of well-educated, Westernized Indians, many of them high-caste Hindus.[25] The independence movement came to harbor two different approaches to achieving its goal. Those of a moderate bent counted on petitioning and lobbying the British authorities, while others preferred more radical, confrontational tactics.*

Gandhi assumed a leading role in the Congress and brought with him his technique of satyagraha, which offered a middle path between the two approaches—more aggressive than the policies the moderates wanted to follow but without the violence that radical initiatives risked. He introduced another innovation that ultimately made the Congress a formidable political force. He transformed it from a small club of the Indian elite into a mass movement[26] that was capable of exerting far greater leverage on India's British rulers than the pre-Gandhi Congress had been able to muster.

As he moved to the center of Indian public affairs in the early 1920s, Gandhi took up a cause dear to the hearts of some of his countrymen. The fall of the Ottoman Empire as a consequence of World War I had unseated its leader, the sultan, who had also been regarded in some quarters as the

---

* B. R. Nanda, *In Search of Gandhi: Essays and Reflections*, New Delhi: Oxford University Press, 2002, p. 73; Ramachandra Guha, *Gandhi: The Years That Changed the World, 1914–1948*, New York: Alfred A. Knopf, 2018, p. xii. A prominent figure among the moderates was Gandhi's friend Gokhale. The leading radical was Bal Gangadhar Tilak. See Stanley Wolpert, *Tilak and Gokhale: Revolution and Reform in the Making of Modern India*, Berkeley, California: The University of California Press, 1962, pp. 299–301. Their deaths—Gokhale's in 1915, Tilak's in 1920—created a vacuum in the leadership of the independence movement that Gandhi did a great deal to fill. Guha, *op. cit.*, p. 108.

political leader of the Muslim world. His domain was called the caliphate, in India the *khilafat*. Indian Muslims came to see the end of the caliphate as a challenge to the religion itself and called for its restoration. Many of them assumed that Great Britain, as a power in the Middle East, could bring this about. In the interest of the kind of Hindu-Muslim solidarity that he had been able to create in South Africa, Gandhi supported the khilafat movement, which did not, however, achieve its aim.[27]

In 1920, he launched a nationwide program of "noncooperation." It rested on the idea that the country's institutions could not function if Indians refused to participate in them. He called, therefore, for government employees in all institutions, from the courts to the military, to leave their jobs and for students to abandon state schools.[28] He expected, and said, that noncooperation would bring swaraj in a year.[29] It did not. Relatively few Indians withdrew from their positions.[30] Gandhi was sent to prison, where he remained for twenty-three months.[31] There he established a routine that he would follow during subsequent periods of incarceration: reading, writing, engaging in wide-ranging correspondence, and occasionally fasting.

He also promoted what he called *swadeshi*. The term meant "self-sufficiency," and for Gandhi it signified the need not only to do without British goods but also to return to the life found in Indian villages that he had come to see as the country's salvation and that the members of his ashram observed. He emphasized the importance of simple, homespun, Indian-made clothing and embarked on a regular routine, including in prison, of spinning cloth himself. The spinning wheel became the symbol of swadeshi.[32]

Gandhi adopted another cause, and a controversial one. In the social and religious hierarchy of the Hindu religion, those at the very bottom were and continue to be known as the "untouchables," so called because for high-caste Hindus mere physical contact with them is considered polluting. Untouchables tend to have the most menial, dirtiest, and least remunerative occupations, and to live under severe social restrictions: in many villages, there were (and still are) temples and other places where they were forbidden to set foot. Gandhi made clear his opposition to the existence of this social category and his conviction that no Indian should be subjected to the indignities and the discrimination that untouchables suffered. He coined his own term for them: *harijans*—"children of God." Although he did not publicly denounce the caste system as a whole, he did call for the abolition of untouchability, which counted as a radical position in a country where traditional religious ideas and practices remained widely popular.[33]

By the end of the 1920s, Mohandas Gandhi had become the most famous and the most revered person in India as well as the most influential Indian. An honorific that the Bengali poet (and Nobel laureate in literature) Rabindranath Tagore initially applied to him[34] came into widespread use. The combination of the Hindi word for "great"—*maha*—and for "soul"—*atma*—made him the Mahatma. His renown spread beyond South Asia. In 1930, the American-based *Time* magazine selected him to be its Man of the Year.

At the end of the decade of the 1920s, the question of how India would be governed, and by whom—that is, what powers Indians themselves would exercise and which ones the British would retain—had become central to the public affairs of the subcontinent, thanks in part to the activities of Gandhi and the Congress. In 1928 a committee of the Congress chaired by Motilal Nehru, a lawyer from northern India and the father of the future prime minister Jawaharlal Nehru, called for dominion status similar to that of Canada and Australia, but a year later the Congress demanded full independence.[35]

To that end Gandhi launched, in 1930, his best-known satyagrahya initiative, an episode known to history as the Salt March. The British government of India obtained some of its revenue from a tax on salt, a commodity that everyone used. Gandhi announced that he would protest the tax in what turned out to be a particularly vivid manner. He would walk 240 miles from Ahmedabad to the coast of the Arabian Sea, which was located in the northern part of the Indian Ocean, gather some salt there, and refuse to pay tax on it. The march, which took place between March and April 1930, captured the imagination of the country. An estimated 2,500 people joined it. After completing it and committing his act of civil disobedience, Gandhi was once again imprisoned.[36]

Meanwhile, the British convened a Round Table Conference in London in November 1930 to discuss India's future with representatives of all sectors of Indian society. The first session having achieved very little, Gandhi was released from prison and represented the Congress at the second session, in 1931.[37] This meeting, too, did not yield a plan for Indian governance to which all parties agreed.

In 1935, therefore, the British parliament, without Indian participation, passed the Government of India Act, which provided for provincial legislatures elected by Indians (on a limited franchise), with the British retaining important powers and prerogatives.[38] The Act led to elections in 1936 and 1937 from which the Congress emerged as the dominant political force in the country.[39]

Even as the Congress and Gandhi were making progress in the struggle with the British, however, they encountered criticism and outright opposition from other Indians. It came most publicly, and ultimately with the farthest-reaching consequences, from Indian Muslims. At the outset of the independence movement, relations between Hindus and Muslims were relatively harmonious, or at least not hostile. Muslims joined the Congress. In the 1920s, political leaders in the two communities began to drift apart on the subject of India's future, and the split widened during the course of the 1930s.[40]

In that decade a London-trained lawyer who practiced in Bombay, Mohammed Ali Jinnah, became the most prominent figure among India's Muslims. He had initially joined the Congress, then resigned and moved to London, then returned to India and began to oppose positions that Congress took. The Congress, and Gandhi in particular, asserted that they represented all Indians—Hindus, Muslims, and all other social and religious categories. Jinnah insisted that only the Muslim League, which had been founded in 1906 and of which he became the leader, could speak for Muslims.[41] He wanted specific provisions for Muslims in any new Indian political order, including reserved seats in legislatures, in order to give them the protection he believed they needed from India's Hindu majority. It did not help matters that Jinnah and Gandhi, although both British-trained lawyers, had poor personal relations.

In the early 1930s, the idea of a separate, independent, Muslim-majority country in South Asia first surfaced, as a proposal by Indian Muslim students in England. The projected country came to be called Pakistan—meaning "land of the pure" and also an acronym for the provinces that were to comprise it.[†] Initially the idea was not taken seriously, but over the course of the decade it began to gain support among the country's Muslims, who constituted about a quarter of India's total population.[42]

[†] Heavily Muslim East Bengal was initially not included. It did ultimately form part of the new country that was created in 1947 but broke away and become independent Bangladesh in 1971.

Opposition to Gandhi came as well from the ranks of the country's untouchables in the person of B. R. Ambedkar, a lawyer educated in both Great Britain and the United States, who represented his community at the London Round Table. Of Gandhi's dislike of untouchability there was no doubt,[43] but Ambedkar believed that he had not made its abolition a sufficiently high priority and was critical as well of Gandhi's failure to oppose the caste system as a whole, of which untouchability was a part.[44] In addition, Ambedkar wanted to reserve places for untouchables in Indian legislatures, a practice entirely unacceptable to Gandhi on the grounds that national groups such as the Congress could adequately represent their interests.[45] In general, Gandhi counted on a change of the prevailing attitudes toward untouchables to relieve their plight. Ambedkar wanted action by the government for this purpose.[46]

A third source of opposition had a lower political profile in the 1930s but played a major role in Gandhi's own life. Decades after his death it became the most potent force in Indian politics: Hindu fundamentalism. Unlike Gandhi, the fundamentalists did not want an India with a government indifferent to religion and tolerant of, indeed hospitable to, other faiths. They believed that it should be an explicitly Hindu country and that non-Hindus living in it would have to accept its sectarian character.[47] They regarded Gandhi—who, although he never renounced Hinduism and was deeply religious in his own way, in important respects was not an orthodox Hindu—as an adversary and an obstacle.

When Great Britain declared war on Germany on September 1, 1939, the British Viceroy, Lord Linlithgow, committed India to the war as well. In making this decision he did not consult the Congress, which responded by insisting that Britain promise complete independence in exchange for Indian support for the war effort. The viceroy offered dominion status but that did not satisfy the Congress, which, at Gandhi's instigation, launched a satyagraha campaign.[48] It involved deliberately violating various wartime regulations, and it spread across India. One prominent member of the Congress, Subhas Chandra Bose, sided with Britain's enemy Japan and devoted himself to recruiting an Indian military force, called the Indian National Army, to assist the Japanese in conquering India.[49]

Fighting for the security of their home islands as well as the preservation of their empire, the British were not disposed to conciliate Gandhi and his colleagues. On August 8, 1942, the Congress passed what came to be known as the "Quit India" resolution, announcing "a mass struggle on non-violent lines on the widest possible scale . . . under the leadership of Gandhiji."[50] Gandhi was arrested and sent to prison, along with most of the Congress leaders.[51] Some of the demonstrations that the resolution triggered turned violent. The British cracked down on them.[52]

The Muslim League did not support the Congress position on the war[53] and, with the Congress leaders imprisoned, faced no competition for the ear of the British and the allegiance of the country's Muslims.[54] Jinnah and the League asserted that British India consisted of two distinct nations—Muslim and Hindu—and that each should, in the spirit of national self-determination, have its own separate political community.[55]

The war itself at first went badly for the British in Asia as well as in Europe. Among other setbacks, the Japanese army drove British forces out of Burma, which brought Japan to the borders of India. To make matters worse, in 1943 Bengal suffered a famine in which more than a million people died,[56] which hardly enhanced Britain's standing among Indians. Eventually, however, in concert with its allies the United States and the Soviet Union and at considerable cost, Britain did manage to win the war.

In the aftermath of the war, a British general election took place that brought to power the Labour Party. Unlike the Conservatives, who had controlled the government from the mid-1930s, Labour sympathized with the Congress and the cause of Indian independence.[57] New elections took place in India in 1946, in which the Congress did well, although the Muslim League dominated the Muslim vote.[58]

The Labour government sent Lord Louis Mountbatten to India as the viceroy in March 1947, and he and the Labour leaders in London concluded that the subcontinent should be divided between a largely Hindu India and a largely Muslim Pakistan.[59] The partition took effect on August 15 of that year. Gandhi had designated a political heir—Jawaharlal Nehru,[60] a British-educated upper-caste Hindu who had himself spent time in prison for his pro-independence activities and who had different ideas about governing independent India from Gandhi's but nonetheless remained steadfastly loyal to him. Nehru became independent India's first prime minister and formed a government. Gandhi himself was not part of it. Nor did he greet independence with joy, because he had strongly opposed dividing British India and because in the previous year massive and deadly communal violence had broken out.[61] The Hindu-Muslim bloodletting had, among other things, made it impossible to keep post-imperial India united.

Gandhi made it his personal mission to try to stop the violence by traveling to the worst-hit areas and appealing for peace by fasting, marching, and meeting with local people. He spent extended time in East Bengal, where Muslims were attacking Hindus, and Bihar, where it was mainly Muslims who were suffering.[62] He did have some success in reducing the violence where he was present,[63] but elsewhere it continued beyond independence and into 1948. On January 30 of that year, Mohandas Gandhi was in Delhi, where a young Hindu fundamentalist accosted him on his way to a prayer meeting and shot him dead.[64]

The Times

Mohandas Gandhi spent all but his final five-and-one-half months as a subject of the British Empire. That Empire had a powerful and pervasive influence on his life and work. As an imperial subject, he was able to live for a time in the imperial capital, London, which changed his life by introducing him to people and ideas he would never have known or known about had he remained in a small town in western India. The scope of British imperial rule made it possible for him then to spend two decades in South Africa, where he developed his views on how economies should be organized and how individuals should live, and discovered his vocation as an agent of political change using nonviolent methods. The Empire furnished him, as well, with the causes for which he became world-renowned and his pursuit of which left a mark on the history of his time: lessening if not abolishing discrimination against Indians in South Africa and ending British rule on the Asian subcontinent.

In London he came in contact with the political culture of Great Britain, with its particular values and institutions, and this served as a source of his ideas. These same values and institutions helped make it possible for him to put those ideas effectively into practice. The tactics the British suffragettes used in campaigning for the right of women to vote, for example, contributed to his development of satyagraha. Britain's commitment to and practice of democracy at home made for a contradiction, since through its imperial rule beyond the home islands (and, before 1922, in Ireland as well), it was denying to Indians and others rights that the British themselves enjoyed.[65] The Indian independence movement exploited that contradiction by pointing out that it was seeking no more than what the

British themselves already enjoyed. In this way the movement gained moral and intellectual power.[66]

Imperial rule rested ultimately on coercion and discrimination, and Gandhi and other imperial subjects experienced that rule as by definition unjust, indeed often oppressive and even cruel. In comparison with other imperial and undemocratic governments elsewhere, however—and empire and autocracy were the rule, not the exception in his era—the British government in India, known as the "raj," counted as relatively restrained. Its relative restraint contributed to what Gandhi was able to achieve. The government of India punished acts of satyagraha when they violated the law, but that government generally followed legal procedures, used—with conspicuous exceptions such as the 1919 shootings in Amritsar—minimal force, and allowed Gandhi and the nationalist movement the freedom to organize. Other imperial powers and autocratic regimes would have crushed the kind of opposition the Congress represented.[†]

The British ruled India in relatively restrained fashion, as well, because there were so few of them on the subcontinent. About 20,000 British personnel had responsibility for governing 300 million Indians. The British needed the tacit acceptance of their presence by the vast majority of Indians and the active collaboration of a smaller but still significant number of them to remain in control.[67] They therefore had to proceed cautiously so as not to drive the people they governed into active and potentially violent opposition, with which, should it take place on a large scale, they would not have been able to cope.[§] The memory of the great Indian Mutiny of 1857, when

---

[†] George Orwell wrote, "It is difficult to see how Gandhi's methods could be applied in a country where opponents of the regime disappear in the middle of the night and are never heard of again. Without a free press and the right of assembly, it is impossible not merely to appeal to outside opinion, but to bring a mass movement into being, or even to make your intentions known to your adversary." Orwell, "Reflections on Gandhi" (1949), in Sonia Orwell and Ian Angus, editors, *The Collected Essays, Journalism and Letters of George Orwell: In Front of Your Nose, 1945–1950*, New York: Harcourt, Brace & World, Inc., 1968, pp. 468–469.

[§] ". . . the structure of [British] rule was as light as possible, and the British saw their role as limited to providing sound government, ready justice, and protecting imperial interests. Even these limited objectives too often proved impossible, and they had no plans for major social interventions or radical economic reform. . . ." Judith M. Brown, *Gandhi: Prisoner of Hope*, New Haven, Connecticut: Yale University Press, 1989, pp. 9–10. "The British had never conquered India, as the Spaniards had South America, for example. The stalwart communities of village and locality remained intact and the British merely slotted into the subcontinent's politics at a comparatively high level of control. . . ." *Ibid.*, pp. 13–14. In

several hundred thousand Indian soldiers rose up against British rule in North India, haunted the imaginations, and affected the policies, of British officials; and that, too, limited the severity of the measures they were prepared to take against Gandhi and the Congress.

Satyagraha explicitly aimed at appealing to the consciences of those whose conduct and policies its practitioners hoped to change. In order to achieve this goal, the people to whom the appeal was being made had to have consciences. The British, on the whole, did; and in the period between the two World Wars a growing number of them, including many influential in the Labour Party, came to believe that India should be free and independent.[68]

Gandhi's political activities and his successes in India may therefore be seen as, among other things, an indirect and unintentional tribute to the relative decency of Britain and the British. While Great Britain's rule in India undoubtedly rested, in the end, on inequality and the threat and the use of force—hardly democratic practices—other countries and their leaders would not have conducted themselves in as restrained a fashion as did the British. Hitler, for example, advised a British minister simply to shoot Gandhi and as many other Congressmen as was necessary to "make it clear that you mean business."[69] He undoubtedly would have done so had he been in charge of India. Hitler did not aspire to govern India, at least not in the short term,[70] but the imperial government of Japan did, and its military forces failed to occupy India only because the British army succeeding in blocking them and then pushing them out of neighboring Burma. Gandhi believed that Japan's only interest in India was defeating Great Britain and that if it had managed to do so it would not have invaded India or molested the Indian people.[71] Had the Japanese managed to occupy India, and had they conducted themselves as they did in China, with severe repression against the Chinese when they controlled parts of it between 1931 and 1945, however, Gandhi's belief would not have been borne out and he probably would not have survived Japanese rule.

When Gandhi joined the Indian independence movement he embraced the political idea behind it, the challenger to the idea and the fact of empire: nationalism. The national idea had a powerful impact on his public career. The idea had its origins in Europe, initially with the French Revolution

Gandhi's era, an Indian villager could go for years, conceivably an entire lifetime, without a direct encounter with a European.

and then with the nineteenth-century consolidations of various German and Italian principalities into single national states. In the twentieth century, nationalism spread around the world, becoming the most potent of all political ideas. It proved to be potent but problematical in the Indian case, and for much of Gandhi's public life after his return from South Africa he struggled with the problems it raised.

While the independence movement sought to form a single Indian state free of British rule, before the British arrived, such an entity had never existed: the subcontinent had never been united under a single authority and the raj itself was scarcely a tight-knit, uniform political unit. A third of it consisted of "princely states," where hereditary rulers held sway under the watchful eye, but usually the loose supervision, of the British.[72] Nor did a strong sense of belonging to a single nation prevail among the 300 million Indians. When Gandhi returned in 1915, the idea of an Indian nation had currency, as had also been the case in Europe in the nineteenth century, almost exclusively among the political and social elite. It had made little headway in the villages, where the vast majority of Indians lived. Gandhi undertook to bring his version of the national idea to the villagers of the subcontinent.

As in Europe and elsewhere, in India social divisions obstructed the unity that a sense of common nationhood implies and that forming a cohesive state usually requires. Cleavages both numerous and deep cut across Indian society. Indians were divided by region, with the south differing in important ways from the rest of the country. They were divided as well by language. While a common language often serves as the basis for a common national identity, India had (and has) many: its post-independence constitution recognizes twenty-two of them, and there are many more regional and local dialects. In political terms, the most significant division, and the one that led to greatest violence, involved religion, with Indian Muslims declaring themselves a distinct nation and demanding, and receiving, their own separate state. Within the majority-Hindu community, moreover, caste divisions generated pervasive inequality and social friction.

Gandhi struggled to overcome these cleavages and to reconcile with one another those whom they divided, with at best mixed success. The British had given the subcontinent a common language—English—although only the elite knew it at all well, but Gandhi considered it an imperial vestige and wanted to eliminate its use. The national government of independent India tried to make Hindi, which is widely spoken in the northern part of the country, the national language at the expense of the regional ones, but met stiff resistance, especially in the south.

Gandhi emphatically opposed creating both a Hindu and a Muslim state out of British India and regarded partition as a tragedy all apart from the bloodletting it triggered. Nor did he make significant progress in abolishing untouchability during his lifetime; and whatever private reservations he may have had about the caste system as a whole that gave rise to it, he did not take a public stance against the social convention of caste.

The two great global conflicts of the first half of the twentieth century also shaped the world in which Gandhi lived and worked. Each brought Indian independence closer, the first mainly through its impact on India itself, the second to a great extent by its effects on Great Britain.

India made a substantial contribution to the war effort in World War I. Almost a million Indians either fought, in Europe and the Middle East, or worked as laborers behind the front lines.[73] The war strained the finances of the raj and caused inflation, which touched everyone on the subcontinent.[74] With the country having rallied to the British cause, the nationalists expected some reward for India's loyalty;[75] and dominion status seemed to many to be the appropriate one.

Expectations for major changes in the governance of the country were all the higher because the postwar peace conference at Paris enshrined the principle of national self-determination as a global political norm—although in the end the victorious powers applied that principle only to the European nations of the multinational empires that had lost the war and not to the overseas subjects of Great Britain and France. The British Empire in fact expanded in the Middle East as a result of the First World War.[76] The economic strains and disappointed expectations produced discontent and unrest in India after 1918, just as Gandhi was becoming active in the independence movement there.[77]

The Second World War substantially weakened the British position in South Asia. British rule had rested in part on Great Britain's image as a mighty military power. The Japanese victories over British forces in Singapore and Burma severely tarnished that image. Six years of war in both Europe and Asia also drained Britain's economic resources and exhausted the British people. At the same time, the price of the Empire seemed likely to rise steeply as the independence movement gathered strength, something that had taken place after the first war. India had largely paid for itself before the war, and the prospect of having to cover the rising expenses of controlling it was not going to sit well with British taxpayers.[78]

In addition, Britain had fought World War II, among other goals, to resist the arbitrary foreign rule that Nazi Germany and Imperial Japan sought to impose in Europe and Asia, respectively. That made it awkward, to say the least, to insist on continuing its own arbitrary rule on the subcontinent. Imperial rule was not only awkward, it was also counterproductive for British relations with its wartime ally the United States, which had emerged as the country with which close economic and military cooperation had the greatest importance for British interests. American leaders generally opposed the perpetuation of the British Empire. Finally, the wartime sacrifices of the British people disposed them to vote into power the political party that was promising to build a welfare state that would, in the eyes of its proponents, justify those sacrifices; and the Labour Party, unlike Winston Churchill and many of his fellow Conservatives, did not regard remaining in India as a supreme national goal.[79] All this meant that, in the wake of World War II, in continuing their campaign for independence Gandhi and the Congress were pushing on an at least half-open British door.

Leadership

Mohandas Gandhi was a man of ideas, but no single large idea or set of ideas governed his thoughts and actions, as Marxism did Lenin's and antisemitism did Hitler's, for his ideas pertained to personal as well as political life. Gandhi drew on a variety of intellectual sources—Eastern and Western.[80] The philosophy of life of the Russian novelist Leo Tolstoy deeply impressed him,[81] and he corresponded with Tolstoy and named one of his South African communities Tolstoy Farm.[82] He also found inspiration in parts of the Hindu tradition and was taken with aspects of Christianity as well.[83] He worked out his personal outlook on life through his reading and his own experiences, and arrived at an eclectic worldview that covered both the political and the personal aspects of human existence.

One of his ideas, swaraj, or self-government, became a reality in no small part through his own leadership of the independence movement. That movement employed, in pursuit of its goal, the practice with which Gandhi is most closely associated and that he himself initiated in South Africa and developed thereafter: satyagraha. He may be said to have been the inventor of nonviolent protest on a large scale, and the success that he and the Congress achieved with it inspired its adoption elsewhere. Satyagraha proved to be not only his most important and original political idea, but also one whose influence spread beyond India and endured after his lifetime.

Gandhi also advocated swadeshi, an economic and social philosophy that entailed a simple, uncluttered, indeed by contemporary standards a Spartan style of life. Underlying this Gandhian idea was the conviction that the products of the Industrial Revolution had made life worse, not better, and that India should do without them.[84] Material possessions, he believed, impeded spiritual health. He himself walked rather than riding in trains or automobiles wherever possible, and the invention he valued most highly was the spinning wheel, which required only human power to operate. To be sure, he was not always able to practice what he preached. His position as the de facto leader of the independence movement and a national and international figure meant that he traveled with an entourage, which had to be supported financially, leading to the wry observation that it cost a lot of money to keep Gandhi in poverty.

He is best known for, and made his impact on the history of the twentieth century through, his ideas about politics and economics—that is, about collective matters. He had ideas, as well, however, which were just as important to him, about how individuals ought to conduct their lives. He devoted considerable time and effort to incorporating those ideas into his own daily routine. He followed a simple vegetarian diet.[85] He did not consider modern medicine, which was just arriving in India during his era, to be an improvement over traditional Indian methods of coping with disease. He avoided it and advised others to do the same and to rely on natural methods of healing.[86] He took a vow of celibacy at the age of 37, believing that abstinence was good for the soul,[87] and observed it for the last four decades of his life.

Concerns about the spiritual well-being of individuals, of the kind that preoccupied Gandhi, are essentially religious rather than political in nature, and in this sense he was a religious figure, although one whose religious ideas and commitments drew him into the public sphere.[88] He himself regarded his two sets of ideas—about collective activity and individual life—as integrally connected.[89] Indeed, he saw satyagraha as a form of spiritual discipline, an exercise in self-mastery for those taking part in it as well as a way to appeal to the consciences of the rulers and a tactic for generating sympathy and support among people not directly involved.

Like the other history-makers of the first half of the twentieth century, Gandhi made his mark by persuading others to adopt his ideas and follow his lead in confronting first the South African authorities and then the government of India. For these purposes he relied heavily on the written word. He wrote extensively, producing a few full-fledged books, many articles (most of them in publications he founded), and a vast correspondence with Indians, Europeans, and others. The collected works of Mohandas Gandhi run to a hundred volumes.[90] He wrote to work out his ideas but also to advance arguments that would convince those who read his writings of the rightness of those ideas and of the utility of the actions that they implied. "I prefer to convert by patient persuasion" he said in 1936,[91] and he did a good deal of converting. Coercion played no part in his leadership.

He had an attractive personality—kind, modest, with a real concern for others and a lively sense of humor—that won him a personal following,[92] although he could be imperious about the rightness of his beliefs. He had two different kinds of followers. One group, many of whom lived in his ashram or traveled with him or both, were his disciples. They embraced his own lifestyle as a path to personal fulfillment. This group regarded him, in effect, as mainly a religious figure and found that his formula for everyday living suited their personal needs. The members of the second group, consisting of those with whom he worked in the independence movement, are best characterized as colleagues. While they, too, were attracted by his personal qualities, they followed his lead because it brought closer the political goal to which they were dedicated: separation from Great Britain.

He inspired many Indians, some of them well-to-do, to support the cause of independence even at the risk of their own personal freedom. In general, he was an effective leader and his political effectiveness rested on his capacity, far greater than that of anyone else, to mobilize the Indian masses living mainly in villages. His broad appeal held the key to his success in promoting swaraj.

Gandhi held large events in which thousands of Indians came to see and hear him. While he often spoke to the audiences he attracted, his speeches did not have the same kind of impact as those of Western leaders such as Hitler, Churchill, and Franklin Roosevelt. For one thing, electronic amplification was not always available. For another, Gandhi did not have a particularly powerful or compelling style of speaking. Finally, in polyglot

India he did not command many of the languages of those at whom his message was aimed.[93]

His appeal, especially to villagers, rested, rather, on his public persona. With his simple clothing, his personal modesty, his disregard for worldly possessions, his regular prayer, and his habit of walking throughout the country, he presented a familiar image to rural, religious Indians: that of the Hindu holy man.[94] What would have appeared eccentric to Westerners gave him an honored status among non-Westernized Indians. For that reason, villagers considered the mere act of being in his presence to be a source of uplift, an experience called *darshan*. It was what Indians saw as Gandhi's saintly persona that gave rise to the honorific that he bore—"mahatma." In earning it he employed a traditional idiom, Hindu holiness, to advance a modern cause, national self-determination.[95]

He achieved a respected, even revered position in Indian society, as well, because, to use a term from a social practice he opposed in principle—warfare—he led from the front. That is, he regularly exposed himself to the risks and penalties that satyagraha entailed. He made going to jail not only an act of patriotism in India but also a qualification for leadership; and in prison he exercised, if anything, more influence than he did when free.

Gandhi provided effective leadership to the Indian independence movement, finally, through his skills as a political strategist. He had a good understanding of his adversary, the British government, and a shrewd sense of how to appeal to the constituency on which its authority ultimately rested, the British public. He had as well a command of an important feature of political leadership: timing—knowing when to take the initiative on a particular issue and when to hold back. He was adept at using the institution that became crucial in twentieth-century politics everywhere: the press.[96] He had a keen sense, as well, of how to rally his own constituency, the Indian masses. His flair for dramatic gestures that could galvanize them on behalf of independence served the Congress well, most vividly in the 1930 Salt March, which called attention to an arbitrary feature of British rule that affected virtually all Indians and thus attracted widespread attention and sympathy across India and beyond. Like other leaders, he made mistakes. The Quit India policy of 1942 had unwanted consequences, not least unintentionally strengthening Jinnah and the Muslim League. In general, though, as one historian of the raj wrote, "Behind the face of the simple prophet-cum-saviour was an astute political brain."[97]

The Personal Imprint

Mohandas Gandhi did more than any other individual to end British rule in the Asian subcontinent.[98] He made two major contributions to this epochal historic development. First, he transformed the Indian National Congress from a debating society for a handful of mainly Westernized, high-caste Hindus (with a sprinkling of Muslims) that the British government could be confident of managing, into a mass movement of Indians capable of exerting substantial and growing pressure on the British to cede power over Indian affairs to the Indians themselves.[99] Gandhi traveled in village India, he spoke to villagers, he identified with them and they with him, and he recruited them to be the (peaceful) foot soldiers of the independence movement. Second, he brought to the subcontinent a novel and unusually effective technique for exerting that pressure: satyagraha. Without him, nonviolent resistance would not have become the favored tactic of the independence movement.

Satyagraha appealed to the consciences of the British and won support for Indian independence both in Great Britain and in the West more broadly (the United States was particularly important here), while at the same time inspiring and mobilizing Indians. The several forms it took— strikes, marches, and resignations from positions involved in administering the country, among others—offered multiple ways in which large numbers of Indians could participate actively in the struggle for independence.

While its nonviolent essence made the cause it served particularly attractive beyond India's borders, and while Gandhi had an unshakable personal commitment to keeping the independence movement entirely peaceful, satyagraha also exerted pressure on the British authorities because it carried with it the implicit threat of violence. Mobilizing hundreds of thousands of Indians in active protest aroused emotions and created confrontations that had the potential to trigger violence; and sometimes acts of civil disobedience, despite Gandhi's wishes, did have that effect.[100] Once it broke out, violence on any scale, the British knew, could easily spread, taxing their capacity to keep control of India and provoking violent responses from the authorities that, like the 1919 shootings at Amritsar, would weaken Britain's standing on the subcontinent.

Just how important was Gandhi in the history of the twentieth century? It is certainly possible to create a counterfactual historical narrative in which India becomes independent without his having played any role at all.[101] History moved sharply in that direction after World War II: within the two decades that followed, the British Empire (and its French, Belgian, and Dutch counterparts as well) all but vanished. Still, it should be noted that India was the first, the largest, and the most important imperial possession to gain independence. Had it not set a precedent by doing so in 1947, the European imperial unwinding, assuming it would still have proceeded, would likely have done so at a slower pace. Indian independence mattered for twentieth-century decolonization. How much did Gandhi matter for Indian independence?

World War II severely weakened Great Britain, and the British would have had difficulty mustering the resources and the political will to retain control of the country even if Gandhi had remained in South Africa. The British Empire did not fall entirely of its own weight, however. It had to be pushed, because the British presence did have important sources of support.

Had Churchill been returned to office in 1945, he certainly would have tried to rally the friends of the raj and would have resisted the dismantling of the empire. How successfully and for how long he could have done so cannot, of course, be known.[102] A sector of British society, although not the majority,[103] was strongly committed to the imperial mission, and the raj had significant support in India itself. Jinnah and the Muslim League embraced the idea of Pakistan because they did not wish to live as a minority in an independent, Hindu-majority state. Presented with the choice between an undivided independent state on the subcontinent and the continuation of British rule, they would have opted to remain under British control.[104] Other minority groups suspected that they would receive more protection from the British than from a Congress-ruled India. Or at least, they knew what they had with the raj but did not know what treatment they would receive after independence.

Similarly, the hereditary monarchs who governed, in traditional fashion, a third of the subcontinent[105] had made their peace with the British and did not know whether they would be able to continue their rule, constrained though it was by British oversight, if the British left. Such fears as they had for their own futures were swiftly borne out. The new Congress government stripped them of their privileges and folded their territories into independent India.

Finally, the civil service, the army, and the police all reported to British authorities and drew their salaries from the Indian treasury that Britain controlled.[106] They worked in the institutions that ran the country. Attitudes toward the raj and independence surely varied among them, but if Britain had tried to stay rather than leave, some number would have remained loyal, and that would have reinforced the British position.

The Labour government did not try to rally these sources of support for the raj, partly out of anti-imperial conviction. What took place on August 15, 1947, was not, however, solely the consequence of the outcome of the 1945 general election in Great Britain. The new government in London could see how powerful were the forces opposing the continuation of British rule in India, and the independence movement was a major part of those opposing forces. All this suggests that the strength of the independence movement made a real difference in the course and pace of events in South Asia, and beyond, after World War II. Since the movement owed much of its strength to Gandhi, it follows that Gandhi himself made a difference in the matter of Indian independence, perhaps a decisive difference.

By strengthening the Congress through his recruitment of large numbers of Indians to its ranks, Gandhi enabled it not only to mount episodes of satyagraha that pressed the British to leave but also to achieve the standing necessary to negotiate effectively with the British authorities on the details of independence. His impact on the independence movement had an additional important consequence: he helped give the Congress a broad enough base, with enough able people in its leadership, to form a coherent government after independence and to govern for more than three decades thereafter, thus launching India on a career—albeit with many problems and shortcomings—as a successful state.[107] For a variety of reasons, Jinnah and the Muslim League did not manage to do as well for Pakistan. Although he took no part in its post-imperial governance, independent India's capacity to function effectively owed something to Gandhi.

He contributed to another major political development in his lifetime, although he did so entirely unintentionally: partition itself. He deeply, indeed desperately, wanted independent India to include all parts of the British raj. He went so far as to suggest that if the country remained united after independence, Jinnah should be its first prime minister, a proposal that attracted no support in any quarter.[108]

The division of the subcontinent's Hindus and Muslims into two separate sovereign states (each one, to be sure, containing people of the other faith) had more than one cause. In retrospect, the Congress, which opposed partition until the last minute, probably made a mistake in not including the Muslim League in the regional governments it formed after the 1937 elections,[109] in not seeking to assemble an all-party government when war broke out in 1939,[110] and in launching the Quit India campaign, which the Muslims declined to join, in 1942.[111] On the Muslim side, Jinnah became increasingly adamant about separation, and less willing to compromise, as time went on. His personality was in some ways a rigid one, which, given his importance among the Muslims, made it difficult to reach compromises that might have kept India together.[112] The British, for their part, sometimes carried out a strategy of "divide and rule" on the subcontinent, playing Hindus off against Muslims for the purpose of weakening opposition to their political supremacy. When reforms provided for elections, for example, the British divided Hindus, Muslims, and others into separate electorates.[113] If the British in India and in London had been more forthcoming earlier in devolving power to the Indians, moreover, it is at least conceivable that partition would have been avoided.[114]

To be sure, no multinational or multiethnic empire in the world survived the end of the rule by a dominant group—in the Indian case, the British—territorially intact. All broke up into more than one successor state, and those successor states themselves sometimes fragmented along ethnic, religious, or national lines, or some combination of these. In the context of twentieth-century history, the partition of the Indian subcontinent appears normal.

Normal, perhaps, but it was not inevitable. Until very late—even, arguably, through the end of World War II—a united independent India seemed possible, perhaps even the likeliest course for the future.[115] Partition came about, first and foremost, because India's Muslims came to fear their fate in a Hindu-majority state;[116] and that fear, whether or not justified, had something to do with Gandhi himself.

Although resolutely ecumenical, and far from orthodox in his religious beliefs and practices, he presented himself to the world as very much a Hindu figure. The habits and appearance of a Hindu holy man that endeared him to the Hindu masses[117] made him seem alien and even vaguely threatening to Muslims.[118] Nehru was a more familiar type, especially to the Muslim elite, but Gandhi was the face of the Congress and it was a decidedly non-Muslim, although not deliberately an anti-Muslim, face.[119] His public persona lent credence to Jinnah's charge that Congress would establish a "Hindu raj."[120] The poor personal relations between

Gandhi and Jinnah shadowed the intensive personal negotiations they conducted in 1944, which failed to reach agreement on India's future.[121] It was surely not an accident that the rise among Muslims of the idea of a separate state coincided with Gandhi's ascendance in the Congress.[122] In this way, the causes of his greatest success—independence—also contributed to what he himself regarded as one of his greatest failures, if not his greatest one: partition.

The Legacy

The Indian nation-state that was born on August 15, 1947, stands as the principal monument to Mohandas Gandhi. Although his transformation of the Congress enabled it to form a viable, and in some ways impressive, modern state, he himself did not take part in the construction of the state apparatus.[123] That was the work above all of Nehru and Vallabhbhai Patel, a lawyer from Ahmedabad who become associated with Gandhi in 1917, rose through the ranks of the Congress, and served as the country's first deputy prime minister. ¶

Gandhi did do a great deal, however—probably more than any other single individual—to make India a nation. It was an unlikely candidate for that status, having, as it did (and does) as much religious, ethnic, and linguistic diversity as all of Europe in addition to lacking any pre-imperial history of being encompassed in a single political jurisdiction.[124] Before the twentieth century the inhabitants of the subcontinent thought of themselves as Hindus, Muslims, or adherents to some other faith, as members of their castes and subcastes, and as residents of their towns and villages—but not as Indians. He promoted the idea of a single India, with a particular national identity, far more effectively than the Westernized leadership of Congress could have done.[125]

Independent India became and has remained, with a brief interruption, a democratic nation-state.[126] Elections in particular, an essential ingredient of democratic government, have become firmly embedded in the fabric of Indian national life.[127] Here, too, much of the credit belongs to Nehru.[128]

¶ Guha, *The Years That Changed the World*, p. 47. "Between 1948 and 1950, Nehru and Patel, and their colleagues in government and administration, tamed a communist insurgency and brought the princely states into the Union, promulgated a constitution assuring equal rights to minorities and women, and mandating a multiparty system based on adult franchise." *Ibid.*, p. 864.

He had enormous authority in the early years and could have sidestepped or overridden democratic norms had he wished to do so, but his belief in democracy was such that he never thought of doing such a thing. Gandhi's leadership of the independence movement also helped to implant democratic norms that continued into the period of statehood,[129] however, in particular through his commitment to and faithful practice of, three elements that are crucial for democratic governance: nonviolence, compromise, and respect for the rights of minorities.[130]

Democracy proved indispensable for the maintenance of independent India's unity, which, given the country's diversity, could not be taken for granted. Compromise resolved, for example, contentious issues arising from the country's many languages without large-scale violence or the secession of any parts of the country.[131] Pakistan, where democratic norms did not take root, had a different experience: its eastern, Bengali wing broke away from the west in 1971 and established independent Bangladesh amid considerable bloodshed.[132]

India also became a secular state, with no religion accorded a privileged position, in no small part because of Gandhi's devotion to that principle. Nehru shared his devotion, and the principle was included in the constitution. Despite occasional communal disturbances, the country has remained generally tolerant of all faiths. A largely Hindu country did not become an avowedly Hindu country. That began to change in the second decade of the twenty-first century with the rise to political primacy of the Hindu nationalist Bharatiya Janata Party (BJP). Its policies placed in jeopardy the principle of nondiscrimination toward any and all religions, about which Gandhi had felt very strongly.[133]

The rise of the BJP coincided with a sharp decline in the electoral fortunes of the Congress Party, the post-independence successor to the Indian National Congress. It was neither feasible nor, from a democratic perspective, desirable for Congress to sustain indefinitely the hegemonic political position it enjoyed in the decades following independence. The rotation of political parties in office is a cardinal feature of democratic governance. The Congress made itself the champion of the secular principle, however, and the decline in its standing weakened secularism in India. Gandhi, of course, had nothing to do with that decline, having been dead for four decades, but the downfall stemmed, among other factors, from two electorally toxic developments that he would certainly have opposed: widespread corruption, a practice entirely at odds with his way of life; and nepotism.[134] Nehru's daughter Indira Gandhi (no relation to Mohandas) became prime minister a few years after he died, her son succeeded her upon her assassination in 1984, and when he, too, was assassinated in 1991, his Italian-born widow became the leading figure in the Congress Party and their son—an unimpressive political figure—became the Congress candidate for prime minister. Gandhi would almost certainly have resisted turning the political party that emerged from the independence movement into the personal fiefdom of one family.

Gandhi also left a legacy beyond South Asia. The independence that India gained through his efforts—although not, to be sure, through his alone—turned out to mark the beginning of the process of decolonization, elsewhere in Asia and also in Africa, that put an end to the great European overseas empires. Many forces combined to undercut these multinational structures, but the Indian precedent surely contributed to this epochal historical development.[135] Of Gandhi's role in the end not only of the British Empire but of the other European empires as well, it might be said what the great physicist of the early twentieth century Ernest Rutherford replied when it was suggested that in his Nobel Prize–winning research he had only been "riding the wave" of discoveries at that time. "But I made the wave, didn't I?"

In 1921, Gandhi proposed a flag for the independence movement. It became the flag of independent India that flies throughout the country and in Indian facilities abroad. It consists of three bands—saffron, white, and green—with a spinning wheel placed in the middle.[136] The flag symbolizes the kind of country he hoped the independent state would be, with the spinning wheel standing for the "swadeshi" he favored: an economy based on village agriculture and handcrafts without the products of the Industrial Revolution that the British had imported.[137] That part of the Gandhian vision never came close to being realized. Nehru and the other Congress leaders did not share it. They wanted, rather, to accelerate industrialization as a way of reducing poverty.

An admirer of the Soviet Union's economy (although not of its political system),[138] Nehru adopted a modified version of the Soviet approach to economic growth, with the state playing a large role, although not as large as in the communist countries.[139] An alternative approach adopted by other countries that emerged from imperial rule after World War II, especially in East Asia, which emphasized exports and the use of free markets in contrast to India's trade restrictions and government planning, achieved higher rates of growth after 1945. In response to an economic crisis in 1991, India moved away from the Nehruvian approach and toward the East Asian model.[140] Neither strategy of economic management, however, corresponded in any significant way to what Gandhi had desired. In independent India his concept of swadeshi turned out to be irrelevant.[141]

Another of Gandhi's causes, his opposition to untouchability, fared better after his death. The Indian constitution set aside seats in legislatures and government jobs for the lowest castes[142] and legislation was enacted to reduce caste discrimination. Still, untouchability did not disappear after independence. A practice that had been deeply embedded in the country's social fabric and religious beliefs for millennia could not be simply and swiftly uprooted. Traditional patterns of caste-related behavior did erode after 1947, but slowly:[143] they became less pronounced in cities, where more and more Indians came to live, and among those with education, whose numbers grew over the decades. Both the government action that Ambedkar had demanded and the change in individuals' beliefs on which Gandhi had counted worked to reduce the role of caste discrimination in Indian life.[144]

On the other hand, caste actually became more salient in the country after independence in two respects.[145] The reservation of jobs for people belonging to lower castes created an incentive to identify as a member of such castes, as well as the demand on the part of entire caste groups to be officially designated as sufficiently disadvantaged to qualify for the allotments of positions the government made available.[146] In addition, caste became a basis for mobilizing voters in elections. Candidates proclaimed their caste identifications for the purpose of attracting the votes of those similarly situated in the social order. Appealing to group solidarity to win political office is a time-honored electoral tactic across the world. In India, it became particularly popular in the case of the members of the lower castes, who, in most places, tended to outnumber those in the upper ranks.[147]

Whatever his indirect and unintended responsibility for partition,[148] it ended Gandhi's quest for a single independent India encompassing all of the subcontinent's Hindus and Muslims. Moreover, it took place amid a massive breach of his cherished principle of nonviolence. As the separation loomed, Hindus left what became Pakistan for India and Muslims living in the areas of what became independent India from which they could more or less easily reach the territory of the new Muslim state moved there. [††]

[††] Millions of Indian Muslims living far from Pakistan could not or at least did not go there. They were far more vulnerable to any depredations their Hindu neighbors might choose

As many as 15 million people became refugees.[149] The population transfers did not take place peacefully. Violence broke out on both sides of what became the new India-Pakistan border, in both Punjab in the west and Bengal in the east, in which an estimated 1 to 2 million people died.[150] The bloodshed, and his efforts to stop it, preoccupied and distressed Gandhi during the last year and a half of his life.[151]

Nor did the two new independent countries on the subcontinent maintain peaceful relations with each other. To the contrary, they were enemies from the beginning and fought four major wars and engaged in numerous lesser border skirmishes in the seventy-five years after 1947. Even within independent India's borders, moreover, the principle of nonviolence did not command universal respect. As in other societies, historically disputes at the village level had often taken a violent turn, and Gandhi's teachings and his example did not put an end to this. ††

Still, the sharp departure from it during partition and in other circumstances notwithstanding, nonviolence as a principled commitment and a political tactic stands, in addition to an independent, democratic India, as Gandhi's most important and enduring legacy;[152] but its most significant flowering after his death took place in other countries. The American movement to end discrimination against people of African descent in the 1960s made extensive and effective use of Gandhian techniques. The Civil Rights movement's sit-ins in segregated facilities, in which African Americans peacefully violated legal restrictions on their presence, as well as its protest marches, resembled Gandhi's campaigns of satyagraha. The Civil Rights movement's principal leader, Martin Luther King Jr., made a trip to India to learn more about the independence movement there and more than once told the story of Gandhi's Salt March to inspire his colleagues and followers.[153] One of the movement's other leaders, Bayard Rustin, counted himself a Gandhian.[154] The campaign to end

---

to inflict on them than were the Muslims of the Punjab and East Bengal, who formed majorities where they lived. This led to the observation that those who needed Pakistan didn't get it and those who got it didn't need it.

†† "Nonviolence has been an influential religious doctrine in certain places and contexts, especially as applied in Gandhian passive resistance. But in the context of most village struggles, violence is a stark fact of life that is partly controlled, partly exploited, partly manipulated, but always a potential factor with which a responsible man must reckon." David G. Mandelbaum, *Society in India, Volume One: Continuity and Change*, Berkeley, California: The University of California Press, 1970, p. 246.

apartheid in South Africa in the 1980s and 1990s also had some Gandhian features, as did the peaceful protests that toppled communist rule in central and eastern Europe in 1989.[155]

Along with the principle and practice of nonviolence, Gandhi's public persona—his renunciation of material possessions, the simplicity of his life, his emphasis on spiritual aspects of human existence, his concern for the poorest members of society—has become part of the public consciousness around the world. He remains the best-known Indian in all of history with the exception of Siddhartha Gautama, a religious leader of the fifth century B.C.E., who is known, like Gandhi, by a honorific: the Buddha. In Mohandas Gandhi's posthumous career as an iconic figure, he resembles Winston Churchill. The association is ironic because the two were adversaries during their lifetimes. Churchill not only opposed any loosening of the British grip on India, he also had a harshly negative view of Gandhi himself, whom he called "a seditious Middle Temple lawyer, now posing as a fakir of a type well-known in the East" and a "malignant subversive fanatic."[156]

Nonetheless, their lives and their afterlives have several features in common. Each led an event-filled and sometimes turbulent life. Each wrote prolifically. Each made a decisive impact on the history of the twentieth century that was, however, circumscribed—Churchill's in time, Gandhi's in space. Churchill refused to bend to Hitler in the crucial months in 1940 and 1941 when Britain was fighting alone against him, which spared the world the awful consequences of a Nazi military victory in Europe. Gandhi forged a mass movement that ended British rule in one specific place: the Asian subcontinent. Finally, and most enduringly, each has lived on after his death as a symbol—Churchill of courage, Gandhi of principled nonviolence—of qualities and values that the world admires and needs and of which it always has far too small a supply.

7

David Ben-Gurion (Gruen)

The Life

David Yosef Gruen was born on October 16, 1886, in Plonsk, a town in Russian-dominated Poland about 40 miles northwest of Warsaw with a population of 7,900, of whom 4,500, like the Gruen family, were Jews.[1] He was his mother's favorite of her five children, but she died when he was 12. His father worked as a purveyor of legal services. By local standards, the Gruens were neither rich nor poor. Young David received a Jewish education, but his formal schooling in Poland ended when he was 13.[2]

From his father, he absorbed a commitment to Zionism, the movement to restore a Jewish homeland where a Jewish commonwealth had flourished in antiquity, a place that was then a province called Palestine in the Middle Eastern Ottoman Empire. In 1896, Theodore Herzl, a Jewish journalist in Vienna, published a book entitled *Der Judenstaat* (The Jewish State) envisioning such a development. The next year, Herzl convened the first Zionist Congress in Basel, Switzerland, and founded an organization dedicated to that purpose. David Gruen identified with Herzl's effort and, having been taught Hebrew by his grandfather, formed a society of Jewish youth in Plonsk to encourage its employment as a spoken language,[3] with the logical place for its everyday use being Palestine. While Hebrew was the language of the Jewish liturgy, it was extremely rare for Jews to speak or write it for other than religious purposes: most of those in Eastern Europe spoke Yiddish.[4]

Gruen went to Warsaw in 1904 and joined Poalei Zion (Workers of Zion), a movement advocating Zionism and socialism: both commanded his allegiance for the rest of his life.[5] In 1906, he decided to move to Palestine and arrived by ship at the Mediterranean port of Jaffa on September 7.[6] He came to regard that day as the most important one of his life.*

Jews had established a number of agricultural settlements in Palestine in the latter part of the nineteenth century and over the next four years David Gruen worked intermittently at several of them.[7] Although by all accounts he neither enjoyed nor had a talent for agricultural work, he came to consider clearing the land and farming it to be the essence of Zionism.[8]

Poalei Zion had sympathizers in Palestine—by one estimate, they numbered 150[9]—and he became active in its affairs. In 1909, he went to Jerusalem to work on a newspaper the group started. He signed one of the articles he wrote for it "David Ben-Gurion:" the original Ben Gurion had been a leader of the Jewish community during the time of the revolt against the Romans in the first century C.E., which led to the end of the last episode, before the twentieth century, of Jewish sovereignty.[10] David Gruen adopted that last name, and it was as Ben-Gurion that the world came to know him.

In 1911, Ben-Gurion moved to Turkey in order to learn the language and study law. He aimed to take an active role on behalf of the Jews in the affairs of the Ottoman Empire, which he assumed would control Palestine indefinitely.[11] World War I interrupted his legal studies, and the Ottoman authorities expelled him from Palestine.[12] He traveled to the United States, arriving on May 16, 1915,[13] where he learned English and attempted, with little success, to persuade American-based Jews to immigrate to Palestine.[14] In America, he produced, in collaboration with others, two books—one a memorial to Jewish pioneers who had died in Palestine, the other a survey of Palestine itself. The second, especially, was widely noted among American Jews[15] and brought Ben-Gurion, for the first time, to the attention of people beyond the membership of Poalei Zion. He spent most of his time in America in New York, where in 1917 he met and married Paula Munweiss, a nurse who had emigrated from Russia. The marriage lasted more than fifty years, until her death in 1968, and produced three children.

---

* The only phrase inscribed on his tombstone is "Emigrated to Eretz Yisrael on September 7, 1906." Ben-Gurion was part of the "Second Aliyah," the second wave of European immigrants to Palestine. Many of them—by Ben-Gurion's estimate, 90 percent—did not remain. Anita Shapira, *Ben-Gurion: Father of Modern Israel*, New Haven, Connecticut: Yale University Press, 2014, p. 19. In the last decades of the nineteenth century and the early years of the twentieth, many Russian Jews emigrated from the tsarist empire, but the vast majority of them went to North America.

Toward the end of the war, Great Britain formed a military unit in which Jews could enlist to fight for the British in the Middle East. Ben-Gurion, who had changed his mind about the durability of Ottoman rule in Palestine, enlisted, received military training, and was sent to the region but did not see action before the war ended.[16] After Great Britain and its allies had won the war, and the Ottoman Empire had disintegrated, the British took control of Palestine under the terms of a Mandate from the new League of Nations. The British assumption of responsibility there had enormously important consequences for Zionism in general and for Ben-Gurion personally.

So, too, did a statement the British government issued during the war. Motivated by a desire to rally the Jewish people of the United States and Russia in support of the war against Germany, as well as by the philo-Semitic sentiments of some members of the British elite,[17] the statement took the form of a November 2, 1917, letter from Arthur Balfour, the foreign secretary, to Lord Rothschild, a leader of the British Jewish community. It read in part, "His Majesty's Government views with favour the establishment of a national home for the Jewish people in Palestine, and will use their best endeavours to facilitate the achievement of this object."[†] The Balfour Declaration was the first official endorsement that the Zionist movement, to which Ben-Gurion had decided to devote his life, had ever received from a leading power; and the British, the new masters of Palestine, were in a position to deliver on what seemed to be their promise to the world's Jews.

In the interwar period, David Ben-Gurion became the most prominent political figure in the Yishuv, as the Jewish community in Palestine was called. He and other Labor Zionists established the political party Achdut Ha'avodah.[18] In 1930, it merged with a similar group, Hapoel Hatzair, to form Mapai,[19] which went on to hold a dominant political position in the

---

[†] Quoted in Howard M. Sachar, *A History of Israel from the Rise of Zionism to Our Time*, New York, Alfred A. Knopf, Second Revised Edition, 1996, p. 109. The sentence continued, "it being clearly understood that nothing shall be done which may prejudice the civil and religious rights of existing non-Jewish communities in Palestine, or the rights and political status enjoyed by Jews in any other country." *Ibid.* A letter from Sir Henry McMahon, the British high commissioner in Egypt, to the sherif of Mecca, an Arab ruler in the Arabian peninsula, in October 1915 stated that Great Britain was prepared, with some exceptions "to recognize and support the independence of the Arabs in all regions within the limits demanded by demanded by the Sherif." *Ibid.*, p. 92.

Yishuv and later in the State of Israel for almost half a century. He also helped to found and became the leader of the Histadrut, a trade union that engaged in a wide variety of activities beyond representing the economic interests of workers—establishing a major bank, for example.[20]

The Zionist movement after World War I had a dual structure. Along with the organizations in the Yishuv in which Ben-Gurion rose to prominence, it included the Zionist Organization that Herzl had founded and that had its headquarters in London. For much of the interwar era, this European wing had, if anything, greater importance in Zionist affairs than the Yishuv itself. It served as the point of contact with the millions of Jews, many in now independent Poland, who did not live in Palestine. It did the bulk of the fundraising on which expanding the Jewish presence in Palestine depended. And it engaged the British government, on which, in the 1920s and 1930s, Zionism's future depended. Dues-paying members of the Zionist Organization, most of them in Eastern Europe, elected delegates to its biannual congresses. The delegates, in turn, elected a directing body known as the Zionist Executive. The Zionist Organization's representative in Palestine was the Jewish Agency. Over the course of the 1930s, Ben-Gurion played an increasingly influential part in the Organization's affairs.

The dominant figure in London was Chaim Weizmann, a German- and Swiss-educated chemist born in Russia in 1874 who held an academic position at the University of Manchester and had played a major role in obtaining the Balfour Declaration.[21] Eloquent, personable, and with a gift for befriending and impressing British and ultimately American political figures,[22] Weizmann came to be widely regarded by Jews and non-Jews alike as the leader of the Zionist movement. He headed the World Zionist Organization almost continuously for the quarter-century beginning in 1920. In 1949, he became the first occupant of the (largely ceremonial) position of president of independent Israel. Ben-Gurion worked closely with Weizmann but also clashed with him. Their conflicts stemmed in part from Ben-Gurion's resentment of Weizmann's higher status during most of the period of the British Mandate, but also from genuine differences over how to advance the Zionist cause. On several occasions, Ben-Gurion came to believe that Weizmann was adopting an excessively conciliatory stance toward the British authorities when their policies were at odds with Zionist interests, and that the older man placed too much faith in Britain and in British good will.[23]

While Weizmann was, for the most part, an ally, Ben-Gurion, a man with a naturally pugnacious character, came into conflict with three other groups. In each case, he did not, in the end, manage to find common ground with them.

One such group, the Revisionist movement, emerged as Labor Zionism's rival for political primacy in the Yishuv. Its leader, Vladimir Ze'ev Jabotinsky, born in Odessa in tsarist Russia in 1880, had had a career as a journalist, poet, and translator. Crucial to his leadership of the Revisionists were his impressive oratorical gifts. The Revisionists opposed the Labor Zionists' socialism and attracted support from urban and middle-class Jews.[24] They opposed, as well, the partition of Palestine—or rather the further partition, since in 1921 the British had carved out from part of the territory it had inherited from the Ottomans the Emirate of Transjordan (later the Kingdom of Jordan) and made a scion of the Hashemite family of the Arabian peninsula, Abdullah, its monarch. Ben-Gurion and Weizmann, unlike Jabotinsky and his followers, were willing to accept partition in order to establish Jewish sovereignty in part of Palestine.

In addition, the Revisionists employed, on the whole, more militant tactics in pursuit of Zionist goals than did the Labor Zionists, and the differences between the two occasionally erupted in violence.[25] In 1934, Ben-Gurion held a series of meetings with Jabotinsky in London in which the two worked out a common program, but the Labor Zionists rejected it.[26] The rivalry between the two Zionist factions continued through the life of the British Mandate and into the period of independence, ultimately becoming the principal cleavage in the electoral politics of the State of Israel.

Ben-Gurion and the Zionist movement as a whole also found themselves at odds with much of the Arab population of Palestine. Politically quiescent before World War I,[27] in the wake of that war the Arabs began to express their rejection of increasing Jewish settlement, let alone prospective Jewish sovereignty. The Zionists, Ben-Gurion included, at first believed that no real conflict of interest existed because the Arabs would benefit substantially from the economic development of Palestine that the Jewish settlers were undertaking.[28] Outbreaks of anti-Jewish violence in 1921, 1929, and then from 1936 to 1939 in what became known as the Arab Revolt, put paid to that optimism. Ben-Gurion met with Arab leaders on several occasions in the 1930s to try, as with the Revisionists, to find common ground. The meetings did not come close to success,[29] and he became persuaded that Zionism would gain Arab acceptance only when the Jewish presence in Palestine had grown too powerful to challenge.[30]

Ben-Gurion and the Zionist movement also clashed with Great Britain. Almost as soon as the Mandate began, the British government started to retreat from the promise of the Balfour Declaration. The overriding reason had to do with geopolitics: since the Arabs adamantly opposed the Zionist project, the British government had to choose between the Arabs and the Jews. The Arabs, in Palestine and throughout the Middle East, far outnumbered the Jews and were thus in a much stronger position to help or harm British interests, or so the British believed: therefore, the British chose the Arabs.[31]

The British authorities periodically imposed limits on Jewish immigration to Palestine and Jewish land purchases there. In 1936, the Peel Commission, one of several ad hoc committees the British government created to assess its policies in Palestine, concluded that a reconciliation between Arabs and Jews was not possible and recommended a partition of the land between the two groups. While the territory allotted to the Jews was so small—roughly 20 percent of the area of Palestine west of the Jordan River—as to call into question its viability as a sovereign political entity, Ben-Gurion and Weizmann accepted the plan in principle.[32] The Arabs rejected it, as they did all subsequent proposals for partition throughout the twentieth century, demanding instead that Jewish sovereignty anywhere in the region be prohibited. They maintained that position even after the establishment of the State of Israel. The anti-Zionist trend in British policy between the two World Wars reached a climax with the issuance of the government White Paper of 1939, which envisioned an independent, Arab-dominated state in Palestine in ten years and imposed severe restrictions on Jewish immigration and acquisition of land.[33]

Then came World War II. Ben-Gurion proclaimed a double-edged policy in response to it: to fight the White Paper as if there were no war and to support Britain against Germany as if there were no White Paper.[34] In fact, the Yishuv did little of either. It could not forcefully oppose the Mandate because it needed British protection from the German army, which looked as if it might conquer the Middle East until the Wehrmacht General Erwin Rommel's forces were stopped at El Alamein, in Egypt, in October 1942.[35] Nor could it make a major contribution to opposing the Germans—although 26,000 Palestinian Jews did serve in the British army[36]—or to rescuing the Jews of Europe, 6 million of whom were murdered by the Nazis.

Ben-Gurion spent much of the war outside Palestine. He was in London for part of the German air campaign against Britain known as the Blitz, and he greatly admired Churchill's wartime leadership.[37] He traveled to the United States in 1940 in an unsuccessful effort to win support for a Jewish army. He was there again in May 1942 for a conference of American Jewry at the Biltmore Hotel in New York City that declared support for a "Jewish commonwealth"—widely understood to mean a sovereign state— in Palestine after the war.[38]

As the war was ending in victory for Great Britain and its allies, a British general election put in power in London a new government, formed by the Labour Party. The Zionists hoped that it would pursue policies in Palestine more favorable to their interests, but in this they were disappointed: the Labor government followed the course its predecessor had charted in the prewar years.[39] The Zionists responded by bringing, illegally, as many Jews as possible to Palestine, some of them survivors of the Holocaust who had made their way to displaced persons camps in the American occupation zone in Germany.

The Yishuv also undertook acts of armed resistance to the British, most of them carried out by the military arm of the Revisionists, the Irgun Zvai Leumi, and its renegade offshoot, Lehi. Ben-Gurion's Labor Zionists supported such operations for a time but then turned against violent tactics.[40]

From the end of the war, Ben-Gurion had weightier issues on his mind than attacking the British. He anticipated that sooner or later Great Britain would leave Palestine, that this would create the opportunity to establish a Jewish state at last, but that that state would have to defend itself against Arab attacks—all of which came to pass. He therefore launched two initiatives to prepare the Yishuv for what was to come. On July 1, 1945, he convened a group of American Jews at the New York home of a businessman named Rudolf Sonnenborn and asked them to raise money to buy the armaments the Haganah, the Zionist military arm, would need. The "Sonnenborn Institute" ultimately collected tens of millions of dollars for this purpose.[41]

Then, between the end of March and the end of May 1947, Ben-Gurion held a series of meetings to discuss the Haganah's organization, strategy, and general fitness for warfare. In these meetings, he made criticisms, sometimes harsh ones, of the state of the Zionist military forces. As a result of what came to be called "The Seminar," those forces underwent a series of changes that made them more effective militarily when war came.[42]

In early February 1947, the British government announced that it would leave Palestine, and it handed responsibility for determining the territory's future to the fledgling United Nations (UN). On November 29, 1947, the UN General Assembly voted to divide Palestine between a Jewish and an Arab state.[43] At a public meeting on May 14 of the following year in Tel Aviv, Ben-Gurion read aloud a statement proclaiming the establishment of the State of Israel, which soon thereafter received recognition from both the United States and the Soviet Union. It was an extraordinary moment: the restoration of Jewish sovereignty where it had once flourished after an interruption of almost 2,000 years. Ben-Gurion wrote in his diary that day: "At 4 p.m. Jewish independence was declared and the state was established. Its fate is in the hands of the defense forces."[44]

In Israel's War of Independence, Ben-Gurion served as commander-in-chief. The war began even before the formal declaration of independence when, shortly after the UN vote, Palestinian Arabs began attacking Jews, Jewish settlements, and Jewish neighborhoods in mixed cities. The Zionists attempted to defend every one of the settlements, but the Arab side scored some military successes. In April 1948, the Zionist forces adopted a more offensive strategy, code-named Plan Dalet (Plan D), and began to make military progress, clearing the lines of communication among the various centers of Jewish population.[45]

With the official proclamation of independence, five Arab armies—from Syria, Iraq, Lebanon, and Egypt and the British-led Arab Legion of Jordan—invaded the new state of Israel. A month of fighting was followed by a month-long truce. During the truce, and over the course of the war, the Haganah became an increasingly effective fighting force, gaining more and better weapons, more training and experience, and more manpower.[46] It made a major effort to defend Jewish Jerusalem, which Arab forces besieged. It succeeded in resupplying the Jews there in the months before independence and ultimately built a road connecting the western part of the city with the rest of Israel. The old city, with its Ottoman-era walls and including its Jewish Quarter, however, fell to the Arab Legion. In the latter stages of the conflict, the Israeli army evicted Arab forces from the Galilee in the north of the country and the Negev in the south. An armistice went into effect in January 1949.[47]

Israel secured its principal aim, its own survival, at the cost of 5,700 to 5,800 dead and 12,000 wounded.[48] It emerged from the conflict with 40 percent more territory than the UN partition resolution had assigned to it.[49] The Jews won because they mustered, by the end, roughly as many troops as did their assailants,[50] because they had shorter lines of supply and communications than their opponents and knew the terrain on which they were fighting better, and because they had higher morale: unlike their adversaries, they were fighting for their lives and their futures and so devoted all the resources at their command to the struggle. Moreover, political divisions afflicted the Arab countries, which had different and sometimes conflicting war aims.[51]

Two episodes in the war had long-lasting repercussions. The Revisionists chartered a ship that they named *The Altalena* (one of Jabotinsky's pen names) to bring into the country, in June 1948, both Jewish immigrants and weapons to be used by the Irgun. Ben-Gurion was determined to prevent the emergence of an armed force independent of the legally constituted authorities of the new state and, when the Revisionist leader Menachem Begin (Jabotinsky had died in 1940 in New York) refused to hand over the weapons, Ben-Gurion ordered the Haganah to fire on the ship. Fifteen people were killed and several dozen wounded.[52] The rift between the Revisionists and the Labor Zionists widened.

In addition, during the course of the war, an estimated 700,000 Arabs left the new state.[53] The Arab countries to which they moved, with the exception of Jordan, refused to accept them as citizens and kept them in special, separate refugee camps while insisting, through the first two decades of the twenty-first century and beyond, that the refugees (and their descendants) be taken back by Israel, even after most of those who had actually lived in Mandatory Palestine had died. The refugee issue became a point of contention in the Arab-Israeli conflict that persisted long after the 1948 war had ended.[54]

The first wave of departures, after the partition resolution, included many of the leaders of the local Arab communities. Their flight proved infectious, and others followed.[55] Arabs fled, as well, out of fear of ill treatment by the Jewish forces, fears magnified by unfounded reports of atrocities, sometimes broadcast by Arab governments.[†] The new Israeli government had no plan or intention to depopulate the country of Arabs,

---

[†] Daniel Gordis, *Israel: A Concise History of a Nation Reborn*, New York: Ecco/HarperCollins, 2016, pp. 159–160; Martin Kramer, "What Happened at Lydda," *Mosaic*, July 1, 2014, https://mosaicmagazine.com/essay/uncategorized/2014/07/what-happened-at-lydda.

but once they had left, Ben-Gurion and his colleagues decided, out of concern for the security of the new state and to ensure a Jewish majority in Israel, not to readmit them.[56] The debate about the responsibility for the Palestinian refugee problem continued for decades. What is clear is that its overriding cause was the war itself, which the Arabs had launched against the new Jewish state and that the Jews had not wanted.[57]

Having secured independence, Israel had to build the structures of a state. For this purpose, the Yishuv had provided a head start by developing many important institutions—Mapai and the Histadrut being outstanding examples—even before full sovereignty. With a heritage of democratic practices from the prestate era, the new country became a democracy, adopting the British parliamentary system but selecting the members of the Israeli parliament—the Knesset—through a system of proportional representation like the one that had governed elections to the Zionist Congresses from their inception.[58] In the first Israeli election, which took place in 1949, Mapai earned the largest number of seats and formed a coalition government that it dominated,[59] with Ben-Gurion as both prime minister and minister of defense.

As the nation-state of the Jewish people, Israel aspired to become the destination for the "ingathering of the exiles"—the return of all Jews to their ancestral homeland and newly established sovereign state. The people whom Ben-Gurion and the other Zionists had expected to populate the state they aimed to create, however—and the Eastern Europeans societies where they had lived—for the most part no longer existed. The Nazis had destroyed Europe's centuries-old Jewish communities—in particular the largest of them, in Poland—and killed most of the Jews who had constituted them. Only a small remnant survived the Holocaust, much of which made its way to Israel after 1945.

After independence, the country did receive a large number of immigrants, but most of them came from a different source. The Jews who had lived for centuries as minorities in the Arab world, with whom Ben-Gurion and the other Zionist leaders had had very little contact and among whom Zionist sentiment was generally weak (where it existed at

---

The Arabs who fled may have feared that the Jews would do to them what the Arab leaders said they planned to do to the Jews. One such leader declared, before the fighting began, "This will be a war of extermination and a momentous massacre which will be spoken of like the Mongolian massacre and the Crusades." Quoted in Sachar, *op. cit.*, p. 333.

all), flooded into the new state. In the Arab countries, they had had a status inferior to that of Muslims but had usually been tolerated; but in the wake of the defeat of the Arab governments by the relatively small Jewish community in Palestine, traditional anti-Jewish discrimination turned into outright and sometimes murderous persecution.[60] The Jews of Islam[61] were forced to flee, in numbers comparable to the Arabs who left Israel as a result of the 1948 war. These Jewish refugees had nowhere to go except Israel. The new government devoted a good deal of its attention and resources to the task of absorbing them. This entailed transporting, housing, feeding, and finding employment for Jewish refugees from Yemen, Egypt, Iraq, Syria, and Morocco as well as other Middle Eastern countries.[62] In its first four years, thanks largely to the influx of Middle Eastern Jews, Israel's Jewish population doubled in size.[63]

As prime minister, Ben-Gurion involved himself deeply in this task, but not to the exclusion of the foreign affairs of the new nation. His principal concern remained the Arab countries, which made it clear that, despite their military defeat, they would not accept a Jewish state as a permanent part of the Middle East and would continue to try to destroy it.

Beyond coping with the ongoing Arab hostility, Ben-Gurion took two other important international initiatives in Israel's first half-decade of existence. The United Nations proposed a special international status, one outside Israel's sovereign jurisdiction, for the city of Jerusalem, since it was a place sacred to Christians and Muslims as well as to Jews. Ben-Gurion did not allow the proposal to be put into practice. He proclaimed Jerusalem the capital of Israel and moved the national government to the western, Israeli-controlled part of the city.[64] In addition, he decided to accept payments from one of the two successor states to Hitler's Third German Reich, the democratic, Western-oriented Federal Republic of Germany, as reparations for the Nazis' crimes against the Jewish people. The decision caused more controversy in Israel than any other post-independence policy with which he was associated.

In 1953, Ben-Gurion resigned as prime minster and went to live on a kibbutz—an agricultural settlement where much of the property is held in common—named Sde Boker in the southern part of the country. He did not give up his seat in the Knesset and just over a year later he returned as defense minister. Mapai emerged from the 1955 election as still the largest party in the Knesset, and he returned to the post of prime minister. The next year, he led the country into the second Arab-Israeli war. That war had its origins, for Israel, in the raids Egyptian forces were conducting on Israeli settlements close to the border between the two countries, which Ben-Gurion was determined to stop.[65] The threat from Egypt increased substantially in his estimation when, in 1955, the government in Cairo, headed by Gamal Abdel Naser, signed an agreement with Czechoslovakia by the terms of which the Czechs promised to deliver weapons to the Egyptian armed forces. Czechoslovakia being a satellite of the Soviet Union, this meant that one of the two nuclear superpowers was effectively aligning itself with the Egyptians.[66]

Ben-Gurion concluded that Israel's security required delivering a sharp military blow to Egypt. He found an ally in France, which opposed Nasser because of his support for the rebellion against French rule in Algeria. The French agreed to supply advanced weapons, notably fighter aircraft, to the Israeli Defense Forces (IDF).[67] The two governments then joined forces with Great Britain, whose interests in the Middle East Nasser had attacked by announcing, in July 1956, the nationalization of the British-operated Suez Canal. The three countries agreed that Israel would undertake a military campaign against Egypt, that France, and Britain would then demand that both sides desist from fighting, and that when, as they expected, Egypt refused to do so, the two European powers would intervene militarily, with the announced purpose of safeguarding the Canal. All three hoped that the anticipated Egyptian military setback would lead to Nasser's fall from power.

On October 29, 1956, Israel launched its attack, quickly routed the Egyptian forces, occupied the Sinai Peninsula and the Gaza Strip, and opened the Straits of Tiran leading to the Red Sea, which Egypt had blockaded. On November 5 and 6, British and French forces arrived in Egypt and began occupying the Canal Zone. The United States opposed the interventions, however, as did virtually every other country, and America applied economic pressure that compelled the British and French to withdraw their troops on December 22. The Israeli forces in Egypt stayed longer, but they, too, left in March 1957.[68]

In June 1963, Ben-Gurion once again, and for the last time, resigned as prime minister.[69] He subsequently formed a new political party, called Rafi, which contested the 1965 elections, with several of his younger proteges, notably the former Army Chief of Staff Moshe Dayan and the former Director-General of the Defense Ministry Shimon Peres, on the list. Although the new party gained ten seats, and Ben-Gurion returned to the Knesset, neither it nor he exerted much influence as an independent force and in 1970 he retired entirely from politics, returning to Sde Boker. He lived to witness three more Arab-Israeli wars: The Six-Day War in June, 1967, the War of Attrition in 1969–1970, and the Yom Kippur War of October 1973. He died a few weeks after the conclusion of the third conflict, on December 1.

The Times

Although he fought in neither conflict, and although the important battles in each took place outside his part of the Middle East and most of them far from the region, the two World Wars had a profound impact on David Ben-Gurion's life and work. World War I resulted in the transfer of Palestine from Ottoman to British control. Before the war (and during its early years as well), Ben-Gurion had anticipated the continuation of Ottoman rule and had learned Turkish and gone to Istanbul to study law in order to prepare himself to take part, on behalf of the Zionist cause, in Ottoman public affairs. If Ottoman rule had in fact continued, however, it seems doubtful that the Zionist project would have succeeded, as it eventually did.

While the Zionists managed to buy land for Jewish settlement in Palestine during the Ottoman period, this was due as much to the endemic corruption in Istanbul as to official approval of the effort. When the war began, the Ottoman authorities expelled a large number of Jews from Palestine;[70] and although the Ottomans did, for most of their empire's existence, tolerate ethnic, national, and religious minorities and sometimes granted them a measure of autonomy (while retaining ultimate power), the Ottoman regime was decidedly unfriendly to attempts to establish full sovereignty by the non-Turkish, non-Muslim peoples it governed.[71]

Zionism had friends in British elite circles, as it did not among Ottoman leaders.[72] Nonetheless, during the three decades of the British Mandate in Palestine, the British authorities did not consistently keep faith with the Balfour Declaration's promise to "use their best efforts to facilitate the achievement" of a Jewish national home there. Yet they did enough, and permitted enough, for the Zionist enterprise to prosper. Affiliation with Britain and its Empire brought economic advances to Palestine, in which the Jewish population shared.[73] Zionist organizations unknown in the Ottoman period came into existence. British administrative methods, above all the rule of law, took root.

Most important of all, through such immigration as was permitted (and also by means of immigrants who reached Palestine in defiance of the British) as well as by natural increase, the Jewish population enjoyed robust growth. In 1918, it had numbered about 60,000. By the end of 1947, it had reached 630,000.[74] That total turned out to be large enough to muster the resources and the manpower necessary to repel the Arab onslaught when the State of Israel was established. An appreciably smaller population probably could not have survived it.

World War II made possible the creation of the State of Israel, and for the same reasons that led to the end of British rule in India a year earlier.[75] The war exhausted the British people, drained the country's resources,[76] and severely weakened the national will to hold on to Palestine, especially because, as in India, internal opposition to British rule was rising.[77]

The opportunity for reestablishing a state was one of the two major consequences of the war for the Jewish people. The other was the Holocaust, the murder of 6 million Jews on the European continent.[§] In the political debate that Israel's creation generated, a theme emerged that connected the two events. The world supported the creation of Israel, it was contended, to compensate for the destruction visited on the Jews by Nazi Germany. The contention became popular among those opposed to the very existence of a Jewish state in the Middle East, especially in the Arab world, where it was claimed that the Palestinian Arabs had been made to suffer for the sins of European Christians.

Ben-Gurion certainly did not regard the Holocaust as an asset for Zionism. To the contrary, it constituted a terrible setback because it deprived Israel of the Jews who, had they lived, would have populated the country.[78] Nor did Holocaust-induced sympathy for the Jewish people tilt the major forces of geopolitics in favor of the Zionist cause. The Soviet Union accorded immediate diplomatic recognition to Israel because its dictator, Josef Stalin, believed that that would weaken the British Empire: capitalist and imperialist Britain was a postwar adversary—although a wartime ally—of the USSR. American recognition came at the behest of President

---

§ "The statistics of the 'Final Solution' numbered 2,800,000 Polish Jews, 800,000 Soviet Jews, 450,000 Hungarian Jews, 350,000 Rumanian Jews, 180,000 German Jews, 60,000 Austrian Jews, 243,000 Czechoslovakian Jews, 110,000 Dutch Jews, 25,000 Belgian Jews, 50,000 Yugoslav Jews, 80,000 Greek Jews, 65,000 French Jews, 10,000 Italian Jews—all liquidated by shooting, gassing, hanging, burning, or starvation and disease." Sachar, *op. cit.*, p. 249.

Harry Truman, who overrode the wishes of the country's foreign policy bureaucracy, which sided with the Arabs for the same geopolitical reasons as did the British.[79] Nor, of course, did the murder of 6 million European Jews have any influence on the policies of Israel's Arab neighbors, who tried to destroy it. The Jewish state managed to survive thanks principally to the sacrifices of its citizens, rather than to international good will arising from the catastrophe of the war years.

Still, the Holocaust did inspire some such good will, which did work to Israel's advantage in some ways. In the UN General Assembly, a number of the votes in favor of partition, and thus for creating a Jewish state, came from Latin American countries that had no particular interests in the Middle East and seemed to have made their decisions at least in part on the basis of sympathy for the recent trials of the Jewish people.[80] The Jewish survivors of the European disaster also generated support for the Zionist cause.[81] Stuck in displaced person camps, understandably unwilling to return to their prewar home countries, almost all of them wished to join the Jewish community in Palestine. The British forbade this, arousing criticism from, among others, President Truman, who urged the government in London to admit the refugees promptly to their preferred destination.[82]

The fact of the Holocaust also motivated the Jewish community in the United States, after the war the largest and richest one in the world, to exert itself on behalf of the Zionist cause. Before the war, few American Jews had had any interest in relocating to Palestine, and for most of them the establishment of a Jewish state there did not have a high priority.[83] Some even opposed the project. The European catastrophe changed many of their minds. After the war, American Jews aided the Zionists by raising money for them,[84] in a few cases by volunteering their military services, and generally by making it clear that they very much wanted their own government to support the new state.[85] The strong bond between American Jews and Israel in succeeding decades had its roots in World War II and its consequences for the Jewish people. ¶

¶ The author's maternal grandfather, Samuel Weiss, told him a story that illustrates the point. In the 1930s, he was living in Tarrytown, New York, which is located in Westchester County a few miles north of New York City. Another member of the town's small Jewish community called on him and said, "We're forming a Zionist organization and want you to join." My grandfather asked, "How much are the dues?" "A dollar a year," he was told. He reached into his wallet, pulled out a dollar, handed it to his visitor, and said, "I give you this dollar so that you won't think that the reason I'm not joining your organization is that

One particular political force powerfully shaped the world in which Ben-Gurion lived and worked, especially in his later years: Arab hostility to the Zionist enterprise. It built steadily during the period of the Mandate and, with the British gone and the state declared, became a pervasive fact of Israel's national life, something of which the Jewish state had to be continually mindful and against which it had constantly to be prepared to defend itself. Ben-Gurion presided over two major Arab-Israeli wars and lived to witness three more. Ethnic and religious conflicts have been distressingly common since the twentieth century, and were hardly unknown before then, but the conflict between Jews and Arabs proved to be unusually long-lasting, for several reasons.

On the Arab side, it had a religious basis, as was clear in 1948.[86] The Arab world objected to a non-Islamic people enjoying sovereignty in the Middle East, a region that Muslims had dominated for the better part of a millennium. The conflict drew its intensity as well from Islam's long rivalry with the Christian West, of which the Arabs saw Zionism, despite the fact that it had nothing to do with Christianity, as a part.[87] The early Zionists came, after all, mainly from Europe, the citadel of Christendom. In the conflict with the West, Muslims had steadily lost ground since Napoleon's invasion of Egypt at the end of the eighteenth century. Zionism appeared to many Arabs to be part of that pattern. The creation of Israel inflicted a particularly painful blow to the Arabs' self-esteem because before the twentieth century they had known the Jews, who had lived among them for many generations, as a poor, weak, inferior, despised people. To have the French and the British control much of the Middle East was bad enough; to suffer defeat at the hands of the Jews was even worse.[88]

The outrage that Zionism provoked and the sting that its victory in 1948 delivered made opposition to Israel central to Arab politics. Virtually every Arab government sought to outdo all the others in its fidelity—always rhetorically and periodically militarily as well—to the anti-Zionist cause. Any leader who seemed insufficiently militant risked being deposed— or worse.[89] Israel had no interest in perpetuating the conflict but for

---

I am too cheap to pay the dues. I am not joining because I am not a Zionist." I asked him, "Why weren't you a Zionist?" "I thought America was the country for the Jews," he replied. Knowing of his support for Israel, I then asked, "What made you change your mind?" He said, "After the war there was no choice."

twenty-five years had no way to end or modify it, as Arab governments refused even to sit in the same room as Israeli officials.

One Arab country broke with this pattern, or at least tried to do so. The Kingdom of Jordan maintained clandestine contacts with the Zionists both before and after 1948. For their own reasons, its monarchs—first Abdullah and then his grandson Hussein—seem genuinely to have wished to stay out of the Arab-Israeli wars of 1948 and 1967. On both occasions, however, the countervailing pressure from the Arab world in general and from the Jordanian population in particular proved too strong for them to resist.[90]

Because the Arabs of the Middle East vastly outnumbered the Jews of Israel, and because Israel had no desire to follow in the footsteps of the Ottomans and govern the entire region, the Arabs could avoid coming to terms with the Jewish state simply by refusing to have anything to do with it beyond attacking it.[91] Yet the Arabs could not end it in the way that they themselves preferred, by defeating Israel. Plagued by rivalries among the different countries into which they were divided, and with societies less suited than was Israel to mustering modern, effective military forces, they lost the five Arab-Israeli wars waged during Ben-Gurion's lifetime. Over time, moreover, and thanks in no small part to Ben-Gurion's personal efforts, the military gap between the two sides widened. Israel became increasingly capable of coping with Arab assaults, but the continuing prospect of such assaults weighed heavily on the life of the state Ben-Gurion had proclaimed in 1948.

Leadership

David Ben-Gurion once said that he had been a Zionist since the age of three. That allegiance lasted for his remaining 84 years. Indeed, it determined the course of his life. The Zionist idea to which he devoted himself combined traditional and modern elements.[92]

The Jewish religion emphasizes the connection of the Jewish people to their ancestral homeland. Its liturgy, religious commentary, and holy-day rituals all make frequent reference to it and to the city of Jerusalem.[††] No one with even a slight acquaintance with Judaism can miss the centrality

---

[††] "... throughout all the centuries of Jewish dispersion until modern times, Zion, hardly less than the Deity, functioned as a binding integument of the Jewish religious and social

of the ancient homeland.[93] Yet it was only in the late nineteenth century that Theodore Herzl created a program for actually returning the people to *Eretz Yisrael*—the land of Israel—and established an organization to bring this about.

In so doing, he was conforming to the spirit of the age: in Herzl's time, the idea that individual nations should live within their own sovereign states was gaining in popularity, and in the twentieth century this became the only widely accepted basis for apportioning sovereignty. It became an international norm that sovereign states should be nation-states, and not multinational empires, which had long dominated the planet and in three of which Ben-Gurion spent his first 62 years. Herzl anticipated Woodrow Wilson's emphasis on the principle of national self-determination[94] by two decades, but the idea was already in the air when the first Zionist Congress met in Basel in 1897.[95] In that sense, Zionism—Jewish nationalism—belongs to the major global political trend of its era, and its rise can be understood as an ordinary, predictable development.

Yet what Herzl set in motion and Ben-Gurion, along with others, brought to fruition counts as something extraordinary as well. The Jewish people had not, after all, had their own state for nineteen centuries. Over that long period, they had dispersed widely: only a small fraction of them actually lived in the territory where Herzl aspired to refound their state. They spoke a number of different languages—at the end of the nineteenth century virtually none used Hebrew, which was to become the national language of Israel, in daily conversation—and practiced widely varying versions of the religion. Some Jewish communities had lost touch with other, distant ones for centuries.

Moreover, from Herzl's era to the establishment of the state and beyond, only a minority of Jews embraced Zionism in that the majority of them worldwide did not move to the Yishuv or later to Israel.[96] Still, in the face of these conditions, and of the opposition of the British and the Arabs and the indifference, at best, of the rest of the world, not to mention the Holocaust, Zionism achieved its goal, thereby demonstrating that it was a very powerful idea indeed.

Ben-Gurion not only embraced Zionism, he considered himself a socialist as well. Far from regarding the two as incompatible, he considered

experience. Rabbinic and midrashic literature, the prayer book, medieval literary treatises, all displayed a uniform preoccupation with the Holy Land." Sachar, *op. cit.*, p. 5.

the second integral to the first. For him, Zionism entailed not only the return of the Jewish people to the land from which they had originally come but also the transformation there of Jewish life, and individual Jews. Traders, merchants, artisans, and sometimes members of the professions in Europe, the Jews, he believed, had to become workers in the Holy Land to sustain themselves there.[97] In particular, in Palestine they had to reclaim, and then work on, the land. He considered the agricultural labor in which he had briefly engaged after his arrival in 1906 to be the heart of the Zionist project.[98]

While he observed the Soviet Union at first hand in the second half of 1923 and had words of praise for Lenin's qualities of leadership, Ben-Gurion was never a communist.[99] He did not believe in the dictatorship of the proletariat through a single, centralized party. Marxist-Leninists scorned mere "trade unionism" as a means to advance workers' interests, but Ben-Gurion built a powerful trade union, the Histadrut.

He did belong to the broader socialist tradition through his egalitarian values and his emphasis on collective rather than individual economic initiative. He spent his last years on a kibbutz, the embodiment of collective economic activity. He had little knowledge of free-market economics[100] and a low regard for businessmen and entrepreneurs.[101] Yet he did not hesitate to raise money from American Jewish capitalists, which demonstrated one of his guiding principles: where Zionism and his version of socialism conflicted, Zionism always prevailed.[102]

The primacy he accorded to the Zionist goal of establishing a Jewish state in Palestine helped him become an important figure in the movement to accomplish this and then the principal leader of the state it created. Personal qualities also put him in that position, but not every feature of Ben-Gurion's personality lent itself to political leadership.

He was not a warm or gregarious person. In his dealings with other people, he often adopted a brusque and sometimes combative manner. He said of himself, "I am a quarrelsome, obstreperous man."[103] He could be petty and vindictive. As prime minister, he denied permission for Jabotinsky to be buried in Israel[104] and for Chaim Weizmann's name to be added to the Declaration of Independence as one of the signatories.[105] (Weizmann had been out of the country on May 14, 1948, on a mission to Washington to persuade the American government to recognize the new Jewish state, which it did.) Indeed, Ben-Gurion had a personality in some ways better suited to making enemies—and he had his share—than friends, of whom, by his own admission, he had very few.[106] In his public and private communications, he was capable of departing from the truth. Still, he managed to win the trust and even the devotion[107] of those who had direct contact with him through traits of personality that compensated for his shortcomings.

He possessed enormous reserves of energy and would spend long hours on the tasks he set for himself. In pursuing his goals, he displayed persistence and determination.[108] He had an unusually large capacity for the often tedious work of starting and managing organizations.[109] Adept, hard-working bureaucrats do not inspire adulation, but others in the organizations in which they function come to depend on them. So it was with Ben-Gurion. In general, he rose to the leadership of the Zionist movement because of his single-minded devotion to it[110] and his success in steering it toward its ultimate aim.[111]

Political leadership in the twentieth century required winning support beyond the circle of people with whom the leader interacted personally. It required appealing to people who saw or heard him or both but did not know him. For this purpose, too, Ben-Gurion carried with him some handicaps. He was not a physically impressive figure: he stood about five feet tall with, as one historian put it, "unruly wings of white hair setting off a large bald head."[112] While he, like other titans of the twentieth century, was a man of the printed word, turning out books and articles[113] as well as keeping a detailed diary for most of his life,[114] leadership in his era generally required oratorical gifts, and here, too, Ben-Gurion was deficient.[115] He lacked the eloquence of the other pioneering Zionist leaders—Herzl, Weizmann, and Jabotinsky—and of his rival, Menachem Begin.

Here, too, however, Ben-Gurion had compensating advantages. People followed him in part because, like Wilson, Churchill, and Franklin Roosevelt, he possessed democratic legitimacy. He gained his positions of leadership in the Yishuv and then in Israel through free and fair elections. The people he led followed him, as well, because they shared his goal: creating and preserving a Jewish state. The passage to statehood and beyond proved to be a difficult, dangerous one. Ben-Gurion had seen Churchill's wartime leadership at firsthand†† and, although he lacked the

---

†† At the time, Ben-Gurion wrote of Churchill, "yet there are moments of crisis, hours when the scales of history waver between life and death, destruction and redemption, victory and defeat. The masses sway back and forth among possibilities, and one mistaken step, small oversight, temporary confusion, or misperception might prove decisive. In such

British prime minister's eloquence, he had the same knack of conveying confidence that the Jews, like the British people before them, would navigate that passage successfully.[116]

Others found his reassurance about the future credible because he had been right about the past. He had the gift of foresight, of seeing around historical corners. He was among the few Zionists to foresee that World War II would create the opportunity to establish a Jewish state,[117] that declaring it would trigger a major war with the Arabs,[118] and that the Yishuv therefore had urgently to prepare for the conflict to come.[119] He also anticipated early on the rising importance of the United States for the world as a whole and for Zionism in particular, and the corresponding decline of Great Britain's geopolitical weight.[120]

He not only foresaw challenges, he also understood what was necessary to meet them, especially the kind of armed forces the Jews of Palestine would need. Moreover, he operated effectively in moments of crisis,[121] when the stakes were high and momentous decisions had to be made quickly on the basis of incomplete information. He had the confidence, indeed the sense of his own personal destiny, to assume the daunting burden of making such decisions.[122] For these reasons, the Israeli public as a whole, like the members of the Mapai Party and Histadrut before them, came to regard him as indispensable.

One particular feature of Ben-Gurion's life contributed to his effectiveness as a leader. He had a passion for owning and reading books and for absorbing ideas and information from them. At his death, he had a library of 18,000 volumes and 5,000 periodicals.[123] He could read books and articles in eight languages, and in his fifties he taught himself ancient Greek and went through many of its classics.[124]

Sometimes he overestimated his grasp of what he had read,[125] but on the whole his eclectic reading of history, philosophy, and biography assisted him in his political career—the more so the higher he climbed and the greater the responsibility he assumed. What he read provided context and

---

an hour, the presence or absence of a leader who is courageous, quick-minded, far-sighted, and accomplished can make the difference between ruin and salvation." Quoted in Martin Kramer, "Ben-Gurion at the Moment of Crisis," *Mosaic*, February 24, 2020, https://mosaicmagazine.com/response/israel-zionism/2020/02/ben-gurion-at-the-moment-of-crisis. In retrospect, he seems to have been describing the standard of leadership that he himself would aspire to meet. "In 1948 he would attempt to emulate Churchill's model." Shapira, *Ben-Gurion*, p. 108.

precedent for, as well as historical examples similar to, the issues with which he had to deal. His acquaintance with the wars and the leaders of the past, with the mistakes and triumphs of other peoples and other leaders at other times, and with the way history can take unexpected turns and can suddenly present decisive moments,[126] while never providing precise formulas for him to follow, deepened his insights and heightened his confidence in his own judgment when he himself had to make decisions. Ben-Gurion the autodidact rendered real service to Ben-Gurion the Zionist leader.

Personal Imprint

Israel survived, and thrived, because it inherited working institutions from the Yishuv, notably functioning political parties and a powerful trade union organization providing a range of services to its many members. Ben-Gurion did not bring these institutions into being and manage them by himself, but no single individual did more than he to establish and develop them.[127] Had he done no more than that, he would have earned a place as one of the important builders of the Jewish state.

Of course, he did much more. He not only worked tirelessly to create the conditions for statehood, he pressed hard to declare a state when the British left Palestine. Other Zionists had doubts, reservations, and hesitations. After the passage of the UN partition resolution on November 29, 1947, when local Arabs began attacking Jewish settlements, the State Department of the United States, the country on which Ben-Gurion counted for support of various kinds, had second thoughts, as did others. The Department suggested that statehood be deferred and Palestine be placed under a United Nations trusteeship.[128] Ben-Gurion would not countenance a delay, and he swept his fellow members of the People's Administration, the decision-making body in the last days of the Yishuv,[129] along with him. (Overruling his advisors, President Truman recognized the new state.)

Ben-Gurion had the greatest influence of all the Zionists in not only laying the foundations of Israel but also declaring its establishment. It was he who publicly read aloud the Declaration of Independence on May 14, 1948, and that document was partly his handiwork: his editing produced the final draft.[§§] The often told story that on the eve of independence a

---

[§§] "While the declaration is identified with Ben-Gurion more than with anyone else, he didn't spend much time on it. He believed there should be a declaration of statehood,

closely divided administration held a vote on whether to proceed and the decision to do so passed narrowly, with Ben-Gurion's the deciding voice, is apparently not true. No such vote took place: by the middle of May, the independence initiative had broad support.[130] Still, in the weeks leading up to May 14, he never wavered in his view that a declaration of independence could not be postponed, and his conviction on this issue had an impact on his colleagues.

Ben-Gurion made his deepest personal imprint on the history of his times in military affairs. Issues of defense and war preoccupied him between 1945 and 1956,[131] and not surprisingly: the continuing existence of the Zionist project to which he had dedicated his life depended on the state's capacity to defend itself.

Between the end of World War II in 1945 and the partition resolution of November 1947, Ben-Gurion devoted his efforts to preparing for the war with the Arabs that he was certain would come. He organized the system by which contributions from overseas Jews, mainly in the United States, went to purchase weapons for the Jews of Palestine. He conducted his two-month-long Seminar in 1947 to investigate every aspect of the Yishuv's armed forces, which led to their reorganization. Ben-Gurion launched both initiatives himself and played a major role in carrying them out.

In the War of Independence, he functioned as the commander-in-chief and, as such, as is common in wartime, he exercised broad authority over how, where, and when the Jewish forces fought. When fighting broke out after the passage of the partition resolution, he decided initially to defend all Jewish settlements. He wanted to buy time to mobilize the military resources that waging the war would require, and he feared that abandoning any of them would damage morale and thus weaken the all-important will to persist in the war.[132] In April 1948, however, he ordered a change of approach. With Plan Dalet, the defense forces adopted offensive tactics,

---

but he let others do the drafting and didn't devote much of any waking day to its content." Martin Kramer, "Three Weeks in May: How the Israeli Declaration of Independence Came Together," *Mosaic*, May 19, 2021, https://mosaicmagazine.com/observation/isr ael-zionism/2021/05/three-weeks-in-may-how-the-israeli-declaration-of-independence-came-together. However, "during the night before the declaration Ben-Gurion took [the previously prepared] text, cut back its length and shifted its tone, and early in the afternoon of the next day presented it to the People's Council as a fait accompli." Martin Kramer, "How Israel's Declaration of Independence Became Its Constitution," *Mosaic*, November 1, 2021, https://mosaicmagazine.com/essay/israel-zionism/2021/11/how-israels-declarat ion-of-independence-became-its-constitution.

which succeeded in pushing back Arab attackers across the country and clearing the lines of communication among the various Jewish population centers.

Throughout, he gave special attention to Jerusalem. The possession of it had potent symbolic value, in addition to which 100,000 Jews lived there.[133] For much of the first part of the war, Arab forces besieged the city, cutting its Jewish population off from the rest of the country. Ben-Gurion ordered repeated and sometimes costly military operations to lift the siege and relieve Jerusalem's Jews. Operation Nachshon, in April 1948, briefly opened the Tel Aviv-Jerusalem road, allowing desperately needed supplies to get through.[134]

Later, at his behest, the Israeli army launched a series of attacks on Latrun, a crucial point controlling the road from Tel Aviv and the coastal plain into the city that Jordan's Arab Legion held, in an effort to break the blockade that the Arabs were imposing. The attacks failed but did have the benefit for Israel of tying down Jordanian troops so that they could not be sent to assist Arab forces fighting elsewhere.[135] Israeli soldiers, engineers, and laborers ultimately succeeded in carving out an alternative road to the city, for the most part working on it clandestinely. It was called the "Burma Road" after an Allied supply route to China in World War II.[136] Still, by the war's end, the Israeli armed forces had liberated only the western part of Jerusalem, leaving its eastern part, including its Old City with its Ottoman walls that included the historic Jewish Quarter, in Jordanian hands.

Perhaps Ben-Gurion's most important decisions for the future of the Jewish state came in the latter part of the war, with Israel gaining the upper hand militarily. He ordered the conquest of the Galilee in the north and the Negev in the south,[137] which both became crucial parts of the Israeli state. His most controversial decision was his refusal to conquer all of Palestine up to the Jordan River, territory that had belonged to the ancient Jewish kingdom and where places of great historical and religious significance for Jews were located. As their armed forces grew stronger, Israel's generals came to believe such a conquest to be feasible.

Ben-Gurion had more than one motive for exercising restraint. He was concerned about an adverse political and conceivably even military reaction from Great Britain and the United States to Israel's occupying and annexing the territory. Nor was he eager to include a large additional Arab population in the new state.[138] Still, he did not oppose in principle incorporating what, after the 1967 War, became known to most of the world as the West Bank (of the Jordan River) and that many Israelis call by their biblical names, Judea and Samaria.

In producing the final draft of the Declaration of Independence, he had deliberately left out any designation of borders, not wishing to confine the new state to those that the UN partition resolution had designated. He regarded Israel's borders at the end of the War of Independence, delineated by what became known as the Green Line, as provisional.[139] When, as a result of the 1967 War, the West Bank did come into Israel's possession, he did not advocate returning it unconditionally to Jordan. He initially said that he would return the territories taken from the neighboring states only in exchange for full peace, which the Arab countries conspicuously did not offer. He later said that he would keep the Golan Heights to the north and the united city of Jerusalem under any circumstances.[140]

As commander-in-chief, Ben-Gurion made it a priority to ensure civilian control of the armed forces of the new state. For that purpose, he ordered the military action against the *Altalena* when his demand that all armaments that the ship carried be turned over to the new government was not met.[141] It was for that same purpose that he disbanded, in October 1948, the Palmach, the elite fighting unit of the Haganah: he feared it might ultimately be tempted to act independently of the legal civilian authority of Israel.[142] Many of the new countries that emerged in the wake of World War II experienced military coups and the disruptive growth of independent militias, making their politics violent and unstable. Whether Israel would have suffered that fate without Ben-Gurion's measures to ensure civilian control of the military cannot be known; but it is a fact that such disruptions, common elsewhere in the Middle East, never occurred in the Jewish state.

After the War of Independence, Ben-Gurion, as both prime minister and defense minister, oversaw the creation of a permanent national army. He became the father of the Israel Defense Forces (IDF).[143] He insisted that they become a Western-style professional force, with a clearly delineated hierarchy. Under his supervision, Israel adopted a manpower system in which every male spent a few years as a full-time soldier and then remained a member of the army's reserves for a couple of decades thereafter, training for one month in each year and subject to immediate mobilization in case of emergency—which happened in both 1967 and 1973.[ε]

[ε] Sachar, *op. cit.*, p. 477. Ben-Gurion also said that "the army must serve as an *educational and pioneering center* for Israel youth—for both those born here and newcomers. It is the

He put his stamp, as well, on the new state's doctrine for employing force, which, given Israel's small size, emphasized waging war on the territory of its adversaries rather than its own. Israel also adopted the practice of responding to border raids with swift and fierce reprisals, with the aim of deterring future incursions.[144] In addition, Ben-Gurion stipulated that, while Israel had to rely only on its own troops in war, for the purpose of obtaining weaponry as well as for political support in the international arena, the state should always have at least one great power as an informal if not formal ally.[145] France filled that role until 1967, after which the United States gradually replaced it.[146]

He made one other important contribution to his country's overall defense policy. He decided that, as a form of insurance against the annihilation its Arab neighbors were threatening to visit on it, Israel needed an atomic bomb. France supplied relevant technical assistance, and the government built a research reactor in Dimona in the southern part of the country. Over the years, according to widely circulated reports, a stockpile of nuclear weapons accumulated. Israel never officially confirmed these reports, saying only that it "would not be the first" to introduce nuclear weapons into the Middle East.[147]

As important as were the military issues he addressed when he dominated the public business of the Yishuv and the new state, Ben-Gurion had to make time as well for nonmilitary matters. None of these was more consequential than immigration. Independent Israel found itself unexpectedly inundated with Jews from predominantly Arab and Muslim countries.

The Jews from Eastern Europe who governed the infant state had reservations about accepting the new immigrants,[148] who followed different customs; spoke unfamiliar languages; had in most cases scant experience with modern, Western ways; and had generally not embraced Zionism in the form envisioned by Herzl and his successors. The Jews of Islam came to Israel not because they sought to build a modern state in the ancestral homeland and only to some extent because of their traditional attachment to that homeland, but mainly because they had no choice: life in the countries where they had resided had become intolerable and they had nowhere else to go.

---

duty of the army to educate a pioneer generation. . . ." Quoted in *ibid.*, p. 478. (Italics in the original.)

Ben-Gurion shared some of these reservations, but he acted on the conviction that the newcomers had to be welcomed and given whatever the state could provide to make them full citizens, wholly integrated into its economic and social life.[149] Israel had, he believed, to be the state of all the Jewish people, and in particular a haven for those persecuted in their home countries. The absence of such a haven had effectively condemned millions of European Jews to death during World War II. He understood, as well, that the state's capacity to defend itself ultimately required as large a population as possible, in order to create as large an economy and as large an army as possible. Since American Jews would not and the Jews of the Soviet Union could not immigrate to Israel, the Jews of the Middle East offered the only near-term prospect for building a more formidable state. So committed was he to these immigrants that he gave funding for transporting, sheltering, and absorbing them priority over defense spending.[150]

As prime minister, he launched three additional initiatives he considered crucial for the state's future. While not personally fond of the city of Jerusalem, he deemed an official Israeli presence there a major political and strategic asset. He therefore moved to nullify the effort in the UN to give it a special international status by declaring it Israel's capital on December 10, 1949, a declaration the Knesset ratified three days later, and locating the government, notably including the Knesset, in West Jerusalem.[151]

Moving the national capital to Jerusalem aroused little controversy in Israel. Accepting reparations from West Germany, by contrast, proved deeply divisive. Demonstrations against the measure became violent.[152] The opposition leader in the Knesset, Menachem Begin, who had lost most of his family in the Holocaust, said, "There are things in life that are worse than death. This is one of them. For this we will give our lives. We will leave our families. We will say goodbye to our children, but there will be no negotiations with Germany. . . ."[153]

The opponents of reparations accused Ben-Gurion of desecrating the memory of the victims of the Holocaust. He stood fast in support of accepting money from a German government, and prevailed. His highest and most urgent obligation, as he saw it, was to the Jews who had survived and in particular to those who were building the new Jewish state, which needed all the financial assistance it could get.[154] The reparations payments came at a time, in the early 1950s, when Israel's finances were under severe strain. They helped to pay for badly needed infrastructure, which formed the basis for the surge in economic growth that the country experienced later in the decade.[155]

Ben-Gurion was not finished with Germany. He authorized, early in 1960, the capture of Adolf Eichmann, the highest-ranking Nazi still at large and a key figure in the systematic murder of 6 million Jews, who was hiding in Argentina. Eichmann was placed on trial in Jerusalem for crimes against the Jewish people and against humanity, as well as for war crimes. He was convicted and executed—the only application of the death penalty in Israel's history. In the Eichmann affair, Ben-Gurion had an educational purpose in mind. He wanted to compel the world to confront, and even more importantly to make known to the generation that had grown up in Israel after World War II and to older Israelis who had not lived through the war in Europe, the details of what had befallen the Jewish people in those terrible years. In this, he succeeded. The trial captured the world's attention, Israelis followed it closely on radio, and the subject of the Holocaust, previously little mentioned in Israel and elsewhere, became a more common subject of discussion.[156]

Finally, Ben-Gurion presided over the second Arab-Israeli war in 1956. The Israeli role in that joint campaign with France and Great Britain came at his personal initiative: he kept the cabinet in the dark about it until the last moment.[157] The Army's Chief of Staff, Moshe Dayan, took the lead in planning and supervising the military operations, but Ben-Gurion made the major political and diplomatic decisions. The war did not achieve all that he had hoped. Israeli forces were compelled to withdraw from the positions they had occupied, the Egyptian leader Gamal Abdel Nasser emerged from the conflict more popular than ever in the Arab world,[158] and Israel's international reputation suffered by the country's association with what came to be seen as the last gasp of European imperialism.

Yet the Sinai Campaign was not, in the end, an unmitigated strategic fiasco for Israel, as it proved to be for Britain and France. It brought some benefits. The military prowess that the Israeli armed forces displayed impressed even countries critical of Israel for having attacked Egypt. Perhaps most importantly, the operation enhanced the confidence of the Israeli people that Arab military power would not be able to crush them. Cross-border attacks against Israeli settlements did diminish.

In return for Israel's ultimate withdrawal from the territory it had gained, the United States gave Israel a guarantee of free passage through the Straits of Tiran, one of the objectives for which it had fought.[159] When in 1967 Egypt once again blocked the Straits, however, the American government did not fulfill its guarantee. That led to another Arab-Israeli war, the first one not fought with Ben-Gurion in charge of Israel's armed forces. The Six-Day War of June 1967 turned out to be more momentous, and had far longer-lasting consequences than the 1956 Sinai campaign.[160]

The Legacy

In common usage, the word "statesman" connotes a skilled, respected political leader. Applied to David Ben-Gurion, it has a more literal meaning. He was a man of the state.[161] He devoted his life to laying the basis for a Jewish state in the Middle East, establishing it, protecting it, and building and strengthening it.[162] Yet seventy-five years after it came into being, and fifty years after he passed from the scene, Ben-Gurion's state had departed in important ways from what he had wanted it to be and anticipated that it would be.

The socialist features of the Yishuv and the state in its early years had all but disappeared. Farmers and workers did not form the core of the country's economy. In income and wealth, it had become less equal than in Ben-Gurion's day. The collective institutions with which he had been closely associated—the kibbutz and the Histadrut—had declined in power and cultural importance.[163] Twenty-first-century Israel did not fit the image of Ben-Gurion's democratic socialism, which had had its origins in Eastern Europe. It had become, instead, a wealthy, modern, Western, urban society that excelled at innovation and the most advanced digital technologies and took full advantage of the increasing volume of cross-border flows of trade and investment known as globalization.

In addition, religion came to have a greater impact on the affairs of the state and the daily lives of Israelis than Ben-Gurion had expected or desired. The rituals of the Jewish religion played a vanishingly small part in his own life.[164] Nonetheless, when the state was established he had made concessions to observant (sometimes called ultra-orthodox) Jews, giving them control over marriage and religious conversion. He also agreed to the enforcement, in official activities, of the Sabbath and dietary laws and to providing state subsidies for young orthodox men to immerse themselves in religious studies without being required to perform military service. He allowed all this because he found the political parties representing the observant Jews to be convenient coalition partners and because he assumed that the beliefs and customs that they had brought from their traditional communities in Europe, with which Ben-Gurion was familiar from Plonsk, would fade away. That assumption proved incorrect. The ultra-orthodox communities sustained high rates of fertility, retained and passed on their traditional way of life, and over the decades became a far more rather than less visible and influential part of Israeli life.[165]

Finally, Ben-Gurion's Labor Zionist political party lost its dominant political position and over time diminished in significance, becoming, by the third decade of the twenty-first century, a marginal presence in the Knesset and in Israeli political life in general. The party descended from Jabotinsky's Revisionist movement, which was initially called Herut and then Likud, first formed a government in 1977 under the leadership of Jabotinsky's loyal follower Menachem Begin, and over the ensuing decades became the leading political force in the state. One of its members, Benjamin Netanyahu, the son of Jabotinsky's secretary, Ben-Zion Netanyahu, eclipsed Ben-Gurion himself as the longest-serving prime minister in the history of the state.

Labor Zionism's political decline had several sources. Its social and economic outlook became decreasingly relevant to twenty-first-century Israel. It suffered electorally from the allegiance to other parties of the Middle Eastern Jews and their descendants, many of whom considered themselves to have been neglected and even mistreated by the Mapai government during their early years in Israel. The strong distrust of anything resembling the socialism under which they had been forced to live in communist countries on the part of the immigrants who arrived from those countries in the 1980s and 1990s further weakened Ben-Gurion's political heirs. In addition, the representatives in the Knesset of the ultra-orthodox Jews came to feel more comfortable in alliance with the secular parties of the right than of the left.

External events also significantly affected Israeli public life, above all the three wars with the Arab states that took place after Ben-Gurion's period in power but during his lifetime. In June 1967, after Nasser closed the Straits of Tiran and threatened Israel with annihilation, the Israeli Defense Forces scored a swift and sweeping military victory. They conquered the Golan Heights from Syria to the north, the West Bank of the Jordan River and Jerusalem from the Kingdom of Jordan to the east, and the Sinai Peninsula and the Gaza Strip to the south from Egypt. The West Bank had formed part of the Jewish state of antiquity, and Israelis began establishing settlements, which grew into towns and small cities, to the east of the 1949 cease-fire line.

In October 1973, Egypt and Syria launched attacks on Israel from the north and south but were repulsed, although with serious Israeli losses. In the wake of that war, negotiations began that led, in 1979, to a peace treaty with Egypt. With the largest Arab state removed from the anti-Israel coalition, major wars against the Jewish state, like the five that had been fought in 1948, 1956, 1967, 1969–1970, and 1973, were no longer feasible. Israel remained in control of the West Bank and Gaza (it withdrew unilaterally from Gaza in 2006) and thus of a large Arab population. This generated pressure both from within and from outside Israel to find a different political status for these territories; and in the 1990s negotiations for that purpose took place between the Israeli government and the Palestine Liberation Organization, headed by Yasir Arafat.

Although the negotiations did produce some alterations in the governance of the territory between the Green Line and the Jordan River, with the Palestinians gaining more control over it, what became known as the "peace process" ended badly. Arafat, it became clear, sought not to make peace with the Jewish state but rather to continue the effort begun in 1947 to destroy it. In 2000, he launched an insurrection that included terrorist attacks against Israeli civilians, which the Israeli army finally suppressed. Prime ministers from Ben-Gurion's Labor Zionists—former generals Yitzhak Rabin and Ehud Barak—had started the negotiations with the Palestinians and had conducted the majority of them. The violence that ensued discredited them and their political party in the eyes of many Israelis. The agent of remarkable success during Ben-Gurion's heyday, the party he had founded and led became identified with weakness, misjudgment, and failure.

Yet Ben-Gurion's most important and enduring institutional legacy was not the Mapai Party, which he, in in any case, left in 1965 to form another, short-lived and unsuccessful one. His chief legacy was, rather, Israel's armed forces, without which Israel would not have survived—in 1948 or thereafter. Ben-Gurion did more than anyone else to create them, and he did so almost from scratch. In the diaspora, the Jewish people had engaged in politics, in economics, and in scientific and cultural pursuits over the centuries, sometimes with distinction; but lacking a state, the Jews had no military tradition. Ben-Gurion founded one.

With his guidance, the IDF trained and, when necessary, mobilized much of the country's adult population. The IDF incorporated and sometimes pioneered the most advanced military technologies of the twentieth and twenty-first centuries, which other countries were eager to purchase. It became the most formidable fighting force in the Middle East, and among the most effective in the world.

Moreover, for all the differences between what Ben-Gurion wanted for the state and what it became, the Israel that developed after 1948 did correspond to the essential features of his vision. It was a sovereign, democratic state[166] with a Jewish majority. Over the years, it grew more populous, wealthier, more powerful, more secure—although it confronted terrorist organizations committed to its destruction on both its northern and southern borders, one of which, Gaza-based Hamas, launched an attack that massacred almost 1,300 Israelis on October 7, 2023. The country also became steadily more widely respected for its achievements.

Those achievements were remarkable. As the distinguished expert on modern Middle Eastern affairs Fouad Ajami put it:

> On a barren, small piece of land, the Zionists built a durable state. It was military but not militaristic. It took in waves of refugees and refashioned them into citizens. It had room for faith but remained a secular enterprise. Under conditions of a long siege, it maintained a deep and abiding democratic ethos.[167]

Zionism began as a utopian, late-nineteenth-century idea held by a few powerless individuals. That idea begat, against daunting obstacles and powerful resistance, a vibrant twenty-first-century nation-state.[†††] In historical perspective, that trajectory seems so unlikely as to qualify as miraculous, which makes David Ben-Gurion, who did more than anyone else to make it happen, a miracle-worker.[168]

---

††† "A diaspora nation that had not had a political tradition for centuries, had learned how to survive in different climates and under a variety of regimes, and lacked its own power base succeeded within a very short time in laying the foundations for existence in a harsh country, far from economic centers and resources of culture and knowledge. Within half a century the Zionists gained international recognition for the entity they had founded, established a state, gathered in its exiles from the four corners of the earth, and created *ex nihilo* a vibrant democracy, a modern economy, an impressive defense force, and a flourishing, challenging culture." Anita Shapira, *Israel: A History*, Lebanon, New Hampshire: University Press of New England/Brandeis University Press, 2012, p. 470.

In his living room at Sde Boker, he had a portrait of Abraham Lincoln,[169] one of the historical figures he most admired. The American president whose public career his most closely resembles, however, is the first one, George Washington. Both he and Ben-Gurion led their people in victorious wars of independence and presided over the establishment of a new state in the wake of that war. Both set their new countries—each of them, as it happens, built by immigrants—on a course of political liberty and economic success. Washington is known as the father of his country. Ben-Gurion deserves the same title for his.

The United States honored Washington by giving his name to its capital city and one of its fifty states, as well as to countless institutions of learning. In a part of the world with a very long history, whose prominent geographic features had already had many names going back to biblical times, Ben-Gurion's name has had a less exalted destiny. Israel has attached it to a university not far from Sde Boker and to the country's major airport.

To appreciate David Ben-Gurion's impact on the world, however, a visitor to Israel arriving at that airport and driving from there into the country it serves would do well to follow the exhortation contained in the Latin inscription for Sir Christopher Wren, perhaps England's greatest architect, in his most prominent creation, St. Paul's Cathedral in London: *Si monumentum requiris circumspice.* If you seek his monument, look around you.

8

Mao Zedong

The Life

Mao Zedong[1] was born on December 26, 1893, in the village of Shaoshan, 30 miles southwest of Changsha, the capital of the province of Hunan in south central China. His father, although far from wealthy, owned more land than most of his peasant neighbors.[2] By his own account, Mao was fond of his mother but had an antagonistic relationship with his father.[3] At the age of 8, he was sent to a local school, where he learned to read and write and became acquainted with the Chinese Confucian classics.[4] He left school at 13 but decided he wanted more education and resumed his career as a student from 1911 to 1918, for most of that time at a normal school in Changsha from which he emerged with qualifications as a teacher.[5] Although he never attended university, Mao was far better educated than almost all Chinese of his generation.[6]

As he grew up, he became acutely aware of the political turmoil that enveloped his country. Having lagged behind the West for more than a century in mastering the techniques of the Industrial Revolution, China was poor. It was also disorderly: the fall of the last imperial dynasty, the Qing, in 1911 led not to a stable government but to the rise of local potentates known as warlords, who asserted their authority, often brutally, amid widespread banditry and violence.[7] This dismayed educated Chinese such as Mao, who were also dismayed, indeed humiliated, by the ongoing control of parts of the country—mainly coastal enclaves—by foreign powers[8] as well as by foreign domination of China's economy. The search for a way for China to escape its degraded condition preoccupied the young Mao and others like him.[9] It was his chief concern as, after finishing his schooling, he spent time in Beijing and Shanghai, worked as a journalist,[10] and joined several study groups of likeminded young people devoted to considering the country's future course.[11] During these years, he also married.*

Mao's search for a path to salvation for China led him to communism.[12] He joined twelve other Chinese and two European envoys from the Soviet Union at the founding Congress of the Chinese Communist Party in July 1921 in Shanghai.[13] With his membership came a commitment to work for a revolution in China like the one the Bolsheviks were making in the Russian Empire,[14] and to that end he became a labor organizer for the Party. Deployed to his home province of Hunan, he began to see, contrary to Bolshevik doctrine that emphasized the urban proletariat as the vehicle of such a revolution, the revolutionary potential of the far more numerous rural peasantry from which he himself came.[15]

Two events transformed his life and the life of the Chinese Communist Party. The Soviet leadership, the patron and guide of China's Communists, ordered the Party to merge with the Kuomintang (KMT),[16] the most prominent national political party, which had played a role in the overthrow of the Qing in 1911 and was attempting, with initial success, to defeat the warlords and unite the country. The KMT, however, under the leadership of Chiang Kai-shek, turned on the Communists in April 1927, killing or imprisoning many of them and forcing others to abandon public political activity and try to survive and operate in hiding.[17] In September of that year, Mao led a rural insurrection in Hunan, which came to be known as the Autumn Harvest Uprising. It failed, and he had to flee.[18]

He and other Communists established, from 1928 to 1934, two safe areas under their control: the first, from 1928 to 1930, near the Jiangguang Mountains on the border between Hunan and Jiangxi Provinces;[19] the second, from 1928 to 1934, in Jiangxi itself.[20] There, Mao built what he had concluded the Chinese Communist movement desperately needed— an armed force.[21] There, he developed the guerrilla tactics that the Communist army used to fight against the larger, better-armed forces

---

* Officially, Mao had four wives during his lifetime. The first marriage was arranged by his parents, was apparently never consummated, and the young lady died at an early age. Mao's second wife was executed by his political enemies, the Kuomintang; his third suffered from mental instability and spent a number of years in the Soviet Union; and his fourth, the former actress Jiang Qing, became a prominent political ally in the last years of his life. Philip Short, *Mao: The Man Who Made China*, Revised Edition, London: I.B. Taurus, 2017, p. 354.

of the Kuomintang, which, under Chiang's leadership, now constituted the national government of China and continued to try to eliminate the Communists. There, he and the other Communists managed to expand the territory that they held. In a preview of what they would do when they succeeded in forming the government of the entire country, they exercised their authority in those years through, among other tactics, the use of terror.[22]

In this period as well, the campaigns of "rectification" commenced, in which allegedly wayward Communists were compelled to confess publicly whatever deviations from Party orthodoxy with which the leadership chose to charge them and then to incur punishment for their political crimes, including execution.[23] Mao and the Communists would continue to employ this practice wherever they held power, which, after 1949, included all of China.

Mao was one of the leading figures in Jiangguang and then Jiangxi, but not the undisputed leader either in the safe areas or in the Communist Party at large. The Party had three centers of power, with Moscow and the cadres who managed to continue to operate in Shanghai serving as sources of doctrinal and organizational authority in addition to the Communist zones in the southwest. In this three-cornered arrangement, as had been the case even before 1928, Mao's standing in the Party rose and fell.[24]

In October 1934, military pressure from the KMT, also known as the Nationalists, forced Mao and the other Jiangxi Communists to flee again.[25] Their retreat, with Chiang's army in pursuit, became known as the Long March. It lasted for a year and four days and covered 6,000 miles, as the Communists moved, mainly on foot, from the far southeast of China first in a westward direction and then to the north, ending in the northwest part of the country. In the course of their journey, they forded twenty-four rivers, crossed five mountain ranges, and fought more than 200 battles.[26] It was during the Long March that Mao became the supreme leader of China's Communists.[27] Out of the 86,000 who began the trek, only 5,000 remained at its conclusion. Communist propaganda later exaggerated and distorted the Long March to make Mao in particular seem more heroic than he had actually been; but even discounting for subsequent embellishments, the Long March counts as a considerable feat of perseverance and ingenuity.

In October 1935, the Communists reached the Yellow Earth Plateau, near the Yellow River in northwest China,[28] where they were out of range of the KMT forces. They made the village of Yan'an their headquarters for the next decade. In Yan'an, Mao sought to establish himself as a major communist theoretician, on a par with the principal Soviet leaders, Lenin and Stalin, through a program of intensive reading and a series of lectures on Marxism-Leninism.[29] The Yan'an period saw the beginning of what would become a full-blown cult of personality around him,[30] with his writings and sayings on politics and social policy treated as definitive blueprints for China's future.[31] In Yan'an, he became the chair of the Party's Central Committee and also of its directing body, the Politburo, giving him the title by which he would become known throughout the world: Chairman Mao. The so-called rectification campaigns and purges of Party members continued as well.[32]

Overshadowing what the Communists said and did in Yan'an, however, was an event that ultimately proved decisive for the Party and the entire country: the Japanese invasion and occupation of much of China. In 1931, Japan took over the northeastern province of Manchuria.[33] With his armed forces far weaker than those the Japanese deployed, Chiang Kai-shek was in no position actively to oppose them. Six years later, a military skirmish between Japanese and Chinese troops near Beijing on July 7, 1937, which came to be known as the Marco Polo Bridge Incident, triggered a Japanese push into north China, which included a successful assault on Chiang's capital city, Nanjing. He retreated up the Yangzi River and moved his capital to Chongqing in Sichuan Province, in the Chinese hinterland. With much of the country under the control of a foreign power, he agreed to suspend his war against the Communists and form a united front against the Japanese invader.

For his part, Mao proclaimed the Communist Party's stalwart opposition to the Japanese invasion and claimed that its People's Liberation Army (PLA) was fighting hard against the occupiers. In fact, Communist forces engaged in little combat against the Japanese, the burden of doing battle with whom fell mainly on Chiang's KMT. Indeed, the Nationalist forces suffered 90 percent of China's casualties in the anti-Japanese effort.[34]

During the Japanese occupation, the Communists, relieved of military pressure from Chiang's forces by the united front policy, expanded both the number of people they controlled and the size of their army. A small, battered band of survivors at the end of the Long March in 1935, a decade later Mao and his associates deployed 900,000 troops and controlled 90 million people, 1.2 million of whom were Party members.[35]

The Communists also succeeded, with help from Western visitors,[†] in presenting Yan'an as an oasis of equality, harmony, and good governance, in contrast to the chaos and suffering in the rest of China.[‡] They told the world that they welcomed diverse political orientations and points of view,[36] and an estimated 100,000 people, many of them well educated, migrated to Yan'an from other parts of China.[37]

Chiang's army did manage to hold out against the Japanese, never surrendering despite the terrible losses it incurred; but it never succeeded in evicting Japanese troops from China. Instead, the naval and air power of the United States ultimately defeated Japan, freeing China from its grip and setting the stage for renewed fighting between the KMT and the Communists.

The United States tried but failed to mediate a settlement between the two Chinese sides, and with that failure the Chinese Civil War began in earnest. At first, the Nationalists held the upper hand. Whereas in the summer of 1945 the KMT had controlled only 15 percent of China, a year later their control had extended to 80 percent of the country.[38] The Communists began to turn the tide by defeating the Nationalists in Manchuria in 1948. From there they surged southward, capturing Beijing in January 1949, Nanjing in April, Shanghai in May, Qingdao in June, and Changsha in August.[39] The PLA moved beyond the ethnically Han heartland of the country to conquer mainly Muslim Xinjiang in 1950 and largely Buddhist Tibet in 1951, thereby giving China borders as expansive as it had ever had in its long history.[40]

The Communists prevailed in the Civil War in part because of the fighting spirit of their troops and the skill of their commanders, in particular

---

[†] The most influential Western visitor was an American journalist named Edgar Snow, who conducted long interviews with Mao and wrote a book based on them entitled *Red Star Over China* that was highly favorable to the Communists and gained a wide readership. On Mao's ability to deceive Westerners about his real political commitments, see Alexander V. Pantsov with Steven I. Levine, *Mao: The Real Story*, New York: Simon & Schuster, 2012, pp. 321, 343–345, and Short, op. cit., p. 385.

[‡] Short, *op. cit.*, p. 339. "The war made between 60 and 90 million Chinese into refugees. Some went to the cities to survive, creating new urban environments, both in the occupied zones and in GMD territory. Crime and exploitation thrived, and life for refugees and city dwellers alike became chaos." Odd Arne Westad, *Restless Empire: China and the World Since 1750*, New York: Basic Books, 2012, p. 270. Between 1937 and 1945, "some 14 million to 20 million Chinese seem to have perished. . . ." Ranan Mitter, *Forgotten Ally: China's World War II, 1937–1945*, Boston: Houghton Mifflin Harcourt, 2013, p. 363.

Lin Biao, later to become defense minister and for a time Mao's designated successor. The shortcomings of Chiang Kai-shek's government and armed forces also made major contributions to the war's outcome. Chiang proved not to be an adept commander-in-chief,[41] the war against Japan had deprived him of his best troops—the Nationalist army had lost an estimated 3 million of them[42]—and rampant inflation cost his government support in China's cities.[43]

Chiang fled, with his senior officials, from the Chinese mainland to the island of Taiwan, 100 miles from the coast of Fujian Province in southeast China, where he established a government in exile. On October 1, 1949, even before the PLA had completed its conquest of the core of China and the non-Han provinces to the west, Mao proclaimed the establishment of the People's Republic of China.

His first order of business as the head of the new regime was to pay a visit to Moscow, the world headquarters of the global communist movement of which, by making the trip, he declared himself a loyal member. There, he met with that movement's undisputed leader, Josef Stalin. The visit, one of two trips Mao made to the Soviet capital (the only times he ever traveled outside China), did not go entirely smoothly, but he did sign a Treaty of Friendship with the Soviet Union and received promises of the economic assistance he sought.[44]

Mao's loyalty to international communism was put to an early test by a war in Korea, a former Japanese possession that had emerged from World War II divided between a communist north and a non-communist south. The war began on June 25, 1950, when North Korea attacked the south. The United States responded by sending troops to support South Korea. The North Korean army made substantial advances at first, overrunning the south's capital of Seoul, but American forces counterattacked, gained the initiative, and moved north across the previous dividing line, approaching the Yalu River, the border between Korea and China. The Communist government in Beijing launched a military intervention against the Americans and drove them back to the south. The war settled into a stalemate, and the fighting finally ended with a truce—although no final peace treaty—in 1953, leaving the Korean peninsula divided roughly where it had been when the fighting began. In all, China suffered an estimated 500,000 casualties, including 147,000 deaths.[45]

Mao had known about the North Korean attack in advance but was at first reluctant to involve his country in the war.[46] The Chinese leadership decided on intervention partly out of loyalty to the international communist cause[47] but mainly out of the fear that a United States that had conquered all of Korea would pose a serious military threat to the Communist government of China.[48] The Chinese intervention in the Korean War had the effect of estranging the People's Republic of China from the United States: for two decades thereafter, the two countries had no official diplomatic relations. The war also secured Chiang Kai-shek's regime on Taiwan: Mao had been planning a military operation to capture the island, but with the outbreak of the fighting in Korea the American president, Harry Truman, sent the American navy's Seventh Fleet into the Taiwan Strait separating the island from the mainland; and the United States committed itself to defend Taiwan, thereby preventing the Communists from taking control of it. The Korean War also helped to consolidate the Communist Party's power in China. Mao's new regime was able to rally the country against the United States, making it easier than it would otherwise have been to carry out its program for governance.[49]

That program consisted of implanting the Soviet political and economic system in China,[50] with an all-powerful Communist Party monopolizing political power and the state controlling all significant economic activity. Under Mao's leadership, the Chinese Communists adopted the Soviet emphasis on building up heavy industry and the Soviet practice of managing the national economy according to centrally imposed five-year plans. Also following the Soviet pattern, China's ruling Communists moved to eliminate private agriculture and herd the country's peasants into government-run collective enterprises. Ultimately, the new rulers all but abolished private property.[51]

Upon taking power, contrary to their promises in Yan'an of welcoming all Chinese to their movement,[52] the Communists also launched a bloody campaign against those they regarded as their "class enemies." The new regime dispossessed landlords and subjected them to public humiliation, persecution, torture, and often execution. The overall death toll probably reached several million.[53] In the first few years of their rule, the Communists also shut down private businesses.[54] In those years as well, almost all foreigners left China.[55]

Also following the Soviet model, the Communist authorities dramatically reduced the scope of individual liberty in China. They imposed strict censorship across the country and determined where Chinese could live and where they had to work. Like Stalin's Soviet Union, Mao's Chinese

People's Republic aspired to, and went a long way toward achieving, total control of the society it governed. Mao installed in China, that is, a totalitarian regime. [§]

In addition to the mass repression, however, by the middle of the 1950s Communist rule had some more attractive achievements to its credit. It had unified China, liberated all of it from foreign control, and restored order throughout the country. After the economically devastating disruption of World War II and the Civil War, both industrial and agricultural production began to increase. By its own standards, at least, the Communist Party of China could consider itself successful.

Mao, however, became dissatisfied. He came to believe that China was making unsatisfactory progress toward the socialism he envisioned for it. In an effort to accelerate that progress, between the end of 1956 and the middle of 1957 the government eased the strict censorship it had imposed and encouraged the Chinese people—which in practice meant Chinese intellectuals—to express their views on what was wrong with the country and what course it should follow. "Let a hundred flowers bloom, let a hundred schools of thought contend" became the slogan of what came to be known as the Hundred Flowers movement.[56]

The experiment in free speech ended abruptly and brutally. The criticism that ensued did not please Mao and the Party, and in July they reversed course by moving to squelch it.[57] They conducted an "anti-rightist" campaign in which those who had spoken out were punished. The repression claimed an estimated 500,000 victims.[58]

[§] "A system of work units, class labels, household registrations, and mass movements fixed each citizen in an organizational cage, within which people exercised political terror over themselves and each other. A pervading bureaucracy governed the economy, politics, ideology, culture, people's private lives, and even many of their private thoughts." Andrew J. Nathan, "Introduction" to Dr. Li Zhisui, *The Private Life of Chairman Mao: The Memoirs of Mao's Personal Physician*, New York: Random House, 1994, p. xi. "This combination of Soviet-style autocracy and ancient Chinese despotism resulted in an abuse of executive power exceeding that of the Soviet Union or of any of China's emperors, controlling politics, the economy, culture and ideology, and every aspect of daily life. The dictatorship's coercive power penetrated every corner of even the most remote village, to every member of every family, into the minds and entrails of every individual. Referring to this system as 'totalitarianism' denotes the expansion of executive power to its ultimate extent and extreme." Yang Jisheng, *Tombstone: The Great Chinese Famine, 1958-1962*, Translated from the Chinese by Stacy Mosher and Guo Jian, New York: Farrar, Straus and Giroux, 2008, p. 17.

On the heels of the Hundred Flowers campaign, Mao launched another and far more deadly initiative. He conceived the idea of increasing industrial and agricultural production so rapidly that China could catch up with the developed world in a relatively short time. The Party set what turned out to be unrealistically ambitious targets for steel and grain production and mobilized the entire country to achieve them.[59] What the Communists called "The Great Leap Forward" led, among other things, to the construction of small-scale "backyard" steel mills. Chinese throughout the country melted down appliances, farm equipment, and even utensils in a largely vain effort to produce usable steel.[60]

The principal result of the Great Leap Forward, however, turned out to be famine on a previously unknown scale. Agricultural output fell to dangerously low levels and, in consequence, by rough estimate 36 to 40 million people died.** The collectivization of agriculture, which destroyed individual incentives to grow as much as possible; the introduction of untried and unworkable agricultural techniques; the large-scale requisitioning of grain to support industrial workers in the cities; and the diversion of agricultural workers to the feckless and fruitless effort to industrialize the countryside all contributed to the precipitous decline in grain production.[61] At a meeting of the Politburo in the city of Lushan in Jiangxi in July and August of 1959, Peng Dehuai, the defense minister, criticized some aspects of the ongoing campaign. Other senior leaders did not join him. Mao had Peng purged.[62] Finally, in January 1961, the Party called a halt to the campaign.[63]

With the disaster of the Great Leap Forward, Mao retreated from the day-to-day direction of Chinese public policy,[64] but he returned with a vengeance in 1966, with another destructive national campaign that came to be called the Great Proletarian Cultural Revolution.[65] The Cultural Revolution counts as one of the most bizarre episodes not just in the long history of China but in the history of any country: a leader—Mao—unleashed a fierce and destructive assault on the political party and the

---

** Edward Friedman and Roderick MacFarquhar, "Introduction" to Yang Jisheng, *op. cit.*, p. x; Yang Jisheng, *op. cit.*, p. 430. "As in famines throughout Chinese history, men sold their wives if there were buyers.... Banditry reappeared. Cannibalism was rife. Bodies were exhumed and eaten. During the winters of 1959 and 1960, when the ground was too hard for burials, corpses littered the roadsides and river banks. Scavengers cut off the flesh and cooked it." Short, *op. cit.*, p. 498.

government that he himself headed, creating chaos throughout his own country.[66]

Mao seems to have had two motives for this, his last great campaign.[67] He wanted to root out the "bourgeois" notions and practices that he had made it his mission to eradicate in China and that he professed to believe had persisted in, or had seeped back into, Chinese life. The Cultural Revolution's announced targets were the "Four Olds:" old ideas, old culture, old customs, and old habits.[68] Concomitantly, he sought to reassert his domination over the Communist Party by removing from power (and sometimes killing) officials who, he had concluded, stood in his way and whom he accused of favoring and protecting all the things that he was determined to crush.[69]

The Cultural Revolution began, fittingly enough, with attacks on culture—initially, in November 1965, on a play that Mao considered to include unacceptable themes.[70] The focus then turned to Beijing, to its Party organization and its university, and ultimately to all figures of authority throughout the country. At a meeting of the Politburo's Standing Committee in March 1966, Mao called for waging class struggle in every educational institution in China.[71] He handpicked suitably radical—and loyal—people to oversee the campaign, including his fourth wife, Jiang Qing. He also called into being shock troops for his campaign in the form of students of all ages, who became known as Red Guards.[72] Eventually, they numbered 13 million. Beginning in Beijing and then spreading throughout the country,[73] they subjected teachers, Party officials, and anyone else suspected of bourgeois tendencies to bouts of harassment and often torture known as "struggle sessions," in the spirit of the recurrent Communist rectification campaigns of the past. The Red Guards also rampaged throughout the country, concentrating on urban areas and destroying whatever they deemed "old" or counterrevolutionary while looting the possessions of those they persecuted.[74]

Ultimately, workers joined the ongoing upheaval, and roving armed bands of workers and students—some radical, some trying to stop the radicals' excesses—clashed with one another.[75] The Mao-sanctioned revolutionaries took over municipal administrations in Shanghai and elsewhere.[76] In many parts of China, the government, the schools, and whole sectors of the economy ceased to function. At his 73rd birthday celebration in December 1966, Mao proposed a toast to "the unfolding of an all-round nationwide civil war."[77]

Having touched off the disruption and encouraged the Red Guards at several huge rallies in Beijing,[78] in late August 1967 Mao began to pull back.[79] In July 1968, he demanded an end to the destruction.[80] The next month the PLA was called in to quell the violence and take back control of the country.[81] Many of the students were dispatched to the countryside, to perform manual labor in harsh conditions.[82] While reliable statistics are lacking, the death toll of the Cultural Revolution probably reached 1.5 million, and perhaps more.[83] Among the dead was Liu Shaoqi, who had held the title of chairman of the People's Republic and was Mao's designated successor. He died a slow, painful death, with Mao's approval.[84] Mao then chose Lin Biao to succeed him, but in 1972, in still unclear circumstances, Lin attempted to flee the country and died in a plane crash.

The major events of China's Maoist era ended with two related foreign policy initiatives. In the first, China disavowed its alliance with the Soviet Union. In the 1950s, and particularly after Stalin's death in 1953 and his successor Nikita Khrushchev's denunciation of him in 1956, the Chinese Communists began to have doubts about the Soviet leadership's doctrinal orthodoxy, doubts that became public. The post-Stalin Soviet leadership, for its part, increasingly had its own reservations about Mao, particularly his seemingly cavalier attitude toward nuclear weapons.[85] In 1960, Khrushchev ordered the withdrawal of the Soviet technicians who were providing assistance of various kinds to the Chinese, having terminated aid to China's nuclear weapons program the year before.[86] Finally, in March 1969, the Sino-Soviet rift erupted into armed conflict. That month troops from the two countries engaged in several skirmishes on Damanskiy (Zhenbao) Island in the Ussuri River, which formed part of the Sino-Soviet border, and other clashes took place over the next several months.[87]

The relationship between the Soviet Union and the Chinese Communists—a relationship that, to be sure, had never been entirely harmonious[88]—erupted into an open conflict that had an ideological dimension. The Chinese opposed what they saw as the post-Stalin Soviet Union's unduly conciliatory approach to the capitalist West and in particular disdained Moscow's policy of "peaceful coexistence" with the West.[89] The Sino-Soviet rift also had a personal element. While Stalin had commanded Mao's sometimes grudging respect, Khrushchev did not; and for their part, Khrushchev and his colleagues regarded Mao's domestic campaigns as crazy and his views on the Cold War as dangerous.[90] Finally, underlying the rift lay an all-but-inevitable conflict. The Soviets considered themselves the leaders and directors of global communism. As communists, the Chinese were willing to defer to them, at least initially; but as Chinese, they were not going to accept a permanently inferior status to Russia—or indeed to any country.[91]

Because in 1969 the Soviet Union had far more powerful military forces than did mainland China, the Communist leadership in Beijing decided that it needed to strengthen its position in the competition with Moscow and did so by effecting a rapprochement with the United States. Diplomatic contacts between the two governments that at first took place secretly led, in February 1972, to a visit to Beijing, amid great fanfare, of the American president, Richard Nixon. By aligning itself geopolitically with the leading capitalist power, Communist China fortified itself in its confrontation with the leading Communist country. Even as Nixon traveled to the Chinese capital, however, Mao's health was visibly declining. He became increasingly decrepit and died on September 9, 1976.

The Times

The steep decline of traditional China formed the backdrop of Mao's early years, and his response to that decline determined the course of his life.[92] As late as the eighteenth century, the Chinese considered their country to be the wealthiest, the most powerful, and culturally the most advanced in the world—and had good reason to do so.[93]

Beginning in the nineteenth century, however, China suffered a series of blows that brought it low. The most destructive of these came from within. The Taiping Rebellion, which lasted from 1850 to 1864, put large parts of southern China outside the control of the ruling Qing dynasty and resulted in 20 million deaths—by that measure, the deadliest civil war in all of history.[94] In Mao's young adulthood, warlords held sway over much of the country and presided over, and themselves perpetrated, widespread violence.

China also suffered incursions from abroad that, while claiming far fewer lives and wreaking far less economic damage than its internal upheavals,[95] humiliated the Chinese by forcing them to cede territory to foreign countries to accommodate the foreigners' economic demands. The Communist regime came to refer to the period between the mid-nineteenth century and the establishment of the People's Republic in 1949 as the country's "century of humiliation." As a result of the Opium Wars of 1839–1842 and 1856–1860, in which Great Britain defeated the imperial Chinese forces, China was required to allow the British and other powers to establish "treaty ports" along the Chinese coast where the foreigners, not the Chinese emperor, held sway.[96] China lost a war to Japan in 1894–1895 as a consequence of which the Japanese took possession of Taiwan, and in Beijing in 1900 foreign troops quelled a Chinese anti-foreign uprising known as the Boxer Rebellion. The China in which Mao came of age, far from being the leading country on the planet, had become backward, chaotic, and the victim of foreign military power.

In the second half of the nineteenth century, in response to the country's decline, Qing officials had tried to implement reforms that aimed at strengthening China while preserving its traditional institutions and values, but they failed.[97] Mao and many in his age cohort believed that the country's salvation, which they were devoted to achieving, could only come about through radical change that discarded China's long-established traditions. For that reason, they looked abroad for inspiration and guidance. The young Mao found both in the Soviet Union. The Russian Revolution was the second historical development that framed his life and work.

It held a strong appeal to Mao as an example to follow because the Bolsheviks did in Russia what he believed was necessary in China. They ousted the old regime, destroyed the existing institutions, declared their opposition to the Western imperialism that plagued China, and were planning a radical economic reconstruction of the country so that it could protect itself, regain its once lofty position in the international system, and spread its revolution beyond its borders. The Russian revolutionaries accomplished all this through the ruthless use of violence, a tactic that Mao would adopt, wielded by a disciplined political party that arrogated all power to itself. Sharing or limiting his own power, as it turned out, formed no part of the Maoist approach to politics and governance.

For Mao and the Communist Party of China, the Russian Revolution served as more than an example. The Soviet Union, the state that the Bolsheviks created, presided over the founding of the Chinese Party, and in the twenty-eight years thereafter, before the establishment of the People's Republic, Moscow provided ideological tutelage and political guidance to its Chinese counterparts. To be sure, Soviet advice was not always sound. It sometimes reflected dogmatic Soviet principles,[98] or an insufficient grasp of Chinese realities, or the requirements of the security of the Soviet state, or the domestic political needs of the moment of Josef Stalin in his battle for primacy with other Bolsheviks.[99] Following Soviet recommendations did not always work to the advantage of the Chinese Communists.[100] For these reasons, Mao came to resent Moscow's interventions into the affairs of the Chinese Party, all the more so because at times the Soviet authorities did not favor him as the Chinese leader,[101] preferring instead Chinese cadres who, unlike Mao, had received training in Moscow.[102]

At other times, however, the relevant Soviet officials, including Stalin, did support Mao, and helped him to gain ascendancy in the Chinese Party.[103] Furthermore, and not least important, they gave that Party financial subventions, without which it could not have continued to function.[104] Moreover, Soviet assistance had a crucial impact during the Chinese Civil War. Soviet forces turned over territory in Manchuria to the People's Liberation Army[105] and supplied it with weapons. For all the weaknesses of the KMT, it is doubtful that the Communist side could have won the war without the support it received from Moscow. After 1949, moreover, Soviet aid rendered substantial assistance to China's economic development.

Mao departed from Leninist orthodoxy in important ways well before coming to power,[106] and he broke decisively with the Soviet Union itself in the late 1950s and 1960s; but the break came, in his own eyes (or at least in his own rhetoric), because of what he saw as the Soviet abandonment of Lenin and Stalin's original revolutionary principles, to which he himself (in his own mind) remained faithful. He repudiated the Soviet Union but not the Revolution that made it.

As with the other twentieth-century political Titans, the World Wars shaped the career of Mao Zedong. The first of them largely bypassed China: the country remained officially neutral for most of it and no major battles took place on Chinese soil.[107] During that war, however, Japan sought to exert extensive control over China through the "Twenty-One Demands" it presented to the Chinese government in January 1915.[108] Later, when the victorious powers at the Paris Peace Conference decided to give Germany's Chinese territory in Shandong to the Japanese, protests by Chinese workers and students erupted on May 4, 1919. Both offenses against China's sovereignty helped to promote the nationalist sentiment that Mao and the Communists were able to use to their advantage.[109]

The second global conflict of the twentieth century, by contrast, had a powerful impact on China, the Communist Party, and Mao himself. As with Lenin's Bolsheviks and World War I, Mao's Communists could not have come to power without World War II.[110] Without that war, the world might very well have taken no notice of Mao, just as without World War I Lenin would have remained an unknown figure, or at most a minor footnote to the history of the twentieth century. The Second World War dramatically weakened Chiang Kai-shek's government,[111] just as World War I had weakened that of the Russian tsar; and Chiang's failure to dislodge the Japanese from China discredited his regime in the eyes of many Chinese.[112]

Just as important for Mao's prospects for winning power, the Japanese assault forced the creation of a united front between the Nationalists and the Communists that gave the Communists some much-needed breathing space.[113] Free of attacks from the KMT forces, they could expand their territory and their army, which made them a far more formidable contender for power in postwar China than they would otherwise have been.[114] In addition, the Communists' portrayal of Yan'an as an oasis of political harmony and governmental efficiency, and their claim that the PLA was offering fierce resistance to the Japanese—although vastly exaggerated in both instances—won sympathy for their cause across China and beyond.

The outcome of World War II also favored the Communists. Japan lost the war, an obviously necessary condition for the Communists to take power throughout the country. Neither they nor the Nationalists defeated the Japanese army, although the KMT bore the brunt of the Chinese resistance to it.[115] The naval and air forces of the United States, operating in the Pacific, not on the Asian mainland, overcame Japan. The American victory made the Soviet Union, the wartime ally of the United States, a victorious power in the war in Asia even though Moscow declared war on Japan only in the war's final days. As part of the winning coalition, the Soviets were in a position to give vital assistance to the Communist side in the Civil War that followed, as they would not have been if World War II had turned out differently.

In the Pacific War, therefore, Mao and the Communists drew enormous benefit from the efforts of other parties that already were or soon became their enemies. The KMT helped to keep Japan from overrunning all of China, and the Americans put an end to the Japanese Empire in Asia, whose largest component was Mao's country.

Leadership

Mao Zedong was a man of the printed word—or rather, the printed character. He read newspapers constantly[116] and almost always had books at hand.[117] He wrote a good deal: journalism, doctrinal disquisitions, even poetry.[118] As with Lenin and Stalin in the Soviet Union, in China at the height of his power his works were treated as holy writ that offered wisdom, insight, and guidance for all Chinese.

Of the ideas he embraced, and about which he wrote, communism had, of course, pride of place. Mao's version of communism, however, owed relatively little to Karl Marx. He had not read much of Marx when he made his commitment to the communist cause[119] and had very limited interest in Marx's detailed analysis of the dynamics of capitalist economies. Properly speaking, Mao was not a Marxist but a Leninist.[120] Like the architect of the Russian Revolution, he was a connoisseur and a technician of power, with a lifelong preoccupation with obtaining it, keeping it, and using it.

However, Mao did not follow Lenin in every respect. In order to take into account the particular features of Chinese politics and economics, his own political thought and practice modified the received Leninist wisdom in two ways.[121] While Lenin, and Marx as well, placed their hopes for revolution in urban workers—the industrial proletariat—Mao saw the Chinese peasantry as the country's revolutionary class and based his strategy for taking power, which ultimately succeeded, on building communist strength in the Chinese countryside.

In addition, Mao concluded that spontaneous uprisings, of the kind that Soviet dogma insisted had brought about the Russian Revolution, would not deliver power to China's Communist Party. To protect itself, to spread its influence, and ultimately to take control of China, the Party needed an army. Mao, along with others, built a Communist army and because, initially, its KMT and Japanese adversaries deployed more and better-armed troops, the Communist forces at first employed guerrilla tactics, avoiding pitched battles and striking their adversaries in hit-and-run raids.[122]

Lenin considered nationalism a retrograde, un-Marxist idea, allegiance to which could only hinder the solidarity of the workers of the world that the global communist revolution that he envisioned required. Mao, however, was a nationalist, albeit in a way that virtually all educated Chinese were.[123] Unlike nineteenth- and twentieth-century nationalism in Europe and elsewhere, the Chinese variety did not seek an independent state for their nation, which had had its own sovereign political community for more than two millennia. Rather, Chinese believed—indeed assumed—that China ought to hold a preeminent position at least in East Asia and eventually elsewhere as well. Although the Chinese Communists rejected virtually every other feature of their country's past, they did not repudiate the presumption of superiority. That presumption lurked in the background of the Sino-Soviet rift and came to play an even larger role in post-Mao China than it did in his era.[124]

Mao also embraced the un-Marxist concept of voluntarism—the idea that human will can overcome material conditions. In so doing, he stood Marx on his head, since the intellectual founder of communism taught that material—that is, economic—conditions determined political institutions and practices. Mao's conviction that the reverse was true, or could sometimes be true, inspired the Great Leap Forward.[125]

Not only his ideas but also his temperament shaped his impact on China. Perhaps stemming from his turbulent childhood relations with his father,[126] Mao encouraged rebellion against authority throughout his life, including when the Communist Party, which he himself at least nominally headed, held power. "To rebel is justified" became one of his best-known aphorisms,[127] and the Cultural Revolution may be understood as a colossal act of rebellion against all established authority in Communist-governed China.

Like Lenin, Mao also had a predilection for violence. He was never reluctant to employ it. Indeed, he seemed to lack any ordinary compassion for other human beings and had a substantial capacity for cruelty, among the many pieces of evidence for which are his sanctioning of the persecution of his one-time designated successor Liu Shaoqi and his prevention of treatment for the cancer that killed his ever-faithful prime minister Zhou Enlai. Violence was his preferred tactic in dealing with those he considered enemies, and his list of enemies was a long one.[128] It included the KMT, Communist Party rivals, landlords, capitalists, the imperialist powers, and anyone he suspected of deviating from what he deemed the correct political path. Such deviants came to include not only the Chinese he caused to be persecuted and often killed but also the Communist Party of the Soviet Union, against which he went to war briefly in 1969.

Mao was able to impose his ideas and his impulses on China because of his mastery of the Chinese Communist Party. That mastery, in turn, had several sources. Not the least important of them was the fact that he managed to survive the unfriendly attentions, over the years, of various warlords, the KMT, and the Japanese, as very many Communists did not. By surviving, he enjoyed the continuing prestige of seniority as a founding member of the Party. In addition, in the debates within the Party during the decades after its founding about what to do to sustain itself and work toward gaining power, Mao's views proved to be correct. He turned out to be right in emphasizing the peasantry, right in waging guerrilla warfare, right in setting up safe areas in Jiangxi and Yan'an, and right in embarking on the Long March. In the course of the Long March, he made several tactical decisions that worked out well for the Communists. In general, being proven correct by events does a great deal for a leader's credibility, and Mao was no exception.

Within the Party, Mao maneuvered skillfully to gain, hold, and increase his personal power.[129] He proved to be adept at intrigue[130]—constantly vigilant in the service of protecting and enhancing his position, skillful at detecting and exploiting the weaknesses of others, and ruthless in pressing home his advantages. He had a gift for deceiving his rivals, actual or potential, who tended to end up obedient, repudiated, cast out, or dead.[131] The second most famous Communist of the Maoist era, long-time prime minister Zhou Enlai, became Mao's slavishly loyal subordinate.

While Mao's successful solutions to the problems the Party faced early on earned him the respect of the other Communists, his skill and brutality at intra-Party maneuvering intimidated them. Indeed, he intimidated even the most senior and experienced officials of the People's Republic,[132] who for the most part did not dare to object to, let alone act to prevent, Maoist schemes that they either expected or learned through bitter experience would end in disaster. The launching of and the persistence with the Great Leap Forward and the Cultural Revolution testify to Mao's hold over China's Communists.

Mao's success in implementing the initiatives he devised depended not only on Party leaders accepting them but also on mobilizing the Chinese people to carry them out. Here, the cult of personality that grew up around him, with his enthusiastic cooperation, played an important role.[133] In the People's Republic, images of him, some of them gigantic, were on display everywhere, an important method of generating political support in a society that in 1949 consisted largely of illiterate peasants. The Chinese public also learned of heroic deeds that Mao allegedly performed: to spark enthusiasm for the Cultural Revolution, he swam in the Yangzi River, moving at a pace that outstripped the fastest ever recorded—or so his official media reported.[134] His collected writings became the Communist equivalent of sacred texts and studying them a universal obligation in China.[135] The printed copies of the *Little Red Book* containing quotations from him reportedly numbered more than a billion,[136] and in the 1960s and 1970s no prudent Chinese allowed him- or herself to be found without a copy.

Lavish tributes to his genius, which would have been considered embarrassing or even pathological, in any other context, became routine. In 1966, Lin Biao asserted that

> "Chairman Mao is a genius. . . . One single sentence of his surpasses 10,000 of ours." The *People's Daily* then took up the cry: "Chairman Mao is the red sun in our hearts. Mao Zedong Thought is the source of our life. . . . Whosoever dares to oppose him shall be hunted down and obliterated." Mao's works, it said, were "more precious than gold"; every sentence is a war drum, every utterance a truth." [††]

By the end of Mao's rule, China had returned to its political roots. He became the communist version of a traditional Chinese emperor: isolated from the everyday life of the country,[137] making occasional ceremonial public appearances, and periodically issuing binding decrees.[138]

Mao mobilized China society to achieve the goals he had set for the country through a series of campaigns that were intended to enlist all Chinese and did, in fact, involve a very great many. The Great Leap Forward and the Great Proletarian Cultural Revolution were the two most consequential—and harmful—but he launched other, lesser ones as well.[139] They also had adverse effects, although less severe ones. In 1957, for example, he initiated a nationwide program to eliminate the "four pests": rats, sparrows, flies, and mosquitoes. The campaign succeeded: China's sparrow population fell sharply. Since sparrows ate the insects that

---

[††] Quoted in Short, *op. cit.*, p. 532. "At workplaces each morning, people stood in formation and bowed three times before Mao's portrait, silently 'asking instructions' for the tasks of the day ahead. They repeated the same ritual each evening, to report on what they had accomplished. Red Guards told their victims to pray to Mao for forgiveness. Thanks was offered to Mao before meals. At city railway stations, passengers had to carry out a 'loyalty dance' on the platform before they were allowed to board the train. In country districts there were 'loyalty pigs', branded with the character *Zhong* (loyalty) to show that even dumb beasts could recognize Mao's genius. Mao's works were referred to as 'treasure books', and special ceremonies were held whenever a consignment went on sale." *Ibid.* p. 546.

otherwise infested crops, however, grain output suffered. China was then reduced to importing sparrows from the Soviet Union.[140]

Mao's efforts to steer China in the directions he favored relied on his unchallenged supremacy in the Party and his ubiquitous and sometimes outlandish cult of personality, and on coercion. People did what the Party told them to do because they knew that the authorities would not hesitate to ruin or even kill them if they failed to do so. The pile of corpses that the Communists generated served as a lesson for everyone. Mao commanded obedience to his decrees in the same way that Stalin did—by his frequent use of one particular form of coercion: terror.

Personal Imprint

Mao Zedong was able to leave a deep and broad imprint on the history of the twentieth century because he was able to accumulate very substantial political power. In his years as an insurgent, he increased his authority within the Chinese Communist Party until, when it took control of the country, he had become its undisputed leader. He continued to exercise supreme power in the Party and therefore in the country, albeit with a few periods of retreat, throughout the remaining twenty-seven years of his life. He enjoyed enormous prestige as both the Lenin and the Stalin of the Chinese Revolution:[141] like Lenin in the Soviet Union, he presided over the Communist seizure of power. Like Lenin's successor Josef Stalin, he oversaw the construction of the Communist regime and its foreign and domestic policies for the next twenty-five years and beyond.

The regime he created, guided, and dominated had, in totalitarian fashion, no check on its authority and reached deeply into the everyday lives of everyone within the borders of the People's Republic. This meant that Mao exercised as much power as any leader in the twentieth century, and therefore, arguably, as much power as any leader anywhere ever has.

Before 1949, it was the Communist Party that bore the stamp of his influence. It was he, more than any other Communist, who emphasized the peasantry as the instrument of revolution in China. Coming as he did from a rural background, he had a deeper acquaintance with peasant life and attitudes than the other early Communists. In addition, his rebellious temperament made him more willing to break with Marxist-Leninist orthodoxy than the other members of the Chinese Party, especially those who, unlike Mao, had trained in Moscow. Since their enemies controlled China's cities, had the Chinese Communists continued to place their faith in the urban proletariat as the vehicle for revolution, they almost certainly would not have gained power.[142]

Nor would they have survived the Party's first two decades without the kind of armed forces that Mao prominently advocated and helped to direct. He did not invent guerrilla warfare,[143] but he saw its relevance for, and adapted it to, Chinese conditions.[144] In the Party's greatest pre-1949 trial, the Long March, Mao also took a leading part. He had a great deal to do with the decision to undertake it and at various points during its course advocated choices that, as it turned out, enabled the band of revolutionaries—in severely reduced numbers—to reach the safety of Yan'an.[145]

Once in control of China, the Communist Party was in a position to conduct the country's foreign policy. As in almost every other sovereign state, in Communist China the leader of the government—Mao—had considerable authority over relations with other countries. The first major foreign policy initiative over which he presided was China's participation in the Korean War, a consequential international event that spread the Cold War from Europe to Asia as well as ratifying the division of the Korean peninsula and separating Taiwan from the People's Republic.[146] China did not start that war, and Mao was initially reluctant to involve his country in it, but he then decided to intervene and persuaded or overcame those in the Communist leadership who continued to have reservations about fighting there.[147]

The Sino-Soviet rift, which changed global geopolitics by transforming the two huge communist countries from allies to adversaries, had causes that went beyond Mao's personal preferences.[148] Still, one of China's declared grievances against Moscow—Soviet deviation from what the Chinese considered orthodox communism, a deviation they called "revisionism"—was a particular preoccupation of the Chairman. His personal disdain for Nikita Khrushchev, in contrast to his respect for Khrushchev's predecessor Josef Stalin,[149] also contributed to the rift;[150] and Mao's power was such that none of China's anti-Soviet initiatives could have taken place without his approval.

Out of its hostile relations with the Soviet Union came China's rapprochement with the United States. President Richard Nixon, in his visit to Beijing in February 1972 to inaugurate it formally, declared his stay in China to be "the week that changed the world." He exaggerated, but the

Sino-American diplomatic initiative did tilt the global political balance away from the Soviet Union and toward the United States and China. Given the size, power, and importance of those countries, this was no small development. It, too, bore Mao's political fingerprints. While he had grown far less vigorous in the early 1970s, his approval was still required for the rapprochement to go forward.[151] The rapprochement earned Mao a reputation among some in the West as an adroit practitioner of foreign policy. It was not entirely deserved. Tilting toward the United States in order to counterbalance the Soviet Union does count as a shrewd if obvious and time-tested geopolitical maneuver. What preceded it, however—confronting both nuclear superpowers simultaneously while dramatically weakening China through the Cultural Revolution—to say the least, does not.

Mao also exerted some influence beyond China in the form of admiration among non-Chinese for his views on revolution and his admirers' efforts to emulate his strategies for bringing it about. Around the world, political radicals in small but not negligible numbers declared themselves to be Maoists. They attempted to practice what he preached, although their interpretations of the Maoism they professed to follow exhibited a certain amount of variation from place to place.[152]

As for China's domestic affairs, a communist party that gained power in that country in 1949 would almost surely have adopted as its economic and political model the Soviet Union, which seemed, at that point in history, to have mastered the tasks of achieving economic growth and international strength. The most Maoist feature of Chinese national life over the next quarter-century, which distinguishes China from the Russian version of communism (and from all other countries as well), the vehicles for Mao's deepest personal impact on the twentieth century, were his several nationwide campaigns of that era. It was he who decided to launch the Hundred Flowers campaign,[153] for example, and he who decided to stop it and punish those who had actually accepted his invitation to express their political opinions publicly.

The two most important and most distinctively Maoist campaigns were the Great Leap Forward and the Great Proletarian Cultural Revolution.[154] They had features in common. Both unfolded on a vast scale. Both wrought immense destruction and suffering: each, in fact, did the kind of damage to China ordinarily inflicted on a country only by an enemy during wartime. Both arose from ideas and inclinations that deserve to be called utopian: in the case of the Great Leap Forward, the conviction that Chinese society, if properly mobilized, could almost instantaneously increase agricultural and industrial production far beyond anything ever achieved anywhere else;[155] for the Cultural Revolution, the belief, more characteristic of the anarchism with which Mao flirted as a young man than of Marxism-Leninism, that smashing a country's governing institutions and bureaucratic structures would somehow lift its people to a higher level of well-being.

These ideas were Mao's—and virtually no one else's, at least not in the Communist Party leadership. Not only did he instigate both campaigns, but no other Chinese leader, perhaps no other leader of any country at any time, would have done so. Odd, eccentric, singular, not to mention damaging though they were, as the supreme leader of Communist China, Mao had the power to put them into practice on a horrifying scale; and only he had the power to call a halt to the campaigns they inspired.

The Great Leap Forward grew out of Mao's extreme voluntarist (and distinctly non-Marxist) view of human society. The other Communist leaders could not prevent or even, without Mao's assent, end it, even when its catastrophic impact could not be concealed. The one leading Communist who raised objections, Peng Dehuai, paid for his candor with his position in the leadership.[156] Mao was not to be contradicted, even when what he believed turned out to be not only false but also extraordinarily costly. [‡‡]

The Cultural Revolution also had its origins in a Maoist obsession, in this case with what he regarded as the deadly and pervasive danger of revisionism: that is, of China somehow, despite the Communist Party's iron control of it, falling back into traditional habits, or succumbing to capitalism, or both.[157] Mao's plotting against the established Communist leadership and his personal approval and encouragement of what the Red Guards did—their assaults across the country, and the chaos they unleashed[158]—made the Cultural Revolution possible. It appalled almost all leading Party officials, and not surprisingly, since it was aimed at them. Pitting himself against virtually the entire structure of authority in China, Mao prevailed. In so doing, and as with the Great Leap Forward, he left a deep scar on his country.

[‡‡] "From February to October [1960], while the state granaries were bulging with grain, most of Mao's colleagues were well aware of the extent of the starvation, yet did nothing. Had they acted to open the grain reserves in order to feed the starving, more than ten million lives might have been saved. They did not because they were unwilling to commit themselves until the Chairman had spoken." Short, *op. cit.*, p. 499. See also *ibid.*, p. 501.

During his lifetime, Mao had his most pronounced personal impact on China in a particularly gruesome way: in the number of premature deaths, often violent ones, that he and his policies caused to take place. The precise number will never be known, but the magnitude is beyond doubt. Through the various campaigns against "counterrevolutionaries" in the almost two decades between the Communists' assumption of power and the end of the Cultural Revolution, the victims of the system of prison camps the regime established and administered, and above all the famine induced by the Great Leap Forward, the toll of fatalities was on the order of 65 million.[159]

To be sure, violence, cruelty, and mass killing in China did not begin with the People's Republic.[160] China's emperors, the Taiping rebels, the post-imperial warlords, and the KMT practiced all three.[161] They did so, however, on a smaller scale than did the Communists and mainly during wartime, as part of an effort to take or hold power. The mass deaths under the rule of the Communist Party took place in peacetime. While Mao did not intend for the Great Leap Forward to kill between 36 and 40 million Chinese, he did insist on continuing the campaign even when its terrible results began to be known and never expressed remorse for what he had caused.[162]

All these deaths stemmed from policies for which he had personal responsibility, and most would certainly not have occurred without his personal initiative. This gives Mao Zedong the distinction of having been, in numerical terms, the greatest mass murderer in all of human history.

The Legacy

As happened with Adolf Hitler in Germany after World War II, in the wake of Mao's death in 1976, what he had built was substantially dismantled and what he had done largely repudiated in China. The reasons for the postwar fates of the two dictators were similar. Just as the devastating impact on Germans of the war that Hitler started created the political impetus and the political space for a sharp departure from the Third Reich, so the damage and disruption of the Cultural Revolution led, after the Chairman had departed, to the end of most of what had been Maoism.[163]

A struggle for power followed his death, in which radicals whom he had promoted and who had enthusiastically supported the Cultural Revolution lost out[164] to Deng Xiaoping, a Party veteran whom Mao had purged no fewer than three times.[165] Under the slogan of the "Four Modernizations"—of agriculture, industry, science and technology, and national defense[166]—Deng presided over major adjustments to China's political and economic direction. He also authorized changes to the Chinese economic system that made it, in comparison with the form it had taken in the Maoist era, almost unrecognizable.

Deng declined to create a Mao-like cult of personality for himself, and well before he himself died in 1997, he stepped away from a number of his responsibilities—while remaining influential behind the scenes. He imposed limits on the time that high-level officials could hold power, and he instituted a more collective form of leadership than the one-man style of the Maoist period.[167] In the Deng era, some of the restraints on individuals that had been implemented after the Communist takeover and had remained in place until Mao's death were eased. The Chinese did not come to enjoy Western-style freedom of speech, for example, but they could speak and even write more freely on a wider range of topics than before. China under Deng did not become a free country, but neither did the Chinese people have to continue to live in the totalitarian cage that Mao, with the enthusiastic assistance of other Communists, including Deng, had built for them.[168]

In economic matters, Deng turned out to be a revolutionary, although Mao would have called what he did—and rightly from the Maoist perspective—counterrevolutionary.[169] During the Cultural Revolution, Mao and the Red Guards accused those they purged and persecuted of the ultimate heresy of trying to lead China to capitalism. The radicals charged those they opposed with being "capitalist roaders." In the wake of that great upheaval, the capitalist road was precisely the path down which Deng guided the country. Just as postwar Germany, both East and West, incorporated the political features that Hitler had despised, so post-Mao China adopted the economic practices that the Chairman had made it his life's work to eradicate.[170] China embraced, on a large scale, free markets and private property, the two institutions that every communist since Marx, including Mao, had identified as the essence of the hated capitalist system.

In the wake of the Great Leap Forward, private agricultural plots on which peasants could grow crops that they could then sell for personal profit had reappeared in China.[171] Private agriculture became far more widespread in the post-Mao era, which saw a sharp reduction in the collective sector in the countryside. As a consequence, agricultural production increased substantially.

In industry, Deng encouraged the creation of what would have been anathema to Mao, a series of "enterprise zones"[172] that were established for the express purpose of attracting precisely the foreign capital that Mao, and Lenin before him, had regarded as the insidious agent of imperialism. China welcomed foreign investment on a large scale and became an integral part of the global trading system, in sharp contrast to the economic autarky of the first three decades of the People's Republic. By joining the global economic order, China gave up the Maoist goal of overturning it, and in that spirit discarded Mao's commitment to fomenting communist revolutions everywhere.

Capitalism requires capitalists, and China under Deng acquired them. He coined the slogan "To get rich is glorious,"[173] and many did. The Communist Party invited successful entrepreneurs to join its ranks. Mao, it is safe to say, would have found both the slogan and the practice repugnant: for him, businessmen were to be rooted out and persecuted, not honored. He had favored, and enforced, the distribution of power and position according to social class and allegiance to Maoist precepts. Those with bourgeois backgrounds or from the wealthy sectors of the peasantry suffered distinct disadvantages at best, regarded as they were as potential or actual enemies of the regime.

In the Deng era, by contrast, upward mobility came to depend on demonstrated ability (as well as on personal connections). During the pre-Mao period, and stretching back centuries into China's imperial past, Chinese had achieved recognition for their abilities through rigorous systems of examination. During the Cultural Revolution, the country's educational institutions had done away with examinations. Deng reinstated them.[174]

Where Mao, during the Cultural Revolution and before, had made the supreme goal of the Communist regime the promotion of ideological purity, as he defined it, Deng elevated economic growth to the top of the national agenda. The economic policies, practices, and institutions over which he presided produced such growth, and on a remarkable scale. For the better part of three decades, China enjoyed, on average, double-digit annual growth. Between 1979, when the economic reforms began in earnest, and 2019, Chinese output grew from $178 billion to $14 trillion.[175] The rising tide of economic growth lifted an estimated 800 million Chinese out of poverty, according to the World Bank.[176]

Thus, post-Mao China achieved, over several decades, the kind of economic advance that Mao had sought to bring about in the Great Leap Forward almost immediately through sheer will power spurred by his own exhortations; but after his death, the country made the dramatic economic progress he had envisioned not by his methods but rather by imitating the capitalist countries that he had regarded as mortal enemies, with political and economic models to be shunned. The Maoist economic strategy yielded the worst-ever famine in a country with a long history of famines. In the capitalist era that Deng inaugurated, starvation was all but unknown.

Amid all the post-Mao changes, however, one central feature of his era remained intact. The Communist Party retained its monopoly of political power. Deng and his successors were no more willing to permit political pluralism than the Chairman had been.[§§] For this reason, because Mao had dominated the Party for four decades, China's Communists could not afford to repudiate him explicitly. Since they were his political heirs, complete repudiation would have called into question their right to hold power,[177] something they made it a high priority to avoid.[178] A huge likeness of him, and his embalmed corpse, therefore remained on prominent display in Tiananmen Square in the heart of Beijing, and his portrait continued to adorn China's currency.[179] The Party issued an official verdict on him that was designed to acknowledge the disasters he had wrought (in which many in the post-Mao leadership had themselves been complicit) while protecting the privileged position of the political party he had built. What the Chairman had done, Deng said in a secret address to the Central Committee in 1978, had been "70 percent correct and 30 percent mistaken."[180]

Post-Mao Chinese public affairs thus entailed the somewhat uneasy coexistence of Western economics and communist politics. In 1989, no doubt in part because Western economics had opened the way for the spread of Western political ideas, the political system faced, and surmounted, a serious challenge. The death that year of Hu Yaobang, a Party leader with a reputation for liberal views, sparked a series of demonstrations, largely

---

[§§] From the perspective of 2022, "[i]n many respects, the CCP has changed little since the party took power in 1949. Now, as then, the party exercises absolute control over China, ruling over its military, its administration, and its rubber-stamp legislature. The party hierarchy, in turn, answers to the Politburo Standing Committee, the top decision-making body in China." Cai Xia, "The Weakness of Xi Jinping," *Foreign Affairs*, September/October 2022, https://www.foreignaffairs.com/china/xi-jinping-china-weakness-hubris-paranoia-threaten-future.

involving students, beginning in April in Tiananmen Square and spreading to an estimated 341 other cities in China.[181] While the demonstrators did not always express coherently the grievances that motivated them, nor were the tens of thousands of them of one mind, they had in common substantial dissatisfaction with the Communist political order.

As the days went by, their numbers grew. At the beginning of June, the Party leadership, with the semi-retired Deng the driving force, decided to crack down on them.[182] It unleashed the army on the demonstrators and at least several hundred of them were killed. Open political dissent in China, having been shown to be lethally dangerous, largely disappeared. In 1992, a few years after what became known as the Tiananmen Massacre, Deng made a trip to Guangdong Province in the south, the purpose of which was to make it clear that he wanted the economic reforms that had been implemented since Mao's death to continue;[183] and they did. For the next two decades, the combination of capitalist economics and communist politics persisted.

In the second decade of the new millennium, however, the man who rose to the pinnacle of the Communist Party hierarchy turned China back in the direction of Maoism, reviving some of the policies that Deng had sought to terminate.[184] Xi Jinping, who came to power in 2011, moved to expand his personal authority, overturning the two-term limit on the positions he held that Deng had introduced, presumably with an eye toward retaining them indefinitely, as Mao had. Xi encouraged the study and celebration of his own speeches, an initiative reminiscent of the Maoist cult of personality.[185] The boundaries of permitted speech in China narrowed, and the regime went to great lengths to control the internet.

Xi initiated purges of Party officials, although the crimes with which the victims were charged had to do with personal corruption (which was indeed rampant in the Party, including among Xi and his close associates) rather than the ideological deviation of Mao's day. Unlike the earlier purges, moreover, very few of those targeted lost their lives. Xi's order locking down tens of millions of people in response to the COVID-19 virus was reminiscent of Mao's campaigns of national mobilization. The Xi economic policies increased the role of the Party[186] and favored the state sector at the expense of private business. Several prominent and wealthy entrepreneurs were singled out for harsh criticism, seemingly for insufficient attention to the wishes of the Party. Under Xi, to get rich was no longer unambiguously glorious.

In foreign policy, Xi continued China's twenty-first-century pattern of high military spending. The Chinese government made extensive, and illegal, territorial claims in the South China Sea and the Pacific Ocean, and its navy conducted aggressive maneuvers in these waters even as the regime stepped up its threats to invade Taiwan. In his public pronouncements, Xi looked forward to what he implied was the not-distant day when China would take its rightful place as the leading country in the world.[187]

Still, he did not seriously attempt to return to high Maoism, with its mass killings, its economic utopianism, its rampaging Red Guards, and its emphasis on ideological fervor over competence and expertise. Xi did not try to reestablish central control of all China's economic activity or abolish all private property. Nor did he profess fidelity to the ideas of Marx and Lenin, or, and despite some similarities to his predecessor, of Mao himself.

Rather, the Xi regime had as its defining characteristics authoritarian (but not totalitarian) politics, a market-based economy with a large role for the government, and a determined nationalism aimed at restoring China's greatness in the world. That program resembled not so much the one Mao had sought to carry out as that of the Chairman's rival of fifty years, Chiang Kai-shek[188]—himself an authoritarian,[189] a capitalist, and a nationalist. In this way, a half-century after Mao's death, China was the kind of country it might well have become if its history had taken a different course. It was the kind of country the twentieth century might well have bequeathed to the twenty-first if the Communists had not won the Civil War, or if Mao Zedong had never lived.

Conclusion

"SOME ARE BORN GREAT," READS a letter introduced in Shakespeare's *Twelfth Night*, "some achieve greatness, and some have greatness thrust upon them."[1] Each of the eight men portrayed in the preceding pages qualifies as great if the term means "supremely important," with no connotation of approbation. In this morally neutral sense, Lenin and Hitler as well as Roosevelt and Gandhi may be said to be "great" historical figures. What made them so?

Only hereditary monarchs are born to greatness, and all eight of the leaders in this book made their careers after monarchies had disappeared or ceased to be powerful. As with all human beings, though, the circumstances of his birth did affect each one's life. Churchill and Roosevelt, born into wealth and privilege, had a head start on the path to political power that all eight eventually followed. None of the other six came from the topmost stratum of his society, nor, however, did any come from the lowest. All began in the middle ranks, in families that, while not wealthy or powerful, were more or less comfortably situated in their communities. None had to fight his way up from the bottom.

In all societies, a person's early childhood, and especially the child's relationship with his or her parents, has a crucial bearing on the individual's subsequent life. Of this formative period, Sigmund Freud said:

> If a man has been his mother's undisputed darling he retains throughout his life the triumphant feeling, the confidence in success, which not seldom brings actual success along with it.

True to that observation, seven of the eight had a warm, loving, supportive mother. The exception is Churchill. He established a close relationship with his own mother as an adult, but when he was a child, she neglected him. In this sense, despite the privileged conditions in which he came into the world, he had to overcome a major obstacle that the other seven Titans did not.

In their families of origin, two of the three tyrannical twentieth-century figures portrayed in this book, Hitler and Mao, had difficult, indeed hostile and even hate-filled relations with their fathers. This raises the possibility that such a relationship conduces to a particularly murderous form of leadership. Unfortunately for this hypothesis, however, the third bloodthirsty tyrant, Lenin, appears to have enjoyed a cordial, or at least not acrimonious, relationship with his own father.

An obstacle to the attainment of power that all but the three democratically elected individuals—Wilson, Churchill, and Roosevelt—faced was the fact that they came from outside the pool of candidates from which leaders of the countries in which they lived were normally drawn. This is not surprising, since their aspirations for sweeping change, the fulfillment of which made them the towering historical figures that they became, put them sharply at odds with the political order into which they lived.*

All overcame the obstacles they faced and achieved the greatness they attained with traits of character that, to one degree or another, they shared: self-confidence, energy, resilience, and perseverance. No doubt, anyone making a mark as a leader in a society in which leadership does not come as a birthright is likely to possess such qualities, which are always useful and perhaps even indispensable for gaining a position of political authority.

The eight Titans achieved greatness, as well, through another feature common to all of them. Words, spoken but especially printed, preoccupied them. All read voraciously. All except Roosevelt wrote extensively, usually for publication. They wrote and spoke to persuade others to give them

---

* A mark of their status as outsiders is the fact that Lenin, Hitler, Gandhi, Ben-Gurion, and Mao all fell afoul, at one time or another, of the governing authorities in the jurisdictions in which they were living. The first three were imprisoned—Lenin was sent into exile—while the last two managed to escape incarceration. Churchill was also briefly jailed, but as a prisoner of war in South Africa, having been captured by the Boers in the Boer War.

power, to adopt their policies, and to follow them in putting those policies into practice. In their era, written words had a singular political importance. Before then, too few people could read for the printed word to play such a major role. Afterward, print had to share the political stage with electronically generated messages and images.

Words are the vehicles for ideas, and the eight lived and worked in the great age of political ideas. The first half of the twentieth century was the era of "isms," to some of which the historical figures of this book gave their names: Wilsonianism, Leninism, Maoism. Previously, men of ideas, who were never particularly numerous, were entirely distinct from men who wielded power, and the two groups had little if anything to do with each other.

For six of the eight figures, political ideas had supreme importance, and theirs were novel, radical, indeed revolutionary ideas. The six made their marks on history by putting these ideas into effect. Lenin and Mao devoted their lives to the pursuit and then the consolidation of a communist revolution. Hitler, by sweeping away the old political order, first in Germany and then in Europe, qualifies as a revolutionary as well. As devoted democrats, Gandhi and Ben-Gurion differed fundamentally from the dictators, but each was the prime mover in creating a political community—independent India and a Jewish state in the Middle East—that had not existed when they began.[2] Wilson sought to transform the ways the international system was organized and national foreign policies conducted.

Churchill and Roosevelt were not revolutionaries. To the contrary, the historical projects that made them twentieth-century Titans are more accurately described as conservative in intent. Churchill sought to conserve British independence and the sovereignty of the countries of Europe, as well as the existence of the British Empire. He succeeded at the first two and failed at the third. Roosevelt contributed to Churchill's first two enterprises and at home preserved the American economic and political systems, which the Great Depression had shaken.

None of the eight, finally, had greatness thrust upon him. All worked hard to achieve the positions of authority in which they became major historical figures. Yet their own efforts alone could not have brought about this result. They were able to become great because of circumstances that made their achievements possible. Specifically, the global social, political, and economic upheavals of the first half of the twentieth century caused by the two World Wars and the Great Depression gave them the opportunity to do what they did. Different as they were in what they sought to achieve, how far they accomplished their aims, and how long their accomplishments endured, the careers of the eight men whose impact on history is the subject of the preceding chapters had that defining feature in common.

The deeds of the leaders who have followed them have not matched the breadth and depth of their accomplishments (not all of which, of course, were desirable) because, in the absence of events as disruptive as the World Wars and the Depression, their successors have not had the political latitude to do so. Perhaps unforeseen events will some day bring back historical conditions comparable to those of the first half of the twentieth century, but by the third decade of the twenty-first, the age of heroic leadership—and even the worst of these eight men were regarded as heroes by millions of their countrymen—had passed. Political initiatives of all kinds had become more incremental, less sweeping in scope. This is not necessarily a bad thing. "Unhappy the land that has no heroes," Galileo's servant, Andrew, in Bertolt Brecht's play *Life of Galileo* says to the great astronomer, to which he replies, "Unhappy the land that needs them."

NOTES

Introduction

1. Israel, Ben-Gurion's country, was and is far smaller than those of the other seven twentieth-century titans. Its creation, however, was as unlikely and remarkable as anything the other seven accomplished and has had an impact that has reverberated throughout the Middle East and beyond.
2. All held formal public office except Gandhi.
3. See pp. 59–63.
4. The most intense personal exaltation of Lenin, complete with the wide dissemination of his image and of items associated with him such as his characteristic cap, came after his death. See p. 54.
5. Outside Europe, the European countries did initially seek to restore or maintain their colonial possessions, many of which Japan had conquered in World War II, but they failed. The French waged two ultimately unsuccessful wars for this purpose.
6. Max Weber, *The Theory of Social and Economic Organization*, Edited with an Introduction by Talcott Parsons, New York: The Free Press, 1964, p. 358.
7. Churchill's supreme goal—to resist and defeat Nazi Germany—and one of Franklin Roosevelt's—to mitigate the effects of the Great Depression on American society—do not qualify as genuinely radical.
8. The oldest of them, Woodrow Wilson, left office in 1921. The youngest, Mao Zedong, died while still in power in 1976.

Chapter 1

1. As a youth, Woodrow Wilson lived through the Civil War, the defeat of the Confederacy in which he lived and that his father supported, and the period of Reconstruction that followed; but these events, central though they were to the history of the United States, seem not to have shaped his adult life or political career. "If the Civil War left a psychological imprint on the boy or the man, it was buried so deep as to be imponderable." John Milton Cooper Jr., *Woodrow Wilson: A Biography*, New York: Alfred A. Knopf, 2009, p. 18.

Wilson's attitudes on race were far from egalitarian—he was a partisan of segregation—but that was not unusual in his era, even in the North.

2. See p. 27.

3. Roosevelt was, like Wilson, a progressive; but rather than diluting Wilson's vote, the Roosevelt candidacy reduced that of his fellow Republican, Taft.

4. Wilson received 435 out of a total of 531 electoral votes. Roosevelt won 27 percent of the popular vote and 88 electoral votes. Taft finished third with 23 percent and 8 electoral votes.

5. Although not coinciding precisely with his time as president, during Wilson's era four amendments of a progressive character were added to the Constitution of the United States: the Sixteenth Amendment, permitting a federal income tax (1908); the Seventeenth, providing for the popular election of senators (1912); the Eighteenth and least clearly progressive of them, prohibiting the manufacture and sale of alcohol (1917); and the Nineteenth, giving women the vote (1919).

6. Wilson defeated his Republican opponent, the former New York governor and Supreme Court justice and future secretary of state Charles Evans Hughes, by 49 to 46 percent in the popular vote and 277 to 254 in the Electoral College.

7. Quoted in George C. Herring, *From Colony to Superpower: U.S. Foreign Relations Since 1776*, New York: Oxford University Press, 2007, p. 399.

8. Some German Americans favored the German side, and some Irish Americans opposed Britain.

9. Robert W. Tucker, *Woodrow Wilson and the Great War: Reconsidering America's Neutrality, 1914–1917*, Charlottesville: University of Virginia Press, 2007, pp. 6, 8, 205; John A. Thompson, *A Sense of Power: The Roots of America's Global Role*, Ithaca, New York: Cornell University Press, 2015, pp. 63, 72; Herring, *op. cit.*, p. 399.

10. "After the horrors of the twentieth century, it requires an effort of historical imagination to understand how appalling this event seemed." Thompson, *op. cit.*, p. 67.

11. He approved a note to the German government saying that the United States would hold it to "a strict accountability" for undersea attacks. Cooper, *op. cit.*, p. 275.

12. "The German government had a twofold rationale for its decision. First, the British blockade was taking an increasing toll both on the country's war effort and on its civilians' daily lives, and the government felt pressure to do something to ease it. Second, the German high command reckoned that, although submarine attacks might well precipitate American entry into the war, German forces could defeat the Allies in Europe before the United States could dispatch enough troops to make a material difference in the fighting." Michael Mandelbaum, *The Four Ages of American Foreign Policy: Weak Power, Great Power, Superpower, Hyperpower*, New York: Oxford University Press, 2022, p. 162.

13. It is academics who use the term Wilsonianism and they have not given it a single authoritative definition: their enumerations of its basic elements

vary, but with considerable overlap. See, for example, Lloyd E. Ambrosius, *Wilsonianism: Woodrow Wilson and His Legacy in American Foreign Relations*, New York: Palgrave Macmillan, 2002, p. 2; G. John Ikenberry, "Woodrow Wilson, the Bush Administration, and the Future of Liberal Internationalism," in Ikenberry et al., *The Crisis of American Foreign Policy: Wilsonianism in the Twenty-first Century*, Princeton, New Jersey: Princeton University Press, 2009, pp. 2, 11–13; and Tony Smith, *Why Wilson Matters: The Origins of American Liberal Internationalism and Its Crisis Today*, Princeton, New Jersey: Princeton University Press, 2017, Introduction.

14. Cooper, *op. cit.*, p. 451.

15. In Wilson's war message, he said: ". . . the menace to . . . peace and freedom lies in the existence of autocratic governments backed by organized force which is controlled wholly by their will, not by the will of their people." https://www.archives.gov/milestone-documents/address-to-congress-declaration-of-war-against-germany.

16. These are the second and third of the Fourteen Points. https://www.archives.gov/milestone-documents/president-woodrow-wilsons-14-points.

17. Number IV of the Fourteen Points. *Ibid.*

18. The last of Wilson's Fourteen Points reads: "A general association of nations must be formed under specific covenants for the purpose of affording mutual guarantees of political independence and territorial integrity to great and small states alike." *Ibid.*

19. Herring, *op. cit.*, p. 420.

20. Orlando left the conference temporarily in protest against the failure to secure some of Italy's demands, during which period the "Big Four" became the "Big Three." Even when Orlando was present, the other three had more influence over the deliberations than he did.

21. In his January 22, 1917 address, he said of the postwar settlement that "it must be a peace without victory." "Victory," he went on, "would mean peace forced upon the loser," which "would leave a sting, a resentment, a bitter memory upon which terms of peace would rest, not permanently, but only as upon quicksand." http://web.mit.edu/21h.102/www/Wilson%20Peace%20Without%20Victory.htm.

22. Just how to apportion responsibility for the outbreak of war in 1914 among Germany and the other belligerent powers has become the subject of a voluminous and ongoing historical controversy, on which no final word has been said and probably never will be. At the very least, a generous share of that responsibility does belong to the Germans. In the matter of the war's origins, they may not have been the only guilty party but they were certainly not innocent.

23. The Lodge reservations are listed in Samuel Flagg Bemis, *A Diplomatic History of the United States*, Fourth Edition, New York: Henry Holt and Company, 1955, p. 653.

24. In 1967, in order to avoid the recurrence of such a circumstance, the 25th Amendment to the Constitution, providing for procedures to follow in the event of presidential incapacity, came into effect.

25. By very rough estimate, the total deaths in the Wars of the French Revolution a century earlier, the bloodiest conflict in Europe to that point and one that continued, off and on, for almost six times as long as World War I, amounted to about 5 million people.
26. See Mandelbaum, *op. cit.*, Chapters 1 and 2.
27. See p. 11.
28. Thompson, *op. cit.*, p. 61.
29. Mandelbaum, *op. cit.*, pp. 134–135.
30. This is the theme of Thompson, *op. cit.*
31. In his "Peace Without Victory" speech, Wilson said, "It is inconceivable that the people of the United States should play no part in that great enterprise [of peacemaking]. To take part in such a service will be the opportunity for which they have sought to prepare themselves by the very principles and purposes of their polity and the approved practices of their Government ever since the day when they set up a new nation in the high and honorable hope that it might in all that it was and did show mankind the way to liberty." http://web.mit.edu/21h.102/www/Wilson%20Peace%20Without%20Vict ory.htm.
32. Herring, *op. cit.*, p. 419; John A. Thompson, *Woodrow Wilson*, London: Longman, 2002, p. 212.
33. Roosevelt's bonhomie did not always pay off. See pp. 154–155.
34. Mandelbaum, *op. cit.*, p. 171.
35. Quoted in Margaret Macmillan, *Paris 1919: Six Months That Changed the World*, New York: Random House, 2001, p. 23.
36. In the United States, prominent Republicans especially favored harsh conditions for Germany. Cooper, *op. cit.*, pp. 443, 446, 448.
37. Ironically, the high cost of World War I made the transformational ideas of Woodrow Wilson seem attractive and plausible but also made one of the policies implicit in them, a generous peace for Germany, unacceptable to public opinion in the countries that won the war.
38. Those arrangements had a short life. Shandong was formally returned to China in 1922 and Japan quit the League in 1933.
39. Herring, *op. cit.*, pp. 419, 427; Cooper, *op. cit.*, p. 457.
40. Cooper, *op. cit.*, p. 83; James Chace, *1912: Wilson, Roosevelt, Taft & Debs—The Election That Changed the Country*, New York: Simon & Schuster, 2004, pp. 128, 246.
41. On Wilson's health and its impact on his policies, see Thomas Knock, *To End All Wars: Woodrow Wilson and the Quest for a New World Order*, Princeton, New Jersey: Princeton University Press, 1992, pp. 264–265; and John Milton Cooper, Jr., *The Warrior and the Priest: Woodrow Wilson and Theodore Roosevelt*, Cambridge, Massachusetts: The Belknap Press of Harvard University Press, 1983, p. 340.
42. In a conversation with his predecessor as president, William Howard Taft, in March 1918, Wilson, according to Taft, "gave it as his opinion that the Senate . . . would be unwilling to enter into an agreement by which the

majority of other nations could tell the United States when they must go to war." Quoted in Knock, *op. cit.*, p. 150.

43. Senator William Borah, quoted in William Widenor, *Henry Cabot Lodge and the Search for an American Foreign Policy*, Berkeley, California: University of California Press, 1980, p. 337.

44. "Harding won the popular vote by 60 to 34 percent and the electoral vote by 404 to 127, delivering to Democrats the most devastating popular-vote defeat ever suffered by either of America's two major parties." Michael Barone, *How America's Political Parties Change (and How They Don't)*, New York: Encounter Books, 2019, p. 17.

45. Quoted in Michael Howard, *The Lessons of History*, New Haven, Connecticut: Yale University Press, 1991, p. 30.

46. It was Lloyd George, not Wilson, who first used the term "national self-determination." Cooper, *Woodrow Wilson*, p. 421.

47. Mandelbaum, *op. cit.*, pp. 65–66.

48. "From mid-1915 onward, [Wilson] would make foreign policy decisions and set directions almost entirely on his own." Cooper, *Woodrow Wilson*, p. 295.

49. "Unless I can improve something," Wilson once said, "I cannot get thoroughly interested." Cited in *ibid.*, p. 116.

50. Evidence of Wilson's religious sensibility is the name for the charter of the League of Nations: a "covenant," the biblical term for the compact between God and the ancient Israelites.

51. Mandelbaum, *op. cit.*, pp. 148–152.

52. Knock, *op. cit.*, p. 272.

53. See pp. 76–77.

54. This assertion became known as the Stimson Doctrine, after Hoover's Secretary of State Henry Stimson, who announced it.

55. Widenor, *op. cit.*, p. 331.

56. Cooper, *Woodrow Wilson*, p. 486; Thompson, *op. cit.*, p. 101; Cooper, *The Warrior and the Priest*, p. 343.

57. The French word for such a salad is *macedoine*, after a region—Macedonia—in the Balkans, a part of the world where different peoples were mixed together.

58. Quoted in Mandelbaum, *op. cit.*, p. 172.

59. On the spread of democracy in the second half of the twentieth century, see Samuel P. Huntington, *The Third Wave: Democratization in the Late Twentieth Century*, Norman: University of Oklahoma Press, 1991; and Michael Mandelbaum, *Democracy's Good Name: The Rise and Risks of the World's Most Popular Form of Government*, New York: PublicAffairs, 2007.

60. On nuclear arms control in the Cold War, see Mandelbaum, *The Four Ages of American Foreign Policy*, pp. 317–320.

61. The assessments are those of Robert W. Tucker, *op. cit.*, p. xi; and George C. Herring, *op. cit.*, p. 379.

62. Richard Nixon, the most "realist" president in his foreign policies since Theodore Roosevelt, called Woodrow Wilson his favorite president because of Wilson's devotion to peace, and hung Wilson's picture in his office.

63. Mandelbaum, *The Four Ages of American Foreign Policy*, pp. 236–237.

64. Mandelbaum, *The Four Ages of American Foreign Policy*, pp. 400–410; Michael Mandelbaum, *Mission Failure: America and the World in the Post-Cold War Era*, New York: Oxford University Press, 2016, Chapter 2.

65. Mandelbaum, *The Four Ages of American Foreign Policy*, Part Four; Mandelbaum, *Mission Failure*, Chapters 1, 2, and 5.

66. This is the theme of Michael Mandelbaum, *The Rise and Fall of Peace on Earth*, New York: Oxford University Press, 2019.

Chapter 2

1. Robert Service, *Lenin: A Biography*, Cambridge, Massachusetts: The Belknap Press of Harvard University Press, 2000, p. 30.

2. Nina Tumarkin, *Lenin Lives! The Lenin Cult in Soviet Russia*, Enlarged Edition, Cambridge, Massachusetts: Harvard University Press, 1997, p. 28.

3. Leonard Schapiro, "Lenin's Intellectual Formation and the Russian Revolutionary Background," in Schapiro, *Russian Studies*, New York: Viking, 1987, p. 191.

4. Service, *op. cit.*, p. 84.

5. Adam B. Ulam, *Lenin and the Bolsheviks: The Intellectual and Political History of the Triumph of Communism in Russia*, London: Secker and Warburg, 1966, p. 525. (Published in the United States in 1965 under the title *The Bolsheviks*.)

6. He subsequently learned German, French, and English.

7. Lenin was to die of a similar affliction at the age of 54. He and his father were the same age at their deaths.

8. Service, *op. cit.*, p. 93.

9. It seems plausible that what happened to his brother influenced his life's path. "Alexander's disappearance had the consequence of hardening the thoughts of a brilliant youth into the posture of a revolutionary activist." *Ibid.*, p. 60.

10. Schapiro, *op. cit.*, p. 217.

11. Martin Malia, *The Soviet Tragedy: A History of Socialism in Russia, 1917–1991*, New York: The Free Press, 1994, p. 36.

12. Revolution, according to Marx, comes when a society's political "super-structure" is out of alignment with its material—that is its economic—base. It is economic change that ultimately drives history. In this sense, Marx was a "historical materialist."

13. Service, *op. cit.*, p. 437.

14. *Ibid.*, pp. 101, 123. He set out this argument most fully in *Imperialism: The Highest Stage of Capitalism*, published in 1916 while World War I was under way.

15. "... the Leninist model in fact amounted to the political expropriation of the proletariat and its subjection to a dictatorial machine operated by the Bolshevik leadership: a leadership which was essentially self-constituted and

irremovable. . . ." George Lichtheim, *Marxism: An Historical and Critical Study*, New York: Frederick A. Praeger, 1965, p. 337.

16. Martin Malia, *History's Locomotives: Revolutions and the Making of the Modern World*, New Haven and London: Yale University Press, 2006, p. 263.

17. The vote count was twenty-four to twenty. Leonard Schapiro, "The Mensheviks," in Schapiro, *op. cit.*, p. 253.

18. Service, *op. cit.*, pp. 153–156; Richard Pipes, *The Russian Revolution*, New York: Alfred A. Knopf, 1990, p. 360.

19. On the events of 1905, see Pipes, *The Russian Revolution*, Chapter 1, and Malia, *The Soviet Tragedy*, pp. 68–69.

20. Norman Stone, *The Eastern Front: 1914–1917*, London: Hodder and Stoughton, 1971, Chapter 13.

21. Ultimately, the tsar and his family were murdered by the Bolsheviks. See Pipes, *The Russian Revolution*, Chapter 17.

22. According to Richard Pipes, the foremost historian of the Russian Revolution, "The mutiny of the Petrograd garrison stimulated disorders among the civilian population unhappy over inflation and shortages. . . . When the generals and Duma politicians persuaded [the tsar] that he had to go to save the army and avert a humiliating capitulation, he acquiesced. Had staying in power been his supreme objective, he could easily have concluded peace with Germany and turned the army loose against the mutineers. The record leaves no doubt that the myth of the tsar being forced from the throne by the rebellious workers and peasants is just that. The tsar yielded not to a rebellious populace but to generals and politicians, and he did so from a sense of patriotic duty." Richard Pipes, *Russia Under the Bolshevik Regime*, New York: Alfred A. Knopf, 1993, p. 497.

23. Service, *op. cit.*, p. 226.

24. *Ibid.*, p. 294; Pipes, *The Russian Revolution*, pp. 410–411; Stephen Kotkin, *Stalin: Paradoxes of Power, 1878–1928*, New York: Penguin Books, 2015, pp. 187–188.

25. Service, *op. cit.*, pp. 260, 262–269; Pipes, *The Russian Revolution*, pp. 393–394.

26. Malia, *The Soviet Tragedy*, p. 93.

27. Pipes, *The Russian Revolution*, p. 504.

28. For overviews of the events of October, see *ibid.*, Chapter 11; Service, *op. cit.*, Chapter 18; and Malia, *The Soviet Tragedy*, Chapter 3.

29. Pipes, *Russia Under the Bolshevik Regime*, pp. 4, 498.

30. Service, *op. cit.*, pp. 317–318.

31. *Ibid.*, pp. 336–337. In the elections for the Assembly, the Bolsheviks received fewer than one-fourth of the votes. Pipes, *Russia Under the Bolshevik Regime*, p. 5.

32. Pipes, *The Russian Revolution*, p. 672; Malia, *History's Locomotives*, p. 272.

33. Malia, *The Soviet Tragedy*, p. 133.

34. Kotkin, *op. cit.*, p. 293.

35. Pipes, *The Russian Revolution*, p. 594.

36. "Russia was required to make major territorial concessions which cost her most of the conquests made since the middle of the seventeenth century: in the west, northwest, and southwest her borders now shrank to those of the Muscovite state. She had given up Poland, Finland, Estonia, Latvia and Lithuania, as well as Transcaucasia, all of which either became sovereign states under a German protectorate or were incorporated into Germany. Moscow also had to recognize the Ukraine as an independent republic. These provisions called for the surrender of 750,000 square kilometers, an area nearly twice that of the German Empire." *Ibid.*, p. 595.

37. Geoffrey Hosking, *Russia and the Russians: A History*, Cambridge, Massachusetts: The Belknap Press of Harvard University Press, 2001, p. 407.

38. Malia, *The Soviet Tragedy*, p. 137.

39. For estimates of the overall costs of the Civil War, see Pipes, *The Russian Revolution*, pp. 138–139. "The Civil War, which tore Russia apart for nearly three years, was the most devastating event in that country's history since the Mongol invasions in the thirteenth century. Unspeakable atrocities were committed from resentment and fear: millions lost their lives in combat as well as from cold, hunger, and disease. As soon as the fighting stopped, Russia was struck by a famine such as no European people had ever experienced . . . in which millions more perished." Pipes, *Russia Under the Bolshevik Regime*, p. 5.

40. "It transpired that a good many old-regime officers were willing to serve in the Red Army. They had deeply resented the shambles to which, in their opinion, the Provisional Government had reduced a once-effective fighting force, and they now welcomed the advent of a regime which took military discipline seriously. Some of them, moreover, considered that the Reds were proving more effective in defending Russia against untrustworthy foreigners than the imperial regime, the Provisional Government, or the Whites." Hosking, *op. cit.*, p. 408.

41. Pipes, *Russia Under the Bolshevik Regime*, p. 138.

42. On the Civil War, see Pipes, *Russia Under the Bolshevik Regime*, Chapters 1 and 2. Referring to the Red Army, Martin Malia writes, "This hastily improvised, poorly structured, and socially fluid force would hardly have been a match for a regular European army. . . . But it was enough to fend off the equally improvised, less ideologically motivated, and even more fluid White armies." Malia, *The Soviet Tragedy*, p. 120.

43. ". . . the defeat of Germany, to which it had made no contribution, not only enabled the Soviet Government to annul the Brest-Litovsk Treaty and recover most of the lands which it had been forced to give up at Brest, but also saved Soviet Russia from being converted into a colony, a kind of Eurasian Africa, which fate Germany had intended for her." Pipes, *The Russian Revolution*, p. 670.

44. Service, *op. cit.*, pp. 331, 441; Pipes, *Russia Under the Bolshevik Regime*, pp. 181–182.

45. On the Polish campaign, see Kotkin, *op. cit.*, pp. 352–364.

46. Service, *op. cit.*, p. 421.
47. On the NEP, see Pipes, *Russia Under the Bolshevik Regime*, Chapter 8.
48. Malia, *The Soviet Tragedy*, p. 146.
49. Malia, *History's Locomotives*, p. 272.
50. Kotkin, *op. cit.*, p. 259.
51. On the history of the idea of socialism, see Malia, *The Soviet Tragedy*, pp. 22–34.
52. On utopian socialism, see Archie Brown, *The Rise and Fall of Communism*, New York: HarperCollins, 2009, pp. 16–18.
53. See pp. 11–12.
54. Alexander Ulianov was studying science in St. Petersburg when he joined the conspiracy to kill the tsar. See p. 40.
55. Malia, *The Soviet Tragedy*, p. 41.
56. Karl Marx, "Theses on Feuerbach," in Karl Marx and Friedrich Engels, *Selected Works*, New York: International Publishers, 1970, p. 30.
57. Pipes, *The Russian Revolution*, pp. 214–216.
58. On the impact of the war and the way it created the opportunity for the Bolsheviks to seize power, see Pipes, *Russia Under the Bolshevik Regime*, pp. 3–5; Service, *op. cit.*, p. 369; Kotkin, *op. cit.*, pp. 172–173; Malia, *The Soviet Tragedy*, p. 89; and Malia, *History's Locomotives* , p. 268.
59. Martin Malia, *Russia Under Western Eyes: From the Bronze Horseman to the Lenin Mausoleum*, Cambridge, Massachusetts: The Belknap Press of Harvard University Press, 1999, pp. 13, 35. "Educational standards [in late-nineteenth-century Russia] were woeful. Legal norms went unheeded. Poverty was awesome. The Romanov police-state banned political parties, trade unions and public protest, and administrative arbitrariness was pervasive." Service, *op. cit.*, p. 2.
60. "At a minimum, most scholars would agree that the fragility of Russia's prerevolutionary civil society made the country exceptionally vulnerable to the impact of modern war, and therefore to takeover by a determined minority, as well as to forcible remolding from above." Martin Malia, "The Hunt for True October," *Commentary*, 92:4, October 1991, p. 25. See also Hosking, *op. cit.*, pp. 5–6.
61. Malia, *The Soviet Tragedy*, pp. 70–71.
62. In February, 1917, the Bolshevik Party "had perhaps ten thousand members throughout Russia." Ulam, *op. cit.*, p. 317.
63. In 1923, Hitler attempted, in the southern German city of Munich, the kind of coup that Lenin had successfully executed in Russia but Hitler's coup failed. He subsequently came to power by legal means. See pp. 67–69.
64. See pp. 41–42.
65. Service, *op. cit.*, pp. 193–194, 236.
66. *Ibid.*, p. 354; Pipes, *The Russian Revolution*, p. 512.
67. "Lenin was a human time-bomb. His intellectual influences thrust him towards Revolution and his inner rage made this impulse frenetic. Lenin had greater passion for destruction than love for the proletariat. . . . His angry outbursts

were legendary throughout the party before 1917; shortly before he died they became so acute that serious questions arose about his mental equilibrium, even his sanity." Service, *op. cit.*, p. 8. See also Pipes, *The Russian Revolution*, pp. 344–345.

68. "He shared a visceral hatred of every social prop of the tsarist political order. He detested the whole Romanov family, the aristocracy, the clergy, the police and the high command. He hated the mercantile middle class and the rising industrial and financial middle class. His zeal to smash down these props by violent methods was something he held in common with [previous Russian revolutionaries]." Service, *op. cit.*, pp. 98–99. See also *ibid.*, pp. 264, 364, and Kotkin, *op. cit.*, pp. 409–410.

69. Service, *op. cit.*, p. 434.

70. He was not so enthusiastic, however, as to take part in acts of violence himself. He let others do the dirty work. *Ibid.*, p. 177. Nor was he personally brave. See Pipes, *The Russian Revolution*, p. 805.

71. "... 'merciless' violence, violence that strove for the destruction of every actual and potential opponent, was for Lenin not only the most effective, but the only way of dealing with problems." Pipes, *Russia Under the Bolshevik Regime*, p. 500.

72. "Lenin owed much of his organizational hold to his intellectual capacity, notably as an interpreter of Marxist economic theorizing." George Lichtheim, "Lives of Lenin," in Lichtheim, *Collected Essays*, New York: The Viking Press, 1974, p. 307. See also Service, *op. cit.*, p. 272.

73. Pipes, *The Russian Revolution*, p. 348. Pipes goes on to quote a contemporary of Lenin's: "... [The Bolsheviks] only followed unquestionably Lenin, the one indisputable leader. Because Lenin alone embodied the phenomenon, rare everywhere but especially in Russia, of a man of iron will, inexhaustible energy, combining a fanatical faith in the movement, in the cause, with an equal faith in himself." *Ibid.*

74. Service, *op. cit.*, p. 195.

75. Ulam, *op. cit.*, p. 470.

76. Pipes, *The Russian Revolution*, pp. 413, 439. Kerensky was defeated politically and sent into exile by Lenin. Trotsky was defeated politically, sent into exile, and murdered by Lenin's successor as the supreme Soviet leader, Josef Stalin. "Both Trotsky and Kerensky were great orators and wretched politicians." Ulam, *op. cit.*, p. 366, note 60.

77. "It was only after the inception of the New Economic Policy in 1921 that [Lenin] became generally famous." Service, *op. cit.*, p. 9.

78. The authoritative account of the Lenin cult is Tumarkin, *op. cit.*

79. The post-Lenin leadership "needed the physical Lenin on permanent exhibit to cater to the popular belief, rooted in Orthodox religion, that the remains of saints were immune to decay." Pipes, *Russia Under the Bolshevik Regime*, p. 487.

80. "Lenin was not merely to be depicted as a heroic figure in the history of Bolshevism and world revolution. He had to enjoy the mythic status of an omniscient revolutionary saint." Service, *op. cit.*, p. 484.

81. "Lenin's writings acquired the status of holy writ; his collected works . . . were accorded a political and cultural significance greater than anything else in print." *Ibid.*, p. 482.

82. Service, *op. cit.*, p. 394; Pipes, *The Russian Revolution*, p. 350.

83. Service, *op. cit.*, p. 487; Tumarkin, *op. cit.*, pp. 256, 259. The Lenin cult reached its apogee in 1970, on the one hundredth anniversary of his birth. "Although the eternal nature of Lenin's spirit was the main message, his spatial pervasiveness was its most striking aspect. Factories, publishing houses, looms, kilns, lawns, bakeries—everything that could produce artifacts—contributed some manner of Leniniana for the occasion. The Soviet Union became a giant display case for busts, statues, posters, poems, banners, bric-a-brac, and commemorative volumes of every description." Tumarkin, *op. cit.*, p. 262.

84. "The full-blown cult of Lenin was an organized system of rites and symbols whose collective function was to arouse in the cult's participants and spectators the reverential mood necessary to create an emotional bond between them and the party personified by Lenin." Tumarkin, *op. cit.*, pp. 2–3. See also Pipes, *The Russian Revolution*, pp. 814–815, and Adam B. Ulam, *Ideologies and Illusions: Revolutionary Thought from Herzen to Solzhenitsyn*, Cambridge, Massachusetts: Harvard University Press, 1976, p. 106.

85. See p. 67.

86. See pp. 234–235.

87. Brown, *op. cit.*, pp. 3–4.

88. Stephane Courtois, "Introduction: The Crimes of Communism," in Stephane Courtois, Nicholas Werth, Jean-Louis Panne, Andrej Pasczkowski, Karel Bartosek, and Jean-Louis Margolin, *The Black Book of Communism*, Cambridge, Massachusetts: Harvard University Press, 1999, p. 4.

89. Service, *op. cit.*, pp. 263, 304; Kotkin, *op. cit.*, p. 214; Pipes, *The Russian Revolution*, pp. 471–473.

90. "Lenin made the Russian Revolution. No one else would have quite had the nerve." John Dunn, *Modern Revolutions: An Introduction to the Analysis of a Political Phenomenon*, Cambridge, UK: Cambridge University Press, 1972, pp. 46–47.

91. Malia, *The Soviet Tragedy*, p. 94.

92. Kotkin, *op. cit.*, p. 223.

93. "There was a single ruling party. There was a politically subordinate legislature, executive and judiciary. The party in reality was the supreme state agency and Lenin in all but name was the supreme leader of that agency." Service, *op. cit.*, p. 391. See also Pipes, *Russia Under the Bolshevik Regime*, p. 504, and Ulam, *Lenin and the Bolsheviks*, p. 365.

94. Service, *op. cit.*, p. 338; Pipes, *The Russian Revolution*, p. 593.

95. Pipes, *The Russian Revolution*, pp. 567, 575, 581.

96. Malia, *The Soviet Tragedy*, p. 115.

97. Service, *op. cit.*, pp. 339–342; Pipes, *The Russian Revolution*, p. 587.

98. Pipes, *Russia Under the Bolshevik Regime*, pp. 182–183; Kotkin, *op. cit.*, p. 377.

99. Pipes, *Russia Under the Bolshevik Regime*, p. 237.

100. "At first, in 1921–1922, the NEP was viewed by most of the Party as a harsh necessity and a forced retreat, and by some as a defeat of socialism, indeed as the failure of the Revolution." Malia, *The Soviet Tragedy*, p. 153.

101. Service, *op. cit.*, pp. 422–427.

102. In this "revisionist" approach to Soviet history, two important texts are Moshe Lewin, *Lenin's Last Struggle*, New York: Pantheon Books, 1968, and Stephen E. Cohen, *Bukharin and the Bolshevik Revolution: A Political Biography, 1888–1938*, New York: Alfred A. Knopf, 1973. On the revisionist project, see Walter Laqueur, "The Long Goodbye," *The New Republic*, April 11, 1994, p. 35, and Malia, *The Soviet Tragedy*, pp. 10–12.

103. Quoted in Service, *op. cit.*, pp. 465 and 469. In the first volume of his authoritative biography of Stalin, Stephen Kotkin casts doubt on whether the note actually came directly from the then grievously ill Lenin. Kotkin, *op. cit.*, pp. 500–501, 527–528.

104. Hosking, *op. cit.*, p. 449.

105. Service, *op. cit.*, p. 465; Ulam, *Ideologies and Illusions*, p. 97.

106. Service, *op. cit.*, pp. 446–447.

107. Malia, *The Soviet Tragedy*, p. 182; Kotkin, *op. cit.*, pp. 411, 413, 419.

108. The Communists "temporarily jettisoned their maximalist program in order to preserve [their] power, so that the Party might live to fight again another day." Malia, *The Soviet Tragedy*, p. 132. "Lenin liked to compare NEP to the Brest-Litovsk treaty, which in its day had also been mistakenly seen as a surrender to German 'imperialism' but was only a step backward: however long it would last, it would not be 'forever.'" Pipes, *Russia Under the Bolshevik Regime*, p. 370.

109. Malia, *The Soviet Tragedy*, pp. 173–174; Malia, *History's Locomotives*, p. 274. In the judgment of Adam Ulam, "Had [Lenin] not been stricken in 1922, it is not improbable that the *Nep* would have ended sooner than it did." Ulam, *Lenin and the Bolsheviks*, p. 477.

110. "If . . . Bolshevik ideology is not just a matter of generalities but involves accepting the inevitable consequences of one's own principles, then Stalin was right to boast himself [sic] the most consistent of all Bolsheviks and Leninists." Leszek Kolakowski, quoted in Malia, *The Soviet Tragedy*, p. 139.

111. Pipes, *Russia Under the Bolshevik Regime*, p. 508.

112. Malia, *The Soviet Tragedy*, p. 114; Kotkin, *op. cit.*, p. 419. At Lenin's behest, the Tenth Congress of the Communist Party, in 1921, issued an order banning all factions within the Party. Malia, *The Soviet Tragedy*, p. 167.

113. Malia, *The Soviet Tragedy*, p. 245.

114. ". . . the total number of deaths for the Stalin epoch was probably around twenty million." *Ibid.*, p. 11.

115. Terror here means "the arbitrary use, by organs of political authority, of severe coercion against individuals or groups, the credible threat of such use, or the arbitrary extermination of such individuals or groups." Quoted in Seweryn Bialer, *Stalin's Successors: Leadership, stability, and change in the Soviet Union*, New York: Cambridge University Press, 1980, pp. 10–11.

116. Pipes, *The Russian Revolution*, p. 838.

117. For an estimate, see *ibid.*

118. Lenin took care not to have to witness personally the carnage he unleashed. Service, *op. cit.*, p. 366.

119. Of the assault that he ordered on the Orthodox Church, Lenin said that "the greater the number of the representatives of reactionary clergy and reactionary bourgeoisie we succeed in shooting . . . the better. It is precisely now that we ought to deliver a lesson to this public so that they won't dare even think about resistance for several decades." Quoted in *ibid.*, p. 442.

120. Service, *op. cit.*, p. 10; Pipes, *The Russian Revolution*, pp. 800–802.

121. Pipes, *The Russian Revolution*, p. 833; Malia, *The Soviet Tragedy*, p. 260.

122. Malia, *The Soviet Tragedy*, p. 199.

123. *Ibid.*; Hosking, *op. cit.*, p. 454. An estimated 40 million people suffered severe hunger in the famine. Kotkin, *op. cit.*, p. 724.

124. Robert Conquest, *The Harvest of Sorrow: Soviet Collectivization and the Terror-Famine*, New York: Oxford University Press, 1986, pp. 46, 47; Malia, *The Soviet Tragedy*, pp. 117–118.

125. Schapiro, *op. cit.*, p. 224; Malia, *The Soviet Tragedy*, pp. 125, 127.

126. Pipes, *The Russian Revolution*, pp. 716, 740.

127. Lenin's "ultimate objective remained to set up socialist collective farms." Service, *op. cit.*, p. 317. See also Kotkin, *op. cit.*, pp. 731–732.

128. Malia, *The Soviet Tragedy*, p. 128; Pipes, *Russia Under the Bolshevik Regime*, p. 504.

129. Service, *op. cit.*, p. 430.

130. Pipes, *Russia Under the Bolshevik Regime*, pp. 424–425.

131. See Michael Mandelbaum, *The Four Ages of American Foreign Policy: Weak Power, Great Power, Superpower, Hyperpower*, New York: Oxford University Press, 2022, pp. 9–11.

132. In keeping with this age-old principle of foreign policy, during World War I, "There can be little doubt that if the Germans had followed through on the recommendations of Ludendorff and Hindenburg [to invade Russia and depose the revolutionary government there], the Bolsheviks, in order to stay in power, would have made common cause with the Allies and allowed them the use of Russian territory for military operations against the Central Powers." Pipes, *The Russian Revolution*, p. 591.

133. "Soviet leaders were justified in claiming that they were ruling within the Leninist tradition and over a Leninist state. From 1917–19 to the late 1980s the edifice was recognizably Lenin's creation." Service, *op. cit.*, p. 491.

134. Malia, *The Soviet Tragedy*, Chapters 11 and 12.

135. Richard Pipes, *The Formation of the Soviet Union*, Cambridge, Massachusetts: Harvard University Press, 1997 (first published in 1954), pp. 296–297; Hosking, *op. cit.*, pp. 428, 433.

Chapter 3

1. Ian Kershaw, *Hitler, 1889–1936: Hubris*, New York: W. W. Norton, 1999, p. 12.

2. *Ibid.*, p. 41; John Lukacs, *The Hitler of History*, New York: Alfred A. Knopf, 1997, p. 49. He was also deeply interested in music, in particular the operas of the German composer Richard Wagner.

3. "Hitler's interest in art was evident throughout his life. He wanted to be a painter; and then an architect." Lukacs, *op. cit.*, p. 101.

4. "Some time in the weeks before Christmas 1909, thin and bedraggled, in filthy, lice-ridden clothes, his feet sore from walking around, Hitler joined the human flotsam and jetsam finding their way to the large, recently established doss-house for the homeless." Kershaw, *op. cit.*, p. 52.

5. Sebastian Haffner, *The Meaning of Hitler*, Translated by Ewald Osers, Cambridge, Massachusetts: Harvard University Press, 1979, p. 10.

6. He formally became a German citizen only in 1932.

7. The war "gave him for the first time in his life a cause, a commitment, comradeship, an external discipline, a sort of regular employment, a sense of well-being, and—more than that—a sense of belonging." Kershaw, *op. cit.*, p. 87.

8. *Ibid.*, p. 102.

9. "The breakthrough experience was his own discovery of his power as an orator, which took place on 24 February 1920, when, with sweeping success, he made his first speech at a mass rally." Haffner, *op. cit.*, p. 14.

10. Kershaw, *op. cit.*, p. 127.

11. Lukacs, *op. cit.*, p. 83; Gordon A. Craig, *Germany 1866–1945*, New York: Oxford University Press, 1978, p. 549.

12. Craig, *op. cit.*, p. 493.

13. On the Nazi program of 1920, see Kershaw, *op. cit.*, pp. 144–145.

14. These views also had a major following in Austria.

15. Kershaw, *op. cit.*, p. 217.

16. *Ibid.*, pp. 363, 369, 390.

17. Craig, *op. cit.*, pp. 573–574.

18. Michael Burleigh, *The Third Reich: A New History*, New York: Hill and Wang, 2000, pp. 154–155.

19. *Ibid.*, pp. 200–201. The term came originally from the British practice during the Boer War in South Africa (1899–1902) of placing Boer farmers and their families in detention centers (often after attacking and burning their farms) so that they could not aid the forces fighting the British. For the Nazi era, the term is often used to denote both the prisons in Germany and the facilities constructed in Poland in 1942 to kill Jews on a massive scale (see p. 74). The second of these are more properly called "death camps."

20. Kershaw, *op. cit.*, pp. 499–517.

21. *Ibid.*, p. 534; Lukacs, *op. cit.*, p. 71; Haffner, *op. cit.*, p. 6.

22. Kershaw, *op. cit.*, pp. 530, 532; Haffner, *op. cit.*, p. 43; Alan Bullock, *Hitler and Stalin: Parallel Lives*, New York: Alfred A. Knopf, 1992, pp. 676–677.

23. An official of the Third Reich said in 1934 that "it is the duty of every single person to attempt, in the spirit of the Führer, to work towards him. Anyone making mistakes will come to notice it soon enough. But the one who works correctly towards the Führer along his lines and towards his aim will in future as previously have the finest reward of one day suddenly attaining the legal confirmation of his work." Quoted in Kershaw, *op. cit.*, p. 529.

24. Barry Eichengreen, *Hall of Mirrors: The Great Depression, The Great Recession, and the Uses—and Misuses—of History*, New York: Oxford University Press, 2015, p. 263.

25. Craig, *op. cit.*, p. 620.

26. Kershaw, *op. cit.*, pp. 550–552; Craig, *op. cit.*, pp. 684–686; Donald Cameron Watt, *How War Came: The Immediate Origins of the Second World War, 1938–1939*, New York: Pantheon, 1989, pp. 21–22.

27. Kershaw, *op. cit.*, pp. 582–589; Craig, *op. cit.*, p. 691.

28. Craig, *op. cit.*, p. 696.

29. Ian Kershaw, *Hitler, 1936–1945: Nemesis*, New York: W. W. Norton, 2000, pp. 78–83.

30. Watt, *op. cit.*, p. 28. Chamberlain, who had never previously flown in an airplane, made all three trips by air.

31. Kershaw, *Nemesis*, pp. 97–118; Craig, *op. cit.*, pp. 706–708. Chamberlain "believed that the European dictators, Hitler and Mussolini, were rational statesmen like himself, or at any rate must be treated as such, and that their discontents could be appeased by rational discussion." A. J. P. Taylor, *English History, 1914–1945*, New York and Oxford: Oxford University Press, 1965, p. 414.

32. Kershaw, *Nemesis*, pp. 133–148. ". . . the night of horror for Germany's Jews had brought the demolition of around 100 synagogues, the burning of several hundred others, the destruction of at least 8000 Jews' shops and vandalizing of countless apartments." *Ibid.*, pp. 140–141.

33. *Ibid.*, pp. 168–172.

34. *Ibid.*, pp. 174–175.

35. *Ibid.*, p. 210.

36. *Ibid.*, p. 236; Craig, *op. cit.*, pp. 715–716.

37. Kershaw, *Nemesis*, pp. 242–243, 246, 248–249, 252.

38. Hence the term for this type of attack: *blitzkrieg* ("lightning war").

39. A detailed description of the Battle of France, and an analysis of the reasons for the stunning German victory, appear in Ernest May, *Strange Victory: Hitler's Conquest of France*, New York: Hill and Wang, 2000.

40. John Strawson, *Hitler As Military Commander*, New York: Barnes and Noble, 1971, p. 236.

41. Kershaw, *Nemesis*, pp. 85–86, 213, 223, 285, 293, 416; John Lukacs, *The Duel: 10 May–31 July 1940: The Eighty-Day Struggle Between Churchill and Hitler*, New York: Ticknor and Fields, 1990, pp. 18–19.

42. Craig, *op. cit.*, pp. 723–724; Strawson, *op. cit.*, p. 114; Kershaw, *op. cit.*, p. 296.

43. The other countries represented included Finland, Romania, Italy, Hungary, Spain, and Slovakia. Bullock, *op. cit.*, p. 726.

44. Kershaw, *Nemesis*, p. 399.
45. *Ibid.*, p. 394. An estimated 5,700,000 Red Army soldiers were captured by the Germans during the course of the war. Of these, an estimated 3,300,000 died in captivity. Burleigh, *op. cit.*, p. 512.
46. Kershaw, *Nemesis*, p. 442.
47. Strawson, *op. cit.*, p. 138.
48. Kershaw, *Nemesis*, p. 357; Craig, *op. cit.*, pp. 729–730.
49. Kershaw, *Nemesis*, p. 463; Craig, *op. cit.*, p. 748.
50. On the distinction between the Nazi treatment of Jews and of the other peoples they persecuted, see Burleigh, *op. cit.*, pp. 571–572.
51. A year after Barbarossa had begun, over a million of the 3.2 million men who had taken part in the initial attack had been killed or wounded or were missing. Kershaw, *Nemesis*, p. 515.
52. *Ibid.*, p. 597.
53. Burleigh, *op. cit.*, p. 508.
54. The Americans called the offensive and their efforts to repel it the "Battle of the Bulge."
55. Kershaw, *Nemesis*, pp. 741–744.
56. Kershaw, *Hubris*, p. 89; Strawson, *op. cit.*, p. 19.
57. Alfred Grosser, *Germany in Our Time: A Political History of the Postwar Years*, Translated by Paul Stephenson, New York: Praeger Publishers, 1971, p. 5.
58. Hajo Holborn, "Diplomats and Diplomacy in the Early Weimar Republic," in Holborn, *Germany and Europe: Historical Essays*, Garden City, New York: Doubleday and Company, 1970, p. 176.
59. *Ibid.*, pp. 188–190.
60. After 1919, "the general aim of German foreign policy was the revision of the treaty of Versailles. It was popular with every party from the extreme right to the extreme left and, one may say, with every individual German." *Ibid.*, p. 208.
61. " . . . the price of a newspaper rose to 200 marks in April, 2,000 in July, 150,000 on September 1, 500,000 on the 15th, 4 million on October 1, 25 million on the 15th, 2,000 million on November 2, and 8,000 million on November 8." Grosser, *op. cit.*, p. 9.
62. "Before [the inflation] had run its course, millions of Germans who had passively accepted the transition from Empire to Republic had suffered deprivations that shattered their faith in the democratic process and left them cynical and alienated." Craig, *op. cit.*, p. 435.
63. See p. 102.
64. Taylor, *op. cit.*, pp. 361–362, 417.
65. *Ibid.*, pp. 387, 425.
66. To be sure, the Pact also provided territorial gains to the Soviet Union, which, like Nazi Germany, wanted to change the post–World War I political arrangements in Europe to its own advantage.
67. Gordon A. Craig, *The Germans*, New York: New American Library, 1982, p. 242; Kershaw, *Nemesis*, pp. 123–124.

68. Craig, *Germany*, pp. 715–716. "... if the Western powers had chosen to do so, they could probably have defeated Germany militarily not only in 1938, when Czechoslovakia would have been an ally, but in 1939, during Germany's four-week war in Poland." May, *op. cit.*, p. 455. See also Williamson Murray, *The Change in the European Balance of Power, 1938–1939: The Path to Ruin*, Princeton, New Jersey: Princeton University Press, 1984.

69. Grosser, *op. cit.*, p. 10.

70. Haffner, *op. cit.*, p. 66.

71. "... without the Depression and the calamitous effect upon Germany ... the Nazi Party may well have broken up and faded into oblivion, remembered essentially as a passing phenomenon of the post-war upheaval." Kershaw, *Hubris*, p. 259.

72. Eichengreen, *op. cit.*, p. 137.

73. "By January 1930, the labour exchanges recorded 3,218,000 unemployed— some 14 per cent of the 'working age' population. The true figure, taking in those on short-time, has been estimated as over 4 1/2 million." Kershaw, *Hubris*, p. 318. The German government, like the governments of other countries, also mistakenly pursued policies of economic austerity. Eichengreen, *op. cit.*, p. 139.

74. "The onset of the 1929 world economic Depression immeasurably radicalized the political climate in Germany." Burleigh, *op. cit.*, 122.

75. Craig, *Germany*, p. 542; Kershaw, *Hubris*, p. 333.

76. Kershaw, *Nemesis*, p. xv.

77. Lukacs, *The Hitler of History*, p. 216; Kershaw, *Hubris*, pp. 424–425.

78. Von Papen served briefly as vice chancellor under Hitler.

79. Lukacs, *The Hitler of History*, p. 88.

80. Many on the right also shared Hitler's antisemitism.

81. Hitler as a revolutionary is a theme of Lukacs, *The Hitler of History*. See pp. 50, 84, 258–259.

82. The man who preceded Hitler as chancellor, Kurt von Schleicher, was murdered on the Night of the Long Knives.

83. Ron Rosenbaum, *Explaining Hitler: The Search for the Origins of His Evil*, New York: Random House, 1998, p. 345; Kershaw, *Hubris*, pp. 371, 380, 419, 424; Craig, *op. cit.*, pp. 568, 569; Burleigh, *op. cit.*, p. 151.

84. "If, as has often been said, the Prussian army made the Prussian state, it is also true that the subsequent political development of Prussia and Germany, was dependent, to a far greater extent than is true of any other country, upon the organization of the army, its relationship to the sovereign power, and the will of its leaders." Gordon A. Craig, *The Politics of the Prussian Army, 1640–1945*, New York: Oxford University Press, 1955, p. xiv.

85. *Ibid.*, p. xviii.

86. Craig, *Germany*, p. 567.

87. "... the significant steps taken since 1933 had in every case been consonant with the interests of the key agencies of power in the regime, above all with those of the Wehrmacht." Kershaw, *Nemesis*, p. 63.

88. Craig, *Germany*, p. 588; Craig, *The Germans*, p. 241; Hajo Holborn, "German Opposition to Hitler," in Holborn, *op. cit.*, pp. 242–243.

89. "Within five years Hitler had accomplished what the liberals of 1848 and 1862 and the republicans and socialists of 1918 had sought to accomplish in vain: he had completely subordinated the army to his own control." Craig, *The Politics of the Prussian Army*, p. xix.

90. ". . . the formidable cohesion and discipline . . . made the German army in 1940 the most efficient in the history of the modern world." Lukacs, *The Duel*, p. 57.

91. Kershaw, *Nemesis*, p. 465.

92. "He was an extreme nationalist—perhaps the most extreme nationalist of all the principal figures of the twentieth century." Lukacs, *The Hitler of History*, p. 127.

93. Rosenbaum, *op. cit.*, p. 352.

94. Haffner, *op. cit.*, pp. 91–92.

95. Burleigh, *op. cit.*, p. 91.

96. Lukacs, *The Hitler of History*, p. 184; Burleigh, *op. cit.*, pp. 770–771.

97. On the subject of the Jews, "there cannot be the slightest doubt, on the basis of his private comments, that Hitler believed in what he said." Kershaw, *Nemesis*, p. 489.

98. Lukacs, *The Hitler of History*, pp. 185, 167; Kershaw, *Hubris*, p. 60; Rosenbaum, *op. cit.*, pp. 83–84.

99. Haffner, *op. cit.*, p. 94.

100. Kershaw, *Nemesis*, pp. xlv, 191, 241; Craig, *Germany*, pp. 676–677; Lukacs, *The Duel*, p. 144. Large-scale population transfer had taken place before and during World War I, especially in and by the Ottoman Empire.

101. Haffner, *op. cit.*, p. 13.

102. Strawson, *op. cit.*, p. 13.

103. Kershaw, *Nemesis*, p. 275.

104. Kershaw, *Hubris*, p. 535; Haffner, *op. cit.*, p. 5.

105. Lukacs, *The Hitler of History*, p. 67. ". . . Hitler would have remained a political nonentity without the patronage and support he obtained from influential circles in Bavaria." Kershaw, *Hubris*, p. 133.

106. Lukacs, *The Hitler of History*, p. 14; Craig, *Germany*, p. 544.

107. Craig, *Germany*, p. 546.

108. *Ibid.*, p. 547; Craig, *The Germans*, p. 68; Burleigh, *op. cit.*, p. 114; Kershaw, *Hubris*, p. 133; Fritz Stern, "Germany 1933: Fifty Years Later," in Stern, *Dreams and Delusions: The Drama of German History*, New York: Alfred A. Knopf, 1987, p. 120.

109. Lukacs, *The Hitler of History*, pp. 48, 69.

110. *Ibid.*, pp. 98, 202.

111. Kershaw, *Hubris*, p. xii.

112. *Ibid.*, p. 294.

113. Craig, *Germany*, p. 544. See also Haffner, *op. cit.*, p. 25; and Craig, *The Germans*, pp. 65–66.

114. "... his most astounding talent was the instant exploitation of opportunities presented to him by others." Fritz Stern, "National Socialism as Temptation," in Stern, *op. cit.*, p. 166.

115. Lukacs, *The Hitler of History*, p. 135; Lukacs, *The Duel*, pp. 35–36.

116. Quoted in Rosenbaum, *op. cit.*, p. 382. "It would always be the same: he only knew all-or-nothing arguments; there was nothing in between, no possibility of reaching a compromise. Always from a maximalist position, with no other way out, he would go for broke." Kershaw, *Hubris*, p. 163. See also *ibid.*, pp. 542, 553.

117. Quoted in Lukacs, *The Hitler of History*, pp. 71–72. See also Kershaw, *Hubris*, p. 198.

118. "The matter for wonder is the largely unquestioning discipline with which most Germans—and perhaps especially the working class—trusted him and held out, demonstrating an astounding measure of national unity, until the last months of the war." Lukacs, *The Hitler of History*, p. 160. See also Strawson, *op. cit.*, pp. 215–216. Germans were hardly unaware of the course of the war as Germany began to lose it, and support for Hitler certainly diminished as the battlefield reverses mounted (Kershaw, *Nemesis*, p. 614), but not in a way that changed his policies. The aftermath of the failed bomb plot of July 1944 "highlighted the extensive reservoir of Hitler's popularity that still existed and could be tapped to bolster the regime at a critical time, despite the increasingly self-evident catastrophic course of the war. The Führer cult was far from extinguished." *Ibid.*, p. 700.

119. See pp. 49–50.

120. "... it was the reversion to barbarism almost as much as the barbarism itself which made Nazi Germany peculiarly hateful...." Taylor, *op. cit.*, p. 419.

121. Kershaw, *Nemesis*, p. xv.

122. "If Hitler had succumbed to an assassination or an accident at the end of 1938, few would hesitate to call him one of the greatest of German statesmen, the consummator of Germany's history." Joachim C. Fest, *Hitler*, Translated by Richard and Clara Winston, New York: Vintage Books, 1975, p. 9.

123. Kershaw, *Nemesis*, p. 599.

124. The historian Hugh Trevor-Roper, author of *The Last Days of Hitler*, stated his "belief that there is something irrational at the heart of Hitler's appeal, something not explicable by the ordinary tools and methods of rational historical and psychological analysis." Rosenbaum, *op. cit.*, pp. 67–68.

125. "The NSDAP of the late twenties was wholly and entirely Hitler's creation...." Haffner, *op. cit.*, p. 25.

126. Craig, *Germany*, p. 700. "Hitler's power was by this time [1939] absolute. He could decide over war and peace." Kershaw, *Nemesis*, p. 188.

127. Kershaw, *Hubris*, p. 542.

128. "... of one thing we can be sure. The Second World War was Hitler's war." Strawson, *op. cit.*, p. 244.

129. "... Hitler, supreme commander though he was, dealt in battalions, not corps and armies...." *Ibid.*, p. 14.

130. "Only in the last four years of his life did Hitler, for the first time, practice a regular activity—as military Commander-in-Chief." Haffner, *op. cit.*, p. 6. See also Kershaw, *Nemesis*, p. 611.

131. Craig, *Germany*, p. 754.

132. May, *op. cit.*, pp. 235–236; Craig, *Germany*, p. 720; Kershaw, *Nemesis*, p. 290.

133. Lukacs, *The Hitler of History*, p. 159; Strawson, *op. cit.*, pp. 145–147. Ian Kershaw's assessment is as follows: "Hitler's early recognition of the dangers of a full-scale collapse of the front, and the utterly ruthless determination with which he resisted demands to retreat, probably did play a part in avoiding a calamity of Napoleonic proportions. But, had he been less inflexible, and paid greater heed to some of the advice coming from his field commanders, the likelihood is that the same end could have been achieved with far smaller loss of life. Moreover, stabilization was finally achieved only after he had relaxed the 'Halt Order' and agreed to a tactical withdrawal to form a new front line." *Nemesis*, p. 456.

134. Kershaw, *Nemesis*, pp. 616, 618.

135. *Ibid.*, p. 648; Lukacs, *The Hitler of History*, p. 136; Strawson, *op. cit.*, p. 17; Craig, *Germany*, p. 755.

136. Kershaw, *Nemesis*, pp. 409–410, 417.

137. "... it is entirely possible that the shape of the conflict would have been profoundly changed if Hitler had been more willing to demand sacrifices of the home front in the first years of the war." Craig, *Germany*, p. 736.

138. Lukacs, *The Duel*, p. 197.

139. Kershaw, *Nemesis*, p. 19.

140. "Economic, military, strategic, and ideological motives were not separable in Hitler's thinking on the Soviet Union. They blended together, and were used by him with different strength at different times in persuading those in his company of the correctness and inevitability of his course of action. The cement holding them in place was, as it had been for nearly two decades, doubtless the imperative to destroy once and for all 'Jewish Bolshevism'—an aim which would at the same time provide the necessary security in 'living-space' and give Germany political and military dominance over the continent of Europe." *Ibid.*, p. 343. See also Bullock, *op. cit.*, pp. 694, 978.

141. Bullock, *op. cit.*, p. 695.

142. John Lukacs, *June, 1941: Hitler and Stalin*, New Haven, Connecticut: Yale University Press, 2006, pp. 117–118; Strawson, *op. cit.*, p. 138.

143. Michael Mandelbaum, *The Four Ages of American Foreign Policy: Weak Power, Great Power, Superpower, Hyperpower*, New York: Oxford University Press, 2022, p. 205; Lukacs, *June, 1941*, p. 18.

144. Lukacs, *The Hitler of History*, pp. 142, 148; Watt, *op. cit.*, p. 619; Kershaw, *Nemesis*, p. 228; Haffner, *op. cit.*, p. 18.

145. Haffner, *op. cit.*, pp. 114–115; Lukacs, *The Hitler of History*, pp. 150–152; Lukacs, *The Duel*, pp. 198–200; Kershaw, *Nemesis*, p. 305; Fest, *op. cit.*, pp. 642–643.

146. Fest, *op. cit.*, p. 655; Brendan Simms and Charlie Laderman, *Hitler's American Gamble: Pearl Harbor and Germany's March to Global War*, New York: Basic Books, 2021, pp. xi–xii; Kershaw, *Nemesis*, p. 364.

147. Taylor, *op. cit.*, pp. 532–533.

148. Haffner, *op. cit.*, pp. 117–118.

149. Simms and Laderman, *op. cit.*, p. 361; Kershaw, *Nemesis*, p. 445.

150. Lukacs, *The Hitler of History*, p. 154.

151. The calculation proved accurate in the sense that American troops did not become involved in land battles in France on a large scale for almost a year after the country's April, 1917 declaration of war. See Mandelbaum, *op. cit.*, pp. 162, 167.

152. Lukacs, *June 1941*, p. 92–93; Lukacs, *The Duel*, pp. 109, 216.

153. Mandelbaum, *op. cit.*, pp. 219–220; Simms and Laderman, *op. cit.*, p. 38; Kershaw, *Nemesis*, p. 448.

154. This is a major theme of Paul Kennedy, *The Rise and Fall of the Great Powers: Economic Change and Political Conflict from 1500 to 2000*, New York: Random House, 1987.

155. Bullock, *op. cit.*, 880; Lukacs, *The Hitler of History*, pp. 157–158. When the news of Franklin Roosevelt's death on April 12, 1945, reached Berlin, Goebbels exulted that a similar scenario was about to come to pass. Lukacs, *The Hitler of History*, p. 158.

156. Had the Nazis not carried out murderous policies against the people they conquered in the Soviet Union, they might have received support and even assistance from local populations, especially non-Russians, who had suffered greatly under communist rule. Bullock, *op. cit.*, pp. 745–746.

157. Lukacs, *The Hitler of History*, pp. 187–189.

158. Kershaw, *Nemesis*, pp. 320–322.

159. Craig, *Germany*, p. 749.

160. Lukacs, *The Hitler of History*, pp. 179, 193; Bullock, *op. cit.*, p. 764; Kershaw, *Nemesis*, pp. 246, 491, 495; Burleigh, *op. cit.*, p. 630

161. Kershaw, *Nemesis*, pp. 473–474.

162. *Ibid.*, pp. 494, 540; Craig, *Germany*, p. 637.

163. Bullock, *op. cit.*, pp. 762, 765.

164. Rosenbaum, *op. cit.*, p. 349.

165. Haffner, *op. cit.*, pp. 99–100.

166. "Never in history has such ruination—physical and moral—been associated with the name of one man." Kershaw, *Nemesis*, p. 841.

167. See Pieter Geyl, *Napoleon: For and Against*, New Haven, Connecticut: Yale University Press, 1967.

168. On Hitler's treatment by historians, see Lukacs, *The Hitler of History*. For a comparison of Hitler and Napoleon, see *ibid.*, pp. 241–250, and Haffner, *op. cit.*, p. 45.

169. Haffner, *op. cit.*, p. 150.

170. Kershaw, *Nemesis*, p. 740.

171. Tony Judt, *Postwar: A History of Europe Since 1945*, New York: The Penguin Press, 2005, pp. 24-26. A total of 13 million ethnic Germans fled westward to West Germany. *Ibid.*, p. 26. "By 1950 there were hardly any Germans left east of the Oder River, a novel condition after eight hundred years." Lukacs, *The Duel*, p. 217.

172. The two most important post-1945 European organizations were both designed to prevent the rise of another Hitler. The European Union was

one. The other was the North Atlantic Treaty Organization (NATO), whose purpose, according to its first secretary-general, the British general Hastings Ismay, was to "keep the Americans in, the Russians out, and the Germans down." Quoted in Mandelbaum, *op. cit.*, p. 261.

173. Ian Kershaw, *The Global Age: Europe, 1950–2017*, New York: Viking, 2018, p. 56; Judt, *op. cit.*, p. 265.

174. Judt, *op. cit.*, pp. 267–269.

175. Craig, *Germany*, pp. 660–661; Haffner, *op. cit.*, p. 104; Istvan Deak, "The Führer Furor," *The New Republic*, December 15,1997, p. 41.

176. Kershaw, *Nemesis*, pp. 402, 405.

177. "In the six months of 'running wild' between Pearl Harbor and the expulsion of the British from Burma between December 1941 and May 1942, the Japanese had succeeded in what five other imperial powers—the Spanish, Dutch, British, French and Russians—had previously attempted but failed to achieve: to make themselves master of all the lands surrounding the seas of China and to link their conquests to a strong central position. Indeed, if China is included among the powers with imperial ambitions in the western Pacific, Japan had exceeded even her achievement." John Keegan, *The Second World War*, New York: Penguin Books, 1990, p. 546.

178. Haffner, *op. cit.*, p. 100.

179. On the origins of the state of Israel, see pp. 195–200.

180. Between 1948 and 1951, 332,000 Jews went from Europe to Israel. Judt, *op. cit.*, p. 32.

181. *Ibid.*, p. 53.

182. *Ibid.*, p. 565; Ian Kershaw, *The Global Age: Europe, 1950–2017*, New York: Viking, 2018.

183. On mass deaths in China during the Maoist era, see p. 245.

184. "No historian has been harsher in his judgement of Stalin. But [Robert] Conquest would later tell me that—if forced to make a comparison between the two—he'd have to say, however hesitantly and subjectively, that Hitler's degree of evil 'just feels worse' than Stalin's." Rosenbaum, *op. cit.*, p. 394. In the 1980s, a controversy among German historians took place about "whether Nazi crimes were unique, a legacy of evil in a class by themselves . . . or whether they are comparable to other national atrocities, especially Stalinist terror." Charles S. Maier, *The Unmasterable Past: History, Holocaust, and German National Identity*, Cambridge, Massachusetts: Harvard University Press, 1988, p. 1. Maier's book describes and analyzes the controversy.

185. Martin Malia, *The Soviet Tragedy: A History of Socialism in Russia, 1917–1991*, New York: The Free Press, 1994, p. 500.

186. "The Final Solution transcended the bounds of modern historical experience. Never before in modern history had one people made the killing of another the fulfillment of an ideology, in whose pursuit means were identical with ends." Lucy S. Dawidowicz, *The War Against the Jews, 1933–1945*, New York: Holt, Rinehart and Winston, 1975, pp. xiv–xv.

187. Lukacs, *The Hitler of History*, p. 266.

Chapter 4

1. The prime minister usually led the House of Commons, but the prime minister of the day, the Marquess of Salisbury, sat in the House of Lords.
2. For many years, it was believed that he had suffered from syphilis. His fatal illness seems, instead, to have been a different disease that affected the brain. Martin Gilbert, *Churchill: A Life*, New York: Henry Holt and Company, 1991, p. 37; Andrew Roberts, *Churchill: Walking With Destiny*, New York: Viking, 2018, p. 28.
3. Gilbert, *op. cit.*, p. 23.
4. He describes his reading in Chapter IX of his 1930 memoir *My Early Life: A Roving Commission*, New York: Charles Scribner's Sons.
5. Geoffrey Best, *Churchill: A Study in Greatness*, London: Hambledon and London, 2001, p. 12.
6. Gilbert, *op. cit.*, pp. 9–11.
7. *Ibid.*, p. 23.
8. Best, *op. cit.*, p. 94.
9. The books are *The Story of the Malakand Field Force* (1898), about the Northwest frontier; *The River War* (1899), about the Sudan; and *Ian Hamilton's March* (1900) and *London to Ladysmith Via Pretoria* (1900), about the Boer War.
10. Best, *op. cit.*, p. 3.
11. *Ibid.*, pp. 317–318.
12. In the year 1934, for example, he wrote fifty articles for magazines and newspapers. Gilbert, *op. cit.*, p. 524. See also Best, *op. cit.*, p. 131.
13. Best, *op. cit.*, p. 35.
14. "He was the most famous man of his [the twentieth] century." Geoffrey Wheatcroft, *Churchill's Shadow: The Life and Afterlife of Winston Churchill*, New York: W. W. Norton, 2021, p. 5.
15. Gilbert, *op. cit.*, pp. 154–157.
16. Best, *op. cit.*, pp. 53–54. At the end of November 1914, the Prime Minister H. H. Asquith created a War Council within the cabinet that included himself, the Chancellor of the Exchequer David Lloyd George, Kitchener, and Churchill. Gilbert, *op. cit.*, p. 289.
17. On the Dardanelles campaign, see Gilbert, *op. cit.*, pp. 291–307; Best, *op. cit.*, pp. 63–69; and Roberts, *op. cit.*, pp. 198–212.
18. Kitchener, for example, seriously underestimated Turkish military prowess. Gilbert, *op. cit.*, p. 307.
19. Best, *op. cit.*, p. 75.
20. See pp. 40–44.
21. See pp. 76–77.
22. Best, *op. cit.*, p. 153. Best reflected Churchill's views in his assessment that "the treaty as a whole was totally unstatesmanlike and imprudent, because it ensured that Germany, a country that no treaty could keep from remaining the largest and potentially most powerful state in Europe, would enter the post-war period with feelings of grievance and a desire for revenge, precisely the results which a wise and (Churchill's constant passion) magnanimous peace treaty

ought to have avoided." *Ibid*. The settlement did produce those feelings and that desire, with ultimately disastrous consequences.

23. Gilbert, *op. cit.*, pp. 408–412. Of the Bolshevik government, he said, "The policy I will always advocate is the overthrow and destruction of that criminal regime." *Ibid.*, p. 426. On the Russian Civil War, see pp. 45–46.

24. The Conservatives' abandonment of tariff policies he disliked smoothed his path back to them. Best, *op. cit.*, p. 114.

25. On Hitler, see Chapter 3. Churchill did for a time have a favorable view of Mussolini, seeing the Italian dictator as, among other things, a bulwark against communism. Roberts, *op. cit.*, pp. 301–302, 318, 325, 366.

26. See pp. 77–79. Churchill described an appeaser as someone who feeds a crocodile in the hope that it will eat him last.

27. On Munich, see p. 70, and Wheatcroft, *op. cit.*, p. 187.

28. On the Norway campaign, see Roberts, *op. cit.*, pp. 488–493.

29. John Lukacs, *The Duel, 10 May–31 July: The Eighty-Day Struggle Between Churchill and Hitler*, New York: Ticknor & Fields, 1991, pp. 32–33.

30. *Ibid.*, p. 6.

31. Gilbert, *op. cit.*, p. 655.

32. The dominions included Canada, Australia, New Zealand, and South Africa.

33. On the Battle of Britain, see Gilbert, *op. cit.*, pp. 670–677. The quote appears on p. 671.

34. Best, *op. cit.*, p. 173.

35. See pp. 89–90.

36. Lukacs, *op. cit.*, pp. 147–148. Stalin did not respond.

37. Best, *op. cit.*, p. 251.

38. Quoted in Wheatcroft, *op. cit.*, p. 237.

39. See pp. 89–90.

40. On the setbacks of 1942, see Best, *op. cit.*, p. 225, and Roberts, *op. cit.*, pp. 692, 718.

41. See pp. 74–75.

42. Of the victory at El Alamein, Churchill said on November 10, 1942, "Now, this is not the end. It is not even the beginning of the end. But it is, perhaps, the end of the beginning." Quoted in Roberts, *op. cit.*, p. 761.

43. Michael Mandelbaum, *The Four Ages of American Foreign Policy: Weak Power, Great Power, Superpower, Hyperpower*, New York: Oxford University Press, 2022, pp. 219–220.

44. Gilbert, *op. cit.*, p. 753.

45. The two did devise an informal plan, which was not revealed until 1953, for apportioning influence in the different countries of the Balkans. Known as the "percentages" agreement, it had no formal status, but the postwar balance of influence in the countries discussed did roughly correspond to what Churchill and Stalin had agreed. Gilbert, *op. cit.*, p. 796.

46. See p. 43.

47. The phrase made its public debut on March 5, 1946, in a speech at Fulton, Missouri, but Churchill had used it previously in private. Gilbert, *op. cit.*, p. 866; Wheatcroft, *op. cit.*, p. 344; Best, *op. cit.*, p. 263.

48. Best, *op. cit.*, p. 288.

49. Gilbert, *op. cit.*, p. 862; Best, *op. cit.*, pp. 284–287.

50. Gilbert, *op. cit.*, pp. 903, 908, 931.

51. The other two were the Duke of Wellington, the conqueror of Napoleon and later prime minister, and William E. Gladstone, a four-time prime minister. Unlike Churchill's funeral, the reigning monarch did not attend theirs. Wheatcroft, *op. cit.*, p. 417.

52. "In the year Churchill was born, General Sir Garnet Wolseley signed a treaty forcing the defeated King Koffee of the Ashanti to end human sacrifice; in the year he died, the spaceship Gemini V orbited the earth and the Beatles released 'Ticket to Ride.'" Roberts, *op. cit.*, p. 966. Churchill entered parliament during the reign of Queen Victoria and left it during the reign of Queen Elizabeth II. He was, needless to say, the only person to achieve that distinction.

53. Best, *op. cit.*, pp. 39–40; Roberts, *op. cit.*, pp. 103–104, 167.

54. The sentence went on "and to trying to maintain the progress of the English people." Quoted in Roberts, *op. cit.*, p. 51.

55. Churchill, *op. cit.*, p. 1.

56. Roberts, *op. cit.*, p. 277. In 1920, Churchill sent "a bunch of roughneck war veterans to reinforce the police and the army against the Irish rebels. The so-called Black and Tans left a trail of murder and mayhem across Ireland. . . ." Ferdinand Mount, "Nasty, Brutish, and Great," *The New York Review of Books*, June 6, 2019, p. 23.

57. Best, *op. cit*, pp. 100–101; Gilbert, *op. cit.*, p. 446.

58. Gilbert, *op. cit.*, p. 103.

59. *Ibid.*, pp. 133–138; Gilbert, *op. cit.*, pp. 495–501, 516–521.

60. Quoted in Roberts, *op. cit.*, p. 354. Churchill had a less than high regard for Gandhi, to whom he once referred as "a seditious Middle Temple lawyer now posing as a fakir of a type well-known in the East, striding half-naked up the steps of the Vice-regal palace. . . ." Quoted in Best, *op. cit.*, p. 135.

61. David Fromkin, *A Peace to End All Peace: Creating the Modern Middle East, 1914–1922*, New York: Henry Holt and Company, 1989, pp. 503–514; Best, *op. cit.*, p. 108.

62. Fromkin, *op. cit.*, pp. 515–529; Roberts, *op. cit.*, pp. 281–283.

63. See p. 194.

64. Best, *op. cit.*, p. 45.

65. Gilbert, *op. cit.*, p. 281.

66. "War was what especially excited him and brought out what was most original and powerful within him." Best, *op. cit.*, p. 141.

67. "No other Prime Minister would have paid so much personal attention to the military uses of science and technology, and no other could have had the same earlier experience of inventing, making and using munitions of war. He had an instinctive 'feel' for the qualities of weaponry." *Ibid.*, p. 199.

68. Best, *op. cit.*, p. 103.

69. Gilbert, *op. cit.*, p. xix.

70. Roberts, *op. cit.*, p. 10.

71. Best, *op. cit.*, p. 20; Gilbert, *op. cit.*, p. 182.

72. Roberts, *op. cit.*, p. 972.

73. In a letter to his wife at the outset of World War I, he wrote: "You know how willingly & proudly I would risk—or give—if need be—my period of existence to keep this country great & famous & prosperous & free." Gilbert, *op. cit.*, p. 268.

74. Best, *op. cit.*, pp. 24, 139.

75. Roberts, *op. cit.*, p. 966.

76. *Ibid.*, p. 470; Gilbert, *op. cit.*, p. 577.

77. Of his first tour at the Admiralty, Churchill subsequently wrote: "The Admiralty yacht *Enchantress* was now to become largely my office, almost my home, and my work my sole occupation and amusement. In all, I spent eight months afloat in the three years before the war. . . . I got to know what everything looked like and where everything was, and how one thing fitted into another. In the end I could put my hand on anything that was wanted and knew thoroughly the current state of our naval affairs." Quoted in Best, *op. cit.*, p. 43.

78. Gilbert, *op. cit.*, p. 373.

79. One younger colleague in the House said to him, "I shall always be grateful— as must be every young man in the house to-day—for the way in which you continually demonstrate to what heights the art of Parliamentary debate can be made to attain." *Ibid.*, p. 577.

80. Best, *op. cit.*, pp. 26, 46, 179–180. In 1940, his wife wrote to him that "One of the men in your entourage (a devoted friend) has been in to me and told me that there is a danger of your being generally disliked by your colleagues and subordinates because of your rough, sarcastic, and overbearing manner." Quoted in Roberts, *op. cit.*, p. 567.

81. Roberts, *op. cit.*, p. 561; Best, *op. cit.*, p. 333.

82. Wheatcroft, *op. cit.*, p. 194.

83. *Ibid.*, p. 121; Roberts, *op. cit.*, p. 978.

84. Wheatcroft, *op. cit.*, p. 113.

85. See, for example, Best, *op. cit.*, p. 34. ". . . Churchill's barbed style made him many enemies. . . ." Gilbert, *op. cit.*, p. 168.

86. Roberts, *op. cit.*, pp. 94–95.

87. Roberts, *op. cit.*, pp. 400–401.

88. In purely electoral terms, Churchill does not qualify as a particularly successful prime minister. He gained the office in the absence of a general election. He then led his party in three such elections—in 1945, 1950, and 1951—only one of which the Conservatives won and in none of which it managed to achieve even a plurality of the total vote. Wheatcroft, *op. cit.*, p. 362.

89. Activism accorded with his temperament as well. "I like things to happen," he once said, "and if they don't happen I like to make them happen." Quoted in Roberts, *op. cit.*, p. 322.

90. Gilbert, *op. cit.*, p. 624.

91. See p. 91.

92. Best, *op. cit.*, pp. 189–190.

93. Throughout his public career, Churchill used "his exceptional mastery of words, and love of language, to convey detailed arguments and essential truths; to inform, to convince, and to inspire." Gilbert, *op. cit.*, p. xx.

94. Quoted in Best, *op. cit.*, p. 188.

95. Quoted in Gilbert, *op. cit.*, p. 656.

96. Quoted in John Lukacs, *Five Days in London May 1940*, New Haven, Connecticut: Yale University Press, 1999, p. 217.

97. Best, *op. cit.*, p. 168.

98. Quoted in A. J. P. Taylor, *English History, 1914–1945*, New York: Oxford University Press, 1965, p. 491.

99. Lukacs, *Five Days in London*, p. 201; Gilbert, *op. cit.*, p. 634. "So hypnotic was the force of his words, so strong his faith, that by the sheer intensity of his eloquence he bound his spell upon [the British people] until it seemed to them that he was indeed speaking what was in their hearts and minds." Isaiah Berlin, *Mr. Churchill in 1940*, Boston: Houghton Mifflin Company, 1964, pp. 26–27.

100. Quoted in Wheatcroft, *op. cit.*, p. 197.

101. Best, *op. cit.*, pp. 119–120.

102. *Ibid.*, p. 47. Churchill presided over the shift from coal to oil as the fleet's principal fuel and proceeded to acquire a controlling share in the Anglo-Persian Oil Company in order to ensure supplies of oil. Wheatcroft, *op. cit.*, p. 66.

103. Best, *op. cit.*, pp. 119–120. Churchill later said that returning to the gold standard was the worst mistake of his life. Wheatcroft, *op. cit.*, p. 115.

104. Best, *op. cit.*, p. 183.

105. *Ibid.*, p. 210; Roberts, op. *cit.*, p. 525; Gilbert, *op. cit.*, pp. 708–709; Eliot A. Cohen, *Supreme Command: Soldiers, Statesmen, and Leadership in Wartime*, New York: The Free Press, 2002, p. 118.

106. Best, *op. cit.*, pp. 259–260. "One of the foreign office contingent described the meeting [at Potsdam] as not so much the Big Three as the Big Two-and-a-Half." *Ibid.*, p. 264. "I realized at Teheran for the first time," Churchill said after that meeting with Roosevelt and Stalin, "what a small nation we are." Roberts, *op. cit.*, p. 805.

107. John Keegan, *The Second World War*, New York: Penguin Books, 1990, p. 483.

108. Best, *op. cit.*, pp. 232–234; Roberts, *op. cit.*, pp. 553, 755–756.

109. Keegan, *op. cit.*, pp. 484, 495.

110. On the debate over the impact of bombing see Best, *op. cit.*, pp. 234–242.

111. Wheatcroft, *op. cit.*, pp. 277–278.

112. Gilbert, *op. cit.*, p. 773.

113. Best, *op. cit.*, p. 216.

114. Roberts, *op. cit.*, pp. 674, 970.

115. Best, *op. cit.*, p. 91. He made a total of twenty-five foreign trips covering over 100,00 miles during the war. Roberts, *op. cit.*, p. 970.

116. The Atlantic Charter "was basically a 374-word U.S.-proposed press release. The British Empire would adhere to little of it for another twenty years, such as calls for self-determination and equal terms of trade." Derek Leebaert, *Unlikely Heroes: Franklin Roosevelt, His Four Lieutenants, and the World They Made*, New York: St. Martin's Press, 2023, p. 320.

117. Gilbert, *op. cit.*, p. 689; Roberts, *op. cit.*, pp. 632–633.

118. "'No one but he' [that is, Churchill] Harold Macmillan [a future Conservative prime minister] wrote in his diary in November 1943, 'and that only with extraordinary patience and skill, could have enticed the Americans into the European war at all.'" Quoted in Roberts, *op. cit.*, p. 822. That assessment is a dubious one.

119. Lukacs, *Five Days in London*, pp. 206–207; Lukacs, *The Duel*, pp. 184, 201. When Churchill came to power, Roosevelt had reservations about him. Lukacs, *The Duel*, pp. 73, 91.

120. Best, *op. cit.*, p. 219. "... the wartime connection between Britain and the US was more tenuous, instrumental and less sentimentally driven than postwar Britain liked to believe. In fact, the two partners were deeply suspicious of one another; their leaders never believed that their interests must converge once Hitler was defeated. They also had sharply different assessments of how to achieve victory. What was striking was not the existence of these differences, but the degree to which they were overcome." Mark Mazower, "The spurious relationship," *Financial Times*, September 12/13, 2009, p. 16.

121. The "percentages" plan he devised with Stalin in October 1944 demonstrated that they could speak the same political language—the language of power politics—and could agree on secondary matters. See Gilbert, *op. cit.*, p. 790.

122. "Had Britain stopped fighting in May 1940, Hitler would have won *his* war. Thus he was never closer to victory than during those five days in May 1940.... Churchill and Britain could not have won the Second World War; in the end America and Russia did. But in May 1940 Churchill was the one who did not lose it." Lukacs, *Five Days in London*, pp. 189–190.

123. "After 10 May 1940, the War Cabinet consisted of five men—Churchill, Halifax, and Chamberlain and the two leaders of Labour, Clement Attlee and Arthur Greenwood, who were brought into the coalition, making it a National Government." Lukacs, *Five Days in London*, p. 68.

124. Gilbert, *op. cit.*, pp. 650–651.

125. Chamberlain died of cancer in November 1940. Churchill sent Halifax to Washington as the British ambassador to the United States in January 1941.

126. The American-born Conservative MP Henry "Chips" Channon, an appeaser who disliked Churchill, recorded in his diary in October,1940, when Churchill became leader of the Conservative Party (in addition to being prime minister) upon Chamberlain's death, that he felt "sad but resigned that this most brilliant, warm-hearted, courageous charlatan should now control the destinies not only of the nation but of the great Conservative Party." Quoted in Martin Pugh, "He's had his chips," *TLS*, September 10, 2021, p. 10.

127. The Labour members of the War Cabinet, Attlee and Greenwood, also opposed making such an approach. Ian Kershaw, *Fateful Choices: Ten Decisions That Changed the World 1940–1941*, New York: Penguin Books, 2008, p. 39.

128. "With Britain supportive of Germany, or at least benevolently neutral towards the Reich, Roosevelt's leanings towards providing material and military backing would have been stopped in their tracks." *Ibid.*, p. 52. See also Roberts, *op. cit.*, pp. 546–547.

129. Lukacs, *Five Days in London*, pp. 181–182.

130. "There can be no doubt that if the War Cabinet had . . . approached Mussolini with a view to mediation, they could not have gone back on that decision. Once the possibility of negotiation had been opened, it could not have been closed, and the government could not have continued to lead the country in outright defiance of German power." P. M. H. Bell, *A Certain Eventuality: Britain and the Fall of France*, London: Saxon House, 1974, p. 48, quoted in Lukacs, *The Duel*, p. 101.

131. Roberts, *op. cit.*, p. 978.

132. Taylor, *op. cit.*, p. 4.

133. On Suez, see John Darwin, *Unfinished Empire: The Global Expansion of Britain*, New York: Bloomsbury Press, 2012, pp. 360–363.

134. Gilbert, *op. cit.*, pp. xix, 191.

135. *Ibid.*, p. 847.

136. Quoted in Roberts, *op. cit.*, p. 763.

137. On Prime Minister Clement Attlee's reasons for giving independence to British India in 1947, see Darwin, *Unfinished Revolution*, p. 348. In general, "the fate of the world-system in which the British Empire was embedded was largely determined by geopolitical forces over which the British themselves had little control." John Darwin, *The Empire Project: The Rise and Fall of the British World-System, 1830–1970*, New York: Cambridge University Press, 2009, p. 649. On the end of the British Empire in South Asia, see pp. 167–170 and 179–181.

138. Even regimes that perpetuated imperial rule in practice denounced it in principle. The People's Republic of China, which governed millions of Muslims and Tibetan Buddhists against their will, claimed to be a staunch opponent of imperialism.

139. Best, *op. cit.*, pp. 136-137.

140. *Ibid.*, p. 303.

141. Two million people were killed and 10 million displaced. Wheatcroft, *op. cit.*, p. 356.

142. "In the long view of world history, Britain's age of world empire was only a phase, an exceptional moment. Its chance was created by one of history's unpredicted conjunctures—when conditions in both Europe and East Asia were simultaneously favourable. A weak and passive East Asia, a Europe precariously in balance between its rival great states, combined with an introverted America and an Islamic world in disarray, provided the perfect conditions for British expansion." Darwin, *Unfinished Empire*, p. 401. Churchill was born and grew up when these conditions were most deeply entrenched. He lived to see them disappear.

143. Mandelbaum, *op. cit.*, pp. 234-236.

144. Darwin, *Unfinished Empire*, p. 390.

145. The army that liberated Burma from the Japanese, perhaps the most impressive feat of British arms largely unaided by Allied support in World War II, was commanded by British officers but Indian and African troops dominated its ranks. Wheatcroft, *op. cit.*, p. 321. On the Burma campaign, see Field-Marshall

Viscount Slim, *Defeat Into Victory*, London: Pan Books, 1999 (first published, 1956).

146. On this general point, see Derek Leebaert, *Grand Improvisation: America Confronts the British Superpower, 1945-1957*, New York: Farrar Straus and Giroux, 2018.

147. Wheatcroft, *op. cit.*, p. 285.

148. Gilbert, *op. cit.*, p. 89; Best, *op. cit.*, p. 215.

149. Best, *op. cit.*, p. 280.

150. See, for example, Wheatcroft, *op. cit.*

151. *Ibid.*, pp. 5–6; Roberts, *op. cit.*, p. 982.

152. During the 2022 Russian invasion of Ukraine, Volodymyr Zelensky, Ukraine's president who led the determined resistance to Russia, was compared to Churchill.

153. In 1916, while serving in the trenches in France, he wrote to his wife: "In great or small station, in Cabinet or in the firing line, alive or dead, my policy is 'Fight on.'" Gilbert, *op. cit.*, p. 346.

154. *Ibid.*, pp. 230, 917; Best, *op. cit.*, p. 71; Anthony Storr, "Churchill: The Man," in Storr, *Churchill's Black Dog, Kafka's Mice, and Other Phenomena of the Human Mind*, New York: Grove Press, 1988, pp. 5, 47.

155. In the first of the three wars, on India's northwest frontier, he was "mentioned in dispatches," a mark of conspicuous gallantry. Gilbert, *op. cit.*, p. 79.

156. Roberts, *op. cit.*, p. 547.

157. "Courage is rightly esteemed the first of human qualities because . . . it is the quality which guarantees all others." Quoted in *Ibid.*, p. 979.

Chapter 5

1. Franklin Roosevelt's father died in 1900 at the age of 72. His mother lived until 1941, when she was 86.

2. As an adult, he had some command of these two languages, could read Spanish, and apparently had some familiarity with Dutch as well. Derek Leebaert, *Unlikely Heroes: FDR, His Four Lieutenants, and a World Made Anew*, New York: St. Martin's Press, 2023, p. 11.

3. Frank Freidel, *Franklin D. Roosevelt: A Rendezvous With Destiny*, Boston: Little, Brown and Company, 1990, p. 7.

4. *Ibid.*, p. 11; Ted Morgan, *FDR: A Biography*, New York: Simon & Schuster, 1985, p. 84.

5. "By 1907, at least, he was telling his fellow law clerks at Carter, Ledyard, and Milburn that 'he wasn't going to practice law forever, that he intended to run for office at the first opportunity, and that he wanted to be, and thought he had a very real chance to be President.'" Robert Dallek, *Franklin D. Roosevelt and American Foreign Policy, 1932–1945*, New York: Oxford University Press, 1979, p. 6.

6. Morgan, *op. cit.*, pp. 206–211.

7. *Ibid.*, p. 57.

8. During the war, "Roosevelt wanted to get into uniform and was under pressure from Theodore Roosevelt to do so, but had no opportunity until the last weeks of the war, when President Wilson informed him it was too late." Freidel, *op. cit.*, p. 30.

9. Leebaert, *op. cit.*, p. 147.

10. "In his grasp of naval affairs, in his limitless energy, in his knack for getting things done and cutting through red tape, Franklin showed himself to be a superb administrator, equal to any task." Morgan, *op. cit.*, p. 222.

11. *Ibid.*, pp. 269–272.

12. *Ibid.*, p. 327.

13. Freidel, *op. cit.*, p. 57.

14. Morgan, *op. cit.*, pp. 303–304, 322.

15. She also learned "to act as his eyes and ears at political meetings." Freidel, *op. cit.*, p. 49.

16. "When the final vote was in, Roosevelt had carried 42 states, and Hoover only 6. The electoral vote was 472 to 59. He received 57.4 percent of the popular vote, and Hoover 39.7 percent." *Ibid.*, p. 78.

17. David M. Kennedy, *Freedom from Fear: The American People in Depression and War, 1929–1945*, New York: Oxford University Press, 1999, pp. 102–103.

18. Freidel, *op. cit.*, pp. 73–74.

19. At the end of the "Hundred Days," "the New Deal had decisively halted the banking panic. It had invented wholly new institutions to restructure vast tracts of the nation's economy, from banking to agriculture to industry to labor relations. It had authorized the biggest public works program in American history. It had earmarked billions of dollars for federal relief to the unemployed." Kennedy, *op. cit.*, p. 153.

20. By the terms of the Twentieth Amendment to the Constitution, ratified in 1933, from 1937 onward the date of the inauguration was January 20.

21. Kennedy, *op. cit.*, p. 202.

22. *Ibid.*, pp. 189, 289, 320; Morgan, *op. cit.*, p. 387.

23. Freidel, *op. cit.*, p. 248.

24. "It was one of the greatest election sweeps in American history. Roosevelt received 27,750,000 votes to 16,680,000 for Landon, and carried the electoral college, 523 to 8. He won every state but Maine and Vermont." Freidel, *op. cit.*, p. 207. In the 1934 midterm elections, the Democratic Party had also done well, increasing its members in the House of Representatives from 313 to 322 and in the Senate from 59 to 69.

25. *Ibid.*, pp. 349–351; Kennedy, *op. cit.*, p. 350.

26. Freidel, *op. cit.*, p. 286. In the 1938 congressional elections, the Democrats lost ground, with the Republicans gaining 80 seats in the House of Representatives and eight in the Senate. *Ibid.*, p. 287. After the 1938 elections, "there came into being—albeit without any coherent legislative program—an informal alliance of Republicans and southern Democrats who dominated the House and the

Senate for twenty years." Michael Barone, *How America's Political Parties Change (and How They Don't)*, New York: Encounter Books, 2019, p. 43.

27. Morgan, *op. cit.*, p. 493.
28. Freidel, *op. cit.*, p. 83; Michael Mandelbaum, *The Four Ages of American Foreign Policy: Weak Power, Great Power, Superpower, Hyperpower*, New York: Oxford University Press, 2022, pp. 183–184.
29. Freidel, *op. cit.*, p. 315.
30. See pp. 30–31.
31. On May 10, 1940, Roosevelt "received a War Department report that the United States could field only five divisions totaling 80,000 men and had equipment for less than 500,000 combat troops." Dallek, *op. cit.*, p. 221.
32. *Ibid.*, pp. 104, 109; Lynne Olson, *Those Angry Days: Roosevelt, Lindbergh, and America's Fight Over World War II, 1939–1941*, New York: Random House Trade Paperback Edition, 2014, p. 89.
33. Leebaert, *op. cit.*, p. 167.
34. Morgan, *op. cit.*, pp. 487, 580; Mandelbaum, *op. cit.*, p. 197; Kennedy, *op. cit.*, p. 390. Opposition was strong, as well, among German Americans who supported their mother country and Irish Americans, who aligned against Great Britain, the country they regarded as their national oppressor.
35. Olson, *op. cit.*, p. 313.
36. Roosevelt was the 32nd president but the 31st person to hold the office. Grover Cleveland's two nonconsecutive terms made him both the 22nd and the 24th chief executive.
37. Quoted in Freidel, *op. cit.*, p. 355.
38. Quoted in *ibid.*, p. 322.
39. Kennedy, *op. cit.*, pp. 468–469; John A. Thompson, *A Sense of Power: The Roots of America's Global Role*, Ithaca, New York: Cornell University Press, 2015, pp. 152–153.
40. Dallek, *op. cit.*, p. 204; Mandelbaum, *op. cit.*, p. 201.
41. Morgan, *op. cit.*, pp, 525–527; Freidel, *op. cit.*, p. 352; Kennedy, *op. cit.*, p. 460; Charles Peters, *Five Days in Philadelphia: The Amazing "We Want Willkie!" Convention of 1940 and How It Freed FDR to Save the Western World*, New York: PublicAffairs, 2005, p. 171.
42. Kennedy, *op. cit.*, pp. 474–475; Peters, *op. cit.*, p. 181.
43. Kennedy, *op. cit.*, p. 496; Mandelbaum, *op. cit.*, p. 202.
44. Morgan, *op. cit.*, p. 523; Freidel, *op. cit.*, pp. 307, 309.
45. Freidel, *op. cit.*, p. 391.
46. Mandelbaum, *op. cit.*, p. 202.
47. Dallek, *op. cit.*, p. 276; Morgan, *op. cit.*, p. 599; Freidel, *op. cit.*, pp. 383–384; Kennedy, *op. cit.*, p. 492. Roosevelt justified an American military presence in Greenland on the cartographically dubious grounds that the island that Denmark had controlled was located in the Western Hemisphere, and the dispatch of forces to prevent Germany from seizing it was therefore a way, consistent with the Monroe Doctrine, of fortifying hemispheric defense.
48. Morgan, *op. cit.*, p. 589.

49. *Ibid.*, p. 601; Freidel, *op. cit.*, p. 391; Leebaert, *op. cit.*, pp. 311, 321; Ian Kershaw, *Fateful Choices: Ten Decisions That Changed the World 1940–1941*, London: Penguin Books, 2007, p. 322.

50. Quoted in Freidel, *op. cit.*, p. 386.

51. *Ibid.*, pp. 382–383.

52. Kennedy, *op. cit.*, pp. 509–511.

53. Freidel, *op. cit.*, p. 360.

54. See, for example, Mandelbaum, *op. cit.*, pp. 213–214. "By 1944, the United States, one of five great powers and several lesser ones at war, manufactured fully forty percent of all the world's armaments." *Ibid.*, p. 213.

55. Kennedy, *op. cit.*, pp. 621–633; John Morton Blum, *V Was for Victory: Politics and American Culture During World War II*, New York: Harcourt Brace Jovanovich, 1976, pp. 121–122.

56. Mandelbaum, *op. cit.*, p. 214; Kennedy, *op. cit.*, pp. 644–646.

57. Mandelbaum, *op. cit.*, p. 225; Dallek, *op. cit.*, pp. 446–447; Morgan, *op. cit.*, pp. 508, 716; Leebaert, *op. cit.*, pp. 177, 178, 235, 236, 357, 412.

58. Mandelbaum, *op. cit.*, pp. 219–220.

59. Mandelbaum, *op. cit.*, p. 216; Kennedy, *op. cit.*, pp. 526–527.

60. Mandelbaum, *op. cit.*, pp. 216–217.

61. *Ibid.*, pp. 216–217. The Japanese also lost 330 airplanes. The United States lost one carrier and 150 airplanes. Freidel, *op. cit.*, pp. 445–446.

62. Freidel, *op. cit.*, p. 581; Blum, *op. cit.*, p. 295.

63. Freidel, *op. cit.*, p. 512; Morgan, *op. cit.*, p. 710.

64. Barry Eichengreen, *Exorbitant Privilege: The Rise and Fall of the Dollar and the Future of the International Monetary System*, New York: Oxford University Press, 2011, p. 34.

65. Barry Eichengreen, *Hall of Mirrors: The Great Depression, the Great Recession, and the Uses—and Misuses—of History*, New York: Oxford University Press, 2015, p. 2. Also aggravating the downturn globally was the inability of Great Britain and the unwillingness of the United States to perform the tasks of economic leadership that major economic crises require. Charles P. Kindleberger, *The World in Depression, 1929–1939*, Berkeley, California: University of California Press, 1973, pp. 28, 292, 306.

66. The statistics are in Conrad Black, *Franklin Delano Roosevelt: Champion of Freedom*, New York: PublicAffairs, 2003, p. 251.

67. Roosevelt called himself "an adopted son of Georgia." Leebaert, *op. cit.*, p. 116.

68. Barone, *op. cit.*, p. 37.

69. Kennedy, *op. cit.*, p. 98.

70. He went on, "It is common sense to take a method and try it: If it fails, admit it frankly and try another. But above all, try something." Quoted in Kennedy, *op. cit.*, p. 104.

71. Peters, *op. cit.*, pp. 123–124.

72. In 1951 that rule was made formal as the Twenty-Second Amendment to the American Constitution.

73. On the 1940 Republican convention, see Peters, *op. cit.*, Chapters 4–9.

74. Four people in particular had prominent roles throughout the Roosevelt presidency: Secretary of Labor Frances Perkins; Secretary of the Interior Harold Ickes; Harry Hopkins, who held a number of positions including Roosevelt's personal emissary to the prime minister of Great Britain, Winston Churchill, and to the leader of the Soviet Union, Josef Stalin; and Henry Wallace, first secretary of agriculture then secretary of commerce after leaving the vice presidency. They are the subjects of Leebaert, *op. cit.*

75. "Over the course of the war, a plethora of other agencies were created to organize production, mobilize opinion at home and abroad, run Lend-Lease, conduct economic warfare, and handle relief programs in liberated areas." Thompson, *op. cit.*, p. 198.

76. Morgan, *op. cit.*, p. 664.

77. Kennedy, *op. cit.*, pp. 457–458.

78. Freidel, *op. cit.*, p. 323; Thompson, *op. cit.*, p. 179; Leebaert, *op. cit.*, p. 223.

79. Olson, *op. cit.*, p. 90.

80. Freidel, *op. cit.*, p. 66; Kennedy, *op. cit.*, p. 124.

81. Leebaert, *op. cit.*, pp. 30, 45, 49.

82. *Ibid.*, pp. 51, 52.

83. Roosevelt "was not hidebound or orthodox. He was prepared to look at an idea on its merits and adopt it. But you had to present it in a way that he could use." Morgan, *op. cit.*, p. 345. " 'At the heart of the New Deal,' according to Richard Hofstader, 'there was not a philosophy but a temperament,' experimental, improvisational, and reactive to events." Quoted in John Lamberton Harper, *American Visions of Europe: Franklin D. Roosevelt, George F. Kennan, and Dean G. Acheson*, New York: Cambridge University Press, 1994, p. 48.

84. Morgan, *op. cit.*, pp. 293, 307, 316, 453.

85. *Ibid.*, pp. 449, 772; Leebaert, *op. cit.*, pp. 146, 220–221.

86. Morgan, *op. cit.*, p. 545.

87. "... historians and biographers have been fascinated by the quicksilver—if one likes, slippery—quality of Franklin Roosevelt's personality. Frances Perkins called him 'the most complicated human being I ever knew'; Ted Morgan, 'a chameleon-like creature.' For Frederick Marks III, he was 'sphinx-like'; for James MacGregor Burns, 'a deeply divided man'; for Waldo Heinrichs, 'the most elusive and dissembling of Presidents'. . . . No one can really claim to have penetrated his 'thickly forested interior'—to use Robert Sherwood's famous phrase." Harper, *op. cit.*, p. 12.

88. Leebaert, *op. cit.*, pp. 60, 62.

89. *Ibid.*, p. 148. Perkins, Ickes, Wallace, and Hopkins fit into this category. See *ibid.*, *passim*.

90. Quoted in Morgan, *op. cit.*, p. 550.

91. Leebaert, *op. cit.*, pp. 107, 146, 206.

92. *Ibid.*, p. 727–730; Freidel, *op. cit.*, pp. 529–537.

93. Freidel, *op. cit.*, pp. 120–121; Leebaert, *op. cit.*, p. 148.

94. "Roosevelt had a talent for governing." Morgan, *op. cit.*, p. 314.

95. *Ibid.*, p. 548.

96. Kennedy, *op. cit.*, p. 137.

97. Quoted in Freidel, *op. cit.*, p. 360.

98. Kennedy, *op. cit.*, p. 137.

99. "Whether listening or talking, in public or private, Roosevelt projected a sense of utter self-confidence and calm mastery." Kennedy, *op. cit.*, p. 114.

100. Roosevelt's impact was almost immediate. "'In one week [after his first inauguration],' [the columnist] Walter Lippmann wrote, 'the nation, which had lost confidence in everything and everybody, has regained confidence in the government and in itself.'" Quoted in Dallek, *op. cit.*, p. 35.

101. "Many of Roosevelt's acquaintances . . . believed that his grim companionship with paralysis gave to this shallow, supercilious youth the precious gift of a purposeful manhood." Kennedy, *op. cit.*, p. 96. See also Morgan, *op. cit.*, pp. 258, 260.

102. Morgan, *op. cit.*, p. 261.

103. Freidel, *op. cit.*, p. 47.

104. ". . . most Americans did not realize until after his death that he was a paraplegic." *Ibid.* Roosevelt "was seen and heard as a man of normal vitality." John Kenneth Galbraith, *Name-Dropping: From FDR On*, Boston: Houghton Mifflin Company, 1999, p. 21.

105. Leebaert, *op. cit.*, p. 218.

106. Freidel, *op. cit.*, p. 98.

107. Roosevelt had, according to some of his associates, "an intellect that was at its sharpest whenever he faced a crucial move in the political game, such as corralling votes." Leebaert, *op. cit.*, p. 101.

108. Quoted in Kennedy, *op. cit.*, p. 357. See also Arthur M. Schlesinger, Jr., *The Crisis of the Old Order*, Boston: Houghton Mifflin Company, 1956, pp. 3–5; Erich Rauchway, *Why the New Deal Matters*, New Haven, Connecticut: Yale University Press, 2021, pp. 3, 37–38; and Saul Bellow, "In the Days of Mr. Roosevelt," in Bellow, *It All Adds Up: From the Dim Past to the Uncertain Future*, New York: Viking, 1994, p. 25.

109. Kennedy, *op. cit.*, pp. 324–343; Morgan, *op. cit.*, pp. 414–415.

110. Kennedy, *op. cit.*, pp. 243–244.

111. Morgan, *op. cit.*, p. 232; Olson, *op. cit.*, p. 344; Thompson, *op. cit.*, p. 154; Dallek, *op. cit.*, p. 16.

112. Churchill reinforced this view, at least in public. On February 9, 1941, he said, in words directed at the United States: "Give us the tools, and we will finish the job." Quoted in Martin Gilbert, *Churchill: A Life*, New York: Henry Holt, 1991, p. 690.

113. Morgan, *op. cit.*, p. 624.

114. He was in regular contact with Admiral William Leahy, his personal military adviser whom he appointed to be the nation's first chairman of the Joint Chiefs of Staff.

115. Kennedy, *op. cit.*, p. 451.

116. The extension of aid to the Soviet Union was "a move in which Roosevelt's personal hand had been both visible and decisive. . . ." Kershaw, *op. cit.*, p. 310.

117. Leebaert, *op. cit.*, p. 316; Morgan, *op. cit.*, p. 599; Dallek, *op. cit.*, p. 278.

118. Morgan, *op. cit.*, p. 577; Leebaert, *op. cit.*, pp. 317–318; Kennedy, *op. cit.*, p. 525; Dallek, *op. cit.*, p. 275.

119. Kennedy, *op. cit.*, pp. 579, 600.

120. Morgan, *op. cit.*, pp. 643–644; Harper, *op. cit.*, p. 83; Freidel, *op. cit.*, pp. 450–451; Dallek, *op. cit.*, p. 321.

121. Freidel, *op. cit.*, pp. 463–464; Kennedy, *op. cit.*, p. 588.

122. Hitler referred to the officials who had surrendered in November 1918 as the "November criminals." See p. 81.

123. Rachel Yarnell Thompson, *Marshall: A Statesman Shaped in the Crucible of War*, Leesburg, Virginia: George C. Marshall International Center, 2017, p. 117.

124. Geoffrey Best, *Churchill: A Study in Greatness*, London: Hambledon and London, 2001, pp. 220–221; Leebaert, *op. cit.*, p. 377. "If Ike deserves the accolade 'great,' it rests on his performance in managing the generals under his command, as fractious and dysfunctional a group of egomaniacs as any war had ever seen." Williamson Murray and Alan R. Millett, *A War to Be Won: Fighting the Second World War*, Cambridge, Massachusetts: The Belknap Press of Harvard University Press, 2000, p. 416. The planning of D-Day, which Eisenhower supervised, was a considerable feat of both imagination and coordination.

125. Kennedy, *op. cit.*, p. 816; Leebaert, *op. cit.*, Chapter 18, p. 498.

126. Kennedy, *op. cit.*, pp. 659–667; Freidel, *op. cit.*, pp. 348–349; Leebaert, *op. cit.*, p. 321.

127. See Michael Mandelbaum, *The Nuclear Question: The United States and Nuclear Weapons, 1946–1976*, New York: Cambridge University Press, 1979.

128. Freidel, *op. cit.*, pp. 443–444; Dallek, *op. cit.*, p. 319. See also p. 109.

129. Leebaert, *op. cit.*, pp. 335–336.

130. "Altogether, Roosevelt and Churchill created organizations for coalition warfare on a global scale." Freidel, *op. cit.*, p. 415.

131. Harper, *op. cit.*, pp. 113–114; Dallek, *op. cit.*, p. 379. In early 1945, "whatever Roosevelt's innermost thoughts about de Gaulle might be, he was seeking a more cordial relationship. . . ." Freidel, *op. cit.*, p. 600.

132. Freidel, *op. cit.*, p. 477.

133. Kennedy, *op. cit.*, pp. 514–515; Rana Mitter, *Forgotten Ally: China's World War II, 1937–1945*, Boston: Houghton Mifflin Harcourt, 2013, p. 6.

134. Dallek, *op. cit.*, pp. 342, 493–494.

135. Morgan, *op. cit.*, p. 700.

136. *Ibid.*, pp. 745–747; Freidel, *op. cit.*, p. 486.

137. Morgan, *op. cit.*, pp. 749–750; Harper, *op. cit.*, p. 119. Roosevelt had domestic political reasons for his emphasis on Poland: Polish Americans formed part of his electoral coalition. It seems unlikely that he had great confidence at Yalta that he could move Stalin on this particular issue.

138. "... in Roosevelt's book the man he couldn't handle was not yet born." Morgan, *op. cit.*, p. 312; Kennedy, *op. cit.*, p. 676.

139. Churchill did no better with Stalin. See p. 121.

140. See p. 12.

141. Barone, *op. cit.*, pp. 155–156.

142. President Eisenhower wrote to his brother Edgar in 1954: "Should any political party attempt to abolish social security, unemployment insurance, and eliminate labor laws and farm programs, you would not hear of that party again in our political history." Quoted in Susan Eisenhower, *How Ike Led: The Principles Behind Eisenhower's Biggest Decisions*, New York: Thomas Dunne Books of St. Martin's Press, 2020, p. 134.

143. Kennedy, *op. cit.*, pp. 377, 379.

144. Freidel, *op. cit.*, pp. 255–256.

145. Morgan, *op. cit.*, p. 639; Dallek, *op. cit.*, p. 342.

146. Mandelbaum, *The Four Ages of American Foreign Policy*, pp. 233–238.

147. *Ibid.*, pp. 263–265. See also Leebaert, *op. cit.*, p. 425, and Dallek, *op. cit.*, p. 534.

148. Mandelbaum, *The Four Ages of American Foreign Policy*, pp. 151–152.

149. On the two approaches, see ibid., pp. 147–155. On Wilson's approach, see pp. 29–30.

150. Harper, *op. cit.*, p. 32; John Milton Cooper, *The Warrior and the Priest: Woodrow Wilson and Theodore Roosevelt*, Cambridge, Massachusetts: The Belknap Press of Harvard University Press, 1983, p. 348.

151. Freidel, *op. cit.*, pp. 357–358.

152. See, for example, Mandelbaum, *The Four Ages of American Foreign Policy*, pp. 400–410, and Michael Mandelbaum, *Mission Failure: America and the World in the Post-Cold War Era*, New York: Oxford University Press, 2016.

153. See Adam Garfinkle and Daniel Pipes, editors, *Friendly Tyrants: An American Dilemma*, New York: Palgrave Macmillan, 1991.

154. Mandelbaum, *The Four Ages of American Foreign Policy*, p. 197; John Thompson, *op. cit.*, pp. 219–220.

155. Mandelbaum, *The Four Ages of American Foreign Policy*, pp. 226–227.

156. Kennedy, *op. cit.*, p. 10.

Chapter 6

1. The caste system may be defined as a "system of hierarchical ranking of kin groups in order of ritual purity." Judith M. Brown, *Gandhi: Prisoner of Hope*, New Haven, Connecticut: Yale University Press, 1989, p. 14. On the working of the caste system, see David G. Mandelbaum, *Society in India: Volume One: Continuity and Change*, Berkeley, California: The University of California Press, 1970, Part III, and Mandelbaum, *Society in India: Volume Two: Change and Continuity*, Berkeley, California: The University of California Press, 1970, Part VI.

2. About a third of the territory of the subcontinent in Gandhi's era had Indian rulers. They governed at the sufferance of the British, who kept watch on them and occasionally intervened in their affairs.

3. Joseph Lelyveld, *Great Soul: Mahatma Gandhi and His Struggle with India*, New York: Alfred A. Knopf, 2011, p. 34.

4. Brown, *op. cit.*, p. 24.

5. Ramachandra Guha, *Gandhi Before India*, New York: Alfred A. Knopf, 2014, pp. 42–43, 49–50.

6. Lelyveld, *op. cit.*, p. 3; Brown, *op. cit.*, pp. 28–29.

7. Guha, *op. cit.*, pp. 135–136.

8. *Ibid.*, pp. 78, 226, 251.

9. Lelyveld, *op. cit.*, pp. 16–18; Guha, *op. cit.*, pp. 204–235, 267, 304–312, 548. "... during the satyagrahas in the Transvaal in 1907–10, some 3,000 Indians courted arrest. They constituted an astonishing 35 percent of the Indians in the colony." *Ibid.*, p. 543.

10. See pp. 187–188.

11. Guha, *op. cit.*, pp. 455, 479–486, 493–494; Lelyveld, *op. cit.*, pp. 20–24, 105–133.

12. Ramachandra Guha, *Gandhi: The Years That Changed the World, 1914–1948*, New York: Alfred A. Knopf, 2018, p. 837.

13. Guha, *Gandhi Before India*, p. 157.

14. *Ibid.*, pp. 335, 433–441.

15. *Ibid.*, pp. 366–367; Brown, *op. cit.*, pp. 66–67. In 1909, he wrote to a friend that "India's salvation consists in unlearning what she has learnt during the past fifty years." Guha, *Gandhi Before India*, p. 365.

16. Lelyveld, *op. cit.*, p. 141.

17. *Ibid.*, pp. 146–147; Guha, *The Years That Changed the World*, p. 21.

18. This was "his first direct experience of peasant life in his homeland." Guha, *The Years That Changed the World*, p. 47. "The urban, Western-educated English-speaker [that is, Gandhi] now saw in all their starkness, villagers' problems of disease, poverty, ignorance and the unequal division of power." Brown, *op. cit.*, p. 111.

19. Judith Brown, *Modern India: The Origins of an Asian Democracy*, New York: Oxford University Press, 1985, p. 209. The Ahmedabad strike is the subject of Erik H. Erikson, *Gandhi's Truth*, New York: W. W. Norton, 1969.

20. Lawrence James, *Raj: The Making and Unmaking of British India*, New York: St. Martin's Press, 1997, pp. 459–460.

21. Guha, *The Years That Changed the World*, pp. 68–70.

22. *Ibid.*, p. 80; Brown, *Modern India*, pp. 211–212.

23. Guha, *The Years That Changed the World*, p. 80.

24. James, *op. cit.*, pp. 471–481.

25. Brown, *Prisoner of Hope*, pp. 11–12.

26. Lloyd I. Rudolph and Susanne Hoeber Rudolph, *The Modernity of Tradition: Political Development in India*, Chicago: The University of Chicago Press, 1967, pp. 231–235; Guha, *The Years That Changed the World*, p. 129.

27. B. R. Nanda, *In Search of Gandhi: Essays and Reflections*, New Delhi: Oxford University Press, 2002, pp. 86–106; Guha, *The Years That Changed the World*, pp. 97–98; Lelyveld, *op. cit.*, p. 157.

28. Lelyveld, *op. cit.*, p. 158; Guha, *The Years That Changed the World*, p. 11.

29. Guha, *The Years That Changed the World*, p. 148.

30. Brown, *Prisoner of Hope*, p. 155.

31. "In March 1922 he stood trial for inciting disaffection towards the legally established government in India, technically on the evidence of articles in *Young India* [a weekly journal that Gandhi published] but in effect for leading a movement of non-co-operation from late 1920 to 1922. He pleaded guilty, calling himself 'an uncompromising disaffectionist and non-co-operator. . . .'" Brown, *Prisoner of Hope*, p. 140.

32. Guha, *The Years That Changed the World*, pp. 82–83; Brown, *Modern India*, p. 207.

33. He wrote in 1920, "I consider untouchability to be a heinous crime against humanity." Guha, *The Years That Changed the World*, p. 119.

34. Lelyveld, *op. cit.*, p. 166.

35. Brown, *Modern India*, p. 256; Guha, *The Years That Changed the World*, p. 310.

36. Guha, *The Years That Changed the World*, pp. 317–339. The march served as "the catalyst for a vast, largely peaceful upheaval that had shaken the pillars of the Raj, resulting in some ninety thousand arrests across India. . . ." Lelyveld, *op. cit.*, p. 205.

37. Guha, *The Years That Changed the World*, pp. 390–395.

38. Brown, *Prisoner of Hope*, pp. 281–282.

39. Guha, *The Years That Changed the World*, p. 504.

40. *Ibid.*, pp. 313–314.

41. *Ibid.*, p. 517.

42. Brown, *Modern India*, p. 303; Penderel Moon, *Divide and Quit*, Berkeley, California: The University of California Press, 1962, p. 270.

43. He said in 1926 that "untouchability for me is more insufferable than British rule." Quoted in Guha, *The Years That Changed the World*, p. 231.

44. Gandhi "was aware of the strength of Hindu orthodoxy and he took care not to equate his campaign against untouchability with the question of caste as a whole, for fear of holding back the work on what he saw as the most vital and urgent reform." Brown, *Prisoner of* Hope, pp. 205–206. See also Lelyveld, *op. cit.*, p. 240. Ambedkar ultimately rejected Hinduism altogether and converted to Buddhism. He was also one of the chief architects of independent India's constitution.

45. Guha, *The Years That Changed the World*, pp. 413–425; Lelyveld, *op. cit.*, pp. 215–217. At one point, Gandhi launched a fast to express his opposition to a separate electorate for untouchables.

46. Guha, *The Years That Changed the World*, p. 754.

47. Brown, *Modern India*, pp. 335–336; Ramachandra Guha, *India After Gandhi: The History of the World's Largest Democracy*, New York: HarperCollins, 2007, pp. 34–36.

48. Guha, *The Years That Changed the World*, pp. 609–610.
49. *Ibid.*, pp. 684–686; James, *op. cit.*, pp. 553–555, 573–578.
50. Guha, *The Years That Changed the World*, p. 646.
51. James, *op. cit.*, p. 564.
52. *Ibid.*, p. 572; Nanda, *op. cit.*, p. 84; Brown, *Modern India*, p. 311.
53. James, *op. cit.*, p. 570.
54. *Ibid.*, p. 583; Brown, *Modern India*, p. 323.
55. Brown, *Modern India*, p. 322.
56. James, *op. cit.*, pp. 578–581. See also p. 110.
57. *Ibid.*, pp. 587–588; Brown, *Prisoner of Hope*, p. 365.
58. James, *op. cit.*, p. 590; Guha, *The Years That Changed the World*, pp. 741–742.
59. James, *op. cit.*, p. 622.
60. Guha, *The Years That Changed the World*, p. 724; Lelyveld, *op. cit.*, p. 308.
61. James, *op. cit.*, pp. 602–604; Nanda, *op. cit.*, p. 151.
62. Lelyveld, *op. cit.*, pp. 318–320, 332; Guha, *The Years That Changed the World*, pp. 763–776.
63. Rudolph and Rudolph, *op. cit.*, p. 210; Guha, *The Years That Changed the World*, pp. 806–807; Nanda, *op. cit.*, p. 156.
64. Gandhi's assassin "was no idiot or maniac but a focused and ideologically driven individual, committed to a form of Hinduism and of nationalism totally opposed to Gandhi's own." Guha, *The Years That Changed the World*, p. 863.
65. The British defense of its South Asian empire in the twentieth century came down to two propositions: first, that Indians lacked the qualifications to govern themselves effectively, an assertion belied by Western-educated Indians such as Gandhi and Nehru; and second, that if the British left, the different communities that inhabited the subcontinent would be at each other's throats, something that did happen in 1946 and 1947. It cannot, of course, be known whether extended British rule, and leaving aside the question of how long it could have lasted, would have substantially reduced the violence. Nor can it be known whether a different British approach to governing the subcontinent would have diminished the violence, or even forestalled partition. See Moon, *op. cit.*, pp. 274–276.
66. "My ambition is no less than to convert the British people through nonviolence," he once wrote, "and thus make them see the wrong they have done to India." Quoted in Lelyveld, *op. cit.*, p. 203.
67. James, *op. cit.*, pp. 490, 645.
68. *Ibid.*, p. 465.
69. *Ibid.*, p. 554. The minister was Lord Halifax, then the foreign secretary, who, as Lord Irwin, had served as Viceroy of India.
70. He wanted to make a grand bargain with the British whereby they would keep their overseas empire in exchange for granting him a free hand in Europe, a bargain that Churchill rejected. See p. 72.
71. Brown, *Prisoner of Hope*, p. 322.
72. See note 2 for this chapter.
73. James, *op. cit.*, pp. 440–446, 457.

74. *Ibid.*, p. 462.

75. *Ibid.*, pp. 456–457.

76. See pp. 101, 110–111, and 201.

77. India "in 1919 was not the country it had been five years before. Like every other participant in the war, it had suffered severe internal strains which had bruised and shaken old social and economic structures." James, *op. cit.*, p. 460. See also *ibid.*, p. 473, and Brown, *Prisoner of Hope*, pp. 102–104.

78. James, *op. cit.*, pp. 587–588; Brown, *Prisoner of Hope*, pp. 353–354.

79. Brown, *Modern India*, p. 320; James, *op. cit.*, p. 556.

80. "Varieties of non-violent resistance had occurred long before Gandhi's South African experiments, and he almost certainly knew of many of them. He used the British suffragette movement, for instance, several times in *Indian Opinion* [the weekly newspaper Gandhi founded in South Africa], and even went back to figures in European history such as Tyler, Hampden, Bunyan and Socrates, as men who had obeyed their consciences rather than bow to the dictates of the ruling authority. Deep within his own Gujarati culture there was also a stress on the positive power of suffering and, surviving into the nineteenth century, a tradition of public action whereby an aggrieved party would publicly call to attention his grievance, shaming the offender, by fasting outside his home." Brown, *Prisoner of Hope*, p. 55.

81. Guha, *Gandhi Before India*, pp. 84–85, 286.

82. He was also influenced by the English writer John Ruskin. Brown, *Prisoner of Hope*, p. 79.

83. Guha, *Gandhi Before India*, p. 45; Lelyveld, *op. cit.*, p. 8.

84. Guha, *Gandhi Before India*, p. 49; Lelyveld, *op. cit.*, p. 261.

85. Guha, *Gandhi Before India*, pp. 445–446.

86. *Ibid.*, p. 289.

87. *Ibid.*, pp. 195–198.

88. In 1919, he wrote, "My bent is not political but religious and I take part in politics because I feel that there is no department of life which can be divorced from religion, and because politics touch the vital being of India almost at every point." Quoted in Brown, *Prisoner of Hope*, p. 155.

89. Rudolph and Rudolph, *op. cit.*, pp. 169–179. He could take the connection, in his own mind, to what would seem to others extreme, indeed eccentric lengths. "... in April 1938 he stated categorically that his own impurity was probably the chief stumbling block to the development of non-violence in India." Brown, *Prisoner of Hope*, p. 285.

90. Guha, *Gandhi Before India*, p. 4.

91. Quoted in Guha, *The Years That Changed the World*, p. 882. See also p. 391.

92. Many of his associates called him *bapu*—"father." Brown *Prisoner of Hope*, pp. 150–151.

93. Lelyveld, *op. cit.*, p. 141.

94. Brown, *Modern India*, pp. 206, 216; Brown, *Prisoner of Hope*, p. 168; Rudolph and Rudolph, *op. cit.*, pp. 167–168; Arthur Lall, *The Emergence of Modern India*, New York: Columbia University Press, 1981, p. 55.

95. Rudolph and Rudolph, *op. cit.*, p. 11.

96. Lelyveld, *op. cit.*, p. 230; Brown, *Prisoner of Hope*, p. 135.

97. James, *op. cit.*, p. 524.

98. Lelyveld, *op. cit.*, p. 26.

99. *Ibid.*, p. 154; Guha, *The Years That Changed the World*, pp. xii, 167.

100. Guha, *The Years That Changed the World*, pp. 150–151; James, *op. cit.*, pp. 487, 527.

101. Brown, *Prisoner of Hope*, p. 385.

102. James, *op. cit.*, pp. 532–533.

103. Brown, *Modern India*, p. 320.

104. Guha, *The Years That Changed the World*, p. 568.

105. Brown, *Prisoner of Hope*, p. 12.

106. *Ibid.*, p. 10.

107. Brown, *Modern India*, p. 358.

108. Guha, *The Years That Changed the World*, pp. 794–795.

109. Moon, *op. cit.*, pp. 14–15.

110. *Ibid.*, p. 24.

111. Guha, *The Years That Changed the World*, p. 810.

112. Moon, *op. cit.*, pp. 286–287; Nanda, *op. cit.*, p. 153.

113. "... these Hindu and Muslim, Christian and Parsi communities were tagged as the eternal elements of Indian society. Defined as majorities and minorities, they were shepherded into communal electorates whose interests the British had to protect from one another." Sunil Khilnani, *The Idea of India*, New York: Farrar, Straus, Giroux, 1997, p. 25. See also Guha, *The Years That Changed the World*, pp. 37, 811.

114. Moon, *op. cit.*, pp. 273–274; 284–285.

115. Brown, *Modern India*, p. 321.

116. Brown, *Prisoner of Hope*, pp. 355–356.

117. Brown, *Modern India*, p. 302.

118. Brown, *Prisoner of Hope*, p. 356.

119. Moon, *op. cit.*, p. 270; Lall, *op. cit.*, pp. 56–57.

120. Lelyveld, *op. cit.*, p. 147.

121. Moon, *op. cit.*, p. 270; Guha, *The Years That Changed the World*, pp. 705–715.

122. Moon, *op. cit.*, p. 278.

123. Nor was Gandhi enthusiastic about building a modern state, but what he wanted in its stead did not receive serious consideration after independence. "The evocative Gandhian vision of an independent India that would dispense with a state altogether and return to traditional habits of rule soon faded from view." Khilnani, *op. cit.*, p. 33.

124. *Ibid.*, pp. 10, 18.

125. Brown, *Prisoner of Hope*, p. 386; Rudolph and Rudolph, *op. cit.*, pp. 218–219.

126. The interruption in democratic governance came in the form of the "Emergency" proclaimed in June 1975 by then Prime Minister Indira Gandhi, Jawaharlal Nehru's daughter. It ended twenty-one months later, in March 1977.

127. This is a major theme of Ruchir Sharma, *Democracy on the Road: A 25-Year Journey through India*, New York: Penguin Random House, 2019.

128. In general, "Constitutional democracy based on universal suffrage did not emerge from popular pressures for it within Indian society, it was not wrested by the people from the state; it was given to them by the political choice of an intellectual elite." Khilnani, *op. cit.*, p. 34.

129. Gandhi and Nehru were both first exposed to democracy as students in Great Britain. So Indian democracy may be seen, in part, as another backhanded tribute to the domestic political values of the imperial country.

130. Guha, *The Years That Changed the World*, p. 881; Lall, *op. cit.*, pp. 108–109.

131. Guha, *India After Gandhi*, p. 206.

132. See pp. 167 and 181.

133. On the rise of the BJP and its sectarian policies, see Christophe Jaffrelot, *Modi's India: Hindu Nationalism and the Rise of Ethnic Democracy*, Princeton, New Jersey: Princeton University Press, 2021.

134. Guha, *India After Gandhi*, p. 469.

135. Brown, *Modern India*, p. 307.

136. Initially, the saffron band represented Hindus, the green stood for Muslims, and the white denoted India's other religions. Guha, *The Years That Changed the World*, p. 131. After independence, the saffron was said to indicate the strength and courage of the country, the white peace and truth, and the green the fertility of the land. https://knowindia.india.gov.in/my-india-my-pride/indian-tricolor.php.

137. Nanda, *op. cit.*, p. 165.

138. Guha, *India After Gandhi*, p. 171.

139. *Ibid.*, p. 228.

140. *Ibid.*, p. 684. On India's post-independence economic trajectory and its change of course in 1991, see Arvid Panagariya, *India: The Emerging Giant*, New York: Oxford University Press, 2008, Part I, especially Chapter 5. See also Michael Mandelbaum, *The Ideas That Conquered the World: Peace, Democracy and Free Markets in the Twenty-first Century*, New York: PublicAffairs, 2002, pp. 281–286.

141. Brown, *Prisoner of Hope*, pp. 390–391; Rudolph and Rudolph, *op. cit.*, p. 217.

142. Guha, *India After Gandhi*, p. 125; Lelyveld, *op. cit.*, p. 210.

143. Lelyveld, *op. cit.*, pp. 237–238.

144. Guha, *The Years That Changed the World*, p. 872.

145. Guha, *India After Gandhi*, pp. 598–609.

146. Khilnani, *op. cit.*, p. 37.

147. *Ibid.*, pp. 56–57.

148. See pp. 180–182.

149. Khilnani, *op. cit.*, p. 129.

150. Guha, *India After Gandhi*, p. 48.

151. See pp. 169–170.

152. Guha, *The Years That Changed the World*, p. 888.

153. Taylor Branch, *Parting the Waters: America in the King Years, 1954–63*, New York: Simon & Schuster, 1988, pp. 250–254, 609.

154. *Ibid.*, pp. 171–172.

155. Nonviolent tactics succeeded where, as in British India, the authorities placed limits on the force they were willing to use against the peaceful protesters. In central and eastern Europe, leaders of the Soviet Union had not hesitated to suppress forcefully public demonstrations opposing communist rule in East Germany in 1952, Hungary in 1956, and Czechoslovakia in 1968. The events of 1989 did not follow this pattern because the Soviet leader at that point, Mikhail Gorbachev, decided not to crack down violently.

156. Guha, *The Years That Changed the World*, p. 366.

Chapter 7

1. Shabtai Teveth, *Ben-Gurion: The Burning Ground, 1886–1948*, Boston: Houghton Mifflin Company, 1987, p. 4.

2. He tried but failed to gain entry to an engineering institute in Warsaw. Michael Bar-Zohar, *Ben-Gurion: A Biography*, New York: Delacorte Press, 1977, p. 8. He later studied law in Istanbul without taking a degree. See p. 190.

3. Bar-Zohar, *op. cit.*, p. 3, 5; Teveth, *op. cit.*, pp. 13–14.

4. On Ben-Gurion's life in Poland, see Anita Shapira, *Ben-Gurion: Father of Modern Israel*, New Haven, Connecticut: Yale University Press, 2014, Chapter 1.

5. Tom Segev, *A State at Any Cost: The Life of David Ben-Gurion*, Translated by Haim Watzman, New York: Picador, 2019, p. 46; Bar-Zohar, *op. cit.*, p. 10; Teveth, *op. cit.*, pp. 27–28.

6. At the time, Palestine had a population of 700,000, of whom about 55,000 were Jews. Teveth, *op. cit.*, p. 40.

7. Shapira, *op. cit.*, p. 26.

8. Bar-Zohar, *op. cit.*, p. 26.

9. Segev, *op. cit.*, p. 26.

10. Teveth, *op. cit.*, p. 73; Bar-Zohar *op. cit.*, p. 28.

11. Shapira, *op. cit.*, pp. 31–36, 40.

12. Ben-Gurion was formally a Russian citizen as well as a Zionist and therefore a doubly suspicious character in the eyes of the Ottoman officials.

13. Teveth, *op. cit.*, p. 99.

14. Bar-Zohar, *op. cit.* p. 34. "One of the few who was won over . . . was a young woman from Milwaukee by the name of Goldie Mabovitch, later to be known as Golda Meir." *Ibid.*, p. 33.

15. "By one estimate twenty-five thousand copies were sold." Segev, *op. cit.*, p. 139.

16. Shapira, *op. cit.*, pp. 51–53; Segev, *op. cit.*, pp. 141–143.

17. Howard M. Sachar, *A History of Israel from the Rise of Zionism to Our Time*, New York, Alfred A. Knopf, Second Revised Edition, 1996, pp. 102, 109.

18. Shapira, *op. cit.*, p. 57; Segev, *op. cit.*, p. 146.

19. Shapira, *op. cit.*, p. 75.

20. Bar-Zohar, *op. cit.*, p. 57; Segev, *op. cit.*, p. 152; Teveth, *op. cit.*, p. 200. "From its inception, the Histadrut was the strongest, and the largest, organization in the

Yishuv." Teveth, *op. cit.*, p. 181. "At its height, the Histadrut was responsible for the armed defense of Palestine's Jews, the establishment of new settlements, and the provision of jobs, health services, and education to tens of thousands of workers." Segev, *op. cit.*, p. 184.

21. Teveth, *op. cit.*, p. 158. On the contributions Weizmann, other Zionists, and the governments of other countries made to that achievement, see Martin Kramer, "The Forgotten Truth About the Balfour Declaration," *Mosaic*, June 5, 2017, https://mosaicmagazine.com/essay/israel-zionism/2017/06/the-forgotten-truth-about-the-balfour-declaration.

22. Teveth, *op. cit.*, p.159; Sachar, *op. cit.*, pp. 97–98.

23. Rick Richman, *Racing Against History: The 1940 Campaign for a Jewish Army to Fight Hitler*, New York: Encounter Books, 2018, pp. 108–109, 115; Shapira, *op. cit.*, pp. 125–126; Bar-Zohar, *op. cit.*, pp. 77–78; Segev, *op. cit.*, pp. 320, 322; Teveth, *op. cit.*, p. 373.

24. Segev, *op. cit.*, p. 234; Teveth, *op. cit.*, p. 373.

25. Teveth, *op. cit.*, p. 369; Bar-Zohar, *op. cit.*, p. 70.

26. Shapira, *op. cit.*, pp. 96–98.

27. Benny Morris, *1948: A History of the First Arab-Israeli War*, New Haven, Connecticut: Yale University Press, 2008, p. 7.

28. Shapira, *op. cit.*, pp. 83–84; Segev, *op. cit.*, p. 132.

29. Shapira, *op. cit.*, p. 95; Bar-Zohar, *op. cit.*, pp. 80–84; Teveth, *op. cit.*, pp. 465–466.

30. Jabotinsky wrote of the need for an "Iron Wall" that would protect the Jews from Arab assault. Ben-Gurion came to the same general conclusion. Daniel Gordis, *Israel: A Concise History of a Nation Reborn*, New York: Ecco/HarperCollins, 2016, pp. 105–106; Segev, *op. cit.*, p. 218; Teveth, *op. cit.*, p. 479; Dennis Ross and David Makovsky, *Be Strong and of Good Courage: How Israel's Most Important Leaders Shaped Its Destiny*, New York: PublicAffairs, 2019, pp. 20–21; Avi Shilon, "The Jabotinsky Paradox," *Mosaic*, August 2, 2021, https://mosaicmagazine.com/essay/israel-zionism/2021/08/the-jabotinsky-paradox.

31. Sachar, *op. cit.*, p. 220.

32. Bar-Zohar, *op. cit.*, pp. 90–92; Teveth, *op. cit.*, pp. 608–614; Sachar, *op. cit.*, pp. 204–205. Weizmann said that the Jews "would be fools not to accept [a state] even if it were the size of a tablecloth." Quoted in Gordis, *op. cit.*, p. 123.

33. Shapira, *op. cit.*, p. 114; Bar-Zohar, *op. cit.*, pp. 87–88.

34. Segev, *op. cit.*, p. 288; Teveth, *op. cit.*, p. 717.

35. Segev, *op. cit.*, p. 336.

36. Morris, *op. cit.*, p. 28.

37. Shapira, *op. cit.*, p. 117; Bar-Zohar, *op. cit.*, pp. 103–104; Segev, *op. cit.*, p. 296.

38. The Biltmore Program also included demands that unrestricted Jewish immigration to Palestine be permitted and that the Jewish Agency be in charge of that immigration. Bar-Zohar, *op. cit.*, p. 107.

39. *Ibid.*, pp. 127–130; Segev, *op. cit.*, pp. 393–394.

40. Shapira, *op. cit.*, pp. 144–145; Bar Zohar, *op. cit.*, p. 132; Eliot A. Cohen, *Supreme Command: Soldiers, Statesmen, and Leadership in Wartime*,

New York: The Free Press, 2002, p. 137. A turning point came with the bombing, on July 22, 1946, of the King David Hotel in Jerusalem, which served as the administrative headquarters of the British Mandate. A total of ninety-one people died. In its wake, violent tactics came to be considered unacceptable and, in the eyes of many Zionists, counterproductive. In the last months of World War II, Ben-Gurion's Labor Zionists had cooperated with the British authorities against the Irgun and Lehi. Bar-Zohar, *op. cit.*, pp. 122–124.

41. Bar-Zohar, *op. cit.*, pp. 126–127; Segev, *op. cit.*, pp. 366–368.

42. For a detailed description and analysis of the motives for and the conclusions and consequences of Ben-Gurion's "Seminar," see Cohen, *op. cit.*, pp. 133–172.

43. The vote was 33 to 13, more than a two-thirds majority.

44. Shapira, *op. cit.*, p. 162.

45. Morris, *op. cit.*, Chapters 3 and 4 and pp. 399–400.

46. Cohen, *op. cit.*, p. 162. ". . . the army was systematically transformed into a modern fighting force." Sachar, *op. cit.*, p. 330.

47. Cohen, *op. cit.*, p. 153. The formal armistice agreement with Egypt was signed at the end of February 1949. Bar-Zohar, *op. cit.*, p. 186.

48. Morris, *op. cit.*, p. 406.

49. Segev, *op. cit.*, p. 458.

50. *Ibid.*, p. 457.

51. Sachar, *op. cit.*, pp. 315–316; Cohen, *op. cit.*, p. 156.

52. Bar-Zohar, *op. cit.*, pp. 170–175.

53. Anita Shapira, *Israel: A History*, Lebanon, New Hampshire: University Press of New England/Brandeis University Press, 2012, p. 157.

54. See Adi Schwartz and Einat Wilf, *The War of Return: How Western Indulgence of the Palestinian Dream Has Obstructed the Path to Peace*, New York: All Points Books, 2020.

55. Benny Morris, *The Birth of the Palestinian Refugee Problem, 1947–1949*, Cambridge, UK: Cambridge University Press, 1987, pp. 286–287.

56. Morris, *The Birth of the Palestinian Refugee Problem*, pp. 289, 291; Sachar, *op. cit.*, p. 335.

57. Morris, *1948*, p. 410.

58. Shapira, *Israel*, p. 181; Sachar, *op. cit.*, pp. 357–358.

59. Gordis, *op. cit.*, p. 195. Mapai-dominated coalitions formed the government after every subsequent election until 1977.

60. Morris, *1948*, pp. 412–415.

61. The phrase is from the book by the eminent scholar of the Middle East and the Islamic world Bernard Lewis: *The Jews of Islam*, Princeton, New Jersey: Princeton University Press, 1984.

62. Sachar, *op. cit.*, pp. 398–403.

63. Shapira, *Ben-Gurion*, p. 175; Bar-Zohar, *op. cit.*, p. 188; Sachar, *op. cit.*, p. 395. By the end of 1956, Israel's population had tripled. Sachar, *op. cit.*, p. 402.

64. Segev, *op. cit.*, p. 483; Sachar, *op. cit.*, pp. 434–435.

65. Sachar, *op. cit.*, p. 475.

66. Segev, *op. cit.*, p. 560.

67. *Ibid.*, p. 574. Ben-Gurion also insisted, if Israel were to join France in a military campaign against Egypt, on a French guarantee of Israel's air defenses. Edward Luttwak and Dan Horowitz, *The Israeli Army, 1948–1973*, Cambridge, Massachusetts: Abt Books, 1983, pp. 125, 198.

68. Gordis, *op. cit.*, pp. 233–234. "In all, the war lasted from October 29 through November 7. Israel lost 231 soldiers with another 900 soldiers wounded. Egyptian losses are estimated at between 1,500 and 3,000, with about 5,000 wounded." *Ibid.*, p. 234.

69. He had become caught up in a complicated controversy known as the Lavon Affair, involving the former Defense Minister Pinchas Lavon, which eroded Ben-Gurion's popularity. Segev, *op. cit.*, pp. 537–540, 617, 622–627; Bar-Zohar, *op. cit.*, pp. 289–297; Amos Perlmutter, *Israel: The Partitioned State*, New York: Charles Scribner's Sons, 1985, Chapter 6.

70. Sachar, *op. cit.*, p. 89. ". . . Djemal Pasha, who had recently been appointed as Ottoman commander of the Egyptian front, made his anti-Zionist stance eminently clear just a few weeks after the Ottomans entered the war. He disbanded a Turkish-loyalist Jewish defense organization, which had been founded by labor leaders Ben-Gurion and Yitzhak Ben-Zvi; he closed down the Zionist newspaper *Ha'achdut*; and he proclaimed every Zionist an enemy of Turkey and liable to death." Gordis, *op. cit.*, p. 90.

71. "While Herzl was still alive he had approached the ruling Turks with his proposals for Jewish settlement in Palestine, which they had flatly refused. . . ." Gordis, *op cit.*, p. 468, note 3.

72. Sachar, *op. cit.*, p. 97.

73. Britain, Ben-Gurion wrote in 1936, "built a harbour at Haifa, and Haifa became a city with a Jewish majority. She built roads connecting the Jewish settlements, and she supported, albeit not sufficiently, Jewish industry." Quoted in Shlomo Avineri, *The Making of Modern Zionism: The Intellectual Origins of the Jewish State*, New York: Basic Books, 1981, p. 211.

74. Morris, *1948*, p. 15. ". . . absent the Balfour Declaration and the postwar British Mandate in Palestine, there could have been no mass immigration." Martin Kramer, "Three Turning Points That Led to the Birth of the State of Israel," *Mosaic*, May 7, 2019, https://mosaicmagazine.com/observation/isr ael-zionism/2019/05/three-turning-points-that-led-to-the-birth-of-the-state-of-israel.

75. See p. 180.

76. ". . . the desperate financial circumstances of the Empire simply could not support the deployment of nearly a hundred thousand troops a year to keep hold of Palestine." Cohen, *op. cit.*, p. 138.

77. The political will to remain in Palestine was, if anything, weaker than in the case of India since India—the "jewel in the crown" of the British Empire—was an imperial possession of greater strategic and economic importance and of longer standing.

78. Teveth, *op. cit.*, p. 854; Segev, *op. cit.*, p. 361; Shapira, *Israel*, p. 471.

79. Jeffrey Herf, "The U.S. State Department's Opposition to Zionist Aspirations during the Early Cold War: George F. Kennan and George C. Marshall in 1947–1948," *Journal of Cold War Studies* 23:4, Fall 2021, pp. 153–180.

80. "The pivotal bloc of votes in favor of the [partition] resolution—not less than 40 percent of the United Nations membership—ultimately was cast by the Latin American delegations. Zionist pressure here was minimal. Nor was the intercession of the United States anywhere apparent in the Latin American stance.... The evidence is compelling that these Latin governments, with few interests either way in the Middle East, accepted the majority report at face value. Simple compassion for the displaced persons unquestionably influenced their decision...." Sachar, *op. cit.*, p. 294.

81. Teveth, *op. cit.*, p. 873; Segev, *op. cit.*, p. 370; Ross and Makovsky, *op. cit.*, pp. 42–43.

82. Shapira, *Ben-Gurion*, p. 136; Sachar, *op. cit.*, p. 283.

83. This is a theme of Richman, *op. cit.*

84. Segev, *op. cit.*, p. 422.

85. Shapira, *Ben-Gurion*, p. 142.

86. "The evidence is abundant and clear that many, if not most, in the Arab world viewed the [1948] war essentially as a holy war." Morris, *1948*, p. 495. The European antisemitism that had underlain the Holocaust infected the Arab world as well. See Jeffrey Herf, *Nazi Propaganda for the Arab World*, New Haven, Connecticut: Yale University Press, 2009 and Amos Elon, *The Israelis: Founders and Sons*, New York: Holt, Rinehart and Winston, 1971, p. 217.

87. Morris, *1948*, p. 394. Islam's rivalry with the Christian West and its impact on the Arab world is a theme of Bernard Lewis, *What Went Wrong? Western Impact and Middle Eastern Response*, New York: Oxford University Press, 2002.

88. Morris, *1948*, p. 419.

89. Sachar, *op. cit.*, p. 285.

90. *Ibid.*, pp. 322–323; Morris, *1948*, pp. 396–397; Ross and Makovsky, *op. cit.*, pp. 54–55; Shapira, *Israel*, p. 280; Martin Kramer, "The Parallel Lives of David Ben-Gurion and Abdullah Bin Hussein," *Mosaic*, November 17, 2020, https://mosaicmagazine.com/observation/israel-zionism/2020/11/the-parallel-lives-of-david-ben-gurion-and-abdullah-bin-hussein.

91. Sachar, *op. cit.*, pp. 453–454.

92. "... in the Zionist idea one can discern both the legacy of Jewish tradition and the challenges of the modern age, the *Sturm und Drang* of nineteenth- and twentieth-century European history combined with a historical heritage going back thousands of years." Avineri, *op. cit.*, p. x.

93. "... Jews were considered by others—and considered themselves—not only a minority, but a minority *in exile*." Avineri, *op. cit.*, p. 3.

94. See p. 15.

95. Other nascent nationalisms helped to inspire Zionism. Sachar, *op. cit.*, p. 10.

96. "The Russian pogroms and anti-Semitic policies of the czarist government caused almost three million Jews to emigrate from Russia between 1882 and

1914. Yet only a small fraction of these, perhaps 1 percent, went to Palestine. The preponderant majority went to the United States, Canada, South America, Australia." Avineri, *op. cit.*, p. 5. "In the peculiar social and ideological world of nineteenth-century Eastern Europe, the more dynamic members of the Jewish minority responded to their oppression in one of several ways: some emigrated to the United States; some entered revolutionary movements; a third and smallest group joined clandestine, usually socialistically oriented Zionist organizations, and hoped eventually to emigrate to Palestine. A few thousand actually did emigrate; many more just talked." Elon, *op. cit.*, p. 37. See also *ibid.*, pp. 58–61.

97. Avineri, *op. cit.*, pp. 200–204; Shapira, *Ben-Gurion*, p. 3.

98. Segev, *op. cit.*, p. 78.

99. Teveth, *op. cit.*, pp. 233–235; Shapira, *Ben-Gurion*, p. 71; Bar-Zohar, *op. cit.*, pp. 51–52; Avineri, *op. cit.*, p. 208.

100. Segev, *op. cit.*, p. 470.

101. Shapira, *Ben-Gurion*, p. 180.

102. Segev, *op. cit.*, p. 179; Bar-Zohar, *op. cit.*, p. 18.

103. Bar-Zohar, *op. cit.*, p. 274.

104. Ben-Gurion's successor as prime minister, Levi Eshkol, authorized the reburial.

105. Gordis, *op. cit.*, p. 169.

106. Segev, *op. cit.*, pp. 205, 212.

107. *Ibid.*, p. 9.

108. "Obstinacy and total dedication to a single objective were the most characteristic traits of David Ben-Gurion." Bar-Zohar, *op. cit.*, p. 77.

109. Perlmutter, *op. cit.*, p. 15; Teveth, *op. cit.*, pp. 149, 150; Segev, *op. cit.*, p. 161.

110. Segev, *op. cit.*, p. 305.

111. He rose to the top of the politics first of the Yishuv and then of the State of Israel for another reason: many of his rivals, actual or potential, predeceased him. *Ibid.*, p. 370; Teveth, *op. cit.*, p. 870.

112. Cohen, *op. cit.*, p. 141.

113. "Almost to the day of his death he published articles in the press and on occasion listed his profession as journalist." Segev, *op. cit.*, p. 593. See also Teveth, *op. cit.*, p. 12.

114. Bar-Zohar, *op. cit.*, p. 56. The published diaries ran to fifty volumes. Teveth, *op. cit.*, p. xi.

115. Shapira, *Ben-Gurion*, p. 44. "Many of his speeches went on for hours; his sentences were long and complex, more fitting for the eye than the ear. His shrill voice and small stature were detrimental to the impression he made." Segev, *op. cit.*, p. 10.

116. Teveth, *op. cit.*, p. 872.

117. Segev, *op. cit.*, pp. 287, 458; Bar-Zohar, *op. cit.*, p. 105.

118. Segev, *op. cit.*, p. 400; Cohen, *op. cit.*, pp. 143, 146.

119. Teveth, *op. cit.*, p. 677; Bar-Zohar, *op. cit.*, p. 101.

120. Teveth, *op. cit.*, p. 787; Segev, *op. cit.*, p. 315; Bar-Zohar, *op. cit.*, p. 80.

121. Shapira, *Ben-Gurion*, pp. 195–196.

122. Segev, *op. cit.*, pp. 428–429, 661–662. This is a major theme of Eran Lerman, "The Greatest Shoulderman—and His Burdens: David Ben-Gurion and the Heroic Decisions that Shaped Israel," Unpublished manuscript.

123. Teveth, *op. cit.*, p. 189.

124. Cohen, *op. cit.*, p. 134; Teveth, *op. cit.*, pp. 750–752.

125. See Amos Oz, *A Tale of Love and Darkness*, Translated by Nicholas de Lange, New York: Harcourt/Harvest Books, 2004, pp. 437–446.

126. Shapira, *Ben-Gurion*, p. 50.

127. Ben-Gurion "was quite simply the doer, the engineer, the forger of the Yishuv. . . . It was Ben-Gurion, at the head of the Socialist Zionist movement, who helped build the physical, social, and political structures that encompass the modern state of Israel." Perlmutter, *op. cit.*, p. 23.

128. Segev, *op. cit.*, p. 413.

129. The People's Administration was the de facto cabinet of the People's Council, on which the political parties of the Yishuv were represented.

130. Martin Kramer, "The May 1948 Vote That Made the State of Israel," *Mosaic*, April 2, 2018, https://mosaicmagazine.com/essay/israel-zionism/2018/04/the-may-1948-vote-that-made-the-state-of-israel.

131. He had taken up military issues before 1945. In 1937, he said, "I am occupied almost exclusively with security matters." Quoted in Segev, *op. cit.*, p. 276.

132. Cohen, *op. cit.*, pp. 158–159; Bar-Zohar, *op. cit.*, p. 146; Gordis, *op. cit.*, p. 157.

133. Cohen, *op. cit.*, p. 159.

134. Shapira, *Ben-Gurion*, p. 158; Gordis, *op. cit.*, p. 159; Bar-Zohar, *op. cit.*, pp. 151–152.

135. Michael Doran, *Pan-Arabism before Nasser: Egyptian Power Politics and the Palestine Question*, New York: Oxford University Press, 1999, pp. 169–170.

136. Cohen, *op. cit.*, p. 161; Gordis, *op. cit.*, p. 174.

137. Bar-Zohar, *op. cit.*, pp. 184–185; Segev, *op. cit.*, p. 446.

138. Cohen, *op. cit.*, p. 162; Gordis, *op. cit.*, pp. 189–190; Bar-Zohar, *op. cit.*, pp. 185, 187; Shapira, *Ben-Gurion*, p. 173.

139. Segev, *op. cit.*, pp. 564–565; Cohen, *op. cit.*, p. 163; Shapira, *Israel*, p. 172.

140. Segev, *op. cit.*, p. 659; Martin Kramer, "Israel's Situation Today Looks Much as Ben-Gurion Envisioned It," *Mosaic*, April 30, 2018, https://mosaicmagazine.com/response/israel-zionism/2018/04/israels-situation-today-looks-much-as-ben-gurion-envisioned-it.

141. Gordis, *op. cit.*, pp. 177–181. Ben-Gurion said at the time, "There are not going to be two States and there are not going to be two armies." Quoted in *ibid.*, p. 179.

142. Luttwak and Horowitz, *op. cit.*, p. 44; Gordis, *op. cit.*, p. 208; Shapira, *Israel*, p. 188.

143. Cohen, *op. cit.*, p. 170. "The IDF was . . . largely his personal achievement." Segev, *op. cit.*, p. 597. On the IDF's virtuosity at innovation see Edward N. Luttwak and Eitan Shamir, *The Art of Military Innovation: Lessons from the Israel Defense Forces*, Cambridge, Massachusetts: Harvard University Press, 2023.

144. Segev, *op. cit.*, p. 508. Ben-Gurion also intended the reprisals to affect Israelis, especially the emigrants from Arab countries. "They have grown used to being . . . helpless victims. . . . Here we have to show them that . . . the Jewish people [have] a state and an army that will no longer permit them to be abused." Quoted in Bar-Zohar, *op. cit.*, p. 219.

145. Bar-Zohar, *op. cit.*, p. 192.

146. Ben-Gurion also pursued a "peripheral" strategy, establishing ties with non-Arab countries in the region including Turkey, Iran, and Ethiopia. *Ibid.*, pp. 261–264.

147. Segev, *op. cit.*, pp. 598–610; Gordis, *op. cit.*, pp. 248–250.

148. Shapira, *Israel*, p. 230.

149. Shapira, *Ben-Gurion*, p. 176; Bar-Zohar, *op. cit.*, pp. 188–189.

150. Cohen, *op. cit.*, p. 172; Gordis, *op. cit.*, pp. 200–201.

151. The Defense Ministry remained in Tel Aviv because that city was less vulnerable to attack.

152. Segev, *op. cit.*, p. 498.

153. Quoted in Sachar, *op. cit.*, p. 373.

154. Shapira, *Israel*, p. 263.

155. Gordis, *op. cit.*, pp. 241–245; Sachar, *op. cit.*, pp. 464–470.

156. Sachar, *op. cit.*, pp. 552–559; Gordis, *op. cit.*, pp. 239–241, 250–257.

157. Perlmutter, *op. cit.*, p. 181; Bar-Zohar, *op. cit.*, p. 244.

158. Sachar, *op. cit.*, p. 513.

159. Gordis, *op. cit.*, p. 234; Sachar, *op. cit.*, pp. 513–514; Bar-Zohar, *op. cit.*, p. 258.

160. On the 1967 War, see Michael B. Oren, *Six Days of War: June 1967 and the Making of the Modern Middle East*, New York: Oxford University Press, 2002.

161. He often used, approvingly, the Hebrew word *mamlachtiyut*, which means, roughly, the "primacy of the state." Avineri, *op. cit.*, p. 213.

162. "He grew determined to impress on Jews of all backgrounds not only the state's political authority, but its moral and cultural centrality as well. In his mind, it was imperative that everyone and everything be subordinate to the newly formed state." Gordis, *op. cit.*, p. 206.

163. Shapira, *Israel*, p. 472.

164. "According to one of Ben-Gurion's letters, his attendance at the bar-mitzvah of [his grandson] was one of the only two times that he had gone to synagogue since his immigration to Palestine." Shapira, *Ben-Gurion*, pp. 152–153.

165. Ben-Gurion subsequently regretted granting the exemptions from military service. Gordis, *op. cit.*, pp. 210–212, 411–413; Shapira, *Ben-Gurion*, p. 191; Sachar, *op. cit.*, p. 367–382; Segev, *op. cit.*, pp. 474–478.

166. Israel's unbroken adherence to democracy is all the more remarkable given that it was "forged out of immigrants who came mostly from nondemocratic countries." Gordis, *op. cit.*, p. 218.

167. Fouad Ajami, "A Reality Check as Israel Turns 60," *U.S. News & World Report*, May 7, 2008.

168. Ben-Gurion himself said that "in Israel, in order to be a realist you have to believe in miracles."

169. Cohen, *op. cit.*, p. 134.

Chapter 8

1. In the text of this chapter, Chinese names are transliterated according to the Pinying rather than the Wade-Giles system (Mao Zedong rather than Mao Tse-tung) except for the Kuomintang (rather than Guomindang) and Chiang Kai-shek (not Jiang Jieshi).

2. Philip Short, *Mao: The Man Who Made China*, Revised Edition, London: I.B. Taurus, 2017, pp. 18–19. Mao later described his father as a "middle peasant." In the rural classification system subsequently used by Mao's Chinese Communists, this placed the father, in wealth, below major landlords but above the more numerous poor peasants.

3. Alexander V. Pantsov with Steven I. Levine, *Mao: The Real Story*, New York: Simon & Schuster, 2012, pp. 16–17.

4. *Ibid.*, p. 15; Short, *op. cit.*, pp. 24–25.

5. Short, *op. cit.*, p. 71.

6. When he resumed his education by entering a junior middle school, "not one child in 200 at that time had access to education of this level." *Ibid.*, p. 33.

7. Pantsov, *op. cit.*, p. 17.

8. Jonathan Spence, *Mao Zedong*, New York: Viking, 1999, p. 1.

9. Short, *op. cit.*, pp. 30, 76.

10. Spence, *op. cit.*, pp. 35–37.

11. Pantsov, *op. cit.*, p. 51; Short, *op. cit.*, p. 92.

12. Pantsov, *op. cit.*, pp. 92–102.

13. *Ibid.*, pp. 102–103; Short, *op. cit.*, pp. 110–113. At the time, the Chinese Communist Party had 53 members. Pantsov, *op. cit.*, p. 102.

14. See pp. 44–45.

15. Pantsov, *op. cit.*, pp. 141–142, 171; Stuart Schram, *The Political Thought of Mao Tse-Tung*, New York: Frederick A. Praeger, 1963, pp. 27, 30.

16. Pantsov, *op. cit.*, pp. 115–116; Short, *op. cit.*, pp. 128–130.

17. Spence, *op. cit.*, p. 73.

18. Short, *op. cit.*, pp. 201–203; Spence, *op. cit.*, p. 75.

19. Pantsov, *op. cit.*, pp. 201–202.

20. Spence, *op. cit.*, pp. 80–81.

21. Pantsov, *op. cit.*, pp. 186, 193; Short, *op. cit.*, p. 197.

22. Pantsov, *op. cit.*, pp. 212, 247.

23. *Ibid.*, pp. 241–242; Short, *op. cit.*, pp. 266, 269–270.

24. Short, *op. cit.*, pp. 235, 285–286, 289; Spence, *op. cit.*, p. 84.

25. Short, *op. cit.*, p. 303.

26. Pantsov, *op. cit.*, p. 288.

27. Short, *op. cit.*, p. 13.

28. Jung Chang and Jon Halliday, *Mao: The Unknown Story*, New York: Alfred A. Knopf, 2005, p. 171.

29. Short, *op. cit.*, p. 342–344.

30. *Ibid.*, p. 376.

31. Spence, *op. cit.*, p. 100. "This was the time when the term 'Mao Zedong Thought' (*Mao Zedong sixiang*) was coined, and when the first versions of his 'Selected Works' were completed. It was then, too that the Maoist anthem, 'The East is Red', was written." Short, *op. cit.*, p. 379.

32. John King Fairbank, *China: A New History*, Cambridge, Massachusetts: The Belknap Press of Harvard University Press, 1992, p. 324; Odd Arne Westad, *Restless Empire: China and the World Since 1750*, New York: Basic Books, 2012, p. 274.

33. Pantsov, *op. cit.*, p. 257.

34. Max Boot, *Invisible Armies: An Epic History of Guerrilla Warfare from Ancient Times to the Present*, New York: Liveright, 2013, p. 344.

35. Short, *op. cit.*, p. 384; Westad, *op. cit.*, p. 272.

36. Short, *op. cit.*, pp. 322–323.

37. Spence, *op. cit.*, p. 92; Ranan Mitter, *Forgotten Ally: China's World War II, 1937–1945*, Boston: Houghton Mifflin Harcourt, pp. 190–191.

38. Short, *op. cit.*, p. 390.

39. Pantsov, *op. cit.*, p. 352; Spence, *op. cit.*, p. 108.

40. "To the historically Chinese-speaking lands the Manchus had added Manchuria, Mongolia, Tibet, and largely Turkic Muslim areas—that is, East Turkestan, or Xinjiang—'new territories' in Chinese. So, when the Republic of China in 1912, and then the People's Republic of China in 1949, laid claim to this real estate, 'China' was twice as large as it had been in 1644, the last year of the Ming dynasty." Charles Horner and Eric Brown, "A Long, Twilight Struggle," *American Purpose*, April 2, 2021, https://www.americanpurpose.com/articles/a-long-twilight-struggle.

41. Jonathan Spence, *The Search for Modern China*, New York: W. W. Norton, 1990, p. 508.

42. Short, *op. cit.*, p. 657; Boot, *op. cit.*, p. 344.

43. Pantsov, *op. cit.*, p. 352; Spence, *The Search for Modern China*, pp. 498, 505.

44. Short, *op. cit.*, pp. 415–419; Pantsov, *op. cit.*, pp. 369–373. "The summit ended in a mixed result for the Chinese visitors. They did get aid and security guarantees. They did get Soviet promises to restore formal Chinese sovereignty in Manchuria. They did not get Mongolia, aid to conquer Taiwan, or a joint revolutionary strategy for East Asia. Worse, the Soviet side consistently forced the Chinese into the role of supplicants, and Stalin, especially, missed no opportunity to lord over his visitors." Odd Arne Westad, "Introduction" to Westad, editor, *Brothers in Arms: The Rise and Fall of the Sino-Soviet Alliance, 1945–1963*, Stanford, California: Stanford University Press, 1998, p. 12.

45. Short, *op. cit.*, p. 427; Pantsov, *op. cit.*, p. 387.

46. Westad, "Introduction" to Westad, editor, *Brothers in Arms*, p. 13.

47. Pantsov, *op. cit.*, p. 374.

48. Sergei N. Goncharov, John W. Lewis, and Xue Litai, *Uncertain Partners: Stalin, Mao, and the Korean War*, Stanford, California: Stanford University Press, 1993, p. 216.

49. Short, *op. cit.*, pp. 429, 432.

50. *Ibid.*, p. 434; Pantsov, *op. cit.*, p. 366.

51. Pantsov, *op. cit.*, p. 425.

52. John Pomfret, *Chinese Lessons: Five Classmates and the Story of the New China*, New York: Henry Holt and Company, 2006, p. 199.

53. Short, *op. cit.*, p. 430.

54. *Ibid.*, p. 441.

55. Spence, *The Search for Modern China*, p. 534.

56. Short, *op. cit.*, pp. 456–457.

57. Pantsov, *op. cit.*, pp. 441–442.

58. Spence, *Mao Zedong*, p. 131. The victims "underwent labour reform or were exiled to the countryside to learn class consciousness from the peasants." Short, *op. cit.*, p. 461.

59. Pantsov, *op. cit.*, pp. 456–457; Short, *op. cit.*, p. 476.

60. Short, *op. cit.*, p. 477.

61. Yang Jisheng, *op. cit.*, pp. 19–20; Jean-Louis Margolin, "China: A Long March Into the Night," in Stephane Courtois, Nicholas Werth, Jean-Louis Panne, Andrej Pasczkowski, Karel Bartosek, and Jean-Louis Margolin, *The Black Book of Communism: Crimes, Terror, Repression*, Translated by Jonathan Murphy and Mark Kramer, Cambridge, Massachusetts: Harvard University Press, 1999, pp. 489–490.

62. Pantsov, *op. cit.*, pp. 464–465.

63. Short, *op. cit.*, p. 500.

64. Pantsov, *op. cit.*, p. 478.

65. For a narrative history of the Cultural Revolution, see Roderick MacFarquhar and Michael Schoenhals, *Mao's Last Revolution*, Cambridge, Massachusetts: The Belknap Press of Harvard University Press, 2006. For the negative impact of the Cultural Revolution on individuals, see Nien Cheng, *Life and Death in Shanghai*, New York: Penguin Books, 1986, and Pomfret, *op. cit.* For an eyewitness account of the Cultural Revolution by a Western diplomat, see George Walden, *Lucky George: Memoirs of an Anti-Politician*, London: Allen Lane The Penguin Press, 1999, Chapter 5, and George Walden, *China: A Wolf in the World?* London: Gibson Square, 2008, Chapter 1.

66. The Cultural Revolution "left a country in ruins, its economy damaged, its international credit destroyed, its education disrupted, its intellectuals humiliated and brutalized, dead between half a million and a million (no one knows exactly) and a legacy of lasting bitterness and disillusion." Percy Cradock, *Experiences of China*, London: John Murray, 1999, p. 33.

67. Short, *op. cit.*, p. 531.

68. Pantsov, *op. cit.*, p. 510.

69. *Ibid.*, pp. 499–500.

70. *Ibid.*, p. 465.

71. *Ibid.*, p. 496.

72. *Ibid.*, pp. 507, 510.

73. *Ibid.*, p. 510; Short, *op. cit.*, p. 539.

74. Pantsov, *op. cit.*, p. 513; Short, *op. cit.*, p. 545.

75. Pantsov, *op. cit.*, p. 526.
76. Short, *op. cit.*, p. 553.
77. Quoted in *ibid.*, p. 547.
78. Spence, *Mao Zedong*, p. 162.
79. Short, *op. cit.*, p. 569.
80. Pantsov, *op. cit.*, p. 531.
81. *Ibid.*, p. 533; Short, *op. cit.*, p. 574.
82. "Beginning in the second half of 1968, some twelve million disillusioned youth were deported to the countryside over the next seven years, most of them to education-through-labor camps where the overwhelming majority remained until . . . 1976." Pantsov, *op. cit.*, p. 533.
83. "The best estimate is that, during the two years the campaign lasted, at least 36 million people were investigated; between 750,000 and 1.5 million were killed, many by what was termed 'enforced suicide'; and an approximately equal number were permanently maimed." Short, *op. cit.*, p. 570.
84. "The most senior victim of the Cultural Revolution, Liu died in November 1969 from medical neglect and physical abuse at the hands of the Central Case Examination Group staff." MacFarquhar and Schoenhals, *op. cit.*, p. 470.
85. Mao scorned the atomic bomb as a "paper tiger." Michael Burleigh, *Small Wars, Faraway Places: Global Insurrection and the Making of the Modern World, 1945–1965*, New York: Viking, 2013, p. 67.
86. Pantsov, *op. cit.*, pp. 468, 472–473.
87. In the Damanskiy battles, the Chinese lost several hundred soldiers. Short, *op. cit.*, p. 580.
88. "At times during the forty years of collaboration, the two parties had disagreed on organizational structure, military strategies, and class analysis; they had suspected each other of betrayal; and they had misunderstood each other's aims because of personal rivalries and cultural differences." Westad, "Introduction," to Westad, editor, *op. cit.*, p. 30.
89. Pantsov, *op. cit.*, p. 473; Short, *op. cit.*, pp. 445–446.
90. Short, *op. cit.*, p. 484.
91. *Ibid.*, p. 444.
92. *Ibid.*, pp. 29–30.
93. The Chinese sense of themselves and of their relationship to the rest of the world found expression in the 1793 message from the Qian Long Emperor to King George III of Great Britain through Lord Macartney, the representative of the British Crown who had traveled to Beijing for the purpose of opening trade with China. "As your Ambassador has seen for himself, we possess all things. I set no value on objects strange and ingenious and have no use for your manufactures. . . . Although your country, O King, lies in the far oceans, yet, inclining your heart towards civilization, you have specially sent an envoy respectfully to present a state message, to kowtow and to present congratulations for the imperial birthday, and also to present local products, thereby showing your sincerity. We have perused the text of your state message, and the wording expresses your earnestness. From it

your sincere humility and obedience can be seen." Quoted in Cradock, *op. cit.*, p. 7.

94. On the Taiping Rebellion, see Jonathan Spence, *God's Chinese Son: The Heavenly Kingdom of Hong Xuiquian*, New York: W. W. Norton, 1995, and Stephen R. Platt, *Autumn in the Heavenly Kingdom: China, the West, and the Epic Story of the Taiping Civil War*, New York: Alfred A. Knopf, 2012.

95. Fairbank, *op. cit.*, p. 216. The Japanese occupation of 1931 to 1945 was an exception to this pattern, but by the time it took place, Mao had charted his life's course.

96. On the first Opium War see Stephen R. Platt, *Imperial Twilight: The Opium War and the End of China's Last Golden Age*, New York: Alfred A. Knopf, 2018. China also yielded territory to France, the United States, Russia, and Austria-Hungary. Rana Mitter, "Barbarians Out!," *The New York Review of Books*, December 7, 2017, p. 42.

97. See Mary Clabaugh Wright, *The Last Stand of Chinese Conservatism: The T'ung-chih Restoration, 1862–1874*, Stanford, California: Stanford University Press, 1962.

98. Pantsov, *op. cit.*, p. 151.

99. Short, *op. cit.*, p. 152.

100. Pantsov, *op. cit.*, p. 182.

101. *Ibid.*, p. 270.

102. *Ibid.*, pp. 238, 254–255; Short, *op. cit.*, p. 249.

103. Pantsov, *op. cit.*, p. 324; Short, *op. cit.*, pp. 287–288.

104. Pantsov, *op. cit.*, pp. 6, 136, 293, 296, 311; Short, *op. cit.*, p. 112.

105. Pantsov, *op. cit.*, p. 348.

106. See pp. 237–238.

107. Arthur Waldron's *From War to Nationalism: China's Turning Point, 1924–1925*, Cambridge, U.K.: Cambridge University Press, 1995, argues that the internal wars of 1924 had a transformative effect on China.

108. Pantsov, *op. cit.*, p. 44.

109. "The May Fourth Incident . . . spawned a nationwide movement for national renewal that spread to every corner of China, triggering a tidal wave of cultural, political and social change. . . ." Short, *op. cit.*, p. 84.

110. "The road to victory for the Chinese Communist Party in 1949 lay within the devastated landscape of China created by the years of war with Japan." Mitter, *Forgotten Ally*, p. 5. On the impact of World War I on Russia and Lenin, see p. 49.

111. ". . . the battered, punch-drunk state that was Nationalist China in 1945 had been fundamentally destroyed by the war with Japan." Mitter, *Forgotten Ally*, p. 13. "Without the war, there would have been a greater possibility of an anti-imperialist, anti-Communist Nationalist government consolidating power." *Ibid.*, p. 377.

112. Short, *op. cit.*, p. 306.

113. *Ibid.*, pp. 361, 364; Westad, *Restless Empire*, p. 272.

114. "When the war broke out, [Mao] was the head of a small party on the run that had been forced into a hideout in the dusty hill country of northwest China. By the end of the war, he would control vast areas of China with its population of some 100 million people, as well as an independent army of nearly a million men." Mitter, *Forgotten Ally*, p. 6.

115. Short, *op. cit.*, pp. 361–362.

116. *Ibid.*, p. 45

117. *Ibid.*, p. 14; Nathan, *op. cit.*, pp. viii-ix.

118. Short, *op. cit.*, pp. 80–81. Arthur Waley, a British translator of Chinese literature who apparently was not an admirer of Mao's literary output, is said to have remarked that Mao's poetry was not as bad as Hitler's painting but not as good as Churchill's. *Ibid.*, p. 639.

119. *Ibid.*, p. 131; Pantsov, *op. cit.*, p. 81.

120. "It cannot be emphasized enough that what inspired the first Chinese Communists was Leninism rather than Marxism." Westad, *Restless Empire*, p. 285.

121. Short, *op. cit.*, p. 131.

122. Mao formulated several principles for conducting guerrilla warfare: "The enemy advances, we retreat; the enemy camps, we harass; the enemy tires, we attack; the enemy retreats, we pursue." Pantsov, *op. cit.*, p. 222.

123. *Ibid.*, p. 42. The borders of the People's Republic, however, were imperial, not national, including as they did non-Han peoples—Uighur Muslims and Tibetan Buddhists—who did not join the Chinese state voluntarily and were generally unhappy to be included in it.

124. Short, *op. cit.*, pp. xxi, 426, 471; Mitter, *Forgotten Ally*, p. 8.

125. Pantsov, *op. cit.*, pp. 423, 449, 453; Short, *op. cit.*, pp. 343, 473. Mao shared a belief in the superior potency of human willpower with Hitler. See p. 88. The best-known sympathetic documentary film about the Nazi movement was entitled *Triumph of the Will*.

126. Pantsov, *op. cit.*, p. 20.

127. *Ibid.*, p. 516; Spence, *Mao Zedong*, p. 161.

128. Schram, *op. cit.*, p. 29.

129. Short, *op. cit.*, p. 2.

130. Pantsov, *op. cit.*, pp. 525, 565.

131. Spence, *The Search for Modern China*, pp. 523–524.; Short, *op. cit.*, pp. 375, 538.

132. "Of all the Chinese leaders Mao purged during his years of power, only Lin Biao attempted to resist." Short, *op. cit.*, p. 604.

133. Walden, *China: A Wolf in the World?*, p. 14.

134. Mao's swim "was a demonstration of vigour, a metaphor for throwing himself back into the fray. Photographs of the 72-year-old Chairman's exploits were printed in all Chinese newspapers, and newsreels shown at cinemas." Short, *op. cit.*, p. 536. See also Spence, *The Search for Modern China*, p. 605, Pantsov, *op. cit.*, pp. 503–505, and Cradock, *op. cit.*, p. 37.

135. Pantsov, *op. cit.*, p. 405.

136. *Ibid.*, p. 488; Short, *op. cit.*, p. 518.

137. "Wherever he went, bombproof villas were built and staffed. He kept himself far from the public, making use later in his career of a system of tunnels linking his residence, the Great Hall of the People, with military headquarters in the western suburbs." Arthur Waldron, "Mao Lives," *Commentary*, October, 2005, pp. 34–35.

138. Pantsov, *op. cit.*, pp. 3, 6; Short, *op. cit.*, pp. 14, 462–463; Cradock, *op. cit.*, pp. 92–93; Nathan, *op. cit.*, p. ix.

139. A list of many of the Maoist campaigns appears in Short, *op. cit.*, p. 497.

140. Short, *op. cit.*, p. 468; Pantsov, *op. cit.*, p. 452.

141. Short, *op. cit.*, p. xxxiv.

142. Benjamin I. Schwartz, *Chinese Communism and the Rise of Mao*, Cambridge, Massachusetts: Harvard University Press, 1951, p. 19; Short, *op. cit.*, pp. 155.

143. For a history of guerrilla warfare, see Boot, *op. cit.*

144. *Ibid.*, pp. 342–343. The Chinese Communists' successful employment of guerrilla tactics had an influence on the communists of Vietnam and on Fidel Castro in Cuba, both of whom used such tactics to win power and establish a communist regime.

145. See, for example, Short, *op. cit.*, pp. 308–309.

146. See Michael Mandelbaum, *The Four Ages of American Foreign Policy: Weak Power, Great Power, Superpower, Hyperpower*, New York: Oxford University Press, 2022, pp. 270–280.

147. Pantsov, *op. cit.*, pp. 380–383; Goncharov et al., *op. cit.*, p. 261; Spence, *Mao Zedong*, pp. 116–117; Short, *op. cit.*, p. 422.

148. See pp. 232–233.

149. In May Day parades in China in 1956, after Khrushchev's speech denouncing his predecessor, giant portraits of Stalin were prominently displayed. Pantsov, *op. cit.*, p. 427.

150. *Ibid.*, p. 7.

151. Short, *op. cit.*, p. 608.

152. "'Maoism' . . . is an umbrella word for the wide range of theory and practice attributed to Mao and his influence over the past eighty years." Julia Lovell, *Maoism: A Global History*, New York: Alfred A. Knopf, 2019, p. 9. See also Walden, *China: A Wolf in the World?*, p. 94.

153. "The 'Hundred Flowers' was Mao's show." Short, *op. cit.*, p. 454.

154. Pantsov, *op. cit.*, p. 7.

155. Mao refused "to recognize that economics has its own logic, partly independent of any broader criteria." Schram, *op. cit.*, p. 84.

156. Spence, *Mao Zedong*, p. 144.

157. Mao was obsessed with "the notion, which would dominate the last years of [his] life, that there was a 'bourgeoisie' inside the Party, which must be ferreted out, regardless of cost, if revolutionary purity was to be preserved." *Ibid.*, p. 493.

158. Spence, *Mao Zedong*, pp. 161–162.

159. Martin Malia, "Foreword: The Uses of Atrocity," in Courtois et al., *op. cit.*, p. ix; Stephane Courtois, "Introduction: The Crimes of Communism," in *ibid.*,

p. 4. Jung Chang and Jon Halliday put the number at "well over 70 million deaths." Chung and Halliday, *op. cit.*, p. 3.

160. Spence, *The Search for Modern China*, p. 210.

161. Short, *op. cit.*, pp. 69–70, 271, 350, 660. On the violent deaths of many of Mao's family members, see Pantsov, *op. cit.*, pp. 388–389.

162. "Undoubtedly it was not Mao's intention to kill so many of his compatriots. But the least one can say is that he seemed little concerned about the death of millions from hunger. Indeed, his main concern in those dark years seems to have been to deny a reality for which he could have been held responsible." Margolin, *op. cit.*, p. 487. See also Friedman and MacFarquhar, *op. cit.*, p. ix. "Having lost children, a brother, and a wife to war and revolution, he seldom seemed moved by the suffering of lovers, children and friends any more than he flinched from imposing misery on the millions of the faceless 'masses' in pursuit of his economic and political schemes. He understood human suffering chiefly as a way to control people." Andrew J. Nathan, "Introduction" to Dr. Li Zhisui, *The Private Life of Chairman Mao: The Memoirs of Mao's Personal Physician*, New York: Random House, 1994, p. viii.

163. Walden, *China: A Wolf in the World?*, pp. 12, 18. According to the Chinese Communist Party's 1981 *Resolution on Party History*: "The 'cultural revolution,' which lasted from May 1966 to October 1976, was responsible for the most severe setback and the heaviest losses suffered by the Party, the state and the people since the founding of the People's Republic. It was initiated and led by Comrade Mao Zedong." Quoted in MacFarquhar and Schoenhals, *op. cit.*, p. 3.

164. The four leading radicals, who included Mao's wife Jiang Qing and were known as the "Gang of Four," were arrested four weeks after Mao's death.

165. Ezra Vogel, *Deng Xiaoping and the Modernization of China*, Cambridge, Massachusetts: The Belknap Press of Harvard University Press, 2011, p. 8.

166. Fairbank *op. cit.*, p. 407.

167. Cai Xia, "The Weakness of Xi Jinping," *Foreign Affairs*, September/October 2022, https://www.foreignaffairs.com/china/xi-jinping-china-weakness-hub ris-paranoia-threaten-future.

168. Short, *op. cit.*, p. xxi.

169. "The Cultural Revolution was so great a disaster that it provoked an even more profound cultural revolution, precisely the one that Mao intended to forestall." MacFarquhar and Schoenhals, *op. cit.*, p. 3.

170. Mao had said, "Our aim is to exterminate capitalism, obliterate it from the face of the earth, and make it a thing of the past." Quoted in Pantsov, *op. cit.*, p. 421.

171. *Ibid.*, pp. 478–479. "By the summer of 1962, between 20 and 30 percent of the land was in the hands of the peasants." *Ibid.*, p. 483.

172. Pomfret, *op. cit.*, p. 120.

173. *Ibid.*, p. 142.

174. Spence, *The Search for Modern China*, p. 656; Vogel, *op. cit.*, pp. 701–702.

175. https://www.macrotrends.net/countries/CHN/china/gdp-gross-domestic-product.

176. https://thedocs.worldbank.org/en/doc/bdadc16a4f5c1c88a839c0f905cde802-0070012022/original/Poverty-Synthesis-Report-final.pdf.

177. "As Deng put it, 'discrediting Comrade Mao Zedong . . . would mean discrediting our Party and state.'" MacFarquhar and Schoenhals, *op. cit.*, p. 457.

178. "State sovereignty, territorial integrity and economic development, the priorities of any state, all are subordinate to the need to keep the Party in power." Richard McGregor, *The Party: The Secret World of China's Communist Rulers*, New York: HarperCollins, 2010, p. xii.

179. Short, *op. cit.*, p. xxii; McGregor, *op. cit.*, p. 244.

180. Quoted in Short, *op. cit.*, p. xxv. Short goes on to write, however, that "Mao was increasingly portrayed on Chinese television and in the cinema as 99 per cent correct and, at most, one per cent mistaken." *Ibid.*

181. Andrew J. Nathan, "Preface to the Paperback Edition" of *The Tiananmen Papers: The Chinese Leadership's Decision to Use Force Against Their Own People – in Their Own Words*, Compiled by Zhang Liang, Edited by Andrew J. Nathan and Perry Link, New York: PublicAffairs, 2002, p. viii.

182. Zhang Liang, "Reflections on June Fourth," in *ibid.*, p. l.

183. Pomfret, *op. cit.*, p. 179.

184. Elizabeth Economy, *The Third Revolution: Xi Jinping and the New Chinese State*, New York: Oxford University Press, 2018, p. 5.

185. Xi Jinping Thought, which "mixes patriotic education with praise for the Chinese Communist party's general secretary, will become part of the national curriculum, from primary school to university, next month." Sun Yu, "Lessons on Xi's Political Philosophy Anger China Parents," *Financial Times*, August 28/29, 2021, p. 4.

186. Economy, *op. cit.*, p. 13.

187. *Ibid.*, p. 4.

188. Chiang's reputation has undergone a degree of rehabilitation on the mainland. Mitter, *op. cit.*, p. 9. See also *ibid.*, p. 12, and Cradock, *op. cit.*, p. 11.

189. Taiwan became a democracy after Chiang's death, but it was far smaller than China and had four decades of experience as part of the largely democratic West, under the protection of the democratic United States.

Conclusion

1. The line appears in Act Two of the play and is part of a joke played on the character Malvolio.

2. A Jewish state had existed in the Middle East in ancient times, but had been discontinued for almost 2,000 years until Israel was founded in 1948.

INDEX

For the benefit of digital users, indexed terms that span two pages (e.g., 52–53) may, on occasion, appear on only one of those pages.

Notes are indicated by "n" following the page number.